PENTON - KTM
WORKSHOP MANUAL
1968-1975
100cc Berkshire
125cc Six-Day
plus
Illustrated parts lists

SACHS
WORKSHOP MANUAL
1968-1975
100cc & 125cc Engines
plus
Illustrated parts list

A Floyd Clymer Publication
This edition published in 2024 by
www.VelocePress.com

All rights reserved. This work may not be reproduced or transmitted in any form without the express written consent of the publisher.

PREFACE

TRADEMARKS & COPYRIGHT

Penton® is the registered trademark of Penton, Inc. This publication is not sponsored by or endorsed by the trademark owner. We recognize that some words, model names and designations, for example, mentioned herein are the property of the trademark holder. We use them for identification purposes only. This is not an official publication however; it may include non-copyright works of the trademark holder.

INTRODUCTION

Welcome to the world of digital publishing ~ the book you now hold in your hand was printed using the latest state of the art digital technology. The advent of print-on-demand has forever changed the publishing process, never has information been so accessible and it is our hope that this book serves your informational needs for years to come. If this is your first exposure to digital publishing, we hope that you are pleased with the results. Many more titles of interest to the classic automobile and motorcycle enthusiast, collector and restorer are available via our website at www.VelocePress.com. We hope that you find this title as interesting as we do.

NOTE FROM THE PUBLISHER

The information presented is true and complete to the best of our knowledge. All recommendations are made without any guarantees on the part of the author or the publisher, who also disclaim all liability incurred with the use of this information.

INFORMATION ON THE USE OF THIS PUBLICATION

This manual is an invaluable resource for those interested in performing their own maintenance. However, in today's information age we are constantly subject to changes in common practice, new technology, availability of improved materials and increased awareness of chemical toxicity. As such, it is advised that the user consult with an experienced professional prior to undertaking any procedure described herein. While every care has been taken to ensure correctness of information, it is obviously not possible to guarantee complete freedom from errors or omissions or to accept liability arising from such errors or omissions. Therefore, any individual that uses the information contained within, or elects to perform or participate in do-it-yourself repairs or modifications acknowledges that there is a risk factor involved and that the publisher or its associates cannot be held responsible for personal injury or property damage resulting from the use of the information or the outcome of such procedures.

WARNING!

One final word of advice, this publication is intended to be used as a reference guide, and when in doubt the reader should consult with a qualified technician.

CONTENTS

CHAPTER ONE - PENTON 100 - 125 WORKSHOP MANUAL

GENERAL INFORMATION 1

Introduction
Specifications
Lubrication
Torque setings
Conversion tables

Controls
Operation & maintenance
Troubleshooting
Owners record

CHAPTER TWO - SACHS WORKSHOP MANUAL (CLYMER)

GENERAL INFORMATION 33

Introduction
Special tools

Engine types

CHAPTER THREE

CYLINDER HEAD, CYLINDER AND PISTON 37

Cylinder head service
Cylinder service

Piston removal and replacement

CHAPTER FOUR

CRANKSHAFT AND CRANKCASE 47

Engine removal
Lower end
Gear selector (one-piece lever)
Gear selector (two-piece lever)
Crankcase separation
Crankshaft removal
Transmission disassembly
Starter mechanism removal
Inspection
Measurement
Crankshaft preassembly

Crankshaft seal replacement
Main bearing replacement
Crankcase reassembly
Ignition installation (Bosch)
Ignition installation (Motoplat)
Drive sprocket installation
Gear selector installation
Drive gear/clutch installation
Clutch side cover installation
Gear selector and kickstarter
Reinstallation, final assembly, and timing

CHAPTER FIVE

TRANSMISSION AND CLUTCH 67

Clutch service
Transmission service

Gear selectors
Shifter set-up and adjustment

CHAPTER SIX

CARBURETOR 87
Operation
Servicing
Adjustment
Air filter

CHAPTER SEVEN

ELECTRICAL SYSTEM 95
Magneto ignition system
Electronic ignition system
Charging system
Wiring diagrams

CHAPTER EIGHT

SPECIFICATIONS 113
1001/5A
1001/6A
1001/6B
1251/5A
1251/6A
1251/6B
1251/6C

CHAPTER NINE

USEFUL FORMULAS AND TABLES 123
Conversion table
Fuel and oil mixtures
Lubricants and sealants
Torque settings - nut and bolt

CHAPTER TEN

SACHS ENGINE 129
Illustrated parts list (1974)

CHAPTER ELEVEN

PENTON 100 - 125 MOTORCYCLES 141
Illustrated frame & components parts list 001 (1968 on)
Illustrated frame & components parts list 002 (1970 on)
Illustrated frame & components parts list 003 (1972 on)

PENTON 100 - 125 WORKSHOP MANUAL

CHAPTER ONE

OPERATION & MAINTENANCE

INTRODUCTION

These are just brief instructions to get this bike running if you are impatient, or know it all, and would like to get this thing racing in a hurry. The following pages have more detailed instructions and we advise reading them.

FRONT FORK: The front forks are already filled with oil. The large forks require 200cc of Hi-Point Fork Oil and the small diameter forks require 135cc.

TRANSMISSION: Already filled, ready to go. Check it nevertheless. Level plug provided at 4 o'clock from kickstart shaft. Capacity: 1 pint.

AIR CLEANER: Filtron, probably it has been oiled but should be oiled again and squeezed out. Filtron air cleaner oil FFC-300, SAE 40 can be used.

POINTS AND IGNITION: OK but it isn't a bad idea to lubricate the point cam a little.

GASOLINE: A mixture of 95 octane, 100% leaded gasoline with Hi-Point two cycle engine oil. Regular two cycle Hi-Point mix 20 to 1. Hi-Point concentrate oil mix 40 to 1. (Follow instructions on labels.)

There is shipping rubber on the transmission filler plug. This we have found from experience can be left on if the machine is being used in extremely wet and muddy conditions. This prevents mud and water from getting into the transmission. Check and tighten all nuts and bolts and check the tires.

FOREWORD

The brief instructions preceding these paragraphs are provided for the customer who feels he knows most of the answers to his new bike and wants to "bug out" in a mad rush. In the following lines, we will start from the front of the bike and try to cover all of the points and conditions of application that most of the customers may need to know. Always bear in mind that you have purchased primarily a competition motorcycle and all instruction will apply mainly to this application.

We are assuming that all owners of a Penton are experienced enough riders to know the positions and use of all controls and have at least general limited knowledge of motorcycles.

The Penton motorcycle, being a competition bike, does not carry a guarantee. We back up our new products and replace all new parts if found to be faulty on the part of manufacturing. If the parts have been used, they will only be replaced on our judgement if returned to us without being tampered with.

For all owners who are mechanically inclined or interested, there is available for purchase a complete up-to-date Service Manual — Shop Manual — Parts Manual consolidation with detailed drawings, photos, and parts explosions.

In so much as this is a competition machine, we are offering these general instructions in hopes that the inexperienced competition rider will read them and benefit. Buddy, this is a competition type motorcycle and it is going to give you as good a service as you give it. It is often said that 500 miles of Jackpine is the equivalent of 10,000 miles of highway touring. Man, you better believe it and then some because I'm speaking from experience. This machine is made to do this and more but you had better do your part because this is the game.

There are four points to being a champion with any good bike.

1. Tighten every single nut and bolt all the time, but don't twist them off.
2. Keep the thing clean inside and out.
3. Service the machine properly.
4. Ride it properly.

We will take one point at a time, in order. I have had riders tell me their engine is falling out. Humbug! This machine has been run by the roughest and toughest guys for six days in a row and the engines were still intact. But, I have news for you. The engine bolts were probably checked and tightened more than once. Also, once the engine is jumping around in the bike, the only thing you can do is start at the beginning and put in new bolts and do the job right. It is the same story with the entire motorcycle. When a rider loses axle nuts, swing arm nuts, seat bolts, gas tank bolts, it is only because he doesn't tighten them.

Next and most important. Cleanliness is next to godliness and boy when it comes to a motorcycle, this is it all the way. Just sink your bike in any mud hole or swamp and then take it home and don't clean the brakes and wheel hubs. Man, in six months you have junk and you'll never win a blasted thing unless it might be a dunce's trophy and a flat pocketbook. If at any time you have had your bike in deep enough to fill the brakes and wheels, take it home and clean them the same week.

I might mention at this time that there are more motorcycles ruined while cleaning them than there are by riding them. When using the pressure guns of today, one must never blow them directly at the wheel bearing seals, into air cleaners, ignition systems, etc. WARNING! Never put a water hose to your machine without first removing the air filter element and removing the breather hose at the carburetor and placing a clean rag tightly in the carburetor intake. The inside of the air box and breather tube should be thoroughly cleaned of water and dirt and checked for air leaks before starting. Never, never wash your machine and just put it away without starting it and riding for 5 or 10 minutes. This dries the condensation out of the engine and other vital parts.

Finally, after securing for the week, remove the ignition cover and let this system completely air and dry out a day or two. I might mention at this time that the two vital parts of the engine are the air cleaning and the ignition. Ninety-nine percent of all engine problems can be traced to these two components. Air cleaning is the first and most critical. These two strokes can be ruined in minutes with dirty air. The rider doesn't always realize this at first but a few weeks later it hits him in the head, with worn out piston rings and fouled plugs. The longevity of the competition two stroke is as great as a four stroke if the air is properly cleaned before entering the engine.

Servicing the unit should be done much more often than a machine used on the highway. As a matter of fact, this is a part of the sport. This writer has never allowed anyone to service his machine and in this way, when trouble is experienced, he has no one to blame but himself. Every moveable part should be constantly lubricated lightly for the best possible control. This service is explained with detail in the further individual component instructions.

Fourth and last comes the riding properly. This one I could write volumes on and still not cover every condition, person, and event. I might mention that with proper clutching, shifting, and treatment in general, you can use this Penton for several years on the same clutch and transmission. In the many years of riding, I have never replaced a clutch or transmission in any of my personal competition bikes. This I contribute only to proper use of the components.

The rear wheel brake shoes are interchangeable with the front and should be cleaned often if used in competition. One should always allow at least one inch up and down play in rear chain with riders performance to lubrication. We say lubricate plenty. Probably the one most important factor on the rear wheel assembly is again making sure to tighten complete assembly after carrying out any necessary adjustments. Always check and double check the axle carrier bushing nuts, brake anchor rod nuts, axle nut, etc. Our experience has shown that 99 times out of 100, when trouble has been experienced with the rear wheel assembly, it was directly due to someone forgetting to tighten something before riding.

THE ENGINE AND RELATED COMPONENTS

Boy, one could write about three books on this subject but we will try to help the rider as much as possible here.

First off, the air cleaner is Filtron of washable type. We recommend washing in petrol, then soap and water after every competition event. Then, squeeze out, allow to dry, and dip in oil. Then squeeze out as little oil as possible and replace. Buddy, this is the heart of the engine. Keep everything clean enough to eat out of. Further, a good idea is to use a brush with grease and completely cover the inside of the air chamber with grease, thus picking up any dirt that should get by.

WARNING! The Penton is fitted with a large air box which is designed to keep water and dirt from the engine and give maximum performance. Air is drawn in from under the seat through the filter and into the still air box into the carburetor. This is as waterproof as possible without completely submerging the bike but should be checked before every event for leaks. A carburetor cover is available as an accessory and should be used when running in enduros or wet and muddy races.

Carburetor is generally set at factory and jet changing should only be done by an experienced mechanic. We recommend the plug that come in the machine (Bosch 260T1) or comparison heat range. Fuel, we recommend Hi Point Concentrate or a good grade SAE 40 weight two stroke oil, using a 20 to 1 mixing ratio.

Point setting is between 12 and 18 thousands of an inch and one should always keep a little lubricant on the point cam pad. Timing of the engine is done by the line at 12 o'clock to the flywheel on the crankcase body edge. One rotates the flywheel clockwise until the piston is .118–.188 inch (3.00–3.5 mm) before top dead center. This is the position where the points should just be breaking. The "0" arrow on the flywheel is top dead center when aligned up with the mark on the crankcase at 12 o'clock. A buzzer usually is used for timing and is very convenient. See the Service Manual for more details.

The piston in the engine employs an "L" type top compression ring for maximum performance. This has proven to be the most reliable and best performance ring to date. But, the one drawback is that it wears rapidly in competition because of dirt. We strongly recommend that with serious and every week competition men, they remove the cylinder every month, clean the ring grooves thoroughly, check ring wear and usually replace the "L" compression ring. Please Note! This "L" ring groove must be clean 100% or you will break the ring every time you try and put it together. This is not a chronic problem with this engine. As a matter of fact, under most extreme hard running road conditions, I have seen the factory run this engine 20,000 kilometers on the same set of rings but, dirt and competition work away at them and it is different.

Transmission oil should be changed every month. There are two drain points, the left hand cover screw at 6 o'clock to the shifter spindle and the 14mm hex screw on bottom side of engine. Refill with Hi Point transmission lube or 20-40 during summertime and automatic transmission fluid type "A" wintertime below 40 degrees F. Capacity is 1 pint.

It must be mentioned and remembered that this being a competition bike is fitted with certain components for performance that naturally don't have the longevity of the street motorcycle. Nonetheless, all major parts are tested and proven and will give you good life with hard but proper use.

FRONT WHEEL AND FORK ASSEMBLY

The front fork should be serviced about every two months. The capacity of the large diameter forks is between 180 and 200cc and 135cc for the small diameter forks. SAE 10 weight spindle oil or to rider's choice and application. Drain plugs are at the lower end and filling is accomplished by removing the large Hex cap at the top, not the screw. Fork sliders are provided for keeping the shafts clean. It may be found that mud and dirt collect under the sliders. When cleaning the machine, these should be loosened and raised and the dirt and mud cleaned off. This is the only service required by the fork and properly executed the fork has many years of trouble-free service designed into it.

The front tire and wheel is conventional and is not provided with a tire lock because of wheel balance and different rider's tastes. This writer has always found screws in the rims as the most effective, but of course, it is up to the individual. Front tire pressure is optional to conditions and riders, ranging from 8 lbs. psi to 25 lbs. psi.

The front fork head should be checked every couple of weeks. This bike has a good set of head bearings but just the same, it is good insurance to keep an eye on them. While the bike is standing still on hard surface, apply front brake, rocking back and forth. Put your finger under the top fork yoke and see if you feel any clicking. If so, tighten firmly, taking out the slack. We strongly recommend packing the head bearings every six months.

HANDLEBAR ASSEMBLY

The Magura control fittings are the best manufactured in the world and have great resistance against breaking. Nevertheless, they should be lubricated often to insure good, free, and smooth action. Our Service Department has found Dri Slide lubricant to be the most effective application for the control levers and cables application. As a matter of fact, we recommend the use of this lubricant on all external working surfaces on our motorcycles.

There is a spring pin provided on the handlebar of each bike. This pin is to lock the handlebars from turning after the rider has chosen his preferred position. It is not absolutely necessary to use this pin but is actually optional. A hole of proper size must be drilled to insert this pin.

REAR SWING ARM AND WHEEL ASSEMBLY

There is not too much to be said about the swing arm as it has proven in competition to be very reliable and has not offered a minute's trouble. The swing arm bushes are automotive type bonded rubber bushing and have many years of life. Nevertheless, the swing arm pivot bolt should definately be kept tight.

Now, a little more about this bloody engine! Comparing it to all 125cc motorcycle engines on the market today, it is second to none. It has been designed to be quite flexible in power, good performance to displacement, reliable, with ease of operation, the latter being the point to emphasize. Shifting this engine under all normal conditons is beautiful but when engaged in intensified competition conditions, some people tend to over shift. This I recognized after extensive use in this area of application. It is no fault of the manufacturer really because they were striving for a gentlemenlike shifting unit which they achieved. This condition can usually be tolerated by the rider getting used to the engine and sometimes by shortening the shifting arm by about 1 to 1½ inches. Of course, I know this is not a full solution. All machines being manufactured now are correct and perfect.

With regard to gearing and sprockets, I might mention that with the wide power range of the engine and five or six speed transmissions, we have found the gearing to be very suitable to almost every event and condition. Of the many machines we have in the field and have tested, we have not yet had any requests for different gearing. However, the 125cc comes with a 14T gearbox sprocket and a 60T or 57T rear wheel sprocket, while the 100cc comes with a 13T engine sprocket and a 60T or 57T rear wheel sprocket. There are available 13T and 14T sprockets for the engines and 40T, 54T, 57T and 60T sprockets for the rear wheel.

Accessories are available for the "Penton" models from your dealer.

INSTALLATION OF ENDURO KITS

The enduro kit was introduced to provide the customer with a much more varied model, more efficiently. Due to the lack of motorcycle knowledge of many dealers and riders, we have had reports of installation problems.

The wiring bit has presented the greatest problems so we will do our best to straighten this out. There are four wires coming out of the engine. The blue wire is ignition which goes to the coil. The yellow wire is the main lighting power which goes to the lighting system. The green wire is for stop light power and can be hooked to a stop light switch if desired. The gray wire can be hooked to a small horn if desired. One must next check out and trace out the wiring harness to the dipper switch because the factory has been known to use many different color combinations for the switch. Nevertheless, the colors from the engine are always correct.

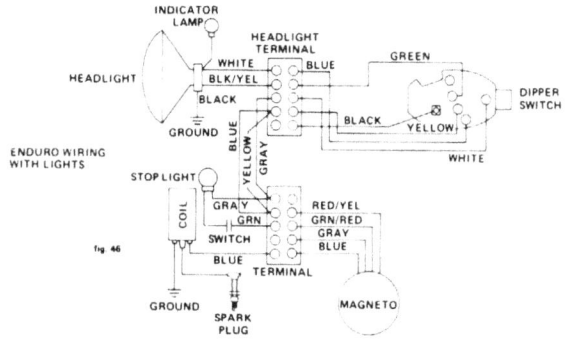

On some enduro kits the lighting kit contains the switch in the headlight housing. This wiring diagram is below.

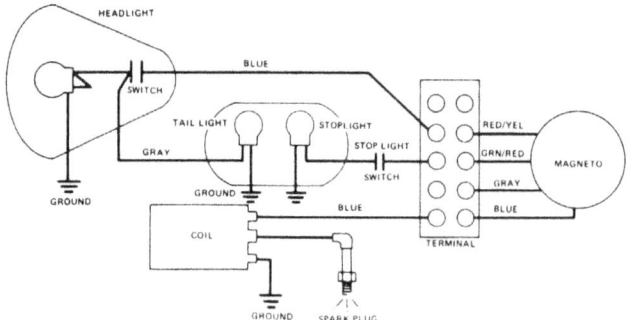

The next thing is the speedo and rear sprocket. These two items are closely related because of the ratio. NOTE! The correct ratios are as follows:

125cc engine sprocket 14T, rear sprocket 54T, Speedo ratio W1.8

125cc engine sprocket 14T, rear sprocket 57T, Speedo ratio W1.95

100cc engine sprocket 13T, rear sprocket 54T, Speedo ratio W1.95

This gearing we have found to be the most adaptable to our enduro work. NOTE!!! The speedo is driven ONLY off of the transmission as the front wheel drive is nylon and too weak to drive the speedo.

The routing of the speedo cable is most important. From the transmission, it should go up and across to the left hand petrol valve and then forward under the tank to the speedo. A rubber band can be applied to hold the cable adjacent to the left hand petrol valve. Plenty of free movement is good for the cable installation.

If after checking the speedo the mileage is found to be incorrect, check and make sure a mistake has not been made in shipping the correct ratio speedo, but only after you make sure that you are using the above correct sprockets.

Please be advised that all speedometer warranty should be adjusted through VDO Instruments, 116 Victor, Detroit, Michigan 48203, as they are the U.S. representatives for the VDO and Penton Imports has no way to adjust these with the VDO Company. If you have a legal warranty claim, pack it up and mail directly to VDO in Detroit with an explanation for warranty claim.

THANK YOU

John A. Penton

JOHN A. PENTON

INTRODUCTION

INTRODUCTION

Congratulations on becoming the proud owner of the Penton Six Day Sport Cycle. You now join the growing number of owners and riders throughout the world who depend on the Penton cycle to bring them the rewards of the sport of cycling.

The Penton is unique in that it was designed and manufactured exclusively for the American competition scene by one of the country's greatest cycle competitors, John Penton, whose name the cycle bears. His knowledge of the sport and industry have revolutionized the sport of small bore racing in the United States.

The Pentons competitive edge over other cycles is maintained by us at the factory who are riding every weekend in the same competitions that you, the rider and owner, are competing in. This continuous testing in conjunction with the International Six Days Trials has enabled us to provide you with a highly dependable and competitive cycle you will be proud to own and ride.

This manual is designed to give you the knowledge necessary to keep your Penton in competitive shape and carry out needed maintenance and repair. This manual is complete in its service to the Penton cycle and should be carried out in the most professional of ways. You, the owner, may prefer to let the dealer who sold you the Penton make needed engine repairs, as this should be carried out only with the proper tools and a good knowledge of mechanics. You, the owner, have a special job in seeing that the Penton is maintained in perfect operating condition. With this, you will always have a competitive cycle and concentration will be on winning rather than finishing.

NOTES

SPECIFICATIONS

TECHNICAL DATA

ENGINE	100 Berkshire	125 Six Day
Type	Single cylinder / Two-stroke piston port / Air cooled	
Bore	1.890 in. (48mm)	2.126 in. (54mm)
Stroke	2.126 in. (54mm)	
Piston displacement	5.980 cu. in. (98cc)	7.505 cu. in. (123cc)
Compression ratio	10:1	
Max. H.P.	16 H.P. (Din)	21 H.P. (Din)
Lubrication	Oil and Gas mixture (See Lubrication)	
CARBURETION		
Type	Bing 27.5mm	Bing 28mm
Main jet	130/135	135/140
Needle jet	35	
Idle jet	276	
Needle	5	
Needle position	3	4
Air cleaner	Twin Air	
	40-404	
ELECTRICAL		
Type	Motoplat (Solid State pointless magneto)	
	headlight 6V, 35 watt, taillight 6V, 35 watt, stoplight 6V, 18 watt	
Ignition timing	2.6 – 3.0mm Before Top Dead Center	
Spark plug	Bosch W 280 MI	
TRANSMISSION		
Gearbox	6 speeds in engine/foot operated	
Gear ratios	1st, 4.60: 2nd, 2.92: 3rd, 2.16: 4th, 1.71: 5th 1.43: 6th, 1.24	
Clutch	Multiple plate clutch	
Transmission ratio engine - gearbox	2:10	
CHASSIS		
Type	Under tank air intake Double down cradle frame - Chrome molybden steel Steering head welded on frame tube	
Suspension front	Ceriani hydraulically dampened telescopic fork	
Suspension rear	Girling	
Brakes	Center line single leading shoe / 38 in. swept area	
Tires	21"x3:00 front (18x3.50 rear 100cc) (18x4.00 rear 125cc)	
Fuel tank	1.4 or 2.8 gallon	
DIMENSIONS		
Length	81 in.	
Width	34 in. at handlebars, 20 in. at footpegs	
Height	42 in.	
Wheel base	55 in.	
Seat height	31 in.	
Ground clearance	9 in.	
Weight	198 lbs.	
Colors	Red	Green

SPECIFICATIONS

LUBRICATION CHART — CAPACITY AND QUALITY

ENGINE	Mixture of 95 octane, 100% leaded gasoline with Hi-Point two cycle engine oil. Regular two cycle Hi-Point mix 20 to 1. Hi-Point concentrate oil mix 40 to 1. (Follow instructions on labels).
FRONT FORKS	190cc of Hi-Point Fork Oil Lubricant in each leg.
GEARBOX	700cc of Hi-Point 20W 40 Motorcycle Transmission Lubricant.
CABLES	Good quality penetrating oil or "Dry-Slide"
WHEEL BEARINGS	Lithium base grease
CHAIN	High quality Hi-Point Chain Oil
SPEEDOMETER DRIVE	Press in approx. 0.07...0.1 fl. oz. high temp. grease
IGNITION	Smear lubrication felt pad for breaker cam with a little lubricant.

TIGHTENING TORQUES FOR BOLTS AND NUTS

Bolts

Qty.	Used on	Dimensions	Tightening torque	
			kpm	ft lb
6	Crankcase	M 6 x 60	0.8...1.0	5.59...7.25
4	Crankcase	M 6 x 75	0.8...1.0	5.59...7.25
3	Armature base plate	M 4 x 14	0.2...0.3	1.45...2.17
2	Selector adjusting plate	M 6 x 20	1.2...1.5	6.86...10.85
4	Crankcase cover — clutch side	M 6 x 65	0.8...1.0	5.59...7.25
2	Crankcase cover — clutch side	M 6 x 38	0.8...1.0	5.59...7.25
1	Crankcase cover — clutch side	M 6 x 52	0.8...1.0	5.59...7.25
4	Cylinder head	M 8 x 40	3.0...3.2	21.70...23.15
4	Crankcase cover — magneto side	M 6 x 60	0.8...1.0	5.59...7.25
3	Clutch box on layshaft wheel	M6 x 15	1.2...1.5	8.68...10.85

Nuts

Qty.	Used on	Dimensions	Tightening torque	
			kpm	ft lb
1	Crankshaft — drive side	M 14 x 1.5	7.0	50.63
1	Clutch boss	M 18 x 1	8.0...9.0	57.86...65.10
4	Cylinder	M 8	2.4...2.6	17.36...18.81
4	Aluminum Cylinder	M 8 x 40	3.1	22.00
1	Crankshaft — magneto side	M 10 x 1 L	3.8...4.0	27.48...28.93
1	Sprocket	M 20 x 1 L	7.0	50.63

SPECIFICATIONS

DECIMAL EQUIVALENTS OF MILLIMETERS

mm.	Inches	mm.	Inches	mm.	Inches	mm.	Inches	mm.	Inches
.01	.00039	.41	.01614	.81	.03189	21	.82677	61	2.40157
.02	.00079	.42	.01654	.82	.03228	22	.86614	62	2.44094
.03	.00118	.43	.01693	.83	.03268	23	.90551	63	2.48031
.04	.00157	.44	.01732	.84	.03307	24	.94488	64	2.51968
.05	.00197	.45	.01772	.85	.03346	25	.98425	65	2.55905
.06	.00236	.46	.01811	.86	.03386	26	1.02362	66	2.59842
.07	.00276	.47	.01850	.87	.03425	27	1.06299	67	2.63779
.08	.00315	.48	.01890	.88	.03465	28	1.10236	68	2.67716
.09	.00354	.49	.01929	.89	.03504	29	1.14173	69	2.71653
.10	.00394	.50	.01969	.90	.03543	30	1.18110	70	2.75590
.11	.00433	.51	.02008	.91	.03583	31	1.22047	71	2.79527
.12	.00472	.52	.02047	.92	.03622	32	1.25984	72	2.83464
.13	.00512	.53	.02087	.93	.03661	33	1.29921	73	2.87401
.14	.00551	.54	.02126	.94	.03701	34	1.33858	74	2.91338
.15	.00591	.55	.02165	.95	.03740	35	1.37795	75	2.95275
.16	.00630	.56	.02205	.96	.03780	36	1.41732	76	2.99212
.17	.00669	.57	.02244	.97	.03819	37	1.45669	77	3.03149
.18	.00709	.58	.02283	.98	.03858	38	1.49606	78	3.07086
.19	.00748	.59	.02323	.99	.03898	39	1.53543	79	3.11023
.20	.00787	.60	.02362	1.00	.03937	40	1.57480	80	3.14960
.21	.00827	.61	.02402	1	.03937	41	1.61417	81	3.18897
.22	.00866	.62	.02441	2	.07874	42	1.65354	82	3.22834
.23	.00906	.63	.02480	3	.11811	43	1.69291	83	3.26771
.24	.00945	.64	.02520	4	.15748	44	1.73228	84	3.30708
.25	.00984	.65	.02559	5	.19685	45	1.77165	85	3.34645
.26	.01024	.66	.02598	6	.23622	46	1.81102	86	3.38582
.27	.01063	.67	.02638	7	.27559	47	1.85039	87	3.42519
.28	.01102	.68	.02677	8	.31496	48	1.88976	88	3.46456
.29	.01142	.69	.02717	9	.35433	49	1.92913	89	3.50393
.30	.01181	.70	.02756	10	.39370	50	1.96850	90	3.54330
.31	.01220	.71	.02795	11	.43307	51	2.00787	91	3.58267
.32	.01260	.72	.02835	12	.47244	52	2.04724	92	3.62204
.33	.01299	.73	.02874	13	.51181	53	2.08661	93	3.66141
.34	.01339	.74	.02913	14	.55118	54	2.12598	94	3.70078
.35	.01378	.75	.02953	15	.59055	55	2.16535	95	3.74015
.36	.01417	.76	.02992	16	.62992	56	2.20472	96	3.77952
.37	.01457	.77	.03032	17	.66929	57	2.24409	97	3.81889
.38	.01496	.78	.03071	18	.70866	58	2.28346	98	3.85826
.39	.01535	.79	.03110	19	.74803	59	2.32283	99	3.89763
.40	.01575	.80	.03150	20	.78740	60	2.36220	100	3.93700

SPECIFICATIONS

DECIMAL EQUIVALENTS

8ths	32nds	64ths	64ths
1/8 = .125	1/32 = .03125	1/64 = .015625	33/64 = .515625
1/4 = .250	3/32 = .09375	3/64 = .046875	35/64 = .546875
3/8 = .375	5/32 = .15625	5/64 = .078125	37/64 = .578125
1/2 = .500	7/32 = .21875	7/64 = .109375	39/64 = .609375
5/8 = .625	9/32 = .28125	9/64 = .140625	41/64 = .640625
3/4 = .750	11/32 = .34375	11/64 = .171875	43/64 = .671875
7/8 = .875	13/32 = .40625	13/64 = .203125	45/64 = .703125
16ths	15/32 = .46875	15/64 = .234370	47/64 = .734375
1/16 = .0625	17/32 = .53125	17/64 = .265625	49/64 = .765625
3/16 = .1875	19/32 = .59375	19/64 = .296875	51/64 = .796875
5/16 = .3125	21/32 = .65625	21/64 = .328125	53/64 = .828125
7/16 = .4375	23/32 = .71875	23/64 = .359375	55/64 = .859375
9/16 = .5625	25/32 = .78125	25/64 = .390625	57/64 = .890625
11/16 = .6875	27/32 = .84375	27/64 = .421875	59/64 = .921875
13/16 = .8125	29/32 = .90625	29/64 = .453125	61/64 = .953125
15/16 = .9375	31/32 = .96875	31/64 = .484375	63/64 = .984375

CONVERSION TABLE

Millimetres (mm) to Inches (in)	1 cm = 10 mm
1 mm = 0.0394 in	Conversion factor 0.0394
e.g. 15.003 mm x 0.0394 = 0.5911182 in	

Square centimetre (cm^2) to Square inch (sq in)	
1 cm^2 = 0.155 in	Conversion factor 0.155
e.g. 1.5 cm^2 x 0.155 = 0.2325 sq in	

Cubic centimetre (cc) to Cubic inch (cu in)	
1 cc = 0.06102 cu in	Conversion factor 0.06102
e.g. 135 cc x 0.06102 = 8.2377 cu in	

Kilograms (kg) to Pounds (lb)	
1 kg = 2.205 lb	Conversion factor 2.205
e.g. 92 kg x 2.205 = 202.86 lb	

Kilopondmetres (mkp) to Foot pounds (ftlb)	
1 mkp = 7.233 ft lb	Conversion factor 7.233
e.g. 1.3 mkp x 7.233 = 9.4029 ft lb	

Litres (l) to US-gallons (US-gall)	
1 l = 0.2642 US-gall	Conversion factor 0.2642
e.g. 9.3l x 0.2642 = 2.45706 US-gall	

Kilograms/square centimetre (kg/cm^2 = atü) to Pounds/square inch (lb/sqin = psi)	
1 atu = 14.22 psi	Conversion factor 14.22
e.g. 1.2 atu x 14.22 = 17.064 psi	

Kilometres (km) to Miles (mil)	
1 km = 0.621 mil	Conversion factor 0.621
e.g. 100 km x 0.621 = 62.1 mil	

Litres/100 Kilometres (l/100 km) to Miles/US-gallon (mil/US-gall)	
$\text{mil/US-gall} = \dfrac{235}{l/100 \text{ km}}$	e.g. $\dfrac{235}{7 l} = 33.57$ mil/US-gall

CONTROLS

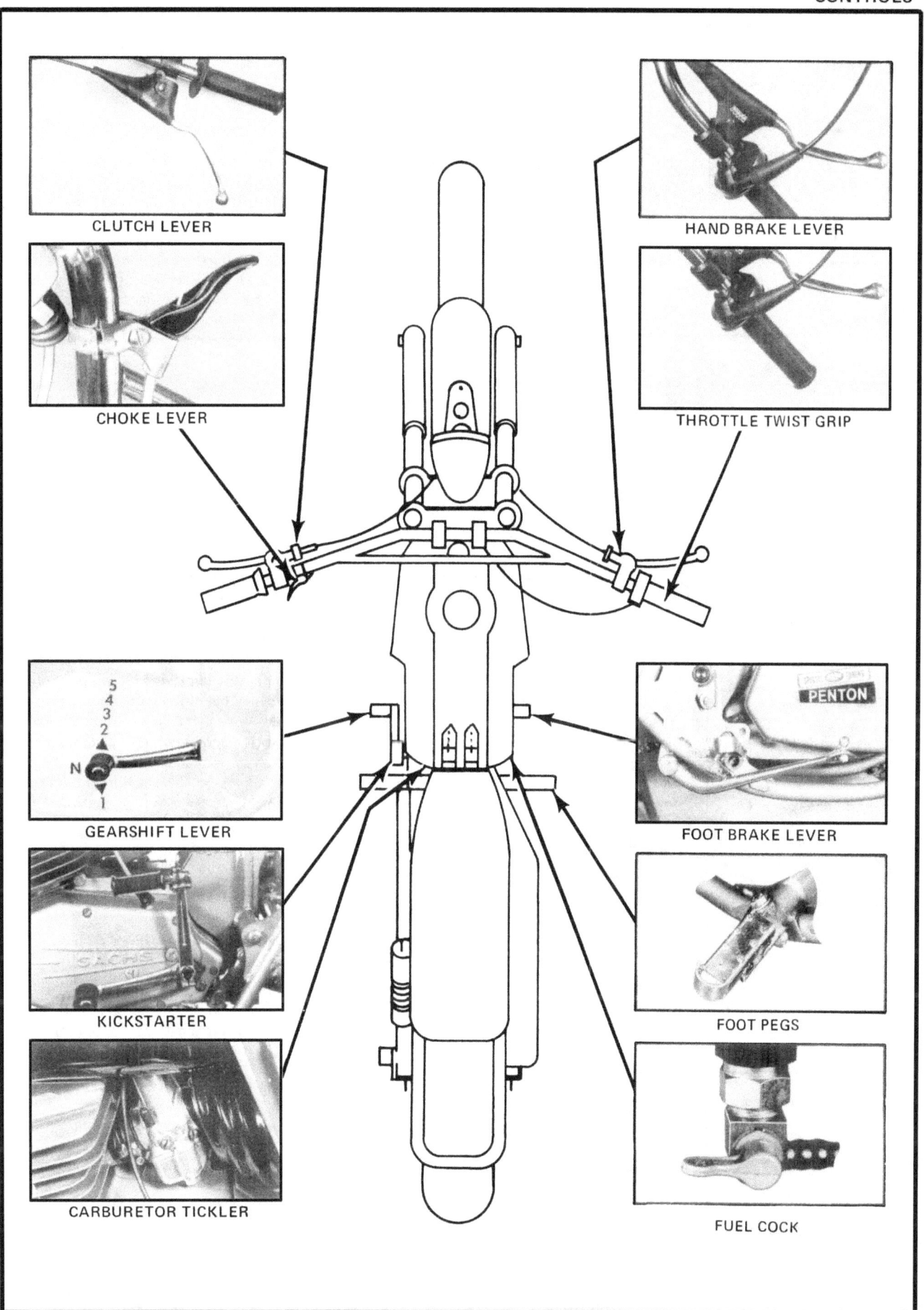

CONTROLS

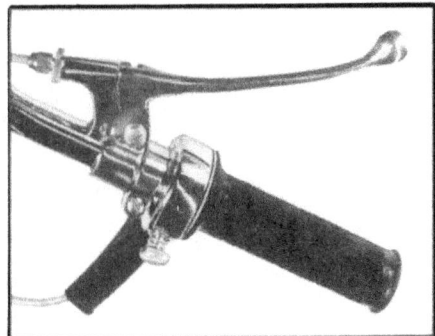
fig. 1

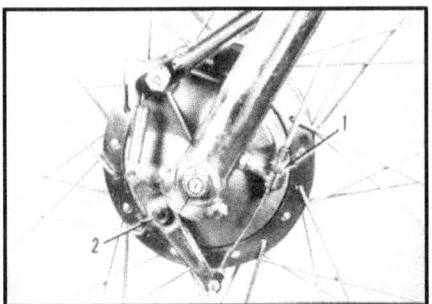
fig. 2

Front Hand Brake Lever

To adjust the brake use the cable adjuster on the hand lever (fig. 1). If the hand lever is impossible to adjust use the adjuster on the brake plate cover (fig. 2/1). Before setting the brake plate adjuster set the hand lever adjuster to approximately mid-position so later adjustment may be made. Due to wear of the brake lining and stretching of the cable both adjusters may no longer tighten the brake. If the lining is in proper condition, the brake plate lever (fig. 2/2) may be moved forward one tooth. To have a good lever effect, the position of the lever must not be understepped or moved forward too far.

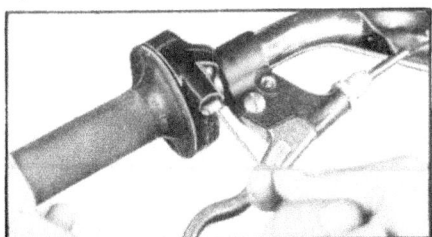
fig. 3

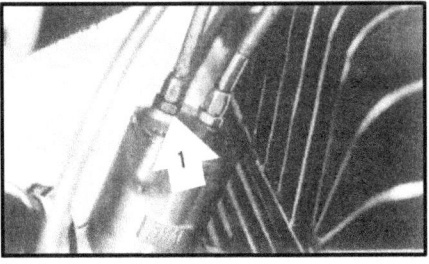
fig. 4

Throttle Twist Grip

The throttle twist grip is located on the right side of the handlebar and is made out of nylon. By removing the threaded screw bushing and rotating the throttle to full close you can remove the cable without taking the throttle apart. You can put in a new throttle the same way. NOTE: The threaded screw bushing should be screwed in all the way in the throttle as this acts as a stop bushing. (Do not make throttle adjustment here.) The throttle cable should have a slight play in it when in the closed position. The play is correct if the cable can be pulled out of the carburetor approximately ⅛" without pulling up the slide. Adjustment of the throttle cable is made by the adjusting screw on top of the carburetor, (1, fig. 4). Secure the locking nut when the proper adjustment is made. Always check this play after adjusting the idle. The throttle cable should be free of binding and routed so as not to catch on anything. Use dry-slide to lubricate cable and throttle.

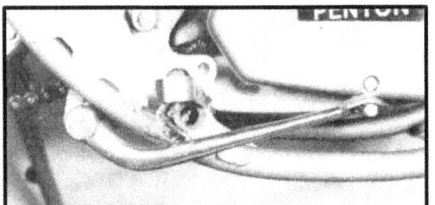
fig. 5

fig. 6

Foot Brake Pedal

The play of the foot brake pedal should be approximately 1" (fig. 5). To adjust the play use the brake rod wing nut (fig. 6). If the play is excessive and the adjusting nut can no longer reset the pedal, reset the brake plate lever (fig. 6/1) backward one notch. Make sure the position of the lever does not over or understep or lever action will be impaired. Before adjusting the brake plate lever check the state of the brake lining. When the rear wheel is adjusted re-check the brake pedal adjustment. Be sure the return spring tension is tight so brake drag does not occur.

CONTROLS

Clutch Lever, Adjusting and Refitting the Cable

The play of the clutch lever, measured at the lever outside (fig. 6-A) should be approximately 1/2". For this adjustment use the cable adjuster (fig. 6-A). If the adjuster is no longer able to take up the play follow this procedure.

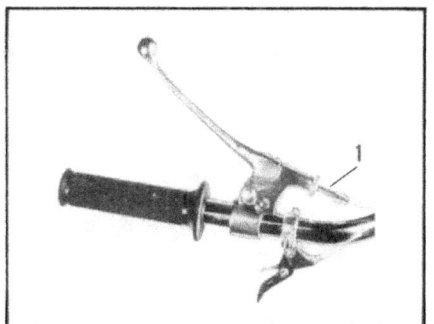

fig. 6A

Adjusting the Clutch - (Also see Chapter 5)

Turn the hand clutch lever adjuster to the bottom position. Remove cross slotted screw plugs and sealing washers (1&2, fig. 7).

The clutch is adjustable by means of the adjusting screw (2, fig. 8) and the control cable adjusting screw (1, fig. 6-A). Slacken lock screw (1, fig. 8) by about 1/2 turn. Screw out the clutch adjustment screw (2, fig. 8) by 1/3 turn.

Check to see whether the clutch lever (3, fig. 8) is resting on the stop (see arrow fig. 8) in the crankcase cover. If this is not the case, the control wire is either too short or the outer casing too long.

While watching the clutch lever (3, fig. 8) screw out the control cable adjusting screw (1, fig. 6-A) again to such an extent that:

(a) clutch lever (3, fig.8) is still bearing on the crankcase cover.
(b) clutch lever (3, fig. 8) lifts off the stop in the crankcase cover when the clutch lever is pulled past the first 1/2" at the handlebar.

Lock the control cable adjusting screw at the handlebar (1, fig. 6-A).

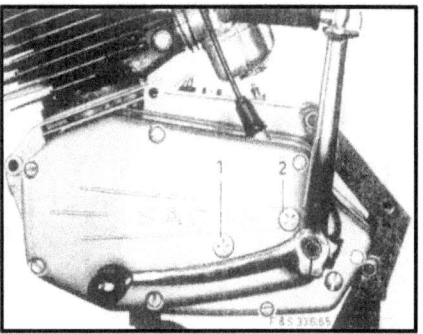

fig. 7

Turn the clutch adjusting screw (2, fig. 8) clockwise until resistance is felt. Ascertain this pressure point accurately by turning the clutch adjusting screw in and out several times. Subsequently, turn the clutch adjusting screw back 1/3 turn. A play of 2-4mm between clutch lever (3, fig. 8) and resistance arrow (fig. 8) results from this. Retighten screw (1, fig. 8).

Take Care of the Proper Clutch Adjustment!

Replace the cross slotted screw plugs and sealing washers.

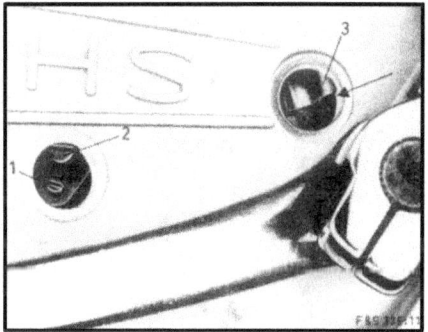

fig. 8

Replacing the Clutch Cable

Remove the cross slotted screw plugs with sealing washers (1&2, fig. 7). Remove the clutch cable at the handlebar control lever.

Lift clutch lever (1, fig. 9) with a small screw driver as shown in the illustration, push control cable (2, fig. 9) down and remove. Pull the cable out the top.

Introduce the control wire, lift clutch lever (1, fig. 9) and attach cable nipple.

Adjust the clutch as described above after removing and fitting the clutch control cable or after its replacement.

The crankcase cover on the clutch side is designed in such a way that cable nipples which may drop off will not drop into the clutch case, but can be removed through the screw plug hole.

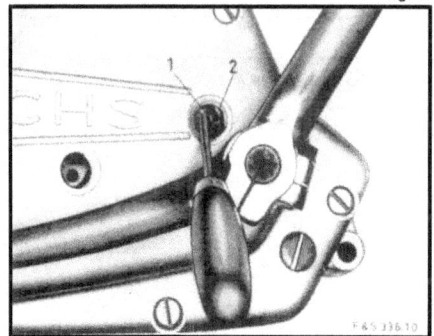

fig. 9

Foot Gear Shift Lever

Gear changes are made as shown in fig. 10. Pedal position may be changed by loosening the fixing screw, removing the pedal and fitting to a new position. The clutch should be used at all times when shifting and a positive movement should be made when changing gears.

With proper clutching, shifting, and treatment in general, you can use this Penton for several years on the same clutch and transmission. If adjustment to the shifting mechanism is required see the section on rebuilding the engine.

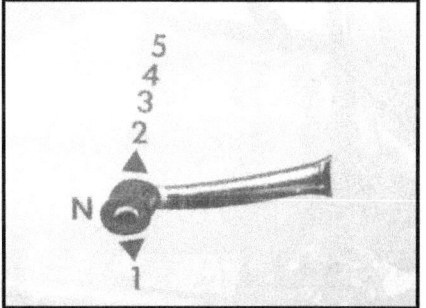

fig. 10

CONTROLS

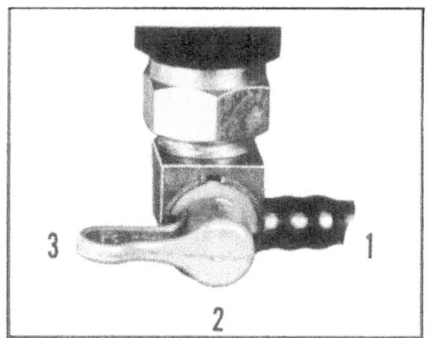
fig. 11

Fuel Cocks

The fuel cocks are located on both sides at the rear of the gas tank. They should both be open when the cycle is running. The fuel cocks have 3 positions: 1-off, 2-on, 3-reserve (fig. 11).

When the cycle is not running, keep fuel cocks closed!

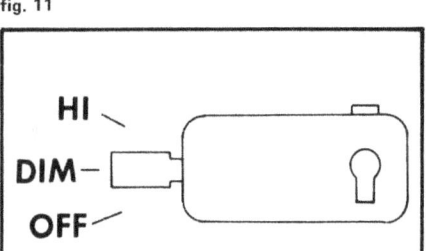
fig. 12

Light Switch

Located on the left handlebar, the control handles all the auxiliary electrical controls. See electrical wiring diagram. (page 26 & Chapter Seven)

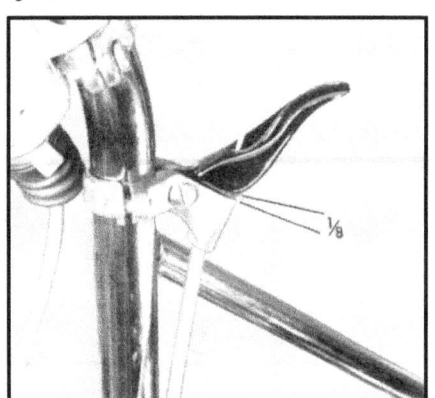
fig. 13

Choke Lever

Located on the left handlebar the choke lever is on when pulled in, and off when released to the normal position. In order to assure that the choke is out of operation during normal running of the engine, the control cable for the choke must have a minimum play of 1/8". This play is measured at the choke lever fig. 13. Adjustment is made at the carburetor by means of the adjusting screw fig. 14. The lever is used when starting a cold engine by pulling in the lever until the engine is warmed up, then releasing the lever.

fig. 14

Handlebar

The handlebar may be adjusted by the rider as his requirements may need. Loosen the nuts beneath the top fork crown, adjust the handlebar and retighten up the nuts securely. After adjusting the handlebars, check all controls and correct if necessary.

OPERATION AND MAINTENANCE

Fuel
The fuel for the Penton should be pre-mixed in a separate gas can. The proper fuel is a 95% octane, 100% leaded gasoline only mixed with Hi-Point 2-cycle engine oil with a ratio of 20 to 1 or with Hi-Point 2-cycle Concentrate at a ratio of 40 to 1. If other oil is used be sure it is 2-cycle air cooled motorcycle engine oil and follow label instructions. Do not run without an oil gas mixture, or use outboard engine oil. The proper oil will eliminate plug fouling, smoke, carbon build-up and prolong your engine life. We recommend Hi-Point 2-Cycle Concentrate available from your Penton Dealer.

Starting Procedure for the Penton
Open both fuel cocks to the open position. Push carburetor tickler until fuel flows from the overflow hole. Close choke lever. With cycle in neutral, kick the starter crank sharply. Use the throttle control for engine speed. Once the engine is running cleanly the choke may be turned off. Keep from overrevving the engine while in neutral.

Breaking In
In breaking in your Penton it is important to follow this procedure: Do not ride on full throttle from the beginning. Gradually increase the stress to the engine and close the throttle entirely for short intervals. In the first hour of riding use only half throttle, gradually work up to full throttle over a several hour period. This will insure proper seating of the rings and a smoother running engine. This will also give you time to get used to riding the Penton. If a new piston or cylinder is fitted follow the same procedure. Be sure to check over the cycle thoroughly after riding and tighten any loose nuts and bolts and make any necessary adjustments to the controls. When subjecting your machine to long stretches of high speed highway or extreme engine stress, we find it useful to close the choke slightly so the bike will run a little richer to eliminate any possibility of seizing, if the engine leans out.

Carburetor, Maintenance and Tuning (Also see Chapter Six)
The carburetor fitted to the Penton and the choice of jet sizes are all determined by means of extensive testing at the factory. The carb setting determined in this way represent the optimum setting, and for this reason it is advisable not to make arbitrary adjustments on your own.

If conditions of climate or altitude cause the bike to run rich (blubbering, won't clean out, especially at low end) or lean (pinging), fine adjustments can be made by varying the jet needle position: .... raising the needle produces a richer air-fuel mixture, lowering it produces a leaner mixture. It must be pointed out that varying the jet needle position alters the richness of the mixture only at low and medium engine speeds.

If, while riding your Penton it is obvious, through bad pinging, that the bike is lean in a portion of the power band, refrain from running there until proper carb adjustment can be made, as hard riding while pinging can cause engine seizure.

With correct carburetor setting, the air filter functioning satisfactorily, and a suitable spark plug, the insulator of the spark plug will be stained brown by burning. If carbon collects on the plug or the plug is wet, it means that the air-fuel mixture is too rich. On the other hand, when the plug becomes white, it is an indication that the mixture is too lean. Of course, the thermal value of the spark plug must be as specified. (See spark plug maintenance)

fig. 18

Tuning the Carburetor
Tune the carburetor while the engine is warm. Unscrew throttle valve stop (3, fig. 18) and set the control cable in such a position that the throttle is completely closed.

Screw in the throttle stop valve (3, fig. 18) until the engine (operating at its normal temperature) runs at an increased idling speed when the twistgrip is closed.

Screw in air adjusting screw (4, fig. 18) until a slightly perceptible stopping occurs, and screw it out (by approximately half a turn) until the engine runs very smoothly.

Unscrew stop screw (3, fig. 18) until the required idling is obtained. We recommend no or little idling if the cycle is used in competition. Check the throttle cable for proper play (see controls section).

OPERATION AND MAINTENANCE

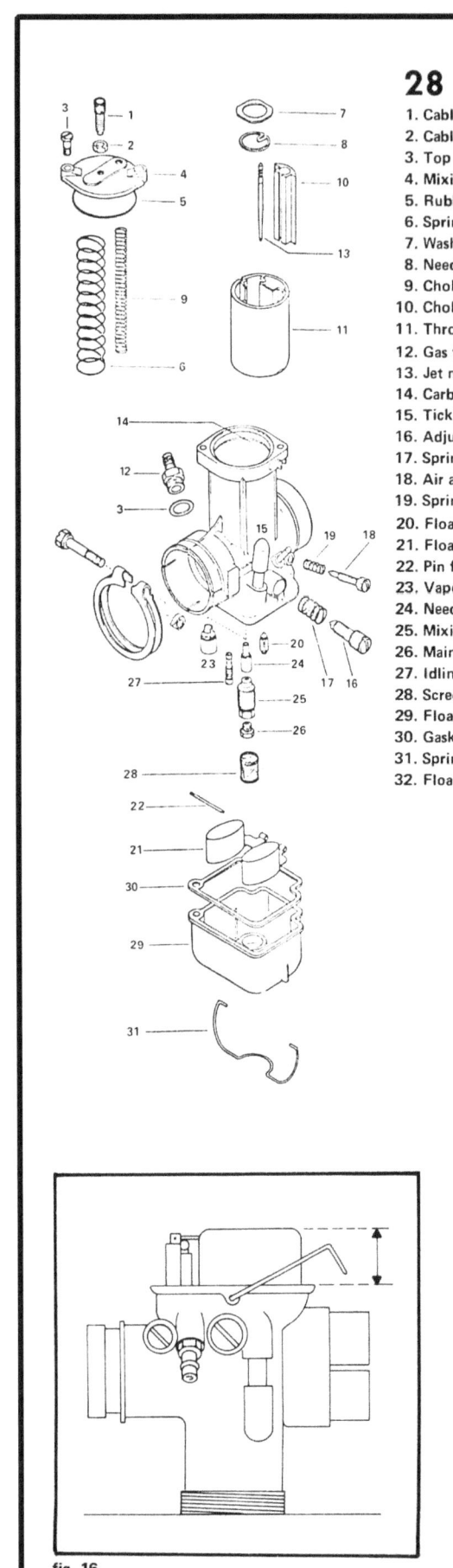

28 Bing
1. Cable adjusters
2. Cable adjuster lock nuts
3. Top screws
4. Mixing chamber top
5. Rubber washer
6. Spring
7. Washer
8. Needle clip
9. Choke spring
10. Choke slide
11. Throttle slide
12. Gas fitting
13. Jet needle
14. Carb body
15. Tickler assy.
16. Adjusting screw
17. Spring
18. Air adjusting screw
19. Spring
20. Float needle
21. Float
22. Pin for float
23. Vaporizer
24. Needle jet
25. Mixing device
26. Main jet
27. Idling jet
28. Screen
29. Float chamber
30. Gasket
31. Spring clip
32. Float nut

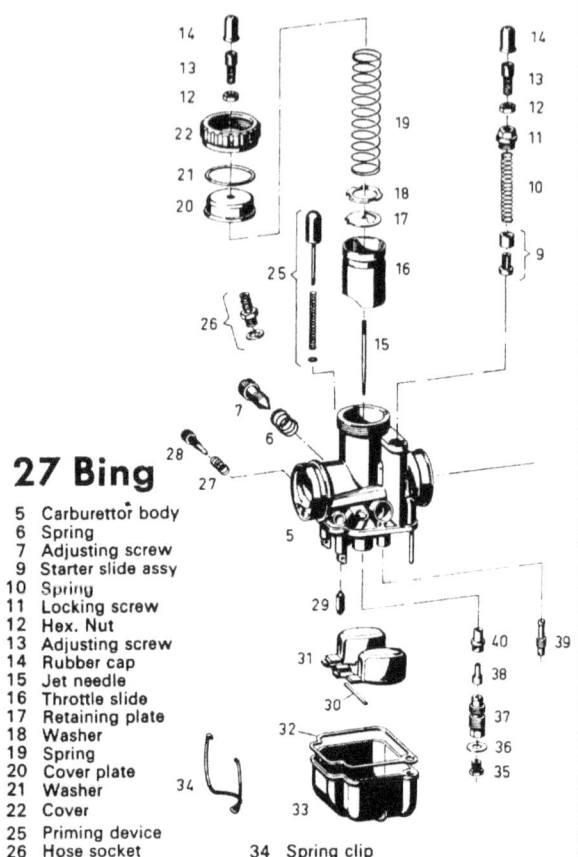

27 Bing
5. Carburettor body
6. Spring
7. Adjusting screw
9. Starter slide assy
10. Spring
11. Locking screw
12. Hex. Nut
13. Adjusting screw
14. Rubber cap
15. Jet needle
16. Throttle slide
17. Retaining plate
18. Washer
19. Spring
20. Cover plate
21. Washer
22. Cover
25. Priming device
26. Hose socket
27. Spring
28. Air adjustment screw
29. Float needle
30. Pin for float
31. Float
32. Gasket
33. Float chamber
34. Spring clip
35. Main jet
36. Washer for main jet
37. Mixing device
38. Needle jet
39. Idling jet

Stripping and Cleaning the Carburetor

It is to your advantage to clean the carburetor from time to time especially after a long endurance run where the carb was subject to a lot of dirt or water.

When disassembling and cleaning, be extra careful not to scratch or nick parts. Clean only with gas or solvent and dry with compressed air. (Do not run wires through parts.) Clean all parts meticulously.

Before reassembling check that all parts are in working condition. Worn float needles, needle jets, jet needles and throttle valves must be replaced by new ones as they have an adverse effect on engine performance and fuel consumption. Check also that all seals and gaskets have been fitted and are in good condition.

Replace the carburetor on the engine, hook up control cables and adjust properly. (See Controls section.)

Checking the Float Level

Before reassembling, the float level should be checked. Place the carb on a level surface as shown in fig. 16. Be sure the float needle is at the bottom of its seat. The level is correct if the float is parallel with the carb body as shown in fig. 16. The brass float tab must just be touching on the spring loaded needle ball. The needle ball must not be pressed down. The level is corrected by bending the brass tab on the float.

fig. 16

OPERATION AND MAINTENANCE

Checking the Chain and Sprockets for Wear and Tension

The easiest way to check and see if the chain can still be used is shown in fig. 19. Press the chain by hand upwards to tension it. If the chain can be lifted from the sprocket by more than 1/2 the diameter of the rollers, the chain must be replaced.

If the sprockets are worn as shown in fig. 20 have them replaced.

With the motorcycle unloaded and in neutral it should be possible to move the lower part of the chain freely about 1 inch (fig. 21). Both excessive and insufficient chain tension will cause unnecessary loading on the chain, sprockets and bearings.

Check to see the chain lines up evenly with both the engine and rear wheel sprockets. Be sure the master link is properly fitted with the closed part in the direction the chain moves. Oil the chain before every event and never run it dry.

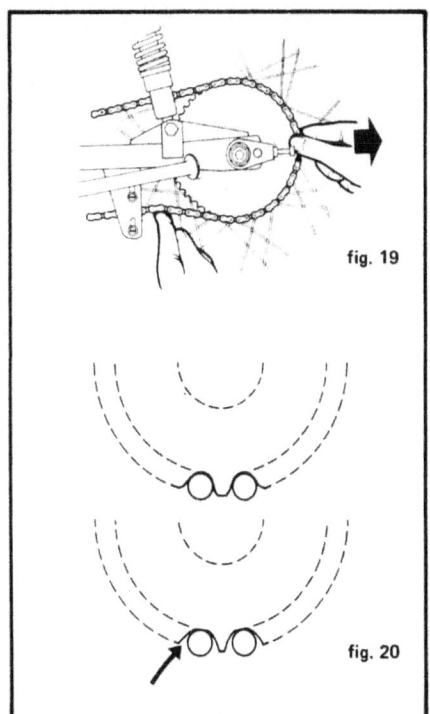

fig. 19

fig. 20

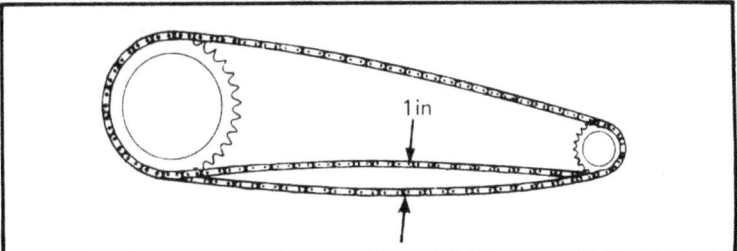

fig. 21

Changing the Gearbox Oil and Maintaining the Level

The gearbox oil should be changed regularly and after every big race or enduro. To drain the oil follow this procedure: Warm the engine up. Remove drain plug (1, fig. 22), oil filler plug (1, fig. 23) drain screw (3, fig. 23) and oil checking screw (2, fig. 23). Have a large enough container to collect the drained oil. Tilt the machine to the clutch side to be sure all oil is drained off. Replace the oil drain plug (1, fig. 22) and the drain screw (3, fig. 23). Through the filler hole put in approximately 700cc, 1½ pint, of Hi-Point Motocycle Transmission Lubricant, or 20-40 during summertime and automatic transmission fluid type "A" in 40 degrees wintertime. The clutch cover can be removed to drain the transmission oil.

The oil level is correct when oil starts to seep out the oil level hole (2, fig. 23) when the engine is in a vertical position. This level should always be checked and maintained. Secure the oil level checking screw and filler plug.

Vent hole in filler plug (1, fig. 23) should be closed either with rubber ring or a round toothpick forced into hole. Crank cases will still vent through clutch cable.

(NOTE: Do not overtighten drain plug.)

fig. 22

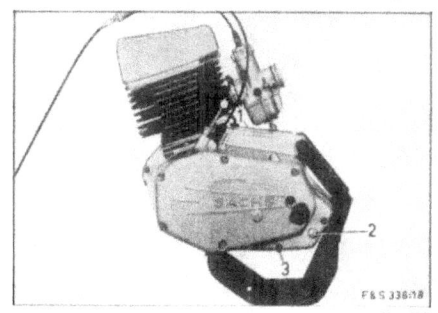

fig. 23

OPERATION AND MAINTENANCE

Front Fork Maintenance and Service

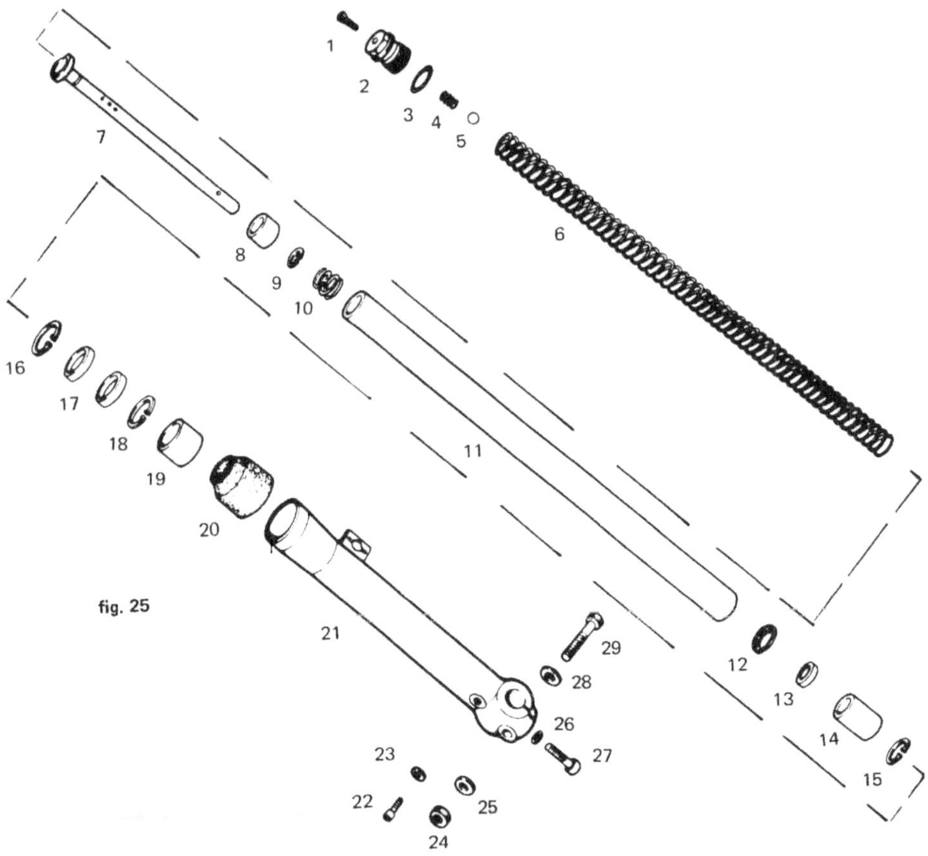

fig. 25

1. Screw
2. Fork tube nut
3. "O" Ring
4. Spring
5. Ball
6. Fork spring
7. Stop valve
8. Bushing
9. Circlip
10. Return spring
11. Fork tube
12. Stop Valve
13. Valve
14. Upper bushing
15. Circlip
16. Circlip
17. Seal
18. Circlip
19. Lower bushing
20. Fork boot
21. Fork leg
22. Drain plug
23. Washer
24. Nut
25. washer
26. Washer
27. Allen head screw
28. washer
29. Hexagon head bolt

fig. 24

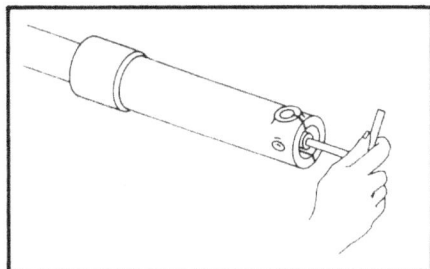

fig. 28

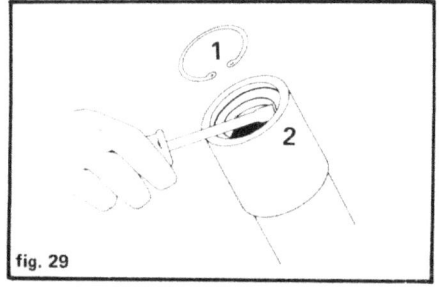

fig. 29

The forks should be maintained whenever poor fork action or excessive breaking around the seals occur. The fork oil should be changed periodically and the fork legs flushed out with a solvent, if found to need it. To change the fork oil, remove oil drain plug screw fig. 24. Let all the oil drain off and spring the forks a couple of times so all oil is drained. Replace the drain screws. Remove the fork tube nuts (2, fig. 25), check and clean these out to make sure the ball check is working properly. Add 185cc of fork oil to each leg at the top fork nut opening. Remember, the lighter weight oil means a softer fork and the heavier weight oil is a stiffer fork. We have developed a new type fork fluid, Hi-Point Silicone, and have had great results with it. It does not break down no matter what the temperature - 10° or + 200° the viscosity stays constant. It also has been found not to leak around the seals. Be sure the air vent screw, spring and ball in the top fork nuts are clear of obstructions (1, 2, 3, 4, fig. 25).

Replacing Fork Seals

Remove the axle pinch bolt.

Remove the allen screw at the bottom of the fork leg (fig. 28). If the allen screw moves but cannot be unscrewed use a piece of round steel of 12 mm diameter and 600 mm length. At one end grind a triangular point and make a handle at the other. The tool is then pressed into the stop valve tube and the allen screw removed.

The forks will now separate.

The upper fork assembly may be removed but does not need to be.

With the lower fork leg in the vise remove the circlip (1, fig. 29). Snap out the 2 seals with a screwdriver by applying heat to the fork leg (2, fig. 29). Replace with new seals.

Reassemble in reverse. Be sure the allen screw at the bottom of the legs are tightly secured, or the fork may separate if the screws fall out while in operation.

OPERATION AND MAINTENANCE

Fork Crown Adjustment and Maintenance

The fork crown on the Penton should always be checked to be sure all pinch bolts and nuts are tightly secured.

Checking and Adjusting Steering Bearings

The play in the steering bearings is checked with the motorcycle blocked up so the front wheel can rotate freely. Grasp the lower part of the fork legs and try to move them forward and backward in line with the machine (fig. 30). If any play can be noticed, this must be taken up on the upper bearing nut. Follow this procedure: Loosen the pinch bolt (2, fig. 31). Loosen the top cap nut (1, fig. 31). It may also be necessary to loosen the fork leg pinch bolts for the upper fork plate.

With a pair of adjustable pliers tighten up the upper nut bearing as shown in (3, fig. 31) then back it off about 1/8 of a turn.

Tighten up the cap nut and pinch bolts if these have been loosened. Check that the bearings move freely and do not bind in any position.

Periodically lubricate the steering bearings with a lithium base grease and be sure the O rings are in good condition. See fig. 32 for exploded view of the fork crown.

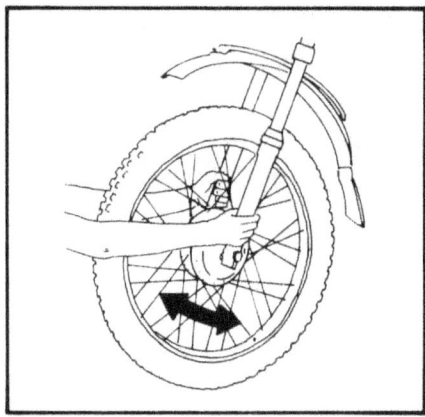

fig. 30

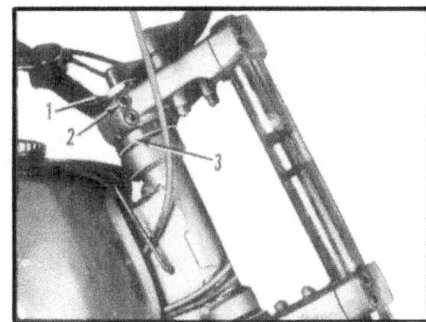

fig. 31

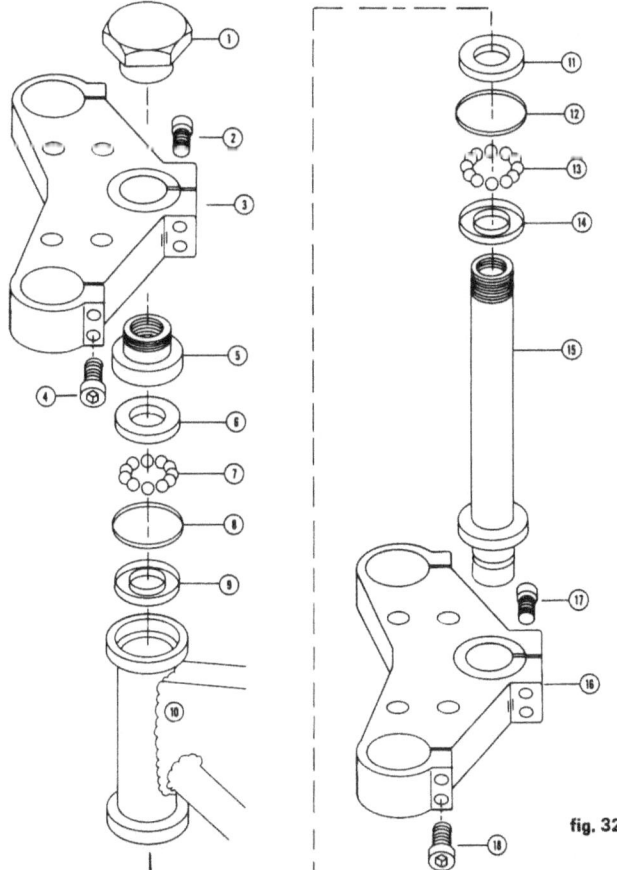

1. Cap nut
2. Pinch bolt
3. Top fork crown
4. Pinch bolts
5. Bearing race nut
6. Bearing race
7. Ball bearings (16)
8. O ring
9. Bearing race
10. Steering head
11. Bearing race
12. O ring
13. Ball bearings (16)
14. Bearing race
15. Fork stem
16. Fork crown, lower
17. Bolt, pinch
18. Pinch bolts

fig. 32

OPERATION AND MAINTENANCE

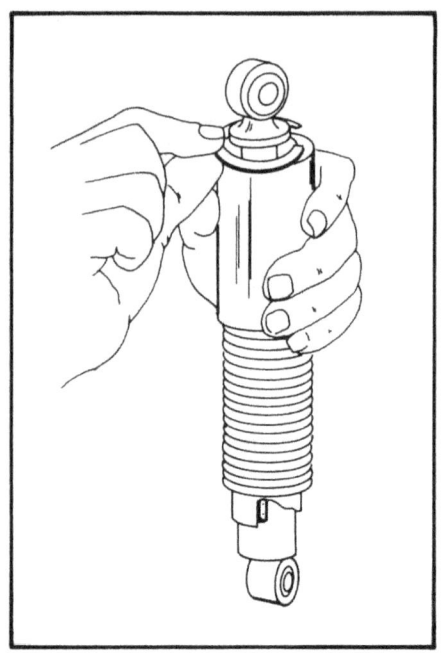

fig. 33

Rear shock absorber adjustment and maintenance

The spring rate on the shocks may be adjusted to 3 different positions by means of the cam ring at the lower end of the shock. A hook spanner is the best tool to use for this job. Different spring rates are also available from your Penton dealer if the springs furnished do not meet a specific job requirement.

Maintenance to the shocks should be carried out periodically. Be sure the rubber bushings are all in good shape and the shock bolts tight. The shock should be straight, if not the plunger is bent and the shock should be replaced.

The shocks should be greased periodically. After removing the shock from the motorcycle, place the lower bolt eye in a vise. Be sure the cam ring is in its lowest position. Push down on the top shield and remove the 2 half round retainers (fig. 33). The shield and spring will now slide off the shock. Clean all the parts and lightly grease the guides, inside the shield and the cam ring. Reassemble the shocks being sure the 2 half round retainers are seated securely.

While the spring is off the shock, check that the plunger rod is straight and that no oil leakage has occured, and that the shock absorber can be easily compressed. On the other hand, when extending the shock absorber there should be a strong resistance. If only light resistance is felt, it may mean there is air in the system. Venting is done by holding the shock upside down and pushing in and pulling out the plunger rod a few times.

If in spite of this no resistance is felt when the plunger rod is pulled out, replace the shock absorber. The rear shocks look rebuildable, but are not.

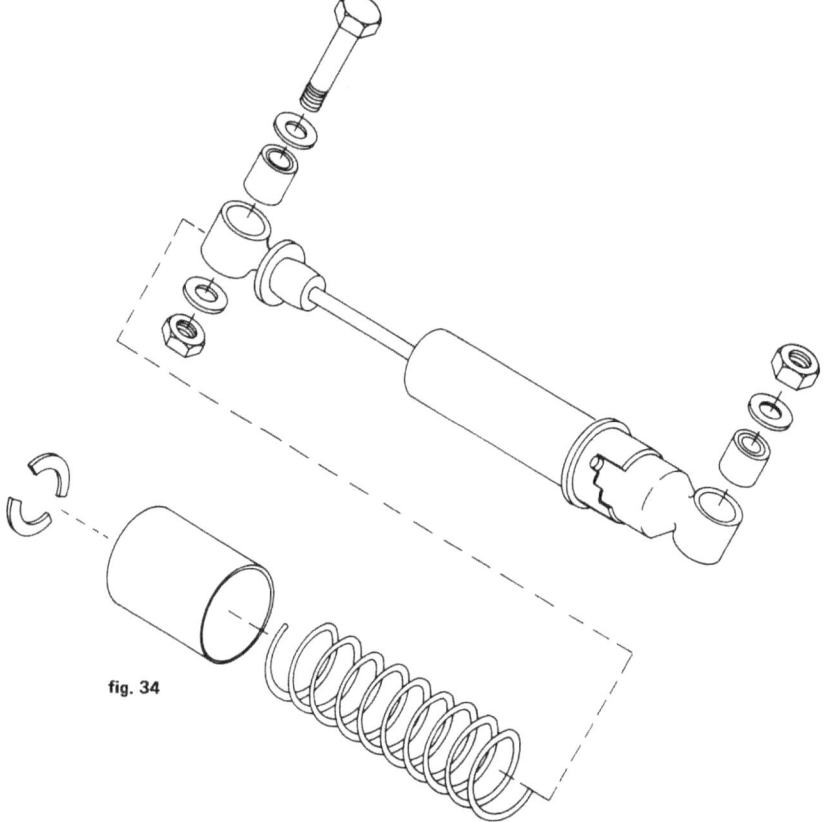

fig. 34

Lubricating The Frame

The Penton frame requires no lubrication. Be sure however to maintain the frame in clean condition and repaint areas that may chip off. For other lubrication see the Lubrication Chart Specifications.

OPERATION AND MAINTENANCE

Front Wheel Maintenance and Removal

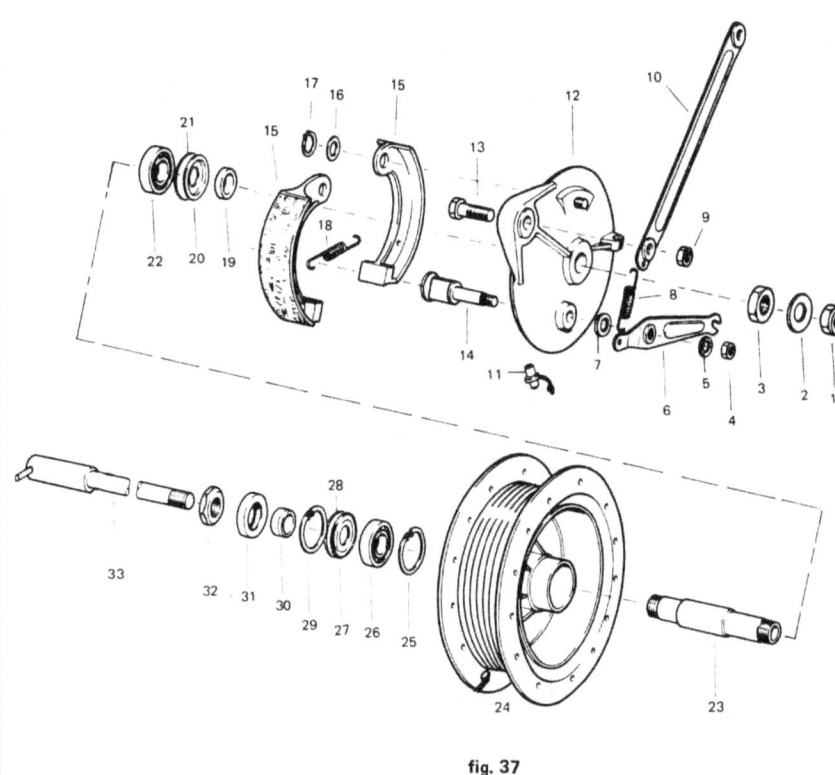

1 Nut	18 Spring
2 Washer	19 Spacer
3 Nut	20 Dust shield
4 Nut	21 Spacer
5 Lock washer	22 Bearing
6 Brake arm	23 Axle
7 PVC washer	24 Hub
8 Spring	25 Circlip
9 Nut	26 Bearing
10 Brake anchor	27 Dust shield
11 Grease fitting	28 Spacer
12 Brake plate	29 Circlip
13 Bolt	30 Bushing
14 Cam	31 Seal
15 Brake shoes	32 Nut
16 Washer	33 Axle
17 Circlip	

fig. 37

Removing the Front Wheel

Secure the motorcycle so the front wheel is off the ground. Remove the front brake cable (1, fig. 35). Remove the front brake anchor arm (2, fig. 35). Loosen the pinch bolts on both fork legs (3, fig. 35). Remove axle nut (4, fig. 35). From the opposite side, pull out the axle bolt completely (fig. 36). Remove the wheel, the front brake assembly will also come out with the wheel. When reassembling the wheel, lightly grease the axle before replacing.

Greasing and Changing the Wheel Bearing

The front wheel bearing should be greased regularly especially after running in water or dust. The bearings should be replaced when needed.

Removing the Wheel Bearings

All numbers refer to exploded view fig. 37.

With the wheel removed, proceed as follows: Remove the brake plate nut (3) from the brake plate (12). Remove brake plate from the wheel housing (24). Remove spacer (19) shims (21) and dust shield (20). Remove axle nut (32) from the opposite side. Knock the axle out toward the brake side; the brake side bearing will come out with the axle.

Opposite the brake side, remove bushing (30) and seal (31). Remove circlips (29) and spacer and dust shield (28 & 27). Knock the bearing out from the opposite side, brake side.

Replace bearings and seals if in poor condition. Regrease and assemble in reverse. Be sure all bearings are fully seated on both sides. Tighten axle nuts finger tight.

Before replacing the brake plate, check the wear on the brake shoes. Replace if necessary.

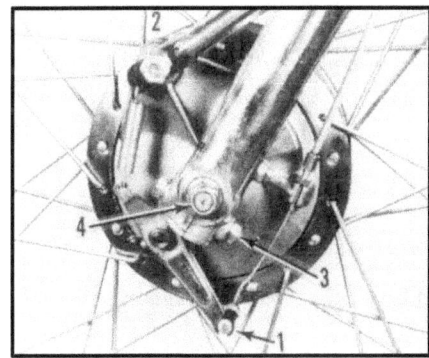

fig. 35

fig. 36

OPERATION AND MAINTENANCE

Rear Wheel Removal and Maintenance

fig. 38

fig. 39

Removing the Rear Wheel

Secure the motorcycle so the rear wheel is off the ground. Remove the brake rod (1, fig. 38). Remove brake anchor arm (2, fig. 38). Remove axle nut (1, fig. 39) top nut only. Pull out axle (3, fig. 38). Remove wheel (sprocket housing will remain on the swing arm). Replace rubber bushings in sprocket housing if any fall out in removing the rear wheel.

Reassemble in reverse.

To remove the sprocket housing undo sprocket housing nut (2, fig. 39) and remove from the swing arm. In reassembling retighten sprocket nut (2, fig. 39) snuggly.

Removing Rear Wheel Bearings

All numbers refer to fig. 40.

With the wheel removed from the motorcycle, remove brake plate (13). From the opposite side, remove snap ring (26). From the side opposite the brake drive out spacer (22) carefully, the bearing (21) will come out with the axle. Carefully drive out bearings (25) from the brake side.

Replace bearings in poor shape. Reassemble in reverse, greasing the bearing liberally with a Lithium based grease. Be sure all bearings are full seated.

NOTE:

When the rear wheel or sprocket housing has been removed the chain tension and wheel alignment should be checked. The chain adjusters (3, fig. 39) are for this purpose. See Checking the chain and sprockets for more information.

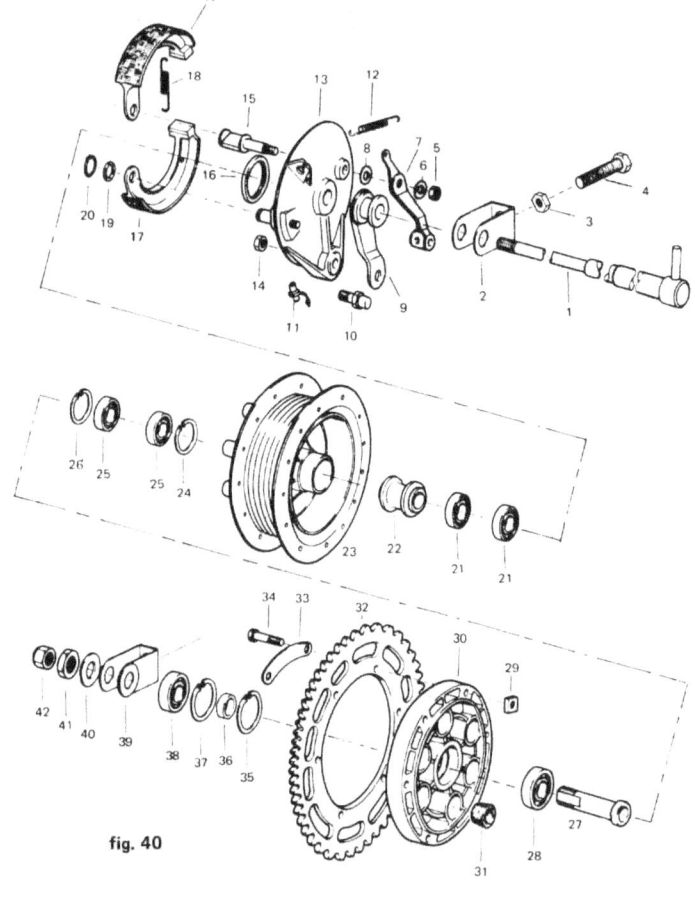

fig. 40

1 Axle	22 Spacer
2 Chain adjuster	23 Hub
3 Nut	24 Circlip
4 Bolt	25 Bearings
5 Nut	26 Circlip
6 Washer	27 Axle
7 Brake arm	28 Bearing
8 PVC washer	29 Nut
9 Spacer	30 Sprocket hub
10 Brake anchor arm bolt	31 Rubber bushings (6)
11 Grease fitting	32 Sprocket
12 Spring	33 Locking plate
13 Brake plate	34 Bolt
14 Nut	35 Circlip
15 Cam	36 Bushing
16 Seal	37 Circlip
17 Brake shoes	38 Bearing
18 Spring	39 Chain adjuster
19 Washer	40 Washer
20 Circlip	41 Nut
21 Bearings	42 Nut

OPERATION AND MAINTENANCE

Removing Sprocket Housing Bearings

All numbers refer to fig. 41.

Remove the sprocket housing from the swing arm by removing bolt (8).

Remove sprocket axle (1) and knock out sprocket bearings from opposite sides. Be sure you don't loose any of the rubber bushing (3).

Replace the bearings if in poor condition. Liberally grease the bearings and reassemble in reverse being sure all bearings are fully seated.

IMPORTANT: Always check rubber bushing drives (3, fig. 41) and maintain in good condition. When worn or fatigued, replace with new rubber bushings.

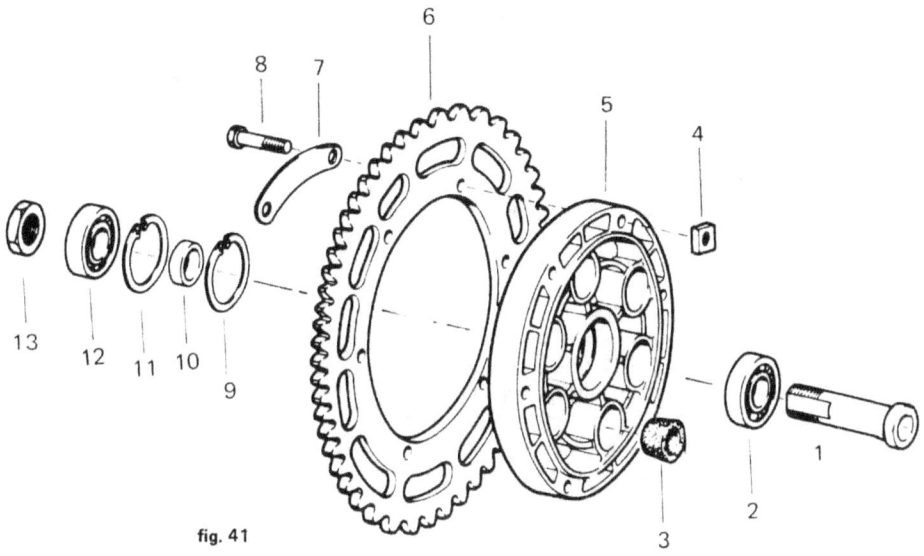

fig. 41

1 Axle	8 Bolt
2 Bearing	9 Circlip
3 Rubber bushing (6)	10 Distance bushing
4 Nut	11 Circlip
5 Sprocket housing	12 Bearing
6 Sprocket	13 Nut
7 Locking plate	

Rims and Spokes Maintenance

Before every event the wheels should be checked to see that the spokes are all tightened, and the inner tube stem straight and capped. Check to see the rims are not damaged and the tires displaced on the rims.

The tire pressure is optional to conditions and rider, pressures from 12 to 25 lbs. psi are recommended. Remember rocks can cause bad rim damage and the tire pressures should be higher than say for riding in mud or sand.

Always replace broken spokes and damaged rims. Tires should be in good shape and tubes should not be over-patched but replaced.

Always check the alignment of the wheels and that all wheel nuts are tight.

NOTE:

Penton cycles do not come with rear tire security bolts. If your Penton is used at low tire pressures, these should be fitted, otherwise tire spinning will take place causing the inner tube valve stem to break.

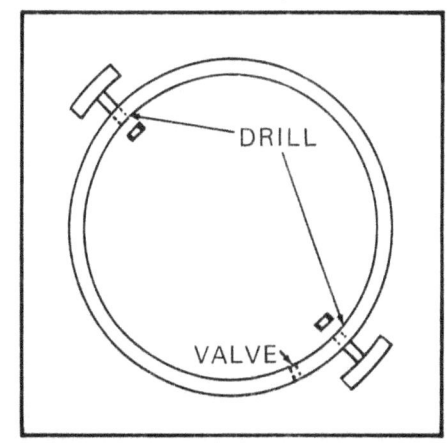

OPERATION AND MAINTENANCE

Decarbonizing the Engine - (Also see Chapter 3)

In any 2-cycle engine a small amount of lubricating oil is burnt and forms carbon deposits in the engine. Decarbonizing is usually needed after 2000 miles/50 hours or when the engine performance drops or four-stroking occurs in spite of proper engine tune.

Decarbonizing properly is a major job and care and thinking must be upper most in your mind when carrying out this job. It is handled easiest with the engine out of the frame, but this is not necessary.

Follow this procedure for the proper job:

The cycle and engine must be clean as possible. Remove the exhaust pipe from the motorcycle. Springs hold the pipe to the engine and a bracket holds it to the frame. With the pipe removed, scrape the exhaust header clean of carbon and use a stiff wire brush to finish it off. Try not to scratch the metal as this will cause carbon deposits to form faster. With the pipe as clean as possible set it aside and return to the engine.

Remove the carburetor and set aside. Remove the spark plug and the 4 cylinder head bolts. Remove the cylinder head. Clean the carbon deposits from the head being very careful not to scratch or nick the metal surface, set aside.

Remove the 4 cylinder nuts from the base of the cylinder and place the engine on its side. This is important to keep dirt and water from falling into the crankcase. Carefully remove the cylinder without rotating the cylinder (so as not to break the piston rings). With the cylinder off, place a clean rag into the crankcase opening to keep out dirt, etc. Remove the piston from the connecting rod (see **Dismantling the Engine** for this procedure.)

Carefully remove the carbon deposits from the exhaust ports in the cylinder and clean meticulously and lightly oil the cylinder liner.

Carefully remove the rings from the piston and clean the ring lands and crown of the piston being careful not to scratch the metal. New rings should always be fitted at this time.

Check the wear of the cylinder by placing the new ring at the piston turning point in the cylinder bore. If the distance exceeds 7 mm or 1/32" it is recommended that the cylinder be rebored and a new piston fitted. Note also that there may be wear on the piston too.

With all the parts thoroughly clean from carbon and dirt you can start reassembling. See **Rebuilding the Engine** for refitting the piston, cylinder and head. All new gaskets should be used. With the piston, cylinder and head all carefully assembled replace the exhaust pipe and all other parts that were removed.

It is important that you keep a record of all the work done to the engine for future reference. Use the forms included in this manual.

OPERATION AND MAINTENANCE

Motoplat (CD Ignition System - Also see Chapter Seven)

We have found in our Test Department that by employing this pointless type ignition, it has increased the power on our 100cc and 125cc engines by better that 1 h.p. Further, these units deliver a stronger spark with increased rpm's and will not start breaking up. Tests show these units to perform perfectly to 20,000 rpm's which is far in excess of anything we need in a motorcycle. As pointed out previously, these units are service free and used properly are a lifetime unit.

Replacement and Checking Ignition Timing

The Motoplat ignition on the engine should never need adjustment as it is set at the factory and should never change. It is good to once in a while pull the mag cover off and let the unit air dry. Also pull the flywheel off and clean the inside as it may build up corrosion.

To remove the unit follow this procedure: Remove mag cover. With magneto holding tool remove M 12 nut (left-hand thread) **(fig. 42)**. Place magneto puller on flywheel and remove flywheel; do not lose key **(fig. 43)**. Remove three screws in center of stator (1, fig.**45**) and remove stator. Screws (2, fig.**46**) remove the stator base plate (this need not be removed).

fig. 42

fig. 43

To Replace and Time Unit:

Place baseplate on engine, turned all the way counterclockwise in slots. (Fig. 46, 1) Tighten screws. Install stator, leaving screws loose enough to allow stator to turn freely in its slots. (Fig. 45, 1) Place the flywheel with key on crankpin. Insert timing pin through flywheel, and turn until it drops into the hole in stator. (Fig. 44, 2) Move flywheel/stator to the proper timing setting 2.6-3.0mm, using a gauge or metric rule inserted through the sparkplug hole. If stator will not move far enough in its screw slots, readjustment of baseplate will be necessary.

Carefully remove pin and flywheel. Tighten stator screws. Replace flywheel and tighten to 40 ft./lb. Recheck timing. If it is off, the timing procedure must be repeated.

Make absolutely positive that you have a good ground to the frame. Make sure all wire connections are perfect and constantly clean the terminals at the coil as they will tend to build up corrosion. Do not use silicone sealer or any other type of sealer on the coil terminal connections.

When not employing lights or a battery in your motorcycle, tape up those leads, but DO NOT GROUND THEM. See the wiring diagram for proper connections.

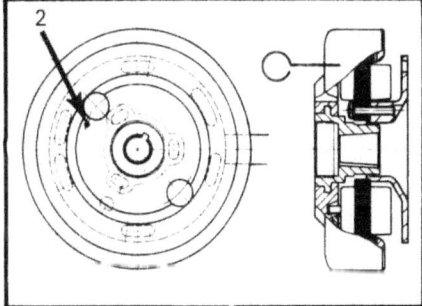

fig. 44

fig. 45

When laying the cycle up till the following week we find it a good practice to remove the ignition cover and let the ignition dry out as it will corrode if not dried out.

fig. 46

OPERATION AND MAINTENANCE

Wiring and Diagrams

The Penton motorcycle is pre-wired, but all wiring should be checked to see that connections are tight, no rubbing of wires or contact with the hot cylinder or head take place. All wiring should be wrapped in electrical tape and secured to the frame to keep from being snagged. All wires that come together should be soldered and taped up.

On the Penton Moto-Cross models no lights are fitted and the wiring is quite simple (fig. 45). Be sure the ground on the coil is tight and contact with bare metal made.

On the Enduro model the wiring is more complicated by the introduction of lights. (fig. 46) is the correct wiring for the Enduro model.

The leads coming from the magneto should be sealed to keep water and dirt from the magneto. Covers are also fitted to the ignition coil and should keep water tight and clean.

The wiring terminal is located under the gas tank (fig. 47). Be sure all the screws are tight and contact is being made.

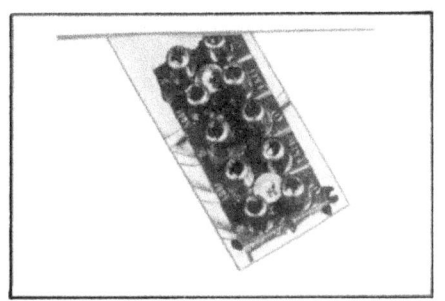

fig. 47

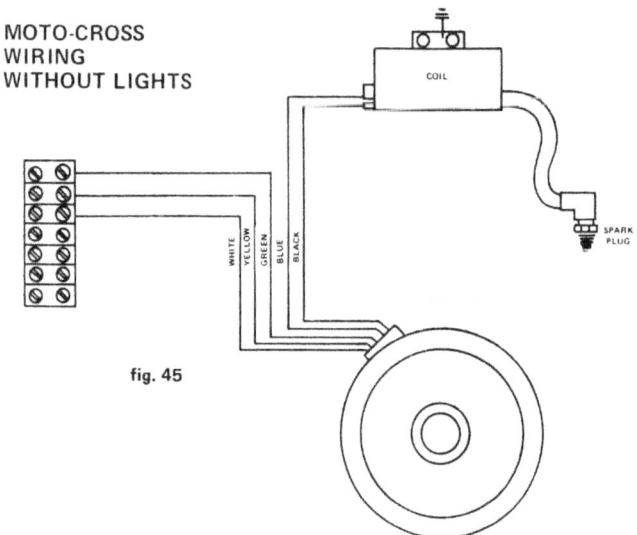

MOTO-CROSS WIRING WITHOUT LIGHTS

fig. 45

WIRES FROM MOTOPLAT
BLUE & BLACK – COIL
YELLOW – HEADLIGHT 6V/35W
GREEN – STOPLIGHT 6V/18W
WHITE – TAILLIGHT 6V/4W

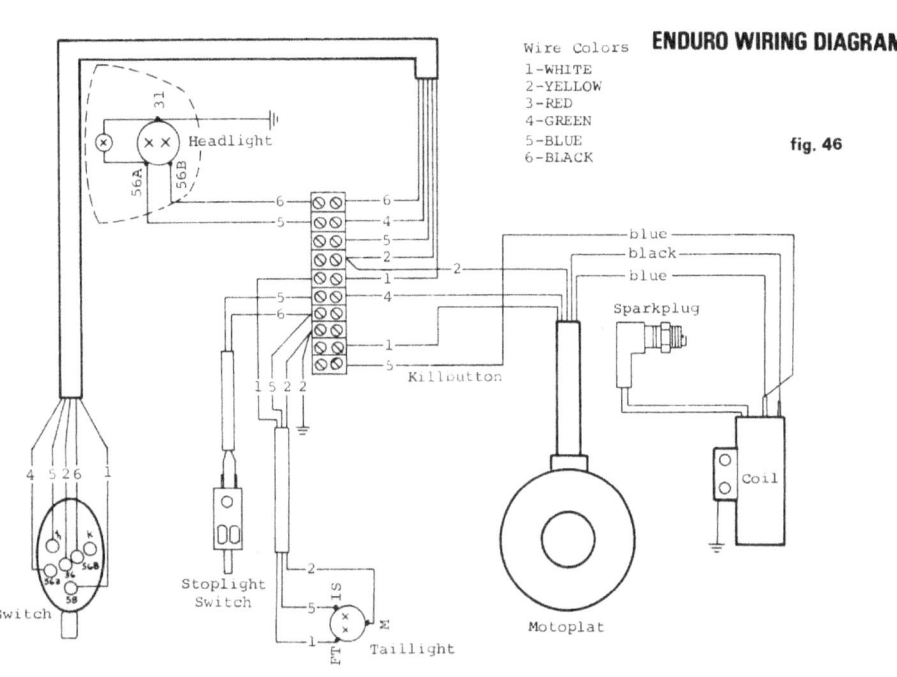

ENDURO WIRING DIAGRAM

Wire Colors
1-WHITE
2-YELLOW
3-RED
4-GREEN
5-BLUE
6-BLACK

fig. 46

OPERATION AND MAINTENANCE

Spark Plug Maintenance

The recommended spark plug is a Bosch W-280-M1 manufactured exclusively for this machine. A Bosch W-260-T1 will also work

Note the plug for the Penton is a short reach plug; never use a long reach plug as engine damage will result to the piston immediately.

The spark plug gap of the electrode should be .020 - .024 in. Use only a wire gauge when checking. Adjustment should be done on the side electrode by bending in or away from the central electrode. The spark plug should be cleaned and gapped before every event and replaced if in doubtful condition.

The heat rating indicates the degree of heat load which a spark plug can withstand. A plug with a high heat range can withstand a higher heat load than one with a lower heat rating. The higher the heat rating, the greater the resistance to glow ignition and the less to carbonizing and oiling up.

A plug with too high a heat rating and which glows, usually causes overheating and piston seizure. In doubtful cases it is better to fit a plug with a cold rating than one with too hot a rating. The engine will not start so easy and will not run as well at low loading in the lower speed range, it will also never be damaged in the way it could be using a plug with too hot a rating.

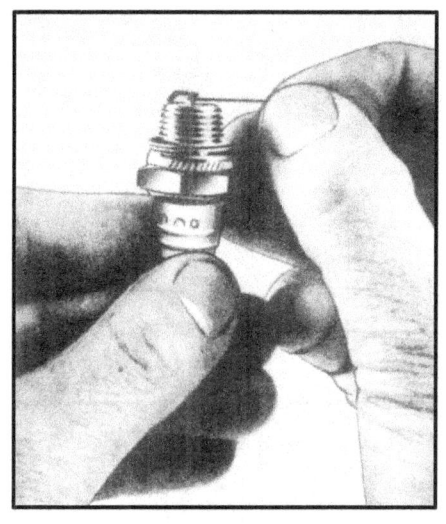

Appearance of the Sparking Plug

Correct Appearance:

Medium-brown insulator base, dark grey socket with grey carbon deposit. No excessive burning of the electrodes.

Incorrect Appearance:	Possible Faults:
Beads on insulator base, which is burnt white. Electrodes "blued".	Heat rating too low. Fuel/air mixture too lean. Ignition too early. Sparking plug insufficiently tightened.
Insulator base, socket and electrodes coated with oil and carbon deposits.	Heat rating too high. Too much oil in the gas.
Insulator base, socket and electrodes coated with dry, black soot.	Heat rating too high. Fuel/air mixture too rich. Air cleaner blocked.
Dry, powder-like coating on socket and part of the insulator base. Insulator base point burnt clean.	Correct heat rating. High lead content in gasoline.
Lead compounds on insulator base. Electrodes heavily corroded.	Heat rating too low and too high a lead content in the gasoline.

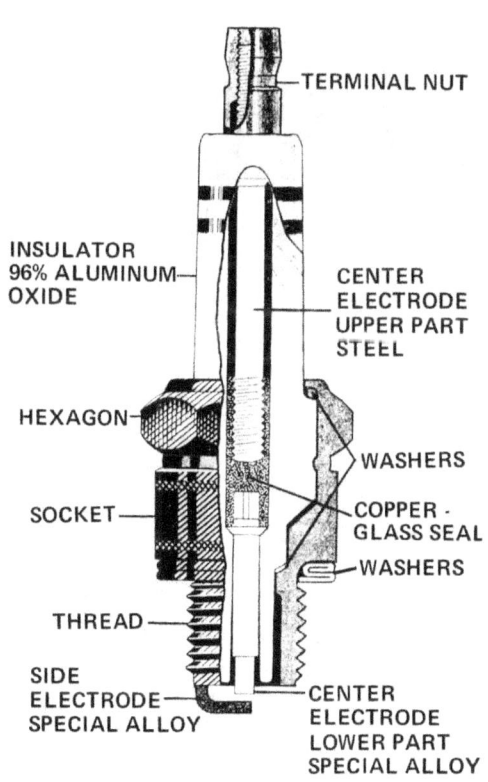

OPERATION AND MAINTENANCE

fig. 48

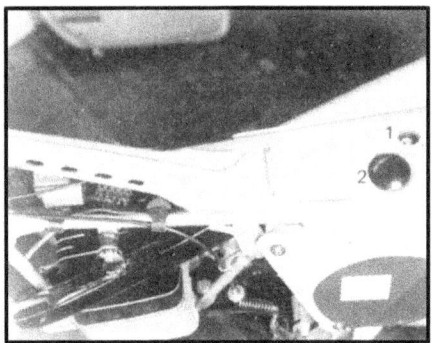
Fig. 49

Air Cleaner Maintenance - (Also see Chapter Six)

The Penton is fitted with a specially designed still air box matched to give the engine its most power.

The air filter is one of the most important maintenance items on your motorcycle and should be constantly maintained before and after every ride. In long enduros and cross country runs, where dirt and water are heavy, it is advisable to change the filter at the halfway point. Having more than one filter handy at one time is a wise thing to do. A good working filter will double the life of your engine and keep your spark plug from whiskering plugs.

The Pentons come with either a paper filter or the foam filter element. You should be aware of the drawbacks and good points of each type and then use your common knowledge as to the one most suitable to you and what type to use on each run.

The Twin Air foam element is very useful in dusty and sandy conditions. It traps most small airborne particles and is popular in desert and dusty motocross racing. The filtron element has no basic fault. If splashed or becomes wet with water, it will pass the water and mud right through. Needless to say, you can imagine what will happen.

The paper is a dual purpose filter. It will work good in dusty conditions, but will sometimes overload with dust and dirt and pass a little. However, it will not pass water and mud unless completely submerged and only cause the filter to become wet making the machine run ragged, but at least not ruin your engine. We recommend the paper filter on enduros where water and mud will be an unknown factor.

The general maintenance of the air box should be to check and clean it meticulously after every race and check for leaks in the air box and connecting hose.

Also check for cracks in the air box itself. A little trick we use is to coat the inside of the air box with a coating of white grease to pick up any dirt that may escape through the filter.

In running where it is muddy and wet, we advise you to purchase the Penton carburetor apron that protects the carb from mud and water.

Remember the air box is probably the most important maintenance item on your bike to insure long engine life.

VERY IMPORTANT!!!! Silicone between boot and air box. Also, tape over top of frame (Fig. 49, 1-2)

(fig. 50)

WASHING your filter.
1. Remove element from screen.
2. Wash with gas, kerosene or soap and water.
3. Squeeze out excess. Let dry. Re-oil per instructions.

OILING your filter before installation.
1. Remove element from screen.
2. Saturate with motor oil. Use petroleum oil only.
3. Squeeze out excess oil.
4. Replace element on screen. Be sure inside sealing edge of foam overlaps screen.
5. Install assembly in air cleaner.

Expansion Chamber/Muffler

The Penton is fitted with a combination expansion chamber/muffler. Fig. 50 shows the muffler in position. This should always be used when riding in enduros and cross country events where the general population may be annoyed by unmuffled motorcycles. It is a courtesy that assures you of being able to ride there again.

(fig. 51)

The muffler is tuned to perform on the cycle and should not be removed. Occasionally you should remove the end and clean out the baffles of oil and grime.

Washing the Cycle

After using the cycle thoroughly wash it down. Best results are obtained by using hot water and detergent after spraying with water. Before spraying, remove the air filter and block the air filter passage with a rag. Do not spray directly into the brake drums.

Take off the rubber protecting covers on the front forks and clean underneath them.

After having wiped the motorcycle dry with a cloth, it is advisable to start the engine. Run the cycle and apply both front and rear brakes lightly so any moisture is dryed-up. Run the engine at a moderately high speed and pump a little oil into the carb at the side of the throttle. This deposits a film of oil on the engine parts and counteracts any rust that may form from condensation.

Remove the magneto casing to enable moisture to evaporate.

In order to prevent unslightly rust marks on the footrests and other parts that the paint is normally rubbed off, it is advisable to lightly wipe with a rag soaked in oil.

Lubricate the drive chain, control cables and associated joints.

Keeping the Penton in Tip-Top Shape

Service and maintenance to your Penton cycle is the most important thing in any competition motorcycle. You should make out a routine service schedule and follow it before and after every outing. You should keep a notebook with all the information you have acquired in servicing and running your Penton.

If parts look like they are in doubtful shape, they should be replaced immediately so they in turn do not effect another good part.

OPERATION AND MAINTENANCE

FAULT TRACING

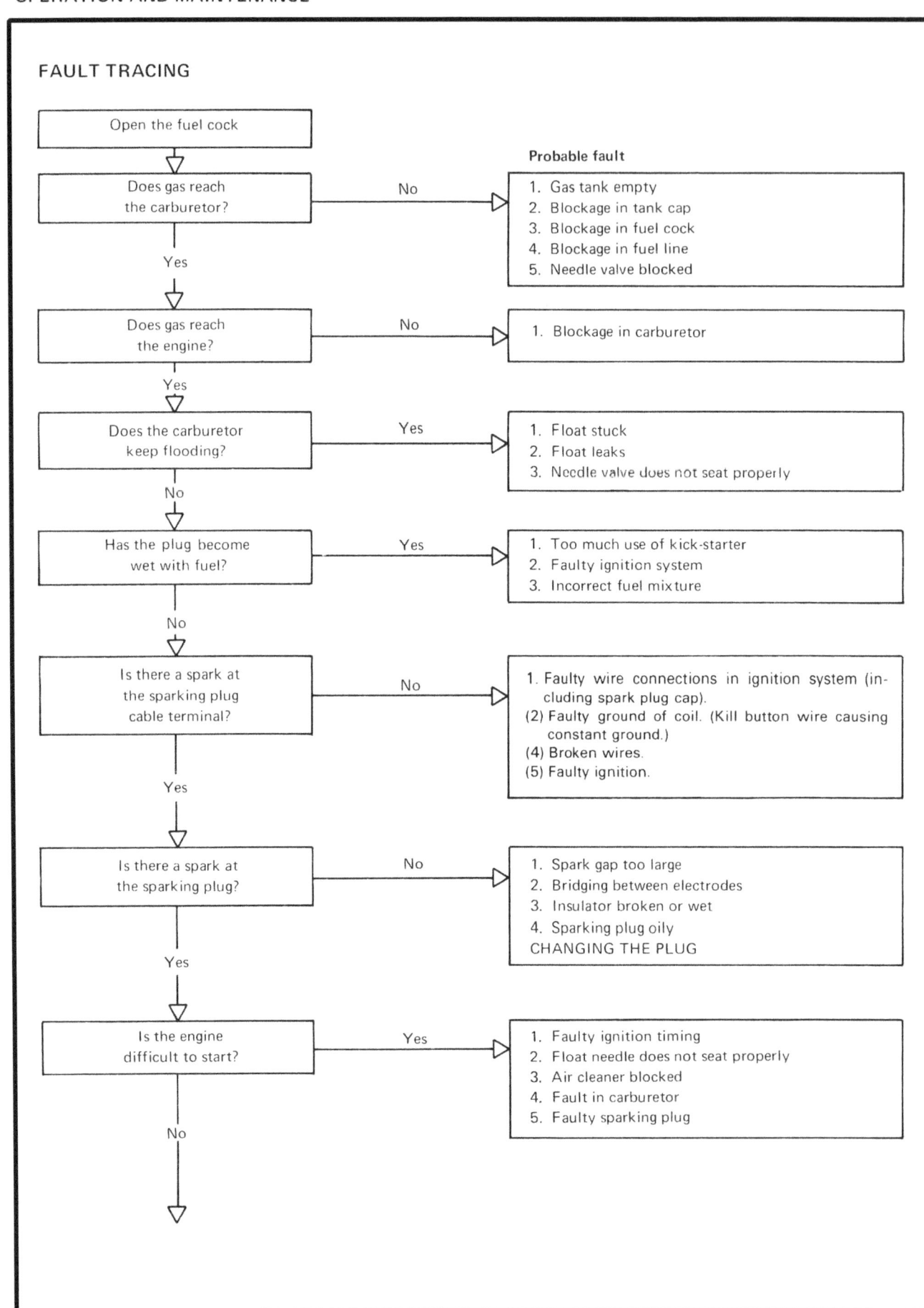

OPERATION AND MAINTENANCE

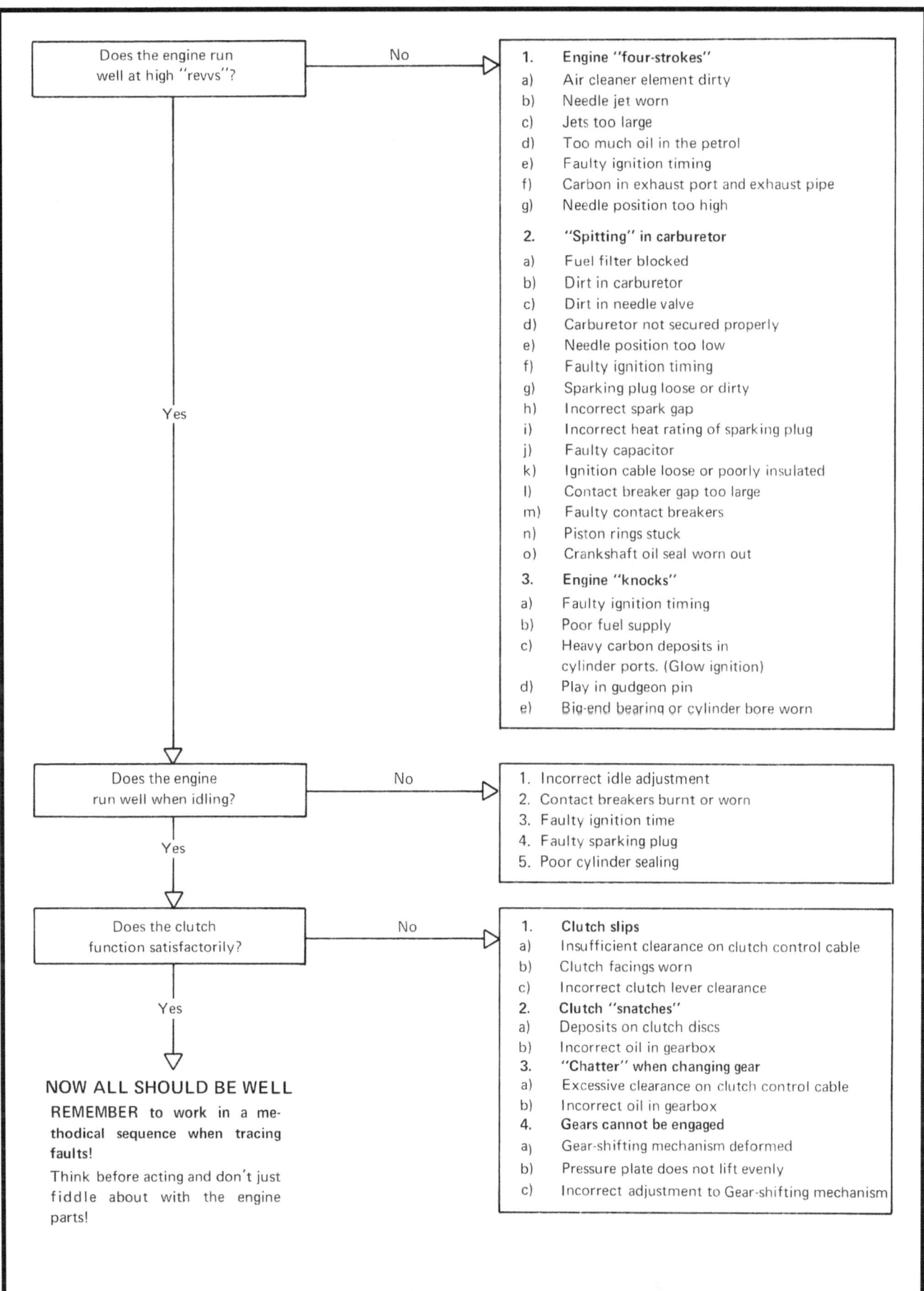

OPERATION AND MAINTENANCE

NOTES ON YOUR PENTON

Whenever work or tuning is performed on your Penton, keep the changes noted here for future reference and forseeing maintenance requirements.

DATE BIKE PURCHASED: _____

DATE OF CHANGE
OR REPAIR

ENGINE
Piston _____
Rings _____
Cylinder _____
Clutch _____
Bearings _____
Con Rod _____
Gears _____
Ignition _____
Overhaul _____
Decarbonized _____
Spark plug _____
Oil changed _____

CARBURETOR
Jets _____
Needle Position _____
Rebuild _____

WHEELS
Front Brake Lining _____
Rear Brake Lining _____
Front Bearings _____
Rear Bearings _____
Sprockets, Engine and Rear _____
Chain _____
Greasing _____

FORKS
Seals _____
Steering Crown _____
Oil _____

REAR SHOCKS
Spring Position _____
Spring Rate _____
Greasing _____
Replacement _____

CONTROLS
Throttle Cable _____
Front Brake Cable _____
Clutch Cable _____
Choke Cable _____

SACHS ENGINE

CHAPTER TWO

GENERAL INFORMATION

INTRODUCTION

Fichtel & Sachs is one of the largest and most experienced builders of proprietary motorcycle engines in the world. Over the years, their engines have been used in virtually hundreds of motorcycle makes. In today's market, Sachs engines are most commonly associated with such motorcycle manufacturers as DKW, Penton, Monark, Tyran, and Dalesman, as well as many limited-production special builders.

The information in this handbook applies to the following models:

    1001/5 A
    1251/5 A
    1001/6 A (no longer in production)
    1251/6 A (no longer in production)
    1001/6 B
    1251/6 B
    1251/6 C

NOTE: The first 3 digits in the engine model number indicate its displacement class.

While all late model Sachs engines of a given displacement are basically identical, variations exist in number of gears (5 or 6), cylinder construction, finning patterns, carburetion, ignition, and exhaust systems. The various engine types are shown in **Figure 2**.

SPECIAL TOOLS

Special tools for servicing Sachs engines are shown in **Figure 1**. In some cases a similar tool that you may already have, such as a gear puller or a timing gauge, may be substituted. As far as possible, use the special tools called for. A jerry-rigged tool could damage a vital component whose replacement cost might be greater than the cost of the special tool required to do the job correctly. The tools may be purchased through dealers handling Sachs-engined products. If you are on good terms with a dealer, you may be able to borrow a tool you need from your dealer's service department.

Much of the labor charge for repairs made by dealers is for removal and disassembly of other parts to reach the defective one. It is frequently possible to do all of this yourself, then take the affected subassembly into the dealer for repair.

Once you decide to tackle a job yourself, read the entire section in this manual pertaining to it. Study the illustrations and the text until you have a good idea of what's involved. If special tools are required, make arrangements to get them before you begin work. It's frustrating to get partly into a job and then find that you are unable to complete it.

REPAIR TOOLS AND MOUNTING JIG

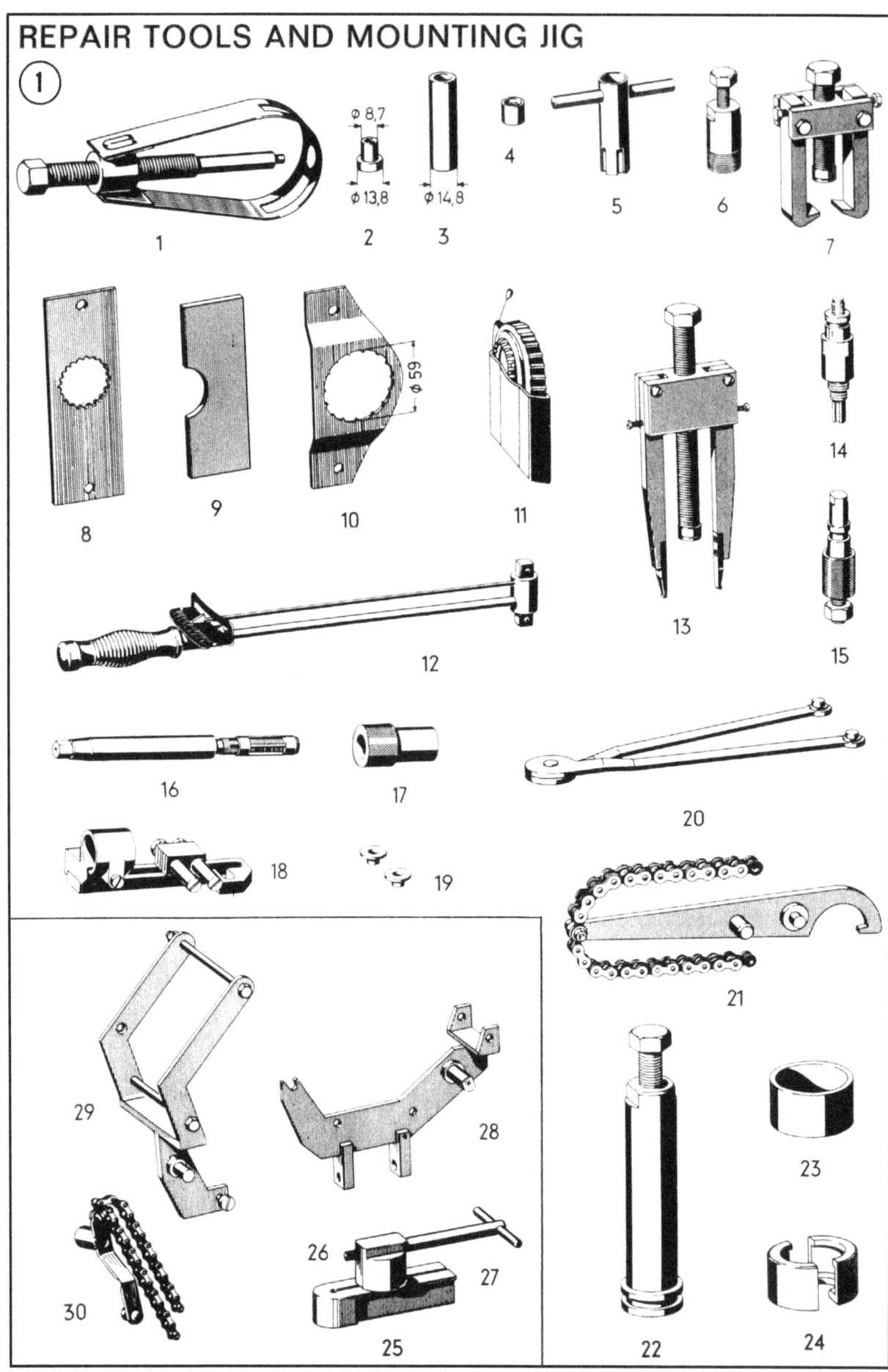

Illustr. No.	Part No.	Description	1001/5 A	1251/5 A	1251/5 B	1001/6 A	1251/6 A	1001/6 B	1251/6 B	1251/6 C
		Repair tools								
1	0276 065 101	Gudgeon pin extractor	x	x	x	x	x	x	x	x
2	0276 122 001	Insert bush for gudgeon pin extractor	x	x	x	x	x	x	x	x
3	0977 053 000	Guide pin for piston	x	x	x	x	x	x	x	x
4	0276 156 000	Protective cap, bore 10 mm (0.394 in.)	x	x	x	x	x	x	x	x
5	0676 021 000	Box spanner (profile)	x	x	x	x	x	x	x	x
6	0276 150 005	Puller for magneto flywheel M 26 x 1.5	x	x	x	x	x	x	x	x
7	0276 179 000	Puller for sprocket	x	x	x	x	x	x	x	x
8	0676 110 100	Locking plate for clutch hub	x	x	x	x	x	x	x	x
9	0276 019 101	Intermediate plate	x	x	x	x	x	x	x	x
10	0676 109 000	Locking plate for driving gear	x	x	x	x	x	x	x	x
11	0276 175 000	Revolution counter	x	x	x	x	x	x	x	x
12	0276 170 000	Torque spanner	x	x	x	x	x	x	x	x
13	0276 161 101	Oil seal extractor	x	x	x	x	x	x	x	x
	0276 164 100	Extractor hook 3 mm (0.118") (1 off) } spare parts for 0276 161 101								
	1476 012 000	Thrust bearing								
14	0276 135 100	Spark advance timing gauge	x	x	x	x	x	x	x	x
15	0676 027 000	Tool for extracting and inserting small end bush	x	x	x	x	x			
16	0276 159 002	Adjustable reamer P 14.0...15.5 mm (0.551...0.610 in.)	x	x	x	x	x			
17	0276 158 001	Guide bush No. 3, bore 17.7 mm (0.697 in.)	x	x	x	x	x			
18	0276 157 000	Guide bar	x	x	x	x	x			
19	0276 160 001	Clamping sleeve, bore 8.2 mm (0.323 in.) (1 off)	x	x	x	x	x			
20	0276 181 000	Adjustable pin spanner	1	1		1	1	1	1	1
21	0277 086 406	Hook spanner	x	x		x	x	x	x	x
	0276 180 002	Hook spanner (without illustration)			x					
22	1476 013 000	Puller sleeve assembly	x	x	x	x	x	x	x	x
	1476 011 000	Threaded sleeve } spare parts for 1476 013 000								
	1440 027 001	Screw, hexagon head								
	1476 012 000	Thrust bearing								
23	1447 009 000	Clamping ring, 58 mm (2.283 in.) I.D.	x	x	x	x	x	x	x	x
24	1476 014 010	Puller shells for inner race of magneto bearing M 20	x	x	x	x	x	x	x	x
		Mounting jig								
25	0276 081 000	Clamping base	x	x	x	x	x	x	x	x
26	0276 082 000	Swivel unit	x	x	x	x	x	x	x	x
27	0276 085 005	Clamping screw	x	x	x	x	x	x	x	x
28	0276 088 006	Mounting bracket	x	x	x	x	x	x	x	x
29	0276 131 000	Mounting bracket	x	x	x	x	x	x	x	x
30	0276 093 205	Lever	x	x	x	x	x	x	x	x

1 = for MOTOPLAT ignition set

② ENGINE VERSIONS

SACHS 1001/5 A
      1251/5 A
(cast iron cylinder)

SACHS 1251/5 B
(aluminium cylinder with sunburst cylinder head)
NHW-Military

SACHS 1001/5 A
      1251/5 A
      1001/6 A
      1251/6 A
      1001/6 B
      1251/6 B
      1251/6 C
(aluminium, large fin cylinder with sunburst cylinder head)

SACHS ENGINE - WORKSHOP MANUAL

CHAPTER THREE

CYLINDER HEAD, CYLINDER & PISTONS

CYLINDER HEAD

Cylinder heads are cast from lightweight aluminum in 3 fin patterns—vertical fins (**Figure 1**), radial or sunburst fins without connecting bridges (**Figure 2**), and sunburst fins with connecting bridges (**Figure 3**).

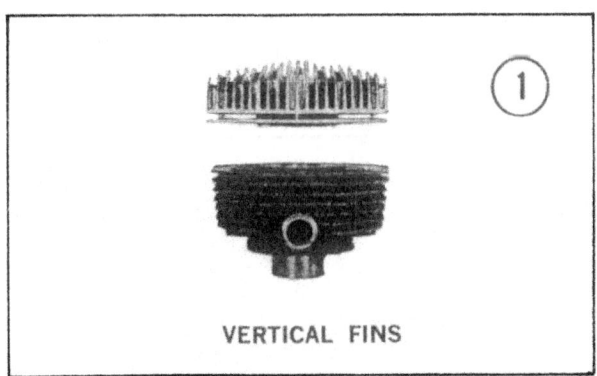

VERTICAL FINS

RADIAL FINS

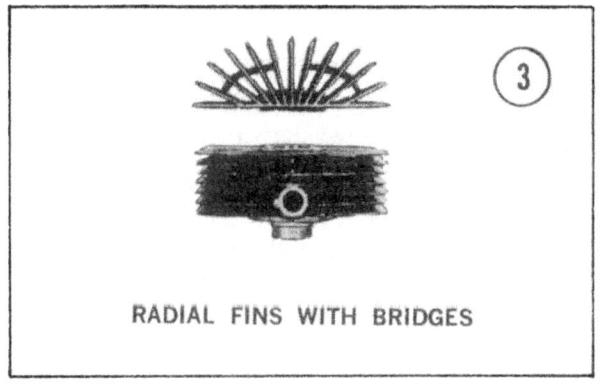

RADIAL FINS WITH BRIDGES

Cylinder Head Removal

To avoid possible distortion of the cylinder head, allow the engine to cool before removal. To remove the head, proceed as follows:

1. If the engine is installed in the motorcycle, shut off the fuel taps, disconnect the lines, and remove the fuel tank from the motorcycle. Unplug the high-tension lead from the spark plug and unscrew the plug from the head. If the coil is situated in such a way that it could be damaged during work on the head, note the location of the primary leads and remove the coil from the motorcycle. On some models, it will also be necessary to remove the exhaust system.

2. Cylinder head nuts must be removed and reinstalled in the sequence specified in **Figure 4**. Loosen each nut one-half turn and repeat the

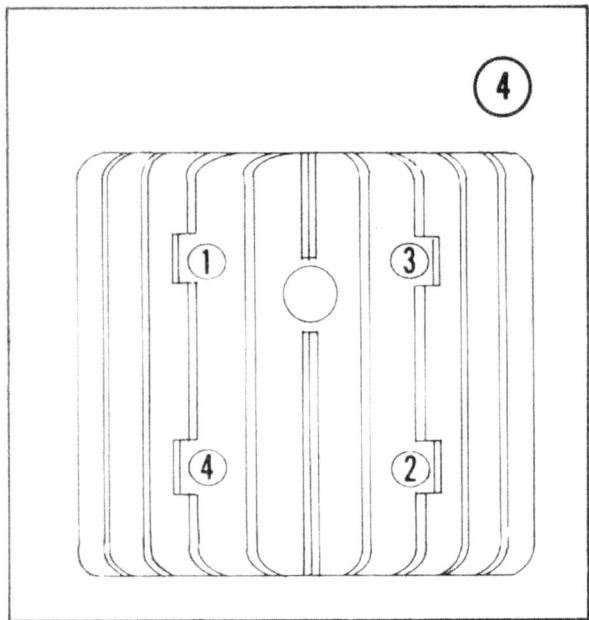

process until each nut has been loosened 2 full turns. Then, remove each nut completely and mark its location so it can be reinstalled on the stud from which it was removed.

3. Lift the cylinder head off of the cylinder, taking care not to drop washers or locating dowels into the cylinder. If necessary, tap the head with a soft-face mallet to loosen it; never pry it off because doing so may damage the fins or the sealing surface. If the engine is equipped with a head gasket, remove it.

Removing Carbon Deposits

Scrape away carbon deposits with the rounded end of a hacksaw blade. Wrap tape around the blade (see **Figure 5**) to provide a comfortable handle and prevent damage to your hand. Be careful not to scar the surface of the combustion chamber or around the seal. Small burrs resulting from gouges in the chamber will create hot spots which will cause pre-ignition and heat erosion. Gouges on the sealing surface will result in an improper seal of the combustion chamber.

After scraping, clean the head in solvent. Carefully clean the spark plug bore with a fine wire brush and blow out carbon particles with an air hose.

Cylinder Head Installation

1. On engines so equipped, install the guide dowels and a new head gasket. The inscription

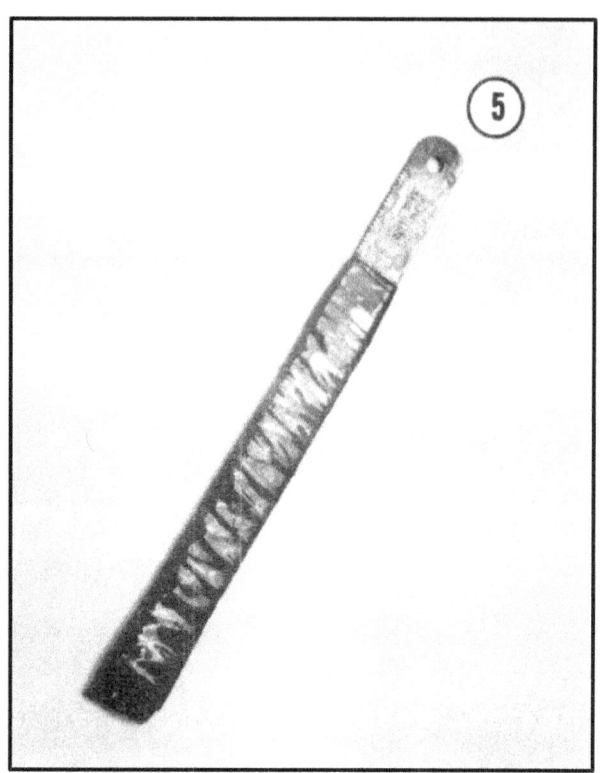

"oben" on the gasket should face up and point toward the exhaust port.

2. Reinstall the head and screw on the nuts (or bolts) making sure each one has a washer.

> NOTE: *For the large sunburst head, make sure the bevelled fin is toward the front and the plug bore to the rear* **(Figure 6)**.

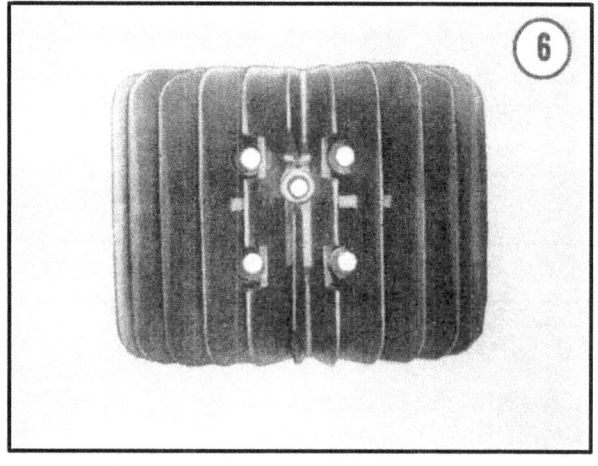

3. Tighten the nuts (bolts) with a torque wrench, in the pattern shown in Figure 4, to 12-15 ft.-lb. (1.7-2.0 kgm). Rotate the crankshaft to move the piston up and down in the cylinder after tightening each nut. Again tighten the nuts in the pattern shown, this time to the appropriate

torque value given in **Table 1**, moving the piston up and down after tightening each nut.

4. Complete the reassembly by reversing the remaining steps for removal.

Table 1 CYLINDER HEAD NUT (BOLT) TORQUE

Type	Torque
Aluminum cylinder with through-studs and nuts	18-22 ft.-lb. (2.5-3.0 kpm)
Cast iron cylinder with head bolts	22-23 ft.-lb. (3.0-3.2 kpm)

CYLINDER

There are 2 cylinder types used on Sachs engines—one-piece cast iron and two-piece cast aluminum with a pressed-in cast iron liner. The integral liner in the cast-iron cylinder is not replaceable; however, the cylinder is designed to accomodate three rebores. The cast-iron liner in aluminum cylinders will also accomodate three rebores and then may be replaced with a new liner to restore the cylinder diameter to the original dimension. Cylinder types for each model are shown in the *Specifications* section.

Cylinder Removal

1. Remove the cylinder head as described previously. In all cases, it is necessary to remove the exhaust system and carburetor.

2. On engines with a flanged cylinder base, unscrew the 4 nuts which hold the cylinder onto the crankcase.

3. Pull the cylinder up and off the studs and piston. Don't rotate the cylinder as you raise it; this could result in breakage of the rings.

Cylinder Inspection

Measure cylinder wall wear at 3 depths within the cylinder, using a cylinder gauge or inside micrometer, as shown in **Figure 7**. Measure parallel and at a right angle to the crankshaft at the locations shown in **Figure 8**. If taper exceeds 0.008 in. (0.20mm), or out-of-round

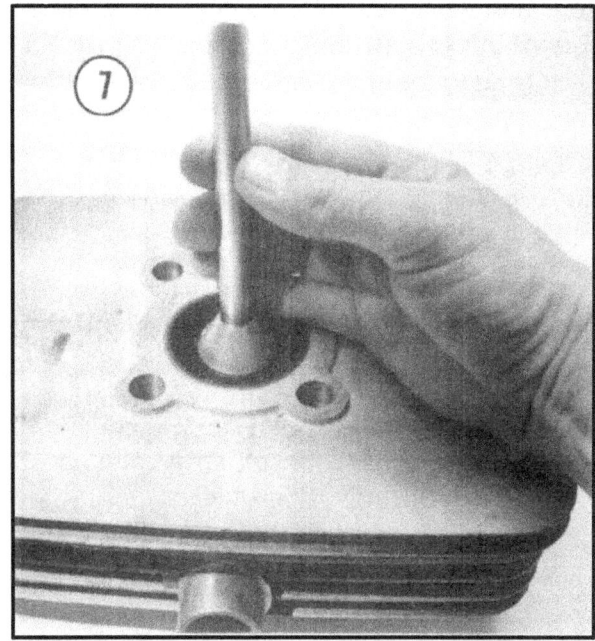

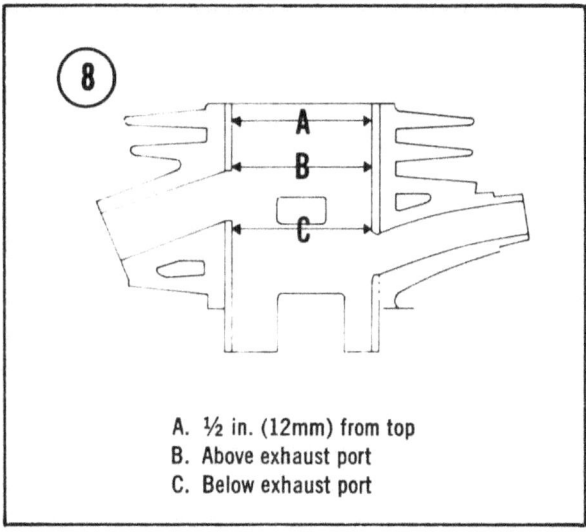

A. ½ in. (12mm) from top
B. Above exhaust port
C. Below exhaust port

exceeds 0.008 in. (0.20mm), rebore and hone the cylinder to the next oversize. After boring, radius the edges of the transfer, intake, and exhaust port (see **Table 2**).

Have the new piston on hand prior to reboring the cylinder so that it may be measured and the cylinder bored to provide the required piston-to-cylinder clearance shown in **Table 3**. Measure the piston just above the bottom of the skirt at a right angle to the pin bosses. Add the result to the desired clearance to determine the final overbore size of the cylinder.

To check the clearance of a run-in piston and bore, measure the piston and cylinder as described above and subtract the piston dimension from the cylinder dimension. If the clearance exceeds 0.008 in. (0.20mm), the cylinder should be rebored to the next oversize and a new piston fitted.

> NOTE: *Because Sachs wrist pins are mounted low in the piston, the wear pattern in the cylinder tends to become barrel shaped* **(Figure 9).** *This condition accelerates ring wear. If this condition exists and only the rings are replaced, they will wear rapidly. If "barreling" is even only slightly evident, rebore the cylinder to the next oversize and fit a new piston.*

Cylinder Installation

1. Install a new cylinder base gasket on the studs in the crankcase (**Figure 10**). On engines with through-studs, install the alignment dowels.

2. Place a wooden block beneath the piston (**Figure 11**).

> NOTE: *The block can be made from a piece of scrap lumber or plywood cut to the dimensions shown in* **Figure 12.**

3. Make sure the rings are seated in the grooves and correctly lined up with the locating pins in the ring grooves (see **Figure 13**).

Table 2   PISTON DIAMETER

Displacement	Standard	First Oversize	Second Oversize	Third Oversize
97cc	48.0mm (1.89 in.)	48.5mm (1.91 in.)	49.0mm (1.93 in.)	49.5mm (1.95 in.)
122cc	54.0mm (2.126 in.)	54.5mm (2.147 in.)	55.0mm (2.167 in.)	55.5mm (2.186 in.)

NOTE: The inch measurement is presented only for general reference. Pistons are sized metrically.

Table 3   PISTON-TO-CYLINDER CLEARANCE

Displacement	Bore Size	Clearance
97cc	Standard 48.0mm (1.89 in.)	0.1198mm (0.00473 in.)
	First Oversize 48.5mm (1.91 in.)	0.1213mm (0.00478 in.)
	Second Oversize 49.0mm (1.93 in.)	0.1226mm (0.00484 in.)
	Third Oversize 49.5mm (1.95 in.)	0.1237mm (0.00488 in.)
122cc	Standard 54.0mm (2.13 in.)	0.1350mm (0.00532 in.)
	First Oversize 54.5mm (2.15 in.)	0.1363mm (0.00537 in.)
	Second Oversize 55.0mm (2.17 in.)	0.1375mm (0.00542 in.)
	Third Oversize 55.5mm (2.19 in.)	0.1388mm (0.00547 in.)

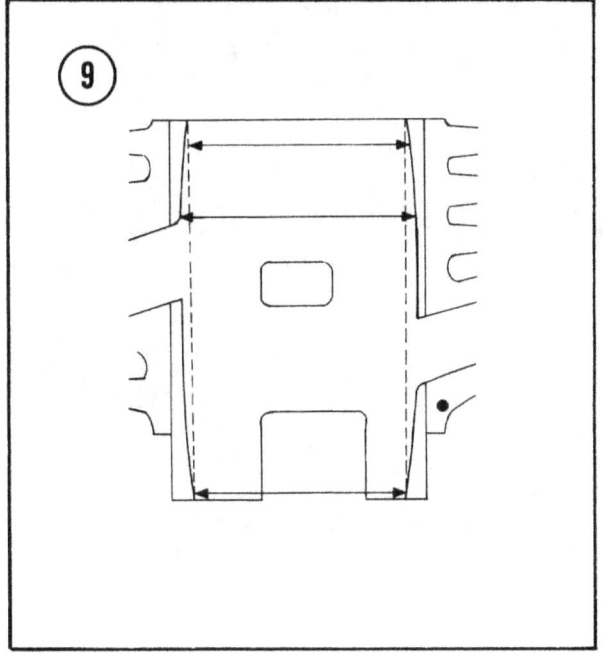

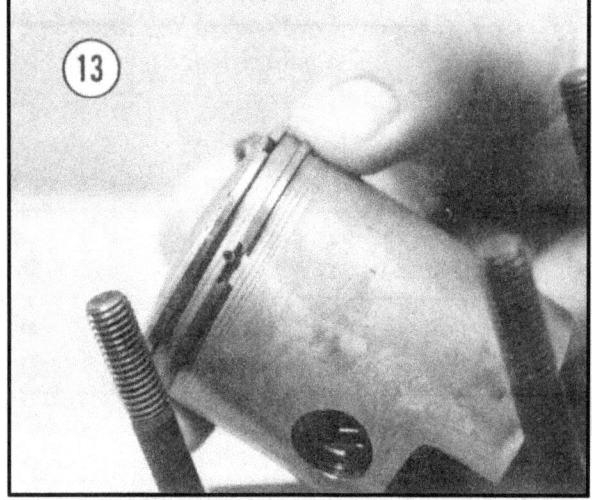

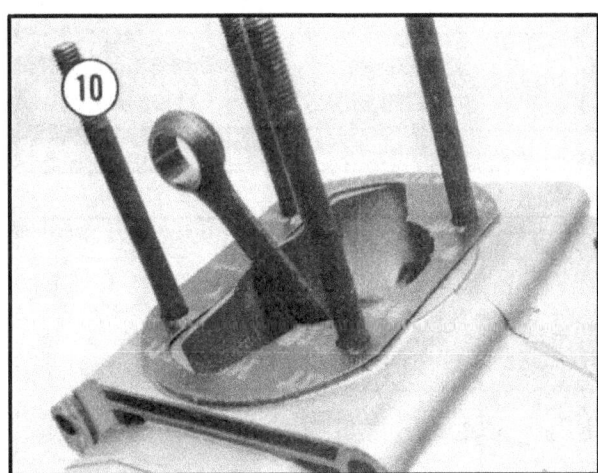

4. Oil the cylinder bore and start the cylinder onto the piston (**Figure 14**). Make sure the cylinder is correctly positioned—intake to the rear.

5. Carefully slide the cylinder down over the rings (**Figure 15**).

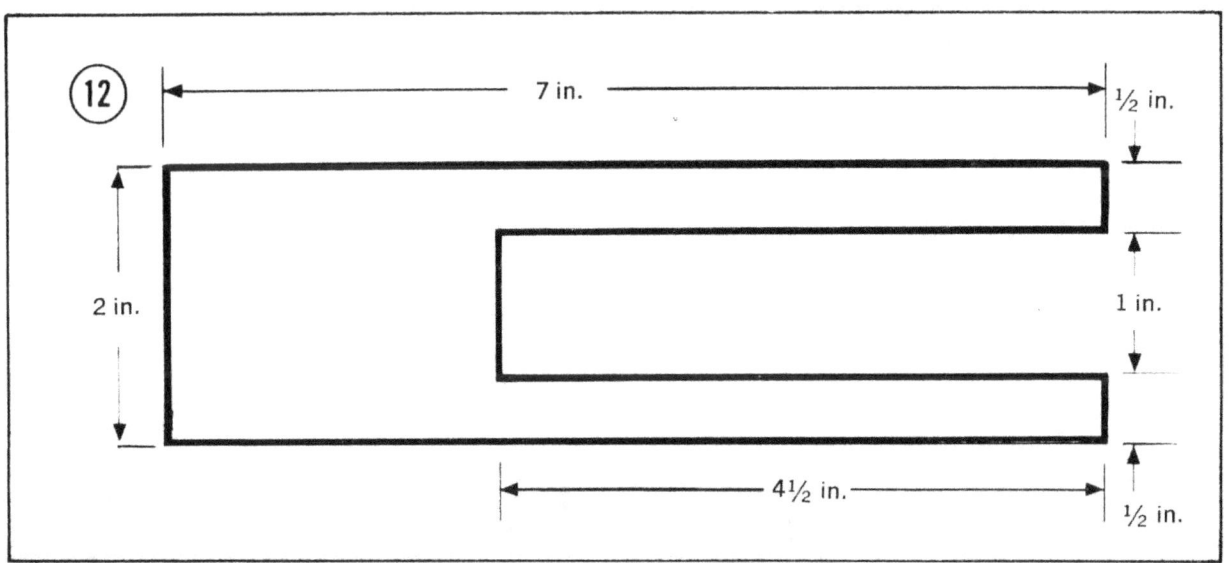

14

15

42

6. Remove the wooden block and push the cylinder all the way down onto the crankcase.

7. On engines with a flanged cylinder, install the 4 washers and nuts on the short studs and tighten the nuts to 17-19 ft.-lb. (2.4-2.6 mkg) in a diagonal pattern. Rotate the crankshaft to move the piston up and down in the cylinder after tightening each nut.

8. Install the cylinder head as discussed previously.

PISTON ASSEMBLY

Sachs pistons (**Figure 16**) are made of aluminum alloy and are fitted with 2 rings—an L or Dykes-pattern top compression ring and a rail type secondary compression ring. The wrist pin is press fitted and retained in the piston with circlips. On engines fitted with an aluminum connecting rod, the wrist pin is connected to the rod with a bronze bushing. On engines fitted with a steel connecting rod, a caged needle bearing is used on the small end of the rod.

Before beginning any work on the cylinder, cylinder head, or piston, thoroughly clean the outside of the engine and adjacent areas with solvent or a good grade of engine cleaner. Flush away dirt and grime with water and thoroughly dry the engine.

Piston Removal

Allow the engine to cool thoroughly to prevent distortion of the cylinder head upon removal, then remove the head and cylinder as discussed previously.

NOTE: *On engines with aluminum connecting rods, check the wear of the pin bushing prior to removing the piston by attempting to rock the piston from side to side along the pin axis. There should be no perceptible rocking movement, although the piston should rotate freely on the axis and slide from side to side slightly.*

1. Stuff a clean, lint-free cloth into the top of the crankcase and place a wooden block beneath the piston. Remove the circlips from both sides of the piston (Figure 11).

2. Push the pin out of the piston with a pin extractor (see **Figure 17**). Be careful not to damage the rings.

3. On engines with steel connecting rods, remove the needle bearing assembly from the rod.

4. If the engine has an aluminum connecting rod and the earlier check of the bushing indicated that it is worn, press out the bushing as shown in **Figure 18** by holding the withdrawal bolt with an open-end wrench and turning the large nut clockwise.

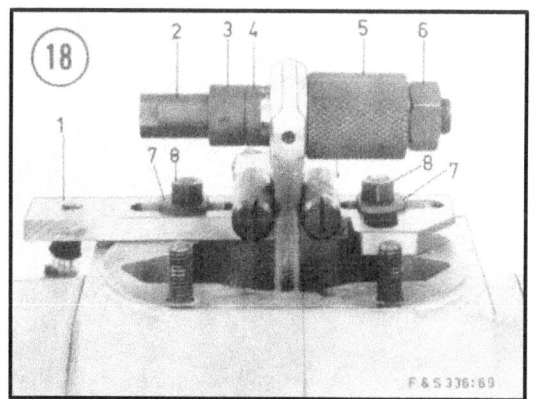

Piston Inspection

Examine the piston carefully for hairline cracks at the top edges of the transfer cutaways (see **Figure 19**). If any cracks are found, replace the piston. Check the ring lands for chips or breaks on the edges. Check the locating pins for wear. Replace the piston if there is any doubt about its condition.

Remove the rings from the piston by spreading the top ring with a thumb on each end, as shown in **Figure 20**. Remove the ring from the top of the piston and repeat the procedure for removing the secondary ring.

Clean the carbon from the top of the piston with the rounded end of a hacksaw blade. Clean the carbon and gum from the ring grooves with a broken ring or a groove cleaner. Any deposits left in the grooves will prevent the rings from seating correctly and may very likely result in piston seizure. Check the top of the piston for erosion of the metal and replace it if any is found. Erosion of the piston crown is very often caused

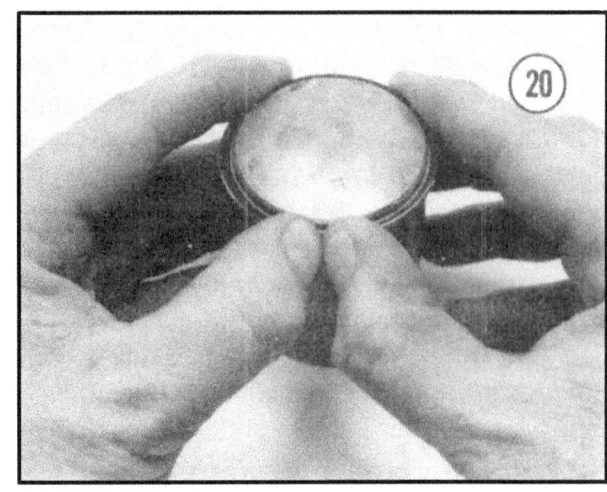

by an extremely lean fuel/air mixture. This condition should be corrected immediately after a new piston has been installed and the engine reassembled.

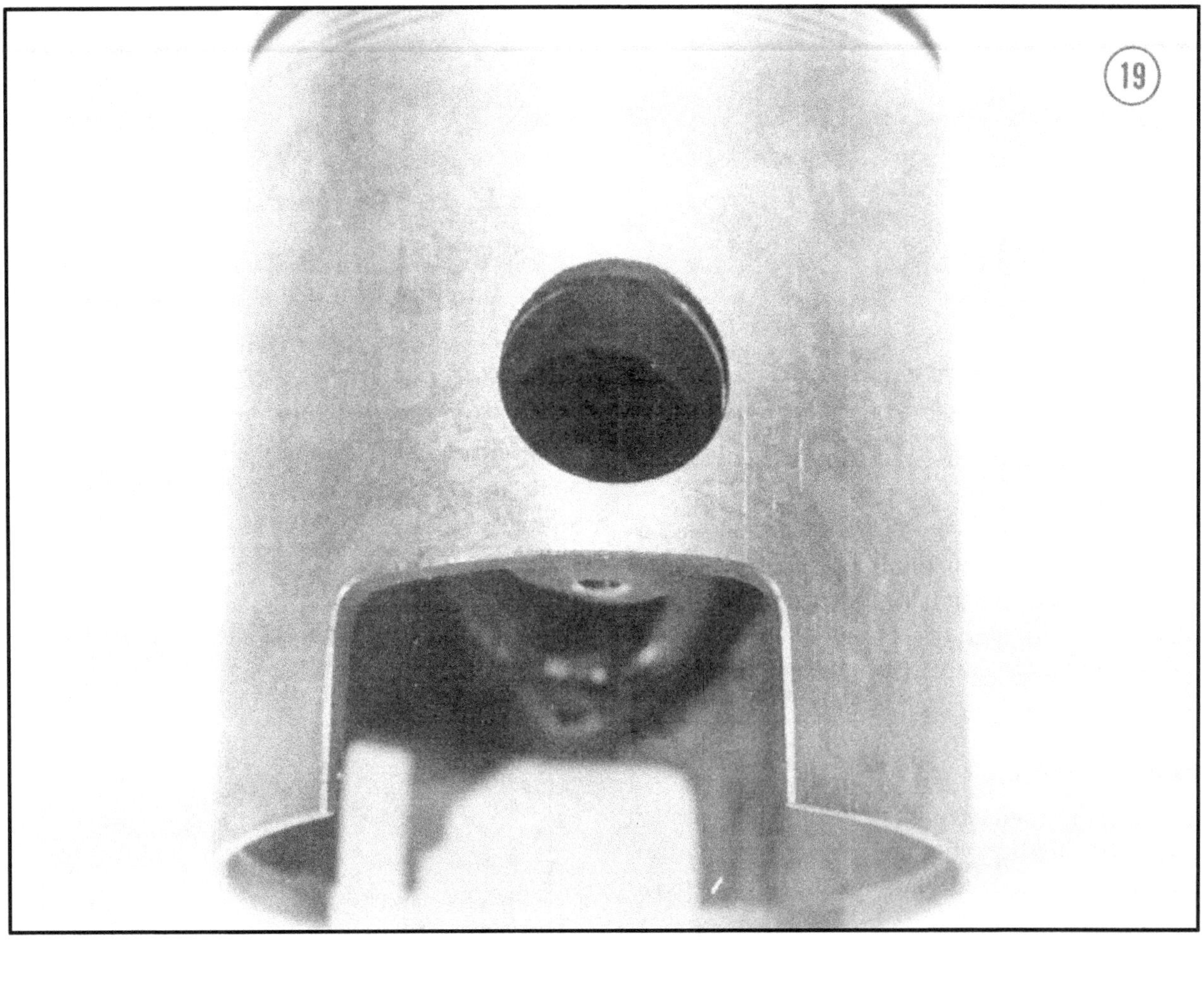

Check the skirt of the piston for brown varnish deposits. More than a slight amount is evidence of worn or sticking rings which should be replaced. Also check the skirt for galling and abrasion—a common symptom of piston seizure. If light galling is present, smooth the affected area with No. 400 emery paper or a fine oilstone. However, if galling is severe or if the piston is deeply scored, replace it.

Measure the piston for clearance in the cylinder as described earlier. Replace the piston and rebore the cylinder as described if the clearance is excessive. Measure the end gap of the rings as shown in **Figure 21**. Insert the ring about 1 in. (40mm) into the cylinder, squaring it up by pushing it into position with the head of the piston. The end gap should be 0.0025-0.0030 in. (0.063-0.076mm) for both rings. If the gap exceeds 0.0030 in. (0.076mm), replace the rings as a set. Check the end gap of new rings in the same manner as for the old.

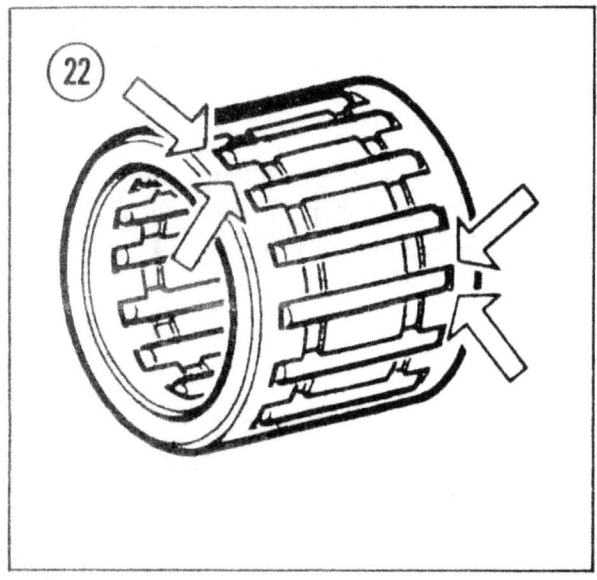

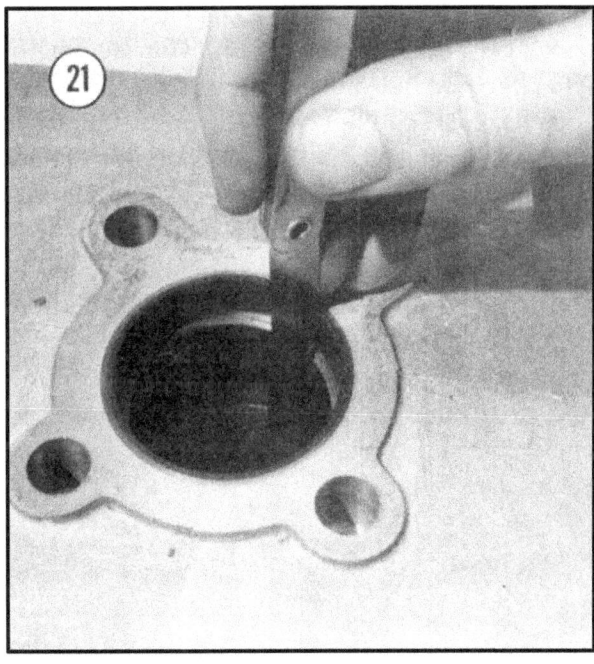

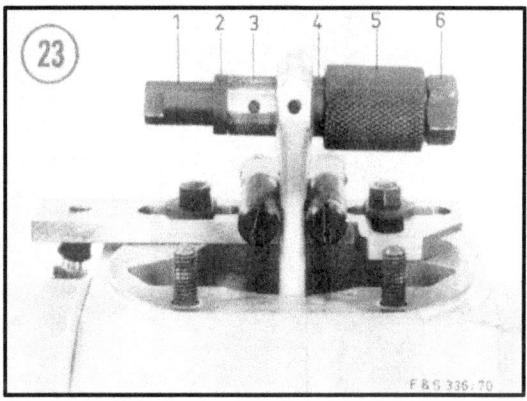

Clean the needle bearing assembly in solvent and dry it thoroughly. With a magnifying glass, examine the bearing assembly for cracks at the corners of the bearing slots, and also on the needles themselves (see **Figure 22**). If any are found, replace the bearing.

Piston Installation

1. Lightly oil the bearing and reinstall it in the upper end of the connecting rod. If the rod is bushed and a new bushing is being fitted, install the bushing and the tool as shown in **Figure 23**.

Make sure the oil hole in the bushing lines up with the oil hole in the rod. Press the bushing into the rod by holding the withdrawal bolt with an open-end wrench and turning the large nut on the tool clockwise.

> NOTE: *The bushing must be reamed to final size — 0.5916-0.5922 in. (15.015-15.030mm). This is a job which should be entrusted to an expert.*

2. Place the slotted wooden block over the top of the crankcase and set the piston on the top of the rod. The arrow on the top of the piston must point forward.

3. Lightly oil the pin and start it into the piston. Set the pin remover/installer tool in place.

4. Align the pin bosses in the piston with the connecting rod and press the pin into the piston by turning the installer bolt clockwise. Stop

when the far end of the pin has reached the inside edge of its circlip groove and remove the installer.

5. Install new circlips in both sides of the piston. Make sure they are completely seated in their grooves by rotating them slightly with the flat of a screwdriver as shown in **Figure 24**.

6. Check the installation by rocking the piston back and forth around the pin axis and from side to side along the axis. It should rotate freely back and forth but not rock from side to side.

7. Install the rings—first the bottom one, then the top—by carefully spreading the ends of the rings with the thumbs and slipping the ring over the top of the piston. Make sure the rings seat completely in the grooves, all the way around the circumference, and the ends are aligned with the locating pins.

8. Install the cylinder and cylinder head and reassemble the remaining components as described previously.

If the rings were replaced, or if the cylinder was rebored and a new piston installed, the engine must be run in at moderate speeds and loads for no less than two hours. Don't exceed 75 percent of normally allowable rpm during run in. After the first half hour, remove the spark plug and check its condition. The electrode should be dry and clean and the color of the insulation should be light to medium tan. If the insulation is white (indicating a too-lean fuel/air mixture) or if it is dark and oily (indicating a too-rich fuel/air mixture ratio), correct the condition with a jet change; both incorrect conditions produce excessive engine heat and can lead to damage of the rings, piston, and cylinder before the engine has had a chance to seat in.

CHAPTER FOUR

CRANKSHAFT AND CRANKCASE

The crankshaft assembly is made up of 2 full-circle flywheels pressed together on a hollow crankpin. The connecting rod big-end bearing on the crankpin is a needle bearing assembly. The crankshaft assembly is supported in 2 roller bearing assemblies on the drive (left) side and a single roller bearing assembly on the ignition (right) side.

The two-piece crankcase splits vertically along the centerline of the connecting rod. Disassembly, or splitting, of the crankcase yields access to both the crankshaft and the transmission. Refer to the exploded master drawing (**Figure 1**) for relationship of the crankcase and crankshaft components.

The procedure which follows is presented as a complete, step-by-step major lower-end rebuild that would be followed if an engine is to be completely reconditioned. However, if you're replacing a known failed part, the disassembly need be carried out only until the failed part is accessible; there's no need to disassemble the engine beyond that point as long as you know the remaining components are in good condition and that they were not affected by the failed part.

ENGINE REMOVAL

Before the crankcase can be split, the engine must be removed from the motorcycle. Prior to beginning work, thoroughly clean, rinse, and dry the motorcycle, paying particular attention to the engine. Refer to Chapter Three for removal of the head and cylinder and then proceed as follows.

1. Disconnect the master link from the drive chain and remove the chain from the motorcycle.
2. Loosen the clutch cable adjuster at the handlebar (**Figure 2**).

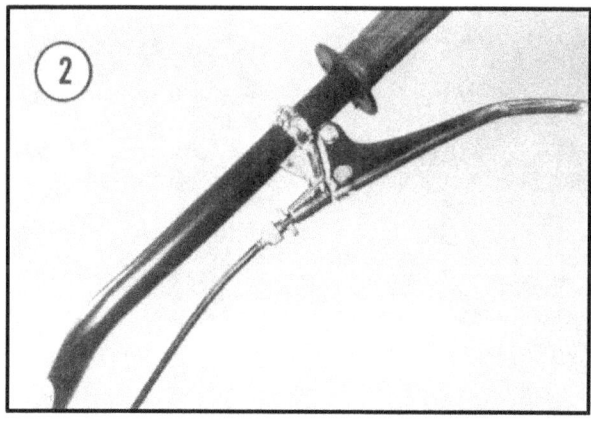

3. Disconnect the speedometer cable from the right side of the transmission (see **Figure 3**).
4. Remove the kickstarter lever (**Figure 4**).
5. Remove the gear selector pedal (**Figure 5**).

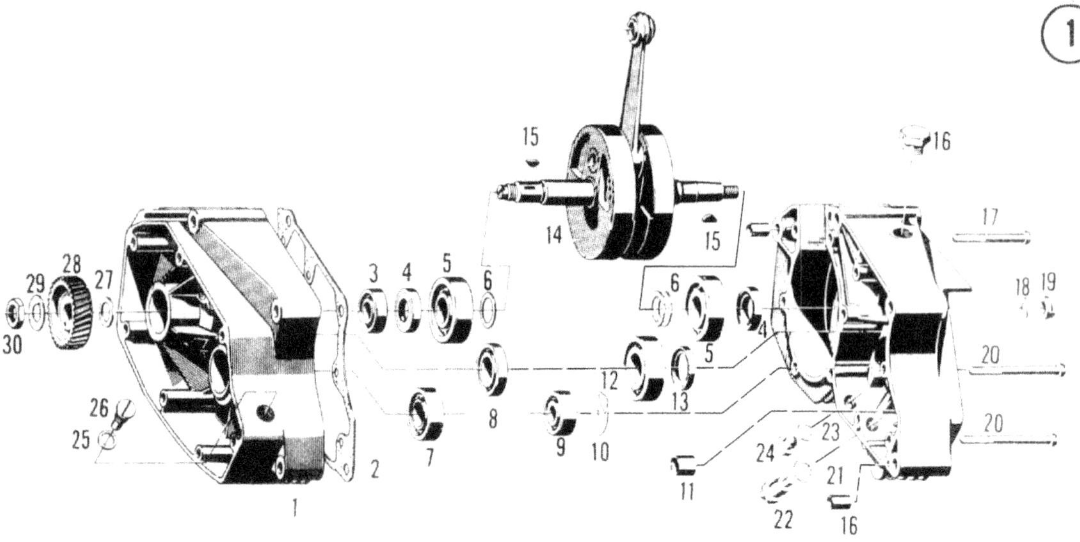

CRANKCASE AND CRANKSHAFT

1. Crankcase assembly
2. Gasket
3. Deep groove ball bearing
4. Oil seal
5. Ball bearing
6. Shim
7. Deep groove ball bearing
8. Deep groove ball bearing
9. Deep groove ball bearing
10. Profile washer
11. Washer
12. Cylindrical roller bearing
13. Oil seal
14. Crankshaft
15. Key
16. Plug screw
17. Screw
18. Spring washer
19. Collar nut
20. Screw
21. Sealing washer
22. Stop screw
23. Sealing washer
24. Oil drain plug
25. Sealing washer
26. Pivot screw
27. Washer
28. Driving pinion
29. Tab washer
30. Nut

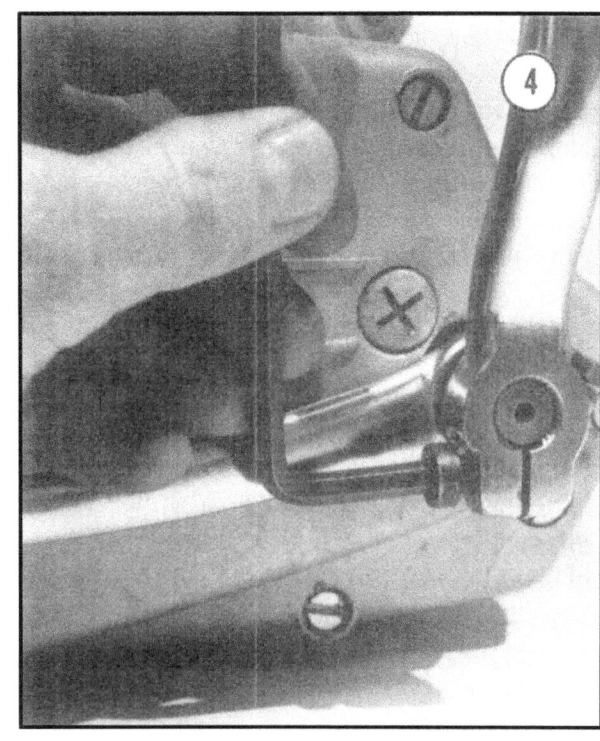

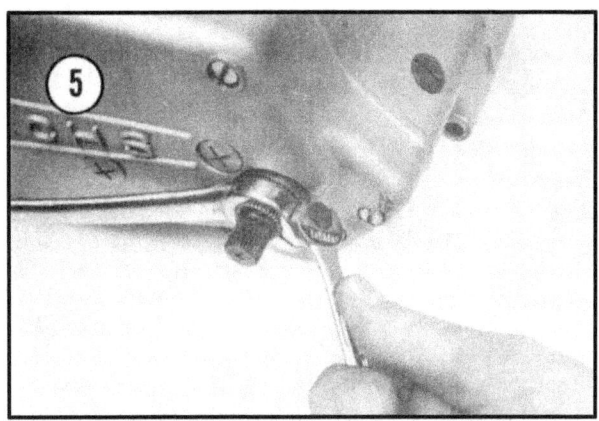

6. Place a drip pan beneath the engine and remove the drain plug (**Figure 6**), the fill plug, and the level and inspection plugs (**Figure 7**).

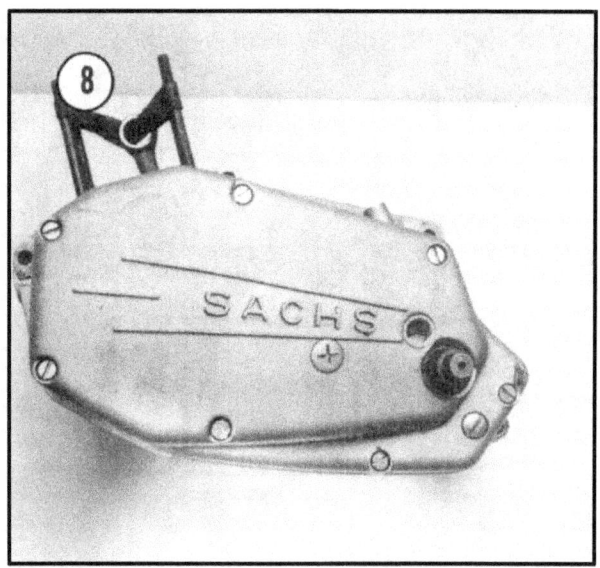

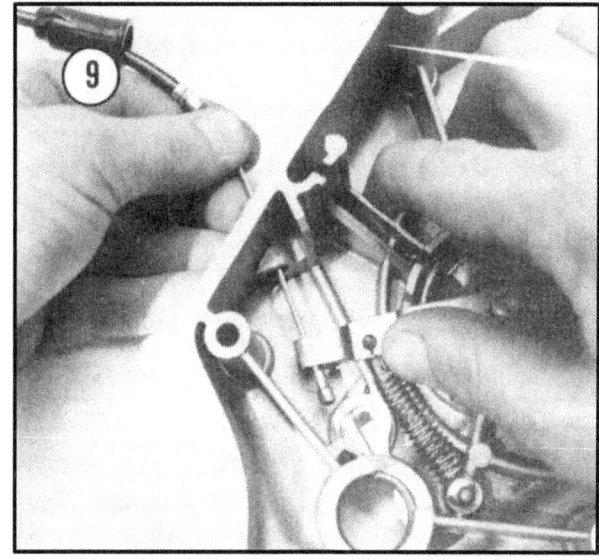

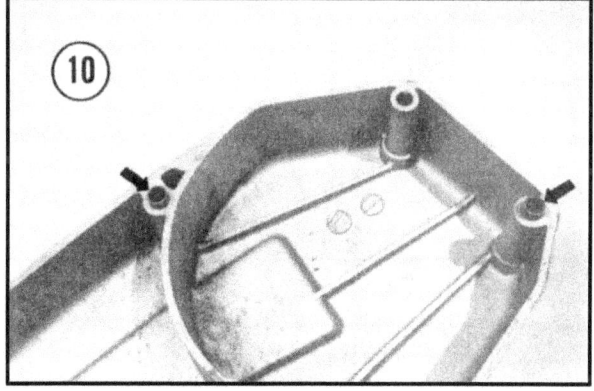

7. Remove the 7 screws from the left engine cover (**Figure 8**), pull the cover out, disconnect the clutch cable from the actuating arm (see **Figure 9**), and remove the cover.

8. Remove the 4 screws from the right engine cover and pull it off. Be careful not to lose the 2 hollow alignment dowels (**Figure 10**).

9. Unscrew the nuts from the ends of the 3 engine mounting bolts (one front, 2 rear), remove the washers, and pull out the bottom rear bolt (see **Figure 11**).

10. Get assistance and lift up the engine to take the tension off the 2 remaining bolts. Pull out

the top rear bolt, then the front bolt, and lift the engine out of the frame (see **Figure 12**).

LOWER END
Disassembly

1. Check the bottom of the engine for dirt and grease embedded between the fins and clean if necessary.

2. Mount the engine in a repair jig.

NOTE: *If a jig is not available, you will need assistance to hold the engine steady during some of the procedures to be carried out. In such case, set the engine on a soft wood surface, such as a piece of plywood, to prevent damage to the fins and cases.*

3. Install the chain lever on the repair jig and lay the chain of the lever over the countershaft sprocket, from left to right, as shown in **Figure 13**. Unscrew the left-hand threaded countershaft nut and remove it and the spring washer.

NOTE: *If the chain lever is not available, or if you are working without a repair jig, remove the countershaft sprocket nut with the engine in the frame before removing the drive chain. Have someone assist you by holding the rear wheel to prevent it from rotating.*

4. Install a puller on the countershaft sprocket and pull it off by turning the puller bolt clockwise (**Figure 14**).

5. Hold the flywheel with a jig lever (**Figure 15**) or a pin wrench and unscrew the left-hand threaded collar nut from the end of the flywheel.

NOTE: *When using a pin wrench to hold the flywheel on engines equipped with Motoplat electronic ignition* (**Figure 16**), *be careful that the pins of the wrench do not touch the timing-signal post at the front of the stator.*

6. Place the protective cap (tool No. 4) over the end of the crankshaft. Install the puller (tool No. 6) and pull off the flywheel by turning

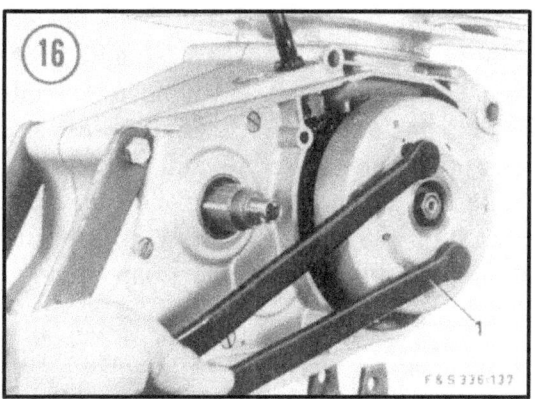

the puller bolt clockwise (**Figure 17**). Remove the puller and protective cap (and the jig lever if it was used) and remove the flywheel from the engine.

7A. On engines equipped with Bosch contact breaker ignition, remove the 3 Phillips head screws and washers from the stator plate (**Figure 18**). Carefully pull the wiring harness and rubber grommet out of the case and remove the assembly from the engine. Insert the stator into the flywheel, wrap the entire unit in clean newspaper, and set it aside.

7B. On engines equipped with Motoplat electronic ignition, remove the 3 slotted screws and

51

washers from the front of stator (**Figure 19**). Carefully pull the wiring harness and rubber grommet out of the case and remove the stator from the engine and insert it into the flywheel. Remove the 3 slotted screws and washers from the base plate (**Figure 20**), remove the base plate and set it on top of the stator. Wrap the entire ignition assembly in clean newspaper and set it aside.

8. If the clutch gear is fitted with a leaf spring mounted outboard of the thrust plate (see **Figure 21**), unscrew the nut holding the spring and remove the spring and plate. The spring may be discarded; it's not essential.

9. Remove the lock spring and shims (**Figure 22**) and pull off the clutch wheel.

10. Remove the shims from the end of the gear selector shaft (**Figure 23**).

11. Tilt the engine to its left and remove the thrust bearing from the clutch hub.
12. Fit the lock (tool No. 8) over the clutch hub splines and secure it with 2 cover retaining bolts as shown in **Figure 24**. Unscrew the clutch hub nut, remove the lock, the clutch, and the key.

13. Fit the lock (tool No. 10) over the crank gear and secure it with two cover bolts as shown in **Figure 25**. Bend back the locking tab and unscrew the sprocket nut. Remove the tab locking plate, the lock tool, the gear, and the key.

> NOTE: *At this stage of disassembly, it's possible to replace the right-side crankshaft seal, provided the special seal puller (tool No. 13) is available. Also, seal removal and replacement can be accomplished with the engine in the motorcycle and without removing the head and cylinder.*

GEAR SELECTOR REMOVAL
ONE-PIECE LEVER

1. Rotate the selector shaft clockwise to engage second gear.
2. Refer to **Figure 26** and unlock the grooved nut and unscrew it.

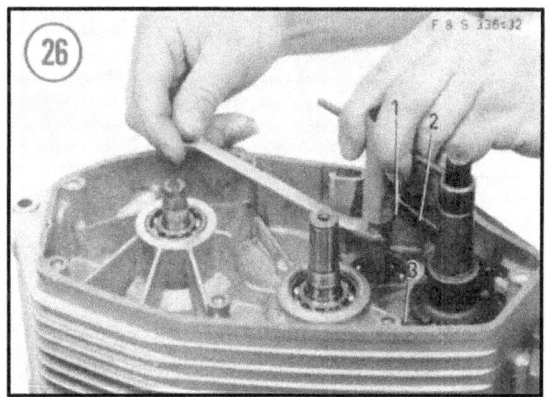

3. Remove the selector fork and slotted nut from the selector lever (**Figure 27**).
4. Remove the 2 Allen bolts and washers from

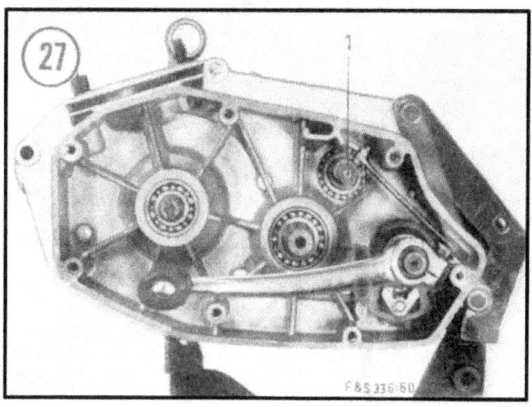

the selector boss (**Figure 28**). Lift the selector lever and pull the selector assembly off the shaft (**Figure 29**), along with the shims. If there is a gear lock on the selector mechanism (see **Figure 30**), unhook the spring and pull it out with the selector assembly.

> NOTE: *It's not necessary to remove the selector lever unless it has been damaged. In such case, remove the pivot bolt, sealing washer, lever, and shims (Figure 31). . When installing the lever, coat the threads of the pivot bolt with Loctite and screw it in with the sealing washer in place. Remember; the spacing washer fits beneath the lever, the shims fit on top.*

GEAR SELECTOR REMOVAL
TWO-PIECE LEVER

1. Rotate the selector shaft counterclockwise to engage first gear.

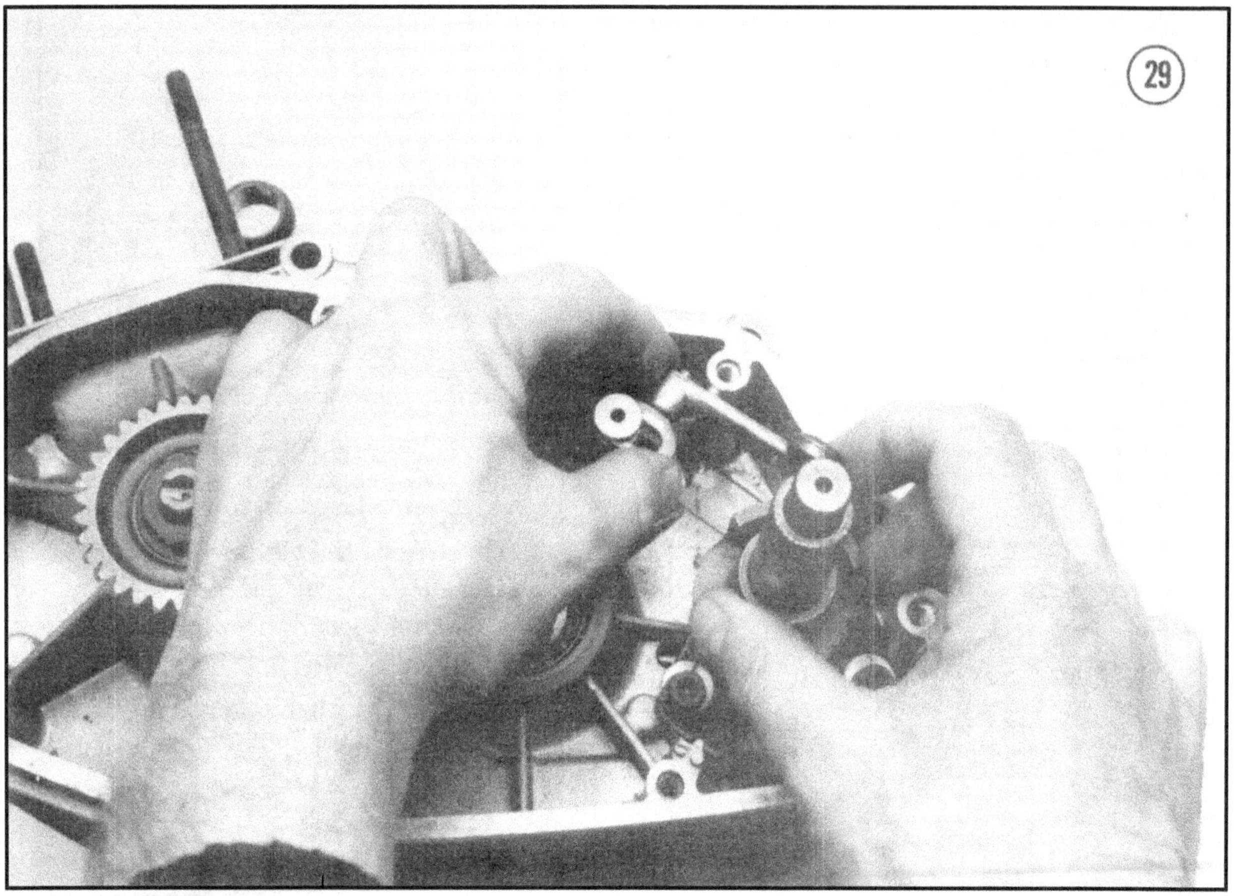

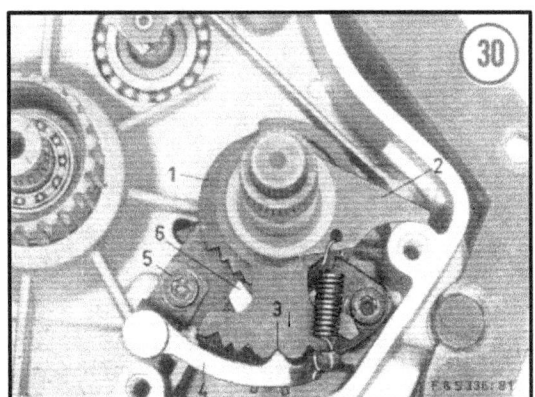

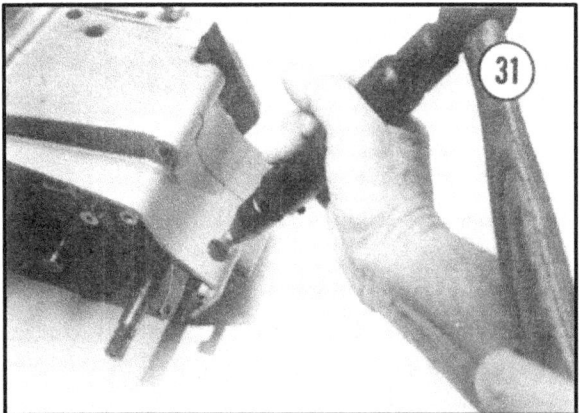

2. Refer to **Figure 32** and unscrew the nut on the top of the selector lever. Remove the lockwasher and the eccentric bolt.

3. Remove the 2 Allen bolts and washers from the selector boss.

4. Lift the selector lever and pull the selector assembly off the shaft.

5. Remove the selector fork from the lever and remove the shims. It's not necessary to remove the selector lever from the case. See the note preceding this section.

CRANKCASE SEPARATION

NOTE: *Before separating the crankcase halves, check the condition of the connecting rod big-end bearing with the crankshaft installed in the crankcase. Refer to the procedure described under* Inspection.

1. Remove the 10 slotted screws from the crankcase (**Figure 33**). The 6 screws located inside the ignition cavity are sealed with liquid sealant and may require the use of an impact screwdriver. Clean the screw threads thoroughly after removal, and remember to apply sealant to them when reassembling the crankcase halves.

2. If a repair jig is being used, remove the crankcase from the jig and reinstall it as shown in **Figure 34**.

3. With assistance, apply pressure to the magneto-side crankcase half and tap lightly on the end of the crankshaft and transmission mainshaft to separate the cases. Lift off the magneto-side crankcase half, taking care not to lose the alignment dowels or shims (**Figure 35**).

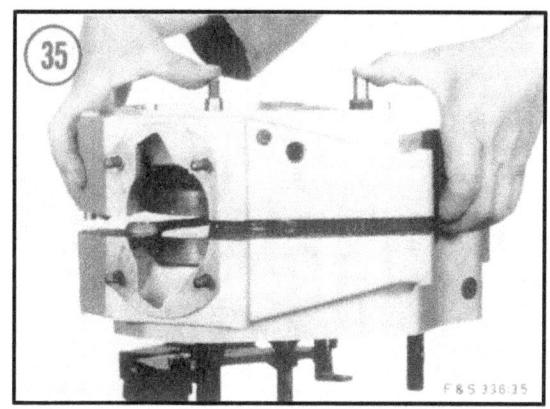

CRANKSHAFT REMOVAL

Remove the crankshaft from the clutch-side crankcase half by pulling the crank assembly straight up with a steady pressure.

TRANSMISSION DISASSEMBLY

1. Remove the layshaft and shims from the crankcase (4, **Figure 36**).

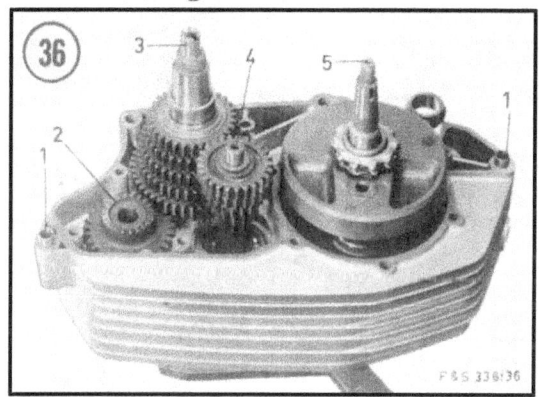

2. Remove the inner bearing race and shims from the main shaft (3, Figure 36).

3. Remove the gears and spacer rings from the main shaft, keeping them in order so they may be reassembled in the same manner (**Figure 37**).

4. Pull the main shaft out of the case, along with the washer and shims.

5. Remove the starter gear along with the thrust washer and shims.

STARTER MECHANISM REMOVAL

1. Install the kickstarter lever on the starter shaft and rotate it until the ratchet wheels lift off the stop screw (**Figure 38**).

2. Rotate the kickstarter lever forward to relax the spring, then remove the lever from the shaft and take the starter mechanism out of the case.

MAIN SHAFT GEARS

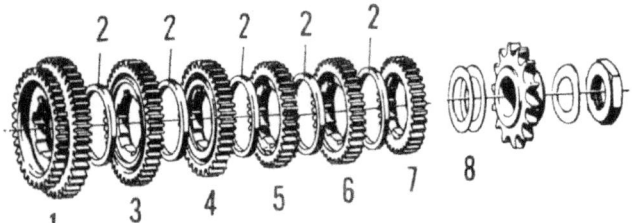

1. Sliding pinion 1st gear
2. Ring
3. Sliding pinion, 2nd gear
4. Sliding pinion, 3rd gear
5. Sliding pinion, 4th gear
6. Sliding pinion, 5th gear
7. Sliding pinion, 6th gear
8. Shim

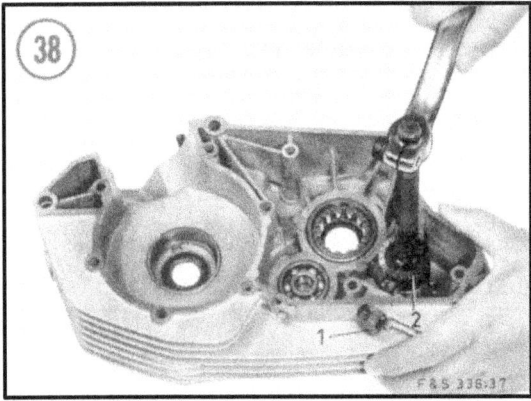

3. Remove the spacer from the case. It isn't necessary to remove the stop bolt (1, Figure 38).

INSPECTION

Check the crankcase halves for cracks or fractures in stiffening webs, around bearing bosses, and at threaded holes. While the likelihood of such damage is rare, it should be checked for, and particularly so following a catastrophic malfunction (i.e., piston breakage, bearing failure, gear breakage) or after a collision or hard spill in which the engine suffers external damage. If cracks or fractures are found, they should be repaired immediately by a reputable shop experienced in and equipped to perform repairs on precision aluminum castings.

Check the condition of the connecting rod big-end bearing by supporting the crankshaft horizontally with the crankpin in the 12 o'clock position.

NOTE: *This check is most easily performed with the crankshaft installed in the crankcase.*

Grasp the connecting rod firmly and pull up on it. Tap sharply on the top of the rod with a soft-face mallet. If the bearing and crankpin are in good condition there should be no movement felt in the rod. If movement is felt, or if there is a sharp, metallic click, the bearing should be replaced. This is a job which should be entrusted to a shop equipped with a press capable of separating and reassembling the crank halves and the pin.

Check the crankshaft and transmission bearings for pitting, galling, and wear. Rotate the bearings and feel for roughness and play. They should turn smoothly and evenly. There should be no radial play in the bearings. If any bearing is found faulty in any way, replace it.

Check the primary drive and transmission gears for chipped, galled, or worn teeth and replace if necessary. If both gears are worn, they should be replaced as a set, even if only one of the gears is damaged; the gears are matched as a set for correct backlash and the mixing of an old worn gear with a new gear is likely to result in premature wear or a failure which could damage other components.

Minor roughness on the surface of gear teeth may be smoothed with a fine oilstone.

MEASUREMENT

There is only one critical measurement involving the crankcase and crankshaft—axial play of the shaft in the case. Permissible axial play is 0.05-0.1mm (0.002-0.004 in.). There are several critical dimensions which must be checked in the transmission, these are covered in Chapter Five.

1. Remove the bearing cages from the main bearings (**Figure 39**).

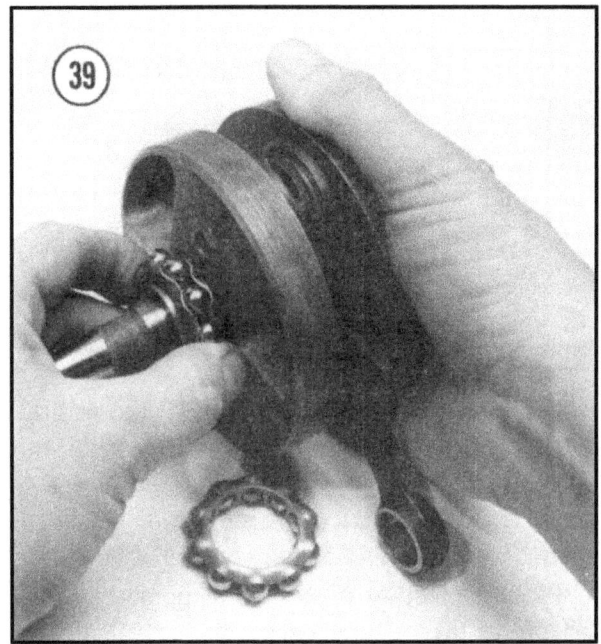

2. Pull the inner races off the crankshaft with puller shells (tool No. 24), the clamping ring (tool No. 23), and the threaded sleeve (tool No. 22) as shown in **Figure 40**. Don't mix the left-side cage or races with the right side.

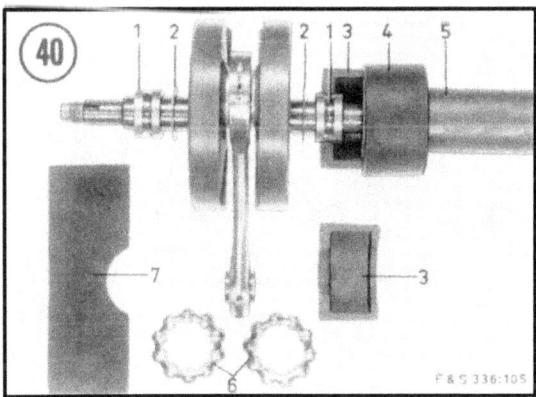

3. Assemble the entire bearings, including inner and outer races and bearing cage, in the crankcase. Make sure the bearing is correctly seated in the bore.
4. Place a gasket on the sealing surface and measure the distance from the gasket surface to the bearing inner race as shown in **Figure 41**.
5. Repeat procedure for opposing bearing.
6. Measure the width of the crankshaft across both webs as shown in **Figure 42**.

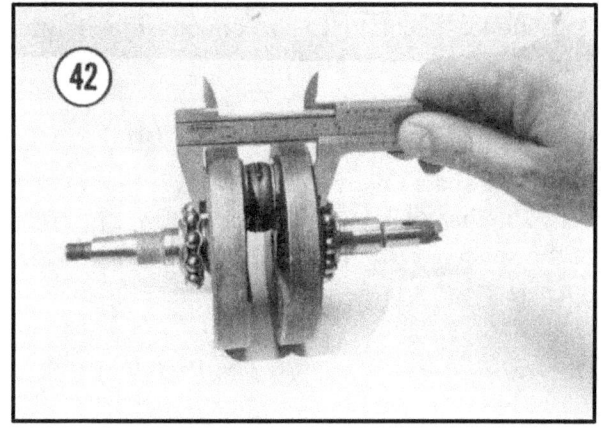

7. Add the dimensions from Steps 4 and 5 and subtract the width of the crank webs from the result to determine the actual axial play.

EXAMPLE

Distance from sealing surface to bearing inner race		
Clutch side	23.30mm	(0.918 in.)
Magneto side	+33.0 mm	(1.300 in.)
	56.30mm	(2.218 in.)
Width of crankshaft across both webs	−54.10mm	(2.131 in.)
Actual axial play	2.20mm	(0.086 in.)
Permissible axial play	−0.10mm	(0.0039 in.)
Difference to be taken up	2.10mm	(0.0827 in.)

8. The difference in axial play is taken up with shims placed between the crank webs and the inner races of the main bearings (2, Figure 40). See **Table 1**.

If possible, the combined shim thickness should be the same for both sides. For instance, in the example above, a 1.0mm and 0.50 shim on each side of the crankshaft would produce

Table 1   SHIM SIZES

Thickness
0.15mm
0.20mm
0.30mm
0.40mm
0.50mm
0.80mm
1.00mm

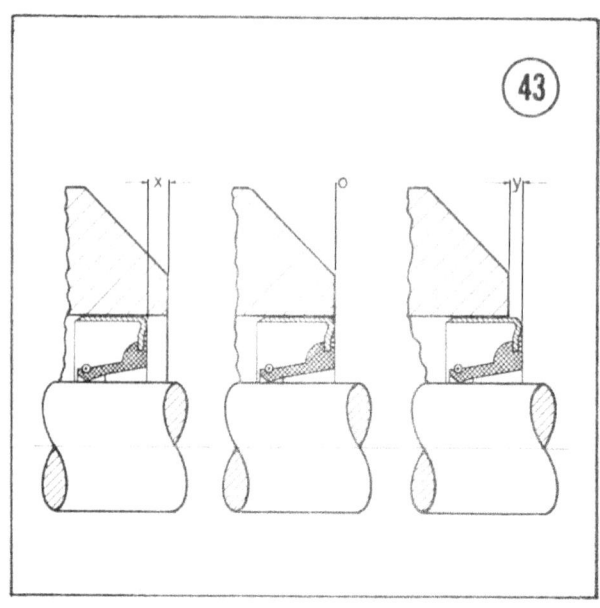

the required play of 2.10mm. If the difference can't be taken up evenly, the thicker combination should be fitted to the clutch side of the crank.

CRANKSHAFT PREASSEMBLY

1. Fit the spacer plate (tool No. 9) (7, Figure 40) between the crank webs and support the ends of the spacer on the bed of a press or across the open jaws of a large vise.

CAUTION
Never clamp the crankshaft ends or webs in a vise, and don't install the inner races by tapping them on; such action will result in the webs being squeezed together. This will damage the big-end bearing and require its replacement.

2. Fit the shims onto the end of the crankshaft.
3. Press the bearing inner race onto the shaft firmly against the shims by screwing the threaded puller bolt into the end of the crankshaft and turning the puller sleeve clockwise (5, Figure 40).
4. Turn the crankshaft over on the bed of the press or vise and repeat the procedure for the other end.
5. Install the bearing cages on the inner races.

CRANKSHAFT SEAL REPLACEMENT

Before removing the seals from the crankcase halves, check their positions in the bores (see **Figure 43**). The new seals must be installed at the same depth as the old ones. Failure to install the seals at the correct depth can result in the seal coming in contact with the rotating bearing race or closure of the oil channel and consequent inadequate lubrication to the bearings and crankshaft.

Removal

1. Place a piece of pipe with a diameter comparable to that of the seal on the seal face and tap it lightly to break any oxide bond that may have formed.

2. Install the seal puller (tool No. 13) so that both hooks are seated behind the steel rim of the seal (**Figure 44**). It may be necessary to partially disassemble the puller (see **Figure 45**) to insert the hooks and then reassemble it.

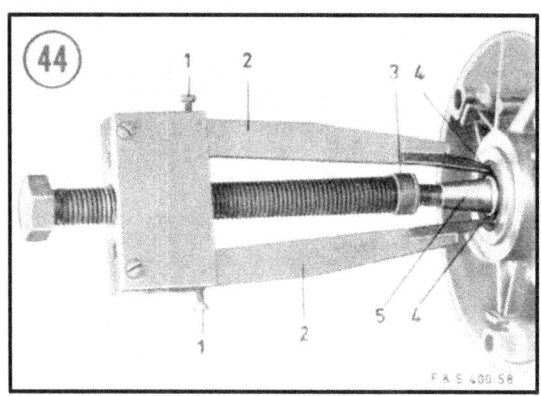

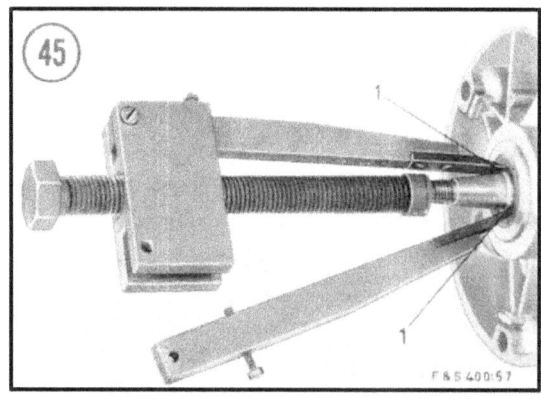

3. Press the puller arms outward equally by turning in the 2 spreader screws (1, **Figure 44**). Make sure the puller bolt and the crankshaft are in a straight line.

4. Hold the puller body to prevent it from turning and remove the seal by screwing the puller bolt clockwise.

Installation

1. Wipe seal bore with clean, lint-free cloth.
2. Fill the inner recess of the seal with high-temperature grease and lightly coat the seal lip.
3. Put a short piece of clear plastic mending tape around the sharp shoulder of the crankshaft to prevent damage to seal lip during installation.
4. Place the seal on the shaft and press it into place with a piece of pipe (**Figure 46**). Press it straight on and to the same depth as the old seal.

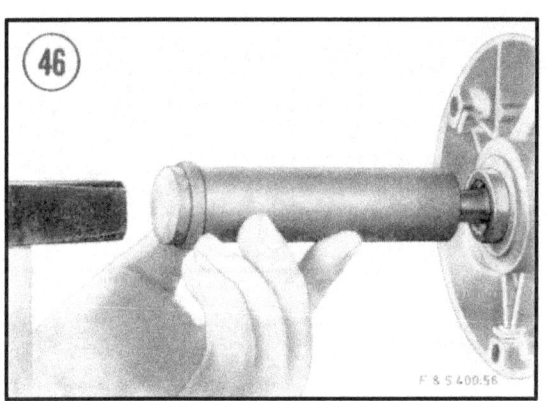

MAIN BEARING REPLACEMENT

Removal and installation of the main bearing inner races is discussed in the section of measuring and correcting crankshaft end-play. If damage has occurred to any of the bearing components—inner race, outer race, or bearing cage—the entire assembly should be replaced.

Outer Race Removal

1. Heat the crankcase halves on a hot plate to 115-140°C (250-300°F).
2. Tap the crankcase half lightly with a rubber mallet to remove the inner race and oil seal.

The transmission main- and layshaft bearings are likely to fall out at the same time. Reinstall these immediately, while the crankcase is still warm, referring to Chapter Five for their locations and positioning if necessary.

Outer Race Installation

1. Fill the recess in the face of the seal with high-temperature grease and lightly coat the seal lip. Press the seal into the bore in the ignition-side case with the sealing lip facing inward until the inner edge of the seal is flush with the inner edge of the seal bore (**Figure 47**).

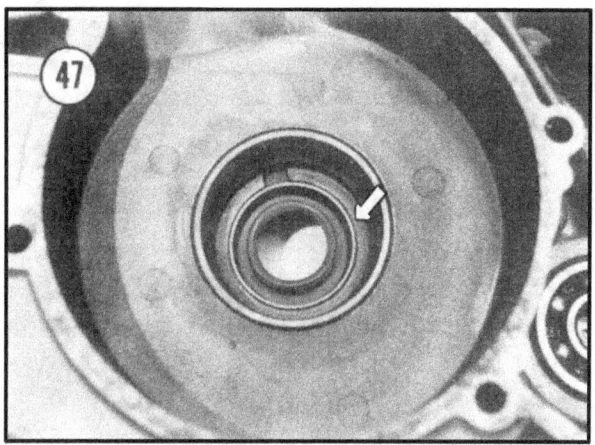

2. Press in the outer race as far as it will go. Its inner edge should contact the shoulder in the bore and its outer edge should be flush with the crankcase wall (see **Figure 48**).

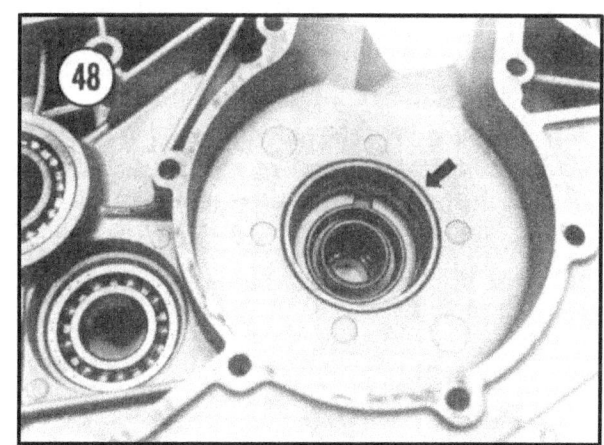

3. Install the seal and main bearing outer race in the clutch-side case in the same manner. Then, with the case still warm, press the outer ball bearing assembly into the case from the outside until its outer edge is flush with the face of the bearing boss (**Figure 49**). Again refer to Chapter Five for installation of the transmission bearings and seals.

NOTE: *Following replacement of the main bearings, measure the axial play of the crankshaft as described earlier and correct it if necessary.*

CRANKCASE REASSEMBLY

Refer to Chapter Five and reassemble the transmission and kickstarter mechanism. Then proceed as follows:

1. Fit the complete crankshaft assembly into the clutch-side case (**Figure 50**).

2. Install the 2 hollow alignment dowels in the clutch-side case.

3. Coat the mating surfaces of both crankcase halves with F&S sealant No. 40 or an equivalent gasket cement and install a new gasket over the alignment dowels. Check to see that all spacers and shims are correctly installed, referring to the disassembly procedure if necessary.

4. Assemble the 2 crankcase halves together, pushing firmly and evenly until they meet along the sealing surface.

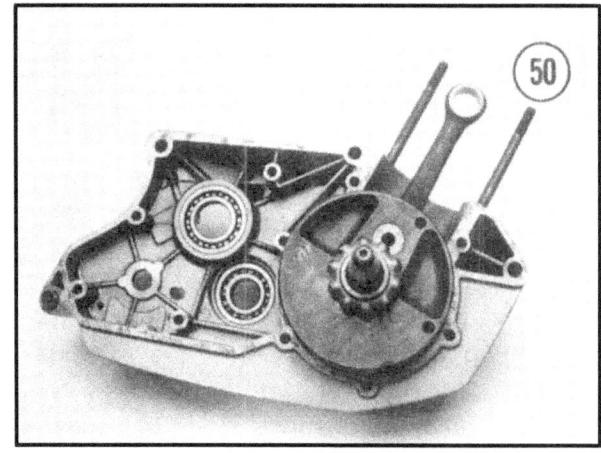

5. Coat the threads of the six 60-millimeter-long (2.36 in.) slotted screws with Diament sealant and screw them into the crankcase (see **Figure 51**).

6. Tighten the screws in the pattern shown in **Figure 52** to 5.8-7.25 ft.-lb. (0.18-1.0 mkg).

7. Screw the four 75-millimeter-long (3.0 in.) screws into the transmission portion of the crankcase (**Figure 53**).

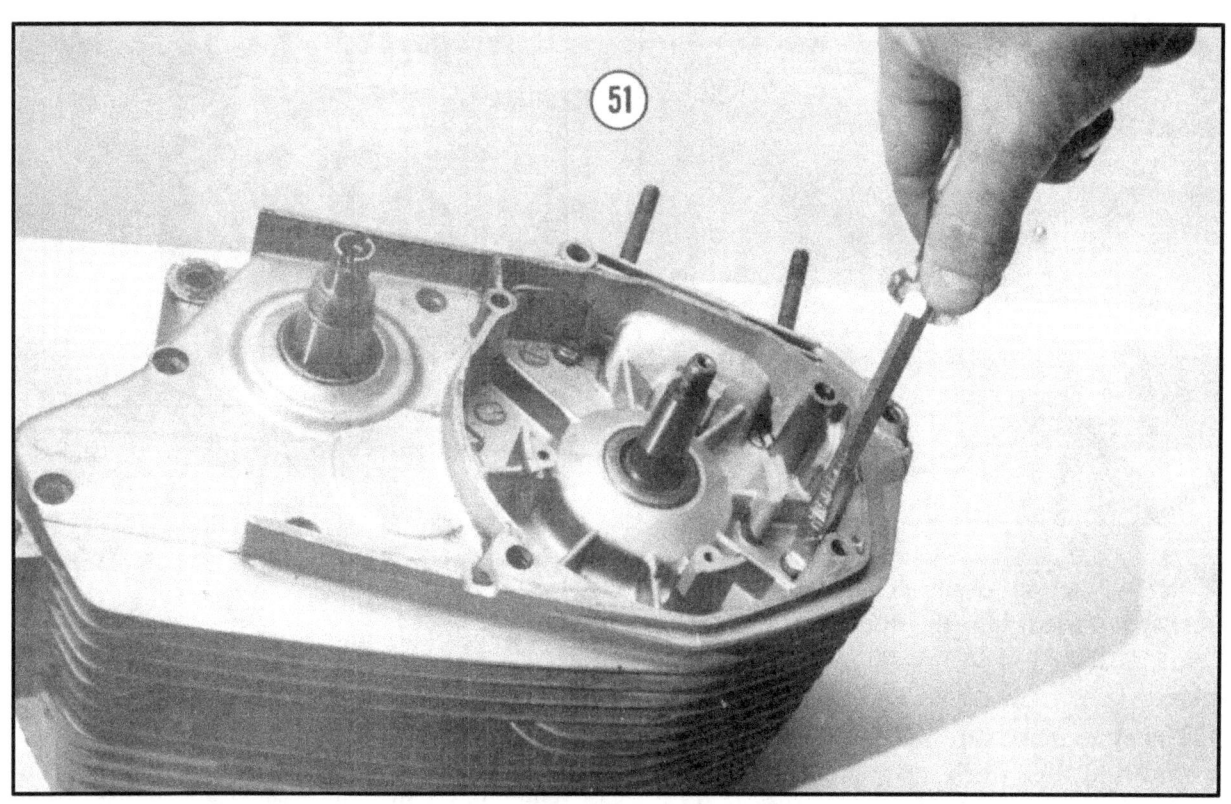

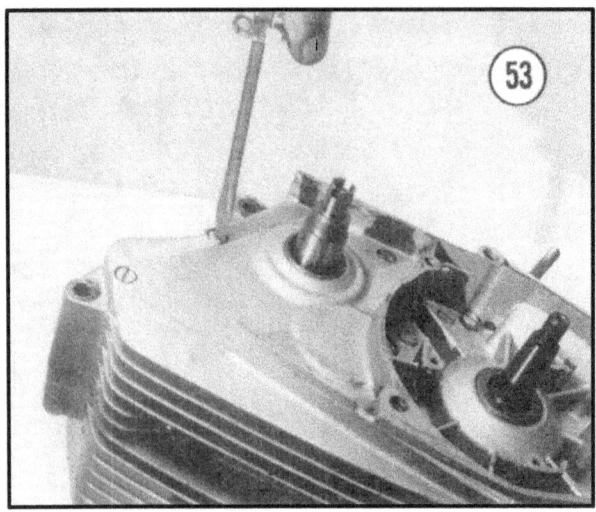

8. Screw the oil drain plug (with a sealing washer installed) into the bottom of the crankcase and tighten it to 9.4-10.85 ft.-lb. (1.3-1.5 mkg).

9. Check to make sure the crankshaft and connecting rod turn freely and smoothly and that the axial play in the shaft is barely perceptible.

IGNITION INSTALLATION (BOSCH)

If you are using a work jig, relocate the engine as shown in **Figure 54**.

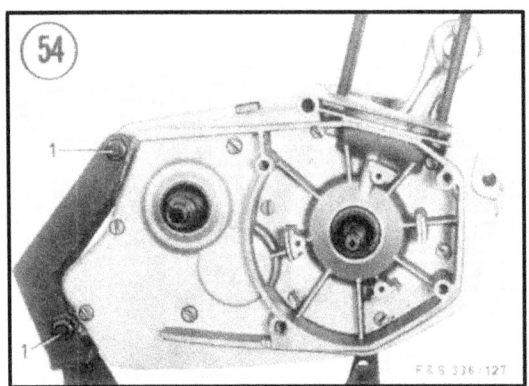

1. Degrease the tapered portion of the crankshaft and the bore in the flywheel.

2. Fit the stator plate over the shaft and onto the case. If the stator plate is not the self-aligning notched type, carefully line up the mark on the plate with the mark on the crankcase (4, **Figure 55**).

3. Coat the threads of the 3 Phillips head screws with Diament sealant and screw them into the case with their washers installed (1, Figure 55).

Tighten the screws to 2.0-4.4 ft.-lb. (0.4-0.6 mkg).

4. Set the key in the slot in the shaft (2, Figure 55) and route the electrical cable through the hole in the case. Press the rubber grommet around the cable into the hole.

5. Install the ignition flywheel on the shaft, taking care to line up the keyway with the key.

6. Hold the flywheel with a jig lever or pin wrench and install the washer and flywheel nut. Remember: it's a left-hand thread. Tighten the nut to 27.5-29 ft.-lb. (3.8-4.0 mkg).

IGNITION INSTALLATION (MOTOPLAT)

1. Degrease the tapered portion of the crankshaft and the bore in the flywheel.

2. Fit the stator plate over the shaft and onto the case. If the stator plate is not self-aligning, carefully line up the mark on the mark on the plate with the mark on the crankcase (2, **Figure 56**).

3. Coat the heads of the 3 slotted screws (1, Figure 56) with Diament sealant and install the screws with their washers. Tighten them to 2.9-4.4 ft.-lb. (0.4-0.6 mkg).

4. Route the cable of the stator body through the hole in the case. Press the rubber grommet around the cable into the hole.

5. Fit the stator body over the end of the shaft. Screw in the 3 slotted screws but don't tighten them; the stator must be able to be turned when the ignition is timed (see Chapter Seven).

6. Set the key in the slot in the shaft. Install the flywheel, taking care to line up the keyway with the key.

7. Install the washer and left-hand-threaded nut. Leave the nut slightly loose until the ignition has been timed.

8. Time the ignition in accordance with the instructions in Chapter Seven.

DRIVE SPROCKET INSTALLATION

1. Degrease the taper on the transmission main shaft and the bore of the drive sprocket.

2. Install the sprocket, washer, and left-hand-threaded nut and tighten it to 50-54 ft.-lb. (7.0-7.5 mkg).

GEAR SELECTOR INSTALLATION

Refer to Chapter Five and install and adjust the gear selector mechanism (and the gear lock if the engine is so equipped).

DRIVE GEAR/CLUTCH INSTALLATION

1. Fit the washer over the end of the crankshaft and insert the key in the keyway (**Figure 57**).

2. Install the drive gear on the shaft, taking care to line up the keyway with the key. Install a lockwasher and nut on the end of the shaft.

3. Fit the locking plate (tool No. 10) over the gear and secure it to the case with 2 screws (**Figure 58**). Tighten the nut to 50-54 ft.-lb. (7.0-7.5 mkg).

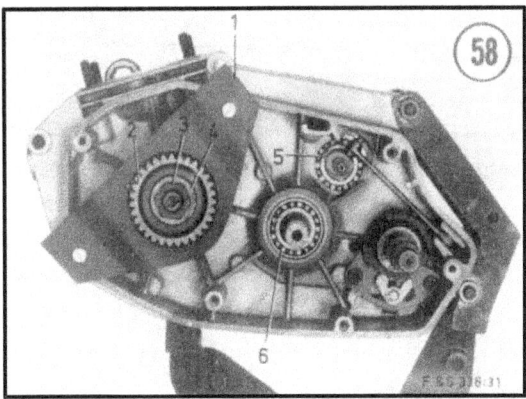

4. Insert the key into the keyway in the layshaft. Install the clutch hub on the shaft, taking care to line up the keyway with the key.

5. Place the flat washer on the shaft and screw on the nut.

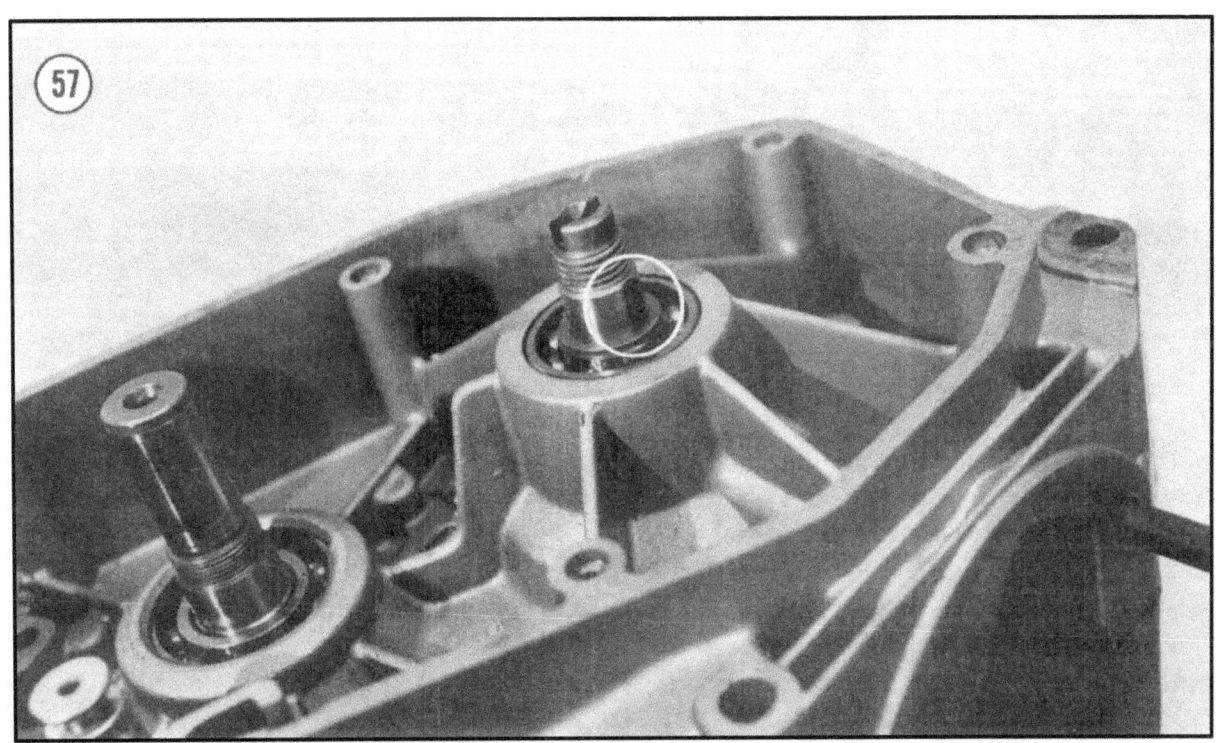

6. Install the locking plate (tool No. 8) on the clutch hub and secure it with 2 screws (**Figure 59**). Tighten the nut on the main shaft to 57-65 ft.-lb. (8-9 mkg).

7. Assemble the thrust plates and ball bearing case onto the shaft (**Figure 60**). The inner plate must have its groove facing outward, and the outer plate must have its groove facing inward.

8. Preassemble the clutch as described in Chapter Five. Oil the clutch hub and fit the clutch onto it (**Figure 61**).

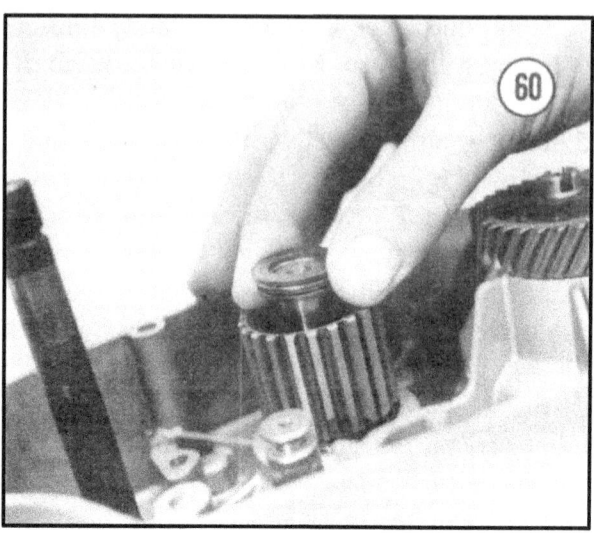

9. Add shims to the end of the shaft, up to the circlip groove, and install the circlip. Check the axial clearance of the clutch with a flat feeler gauge (**Figure 62**). It should be 0.004 (0.1 millimeter). If necessary, remove the circlip and correct the axial play by adding or removing shims as required. (See **Table 2**).

Table 2 SHIM SIZES

0.15 mm (0.006 in.)
0.3 mm (0.012 in.)
0.5 mm (0.020 in.)
1.0 mm (0.40 in.)

10. Fit the pressure plate onto the clutch and install the 2 hollow alignment dowels in the case.

CLUTCH-SIDE COVER INSTALLATION

Coat the mating surface of the crankcase and the cover with F&S sealant No. 40 or an equivalent gasket cement and install the gasket over the alignment dowels in the crankcase. Set the cover in place and install the 7 slotted screws as shown in **Figure 63**. The bottommost screw must be fitted with a sealing washer because it serves as an oil drain. Tighten the screws in the pattern shown 6-7 ft.-lb. (0.8-1.0 mkg).

GEAR SELECTOR AND KICKSTARTER

Position the gear selector pedal on its shaft so it's about horizontal and install it (**Figure 64**). Slide the O-ring seal onto the shaft (**Figure 65**) and install the kickstarter lever. Tighten the pinch bolts in both levers.

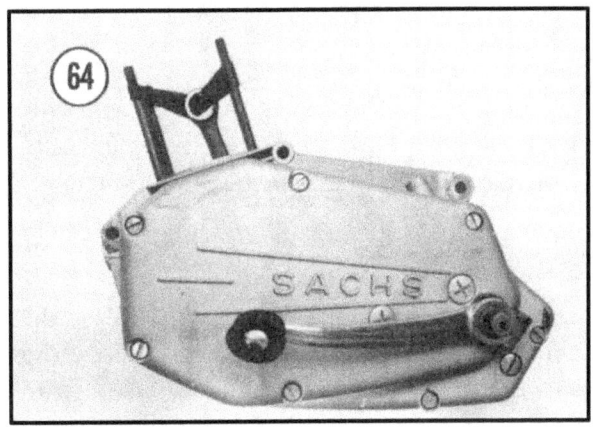

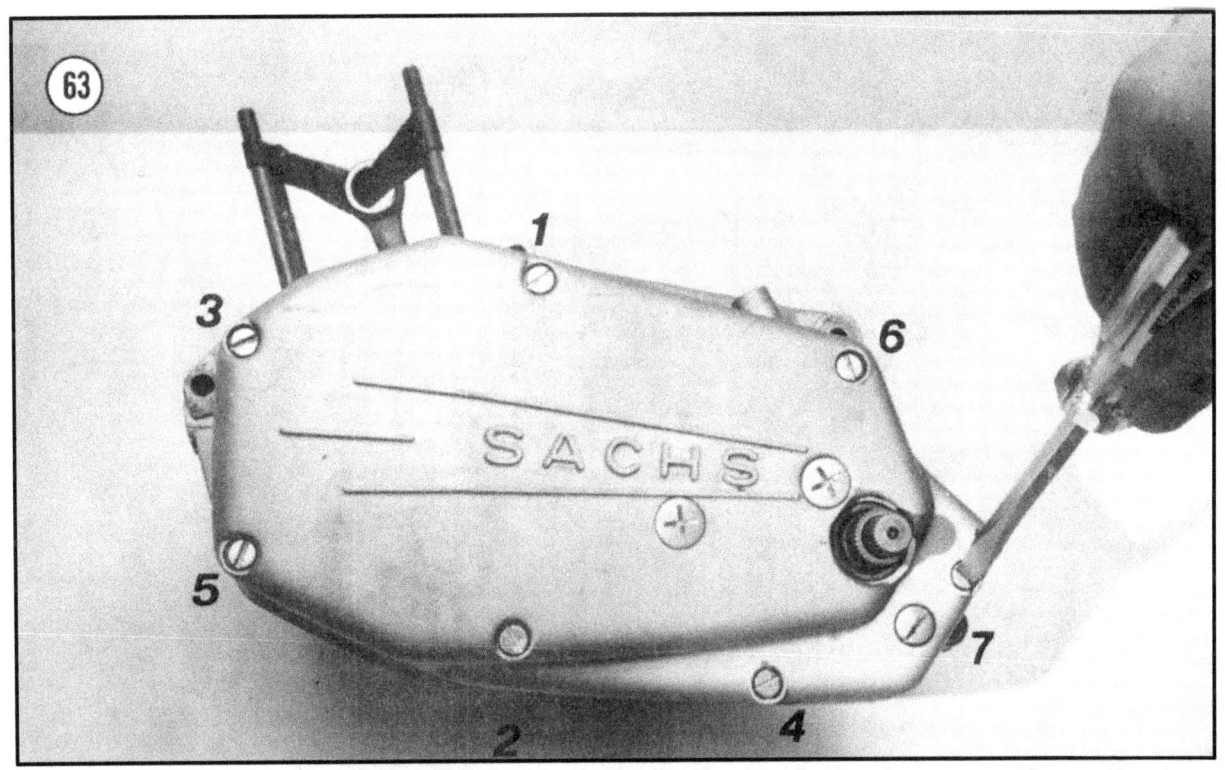

REINSTALLATION, FINAL ASSEMBLY, AND TIMING

The engine may be reinstalled in the motorcycle at this point. Reverse the removal procedure and reassemble the upper end, referring to the procedure in Chapter Three. Fill the gearbox (see specifications for details). Prior to installing the ignition-side cover on the engine, time the ignition in accordance with the instructions in Chapter Seven.

Install the hollow alignment dowels in the right side of the crankcase and coat the mating surfaces of the crankcase and the cover with F&S sealant No. 40 or an equivalent gasket cement. Set the gasket in place over the alignment dowels. Set the cover in place, making sure the tangs inside the beveled speedometer drive gear (**Figure 66**) fit into the slot in the end of the mainshaft (**Figure 67**).

Screw in the four 60-millimeter-long (2.36 in.) slotted screws and tighten them to 5.6-7.3 ft.-lb. (0.8-1.0 mkg).

Reassemble the rest of the motorcycle by reversing the disassembly steps presented earlier.

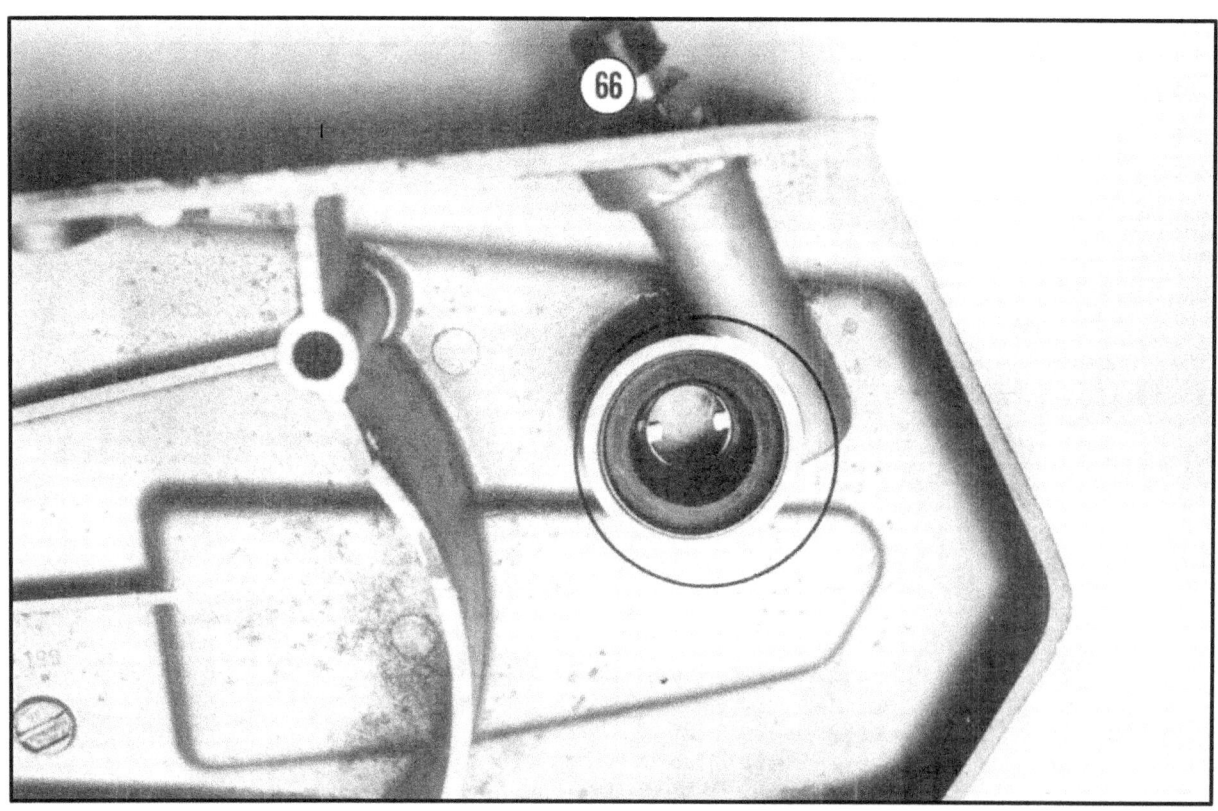

CHAPTER FIVE

TRANSMISSION AND CLUTCH

Two transmission types are used in Sachs engines—a 5-speed (**Figure 1**) and a 6-speed (**Figure 2**). Most service procedures are identical for both types. Where exceptions exist, they're noted in the text and figures. Clutches (**Figure 3**) in all models are the same.

CLUTCH

The clutch may be removed, serviced, installed, and adjusted with the engine in the motorcycle.

Removal

Removal of the clutch is discussed in Chapter Four. Be sure to drain the primary case and transmission before removing the outer cover.

Disassembly

1. Unscrew the 3 locknuts from the outer face of the layshaft gear and unscrew the 3 Allen screws which hold the clutch box on the gear (**Figure 4**). The screws should be unscrewed

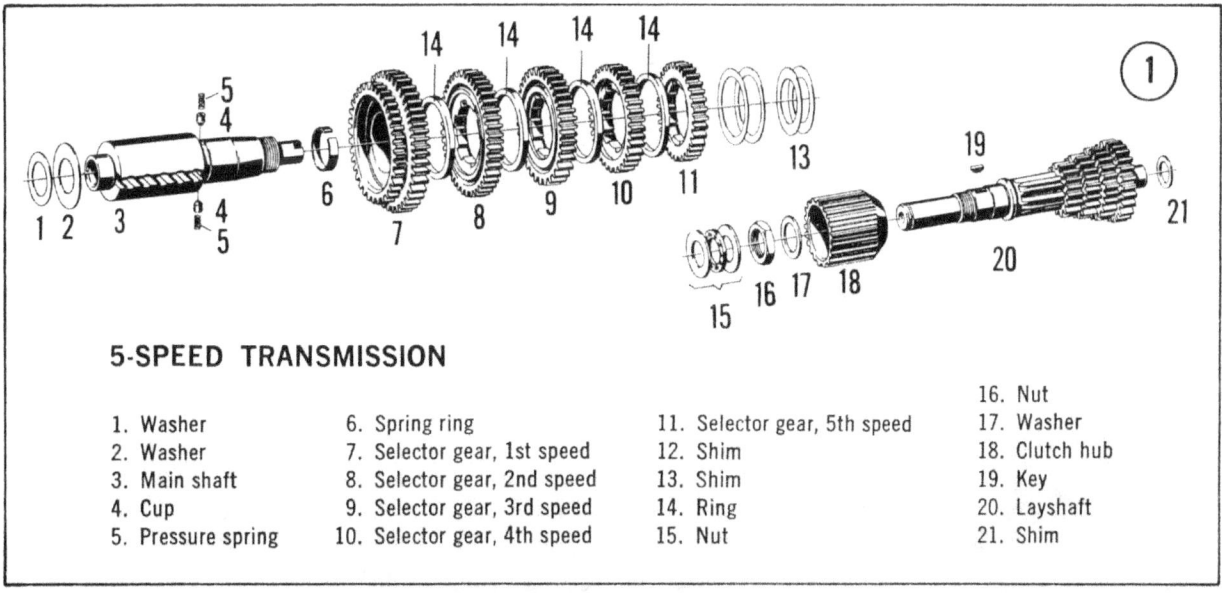

5-SPEED TRANSMISSION

1. Washer
2. Washer
3. Main shaft
4. Cup
5. Pressure spring
6. Spring ring
7. Selector gear, 1st speed
8. Selector gear, 2nd speed
9. Selector gear, 3rd speed
10. Selector gear, 4th speed
11. Selector gear, 5th speed
12. Shim
13. Shim
14. Ring
15. Nut
16. Nut
17. Washer
18. Clutch hub
19. Key
20. Layshaft
21. Shim

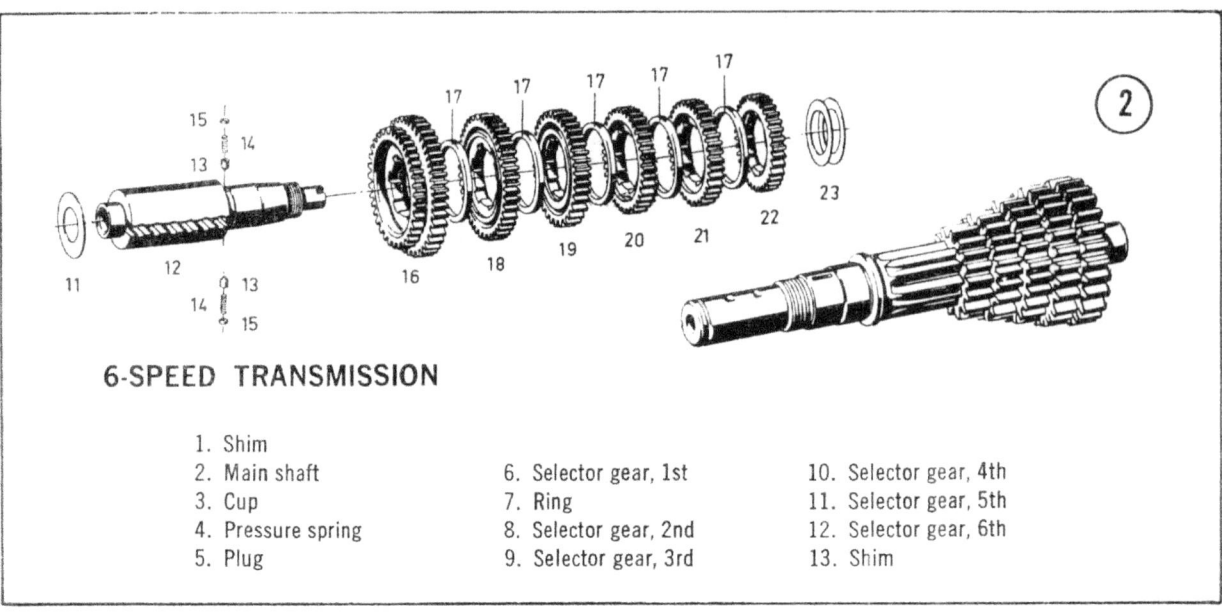

6-SPEED TRANSMISSION

1. Shim
2. Main shaft
3. Cup
4. Pressure spring
5. Plug
6. Selector gear, 1st
7. Ring
8. Selector gear, 2nd
9. Selector gear, 3rd
10. Selector gear, 4th
11. Selector gear, 5th
12. Selector gear, 6th
13. Shim

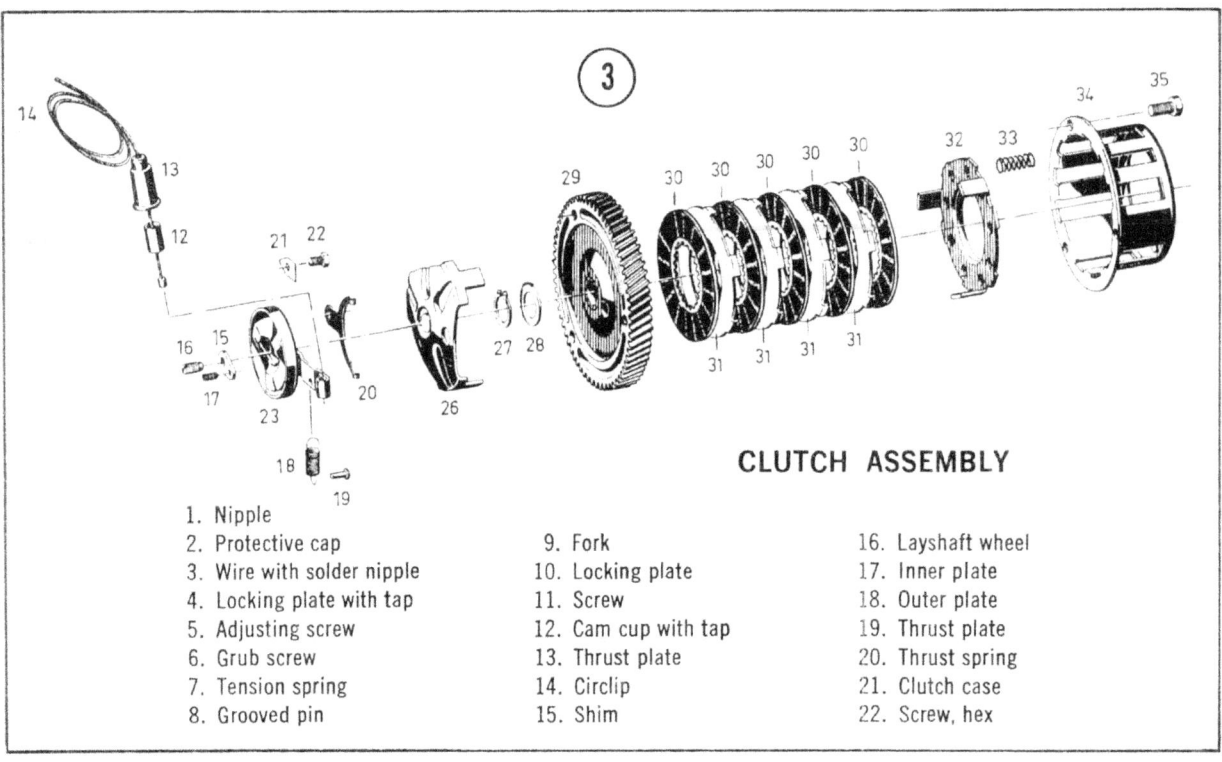

CLUTCH ASSEMBLY

1. Nipple
2. Protective cap
3. Wire with solder nipple
4. Locking plate with tap
5. Adjusting screw
6. Grub screw
7. Tension spring
8. Grooved pin
9. Fork
10. Locking plate
11. Screw
12. Cam cup with tap
13. Thrust plate
14. Circlip
15. Shim
16. Layshaft wheel
17. Inner plate
18. Outer plate
19. Thrust plate
20. Thrust spring
21. Clutch case
22. Screw, hex

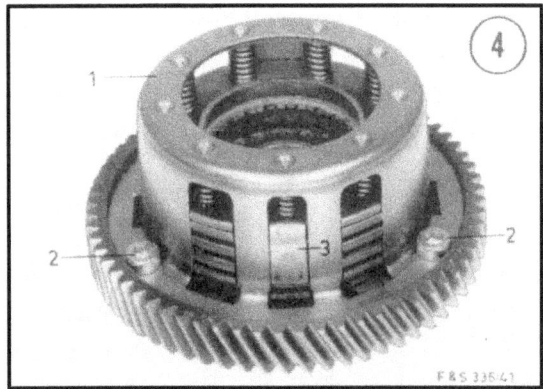

evenly, about one-half turn at a time until the spring tension has been relieved.

2. Pull off the clutch box and remove the springs and plates.

Inspection

1. Check the resiliency of the springs. They should be firm and the spacing between the coils should be even. The springs should be equal in length (**Figure 5**).

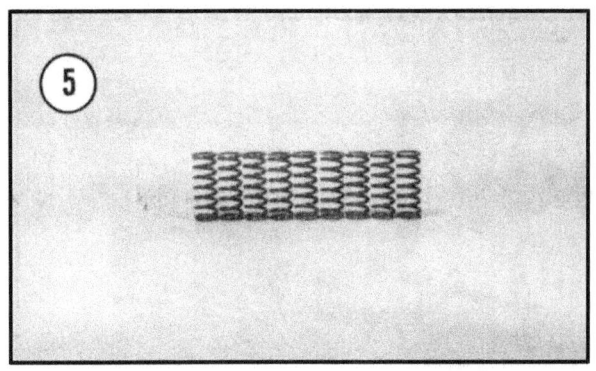

2. Examine the steel plates for galling or grooves. The friction material on the alternate plates should be uniform in thickness. If the condition of the plates is in doubt, or if the plates can be separated by pushing on the pressure plate with the clutch assembled, the plates and the springs should be replaced.

Assembly

1. Place the clutch hub over the boss on the layshaft gear (**Figure 6**) and install the plates beginning with a friction plate, alternating with a steel plate, another friction plate, and so on until all of the plates are installed. The tabs on the steel plates must point upward.

2. Install the inner pressure plate and apply a dab of grease to each of the 9 nubs. Set the springs on the pressure plate, one on each nub (**Figure 7**).

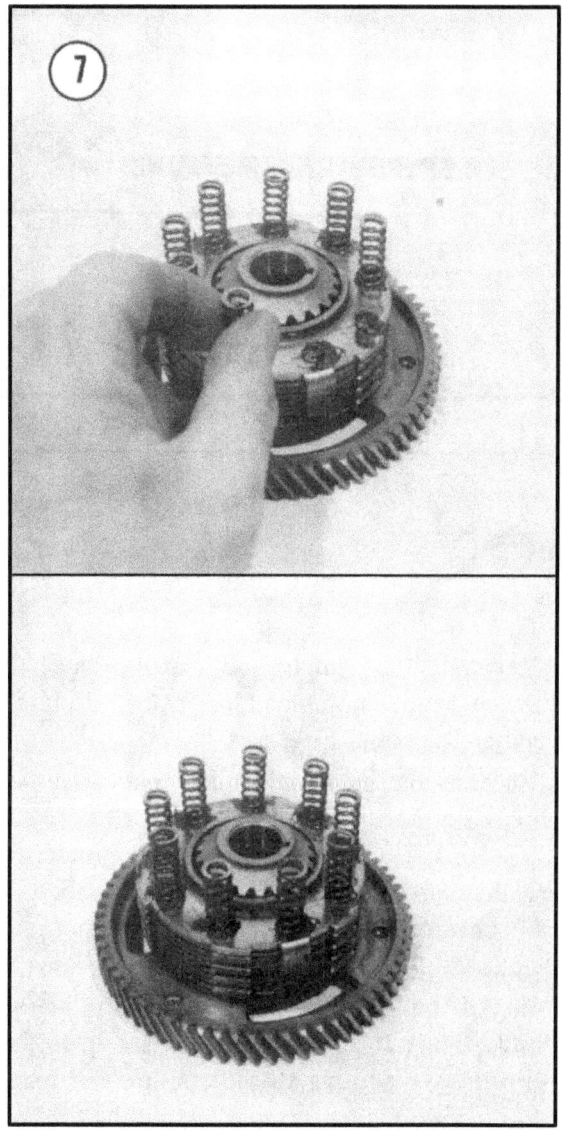

3. Install the clutch box so that its nubs engage the ends of the springs and its 3 narrow slots straddle the 3 tabs in the pressure plate (**Figure 8**). Line up the 3 holes in the flange of the clutch box with the tapped holes in the layshaft gear.

4. Coat the threads of the 3 Allen screws with liquid locking compound and screw them in evenly but not tight.

5. Reinstall the clutch hub on the layshaft and then install the assembled gear and clutch to center the plates.

6. Remove the gear and clutch assembly and tighten the 3 Allen screws to 8-7.10.8 ft.-lb. (1.2-1.5 mkg). Coat the protruding threads of the Allen screws with liquid locking compound and screw on the locknuts. Tighten them to 8-8.7 ft.-lb. (0.5-0.6 mkg).

7. Install the gear and clutch assembly, fit the shim or shims on the end of the shaft up to the circlip groove and install the circlip. The axial play of the clutch on the shaft should be 0.0039 in. (0.1mm). To check the play, push in on the clutch and insert a flat feeler gauge between the circlip and the top shim.

8. Install the outer pressure plate with its lugs engaging the inner pressure plate lugs through the slots in the layshaft gear.

9. Install the hollow alignment dowels in the crankcase and coat the sealing surface with gasket cement. Install the gasket and the outer cover. Install the 7 slotted screws (4 longest screws in the 4 forward holes) and tighten them to 5.6-7.25 ft.-lb. (0.8-1.0 kpm).

Adjustment

Adjust the clutch in accordance with the instructions in the Penton workshop manual.

TRANSMISSION

Major transmission service requires that the engine be removed from the motorcycle, the crankcase split, and the gear train removed in accordance with the instructions provided in Chapter Four.

Service and adjustment of the gear selector mechanism (with the exeception of the selector rod and selector key), which is presented later in this chapter, can be carried out with the engine installed in the motorcycle.

Disassembly

The layshaft and its gears are a single assembly (**Figure 9**). The main shaft and its gears and spacers can be disassembled by sliding them off the drive end of the shaft with the sprocket removed (Figures 1 and 2).

The main shaft and selector rod and key are disassembled as follows:

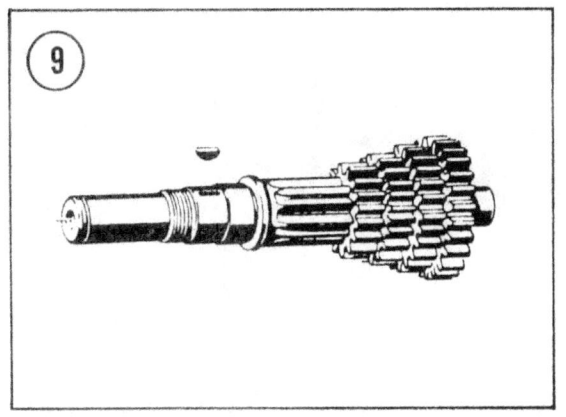

1. Gently clamp the main shaft in a vise fitted with soft jaws and unscrew (left-hand thread) the selector rod (**Figure 10**).

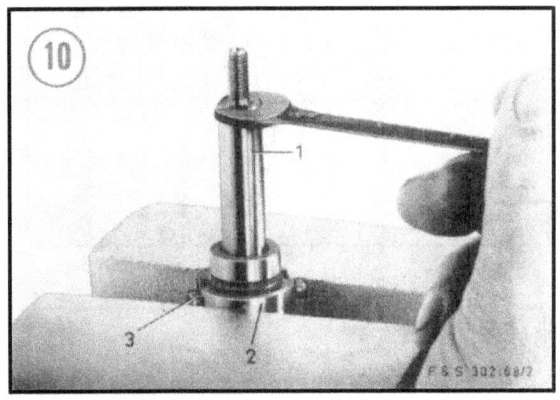

2A. If the main shaft is fitted with a spring retainer for the springs and cups (A, **Figure 11**), slide the spring back and remove the springs and cups from the shaft.

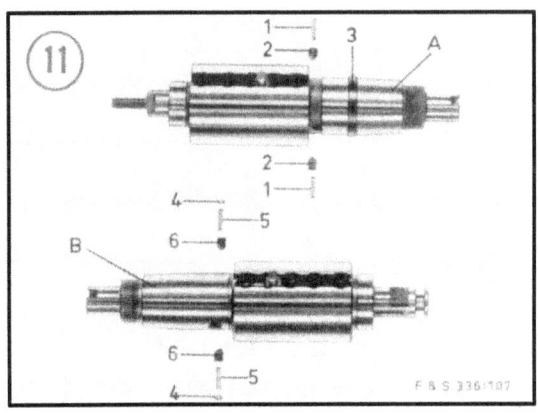

2B. If the main shaft is fitted with plugs to retain the springs and cups (B, **Figure 11**), remove the plugs and then the springs and cups.

3. Remove the rod and key from the main shaft.

Inspection

1. Check the gears for wear, pitting, galling, and chipped or fractured teeth and replace as necessary.

2. Check the bores in the inner bearing races for scores or galling. Rotate the bearings and feel for roughness and radial play. If either condition is present, the bearing should be replaced as described later.

3. Examine the selector rod, key, and cups for wear and replace as necessary.

> NOTE: *If bearing replacement is required, the following measurements should be performed after the new bearings have been installed.*

4. Place a new gasket on the magneto-side crankcase half and measure the distance between the inner race of the main shaft bearing and the mating surface of the crankcase as shown in **Figure 12**.

5. Measure the distance between the inner race of the main shaft bearing and the mating surface in the clutch-side crankcase half (**Figure 13**).

6. Measure the large-diameter portion of the main shaft (A or B, **Figure 14**).

7. Add the dimensions from Steps 4 and 5 and subtract the dimension determined in Step 6 from their sum.

EXAMPLE

Magneto side	42.9mm
Clutch side	12.1mm
	55.0mm
Less mainshaft width	54.1mm
Actual axial play	0.9mm
Allowable axial play	0.1mm
Difference to be compensated for	0.8mm

Appropriate shims must be fitted to the clutch side of the main shaft when the transmission is reassembled and installed in the crankcase.

8. The axial play of the layshaft should also be 0.1mm (0.0039 in.) and is determined in a

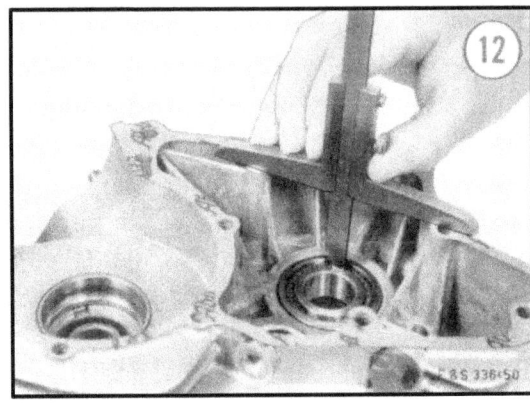

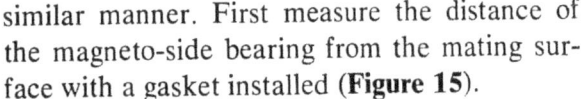

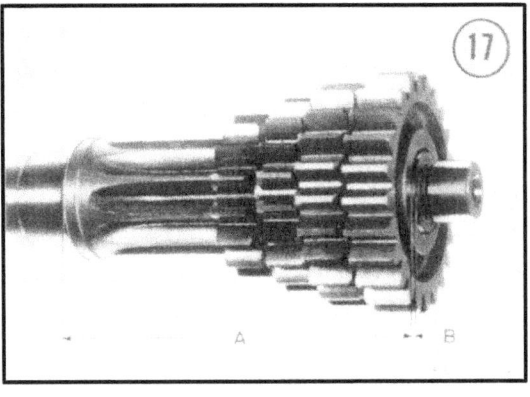

similar manner. First measure the distance of the magneto-side bearing from the mating surface with a gasket installed (**Figure 15**).

9. Measure the distance from the clutch-side bearing and the mating surface without a gasket (**Figure 16**) and add the 2 dimensions.

10. Measure the layshaft (dimension A plus dimension B in **Figure 17**) and subtract the result from the sum of the dimensions determined in Steps 8 and 9. This is the actual axial play of the layshaft. It can be corrected to the allowable axial play by adding or removing shims from the magneto-side end of the layshaft when the transmission is reassembled and installed in the crankcase. See **Table 1**.

11. The axial play of the starter shaft is also 0.1mm (0.0039 in.) and it's determined in a similar manner to that for the main shaft and layshaft. Measure the distance from the mating surface of the magneto side of the crankcase with a gasket installed (**Figure 18**).

12. Measure the distance from mating surface of the clutch-side crankcase half without a gasket to the rim of the bore for the starter ratchet (**Figure 19**).

13. Measure the starter shaft as shown in **Figure 20**. Subtract this dimension from the sum

Table 1 SHIM SIZES

Mainshaft

Five-speed
(large diameter) 0.3mm (0.012 in.)
0.5mm (0.020 in.)
0.6mm (0.024 in.)
0.8mm (0.032 in.)
1.0mm (0.039 in.)

(small diameter) 0.2mm (0.008 in.)
0.3mm (0.012 in.)
0.5mm (0.020 in.)
0.8mm (0.032 in.)
1.0mm (0.039 in.)

Six-speed
(same as small diameter for five-speed)

Layshaft

All transmissions 0.2mm (0.008 in.)
0.5mm (0.020 in.)
1.0mm (0.039 in.)
1.5mm (0.060 in.)

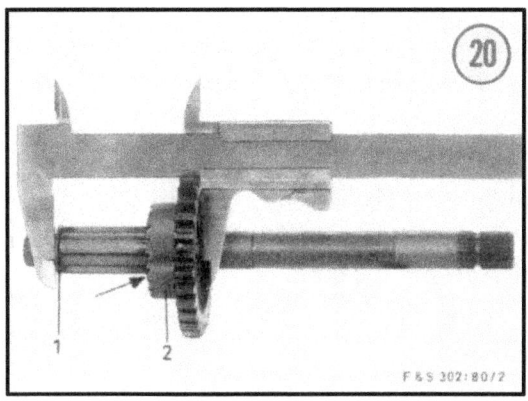

of the dimensions determined in Steps 11 and 12. This is the actual play of the starter shaft. It can be corrected by adding or removing shims between the rim of the starter bore in the clutch side of the crankcase and the ratchet gear (**Figure 21**).

Bearing Replacement

1. Heat each crankcase half to 115-140°C (250-300°F) and tap it with a soft mallet to knock out the bearings and seals. Note the location of the washer outboard of the layshaft bearing in the magneto side case so it may be reinstalled correctly (**Figure 22**).

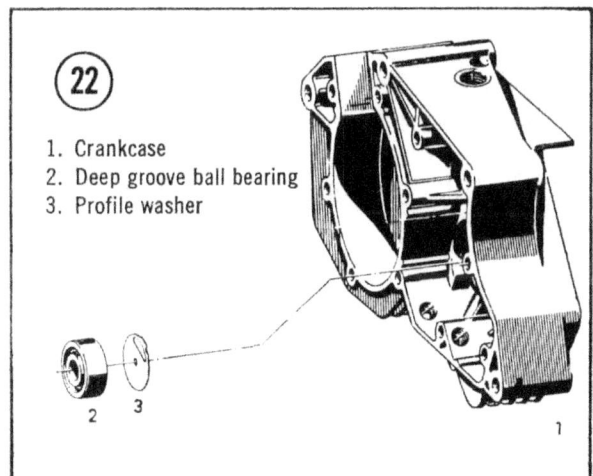

1. Crankcase
2. Deep groove ball bearing
3. Profile washer

2. Clean and deburr the bearing bores in the crankcases.

3. Fill the grooves in the oil seals with high-temperature grease and oil the seal lips.

4. Press the bearings and seals into the case while it is still hot. The seal lips must point inward and the outer surface of the seals must be flush with the outer edge of the bores in the cases. The flat surface of the profile washer in the layshaft bore in the magneto-side case must face inward and the washer's tab must engage the recess in the bore.

5. After the cases have cooled, repress the bearings.

> NOTE: *If the crankshaft bearings and seals were knocked out along with the transmission bearings and seals, refer to Chapter Four and reinstall them in accordance with the instructions.*

6. Refer to the section on inspection to select the appropriate shims for the transmission shafts.

Reassembly

1. Reassemble the main shaft and selector rod and key by reversing the steps for disassembly (**Figure 23**). Lightly oil all of the parts as they are assembled. Make certain the selector rod moves smoothly in the main shaft and that the detent action of the springs and cups is positive on each of the recesses in the rod. Apply liquid locking compound to the threads of the selector rod and tighten it in the selector key to 40 ft.-lb. (5.5 mkg).

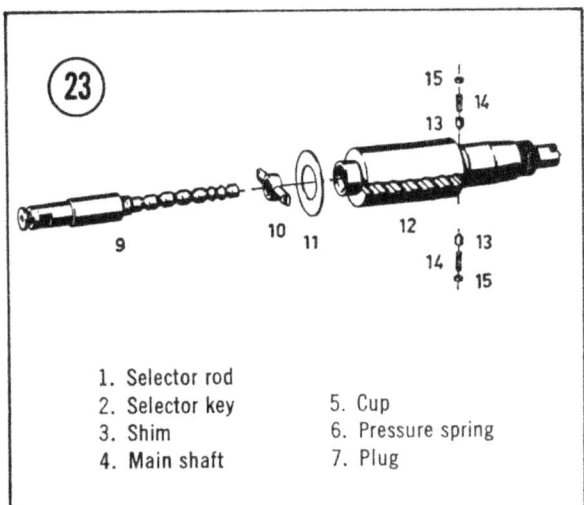

1. Selector rod
2. Selector key
3. Shim
4. Main shaft
5. Cup
6. Pressure spring
7. Plug

2. Place the shim(s) on the main shaft bearing in the clutch-side case and install the main shaft (**Figure 24**). The chamfered side of the shim must point inward.

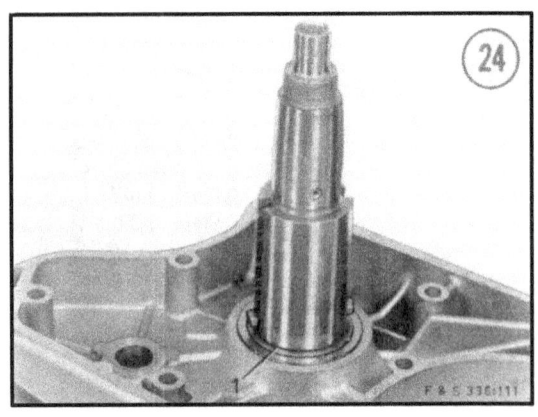

3. Oil the gears and spacers for the main shaft and install them on the shaft, beginning with the largest gear (the smaller gear of this double gear must face outward). Install a spacer and then the next smaller gear, alternating spacers with gears until they are all installed.

> NOTE: *On 5-speed transmissions, second, third, and fourth gears are reversible (not interchangeable) on the shaft. Fifth gear is recessed on the side facing fourth gear and its outer side is flat. In 6-speed transmissions, second, third, and fifth gears are reversible. Fourth gear is recessed on the side facing third gear. Sixth gear is recessed on the side facing fifth gear and its outer side is flat.*

4. Install the appropriate shim(s) beginning with the chamfered shim (chamfer facing the main-shaft collar) and install the inner race of the mainshaft bearing.

5. Install the layshaft in the transmission and fit the appropriate shims to its outer end.

6. Add the appropriate shims to the rim of the bore for the layshaft after coating them with grease and install the starter ratchet. Set the thrust washer in place on the ratchet (Figure 21).

7. Grease the rim of the starter shaft bore in the magneto-side case and install the 1mm thrust washer. Install the starter return spring in the case with the extended tang against the bottom stop in the case (**Figure 25**).

8. Slide the ratchet over the spring and engage the parallel end of the spring in the small hole in the ratchet.

9. Install the starter shaft through the ratchet and into the bore in the case. Make sure it passes through the thrust washer and is seated correctly in the case.

10. Install the kickstarter lever on the end of the shaft and turn it about ¾ turn in the starting direction. Press the ratchet down until it can be engaged with the stop screw in the case and remove the kickstarter lever.

11. Assemble the 2 crankcase halves, reassemble the rest of the engine, and install it in the motorcycle in accordance with the instructions in Chapter Four.

GEAR SELECTORS

There are 2 gear selector designs used on Sachs engines. On 100cc engines up to No. 5692 842 and 125cc engines up to No. 6318 754, the mechanism is distinguished by a one-piece lever (**Figure 26**). On subsequent engines, with both 5- and 6-speed transmissions, a 2-piece lever is used (**Figure 27**). Service and adjustment procedures for the 2 designs are distinctly different.

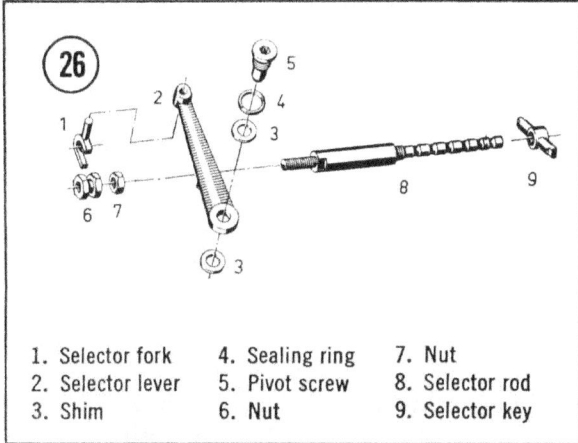

1. Selector fork
2. Selector lever
3. Shim
4. Sealing ring
5. Pivot screw
6. Nut
7. Nut
8. Selector rod
9. Selector key

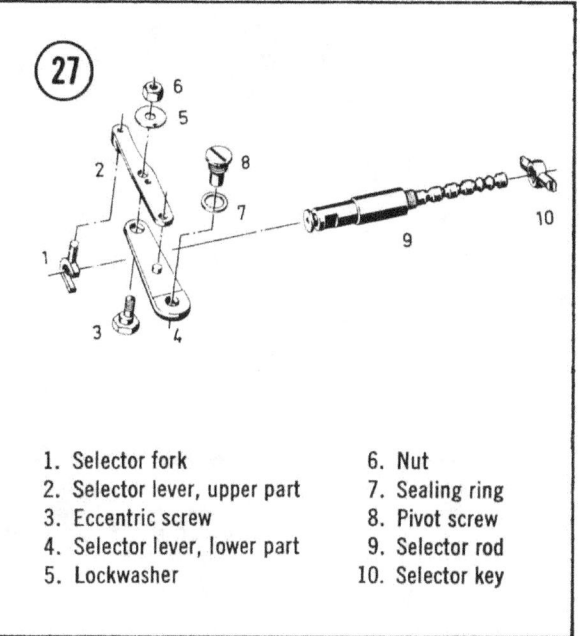

1. Selector fork
2. Selector lever, upper part
3. Eccentric screw
4. Selector lever, lower part
5. Lockwasher
6. Nut
7. Sealing ring
8. Pivot screw
9. Selector rod
10. Selector key

GEAR SELECTOR (ONE-PIECE)

Removal

Removal of the gear selector mechanism is described in Chapter Four.

Inspection

1. Check the resiliency of the springs and replace them if they are weak.

2. Examine the teeth of the pawl and selector boss for chips and wear.

3. Install the selector assembly on the kickstarter shaft and press in the adjusting plate (**Figure 28**). There should be no apparent axial play of the selector. If play exists, an appropriate shim must be installed on the shaft behind the selector mechanism; however, the selector must rotate freely on the shaft without binding.

4. Check the pathway (spiral groove) in the selector boss for wear. The edges should be sharp and even. If they are not, the selector boss should be replaced. In such cases, refer to **Figure 29** and remove the large circlip from the end of the shaft. Remove the outer shims, the selector boss, the inner shim and the pawl spring. Remove the small circlip from the end of the pawl shaft and remove the outer shims, pawl, and inner shim. Relax the spring and remove it. Remove the adjusting plate and the shim behind it and pull the selector shaft off of the kickstarter shaft.

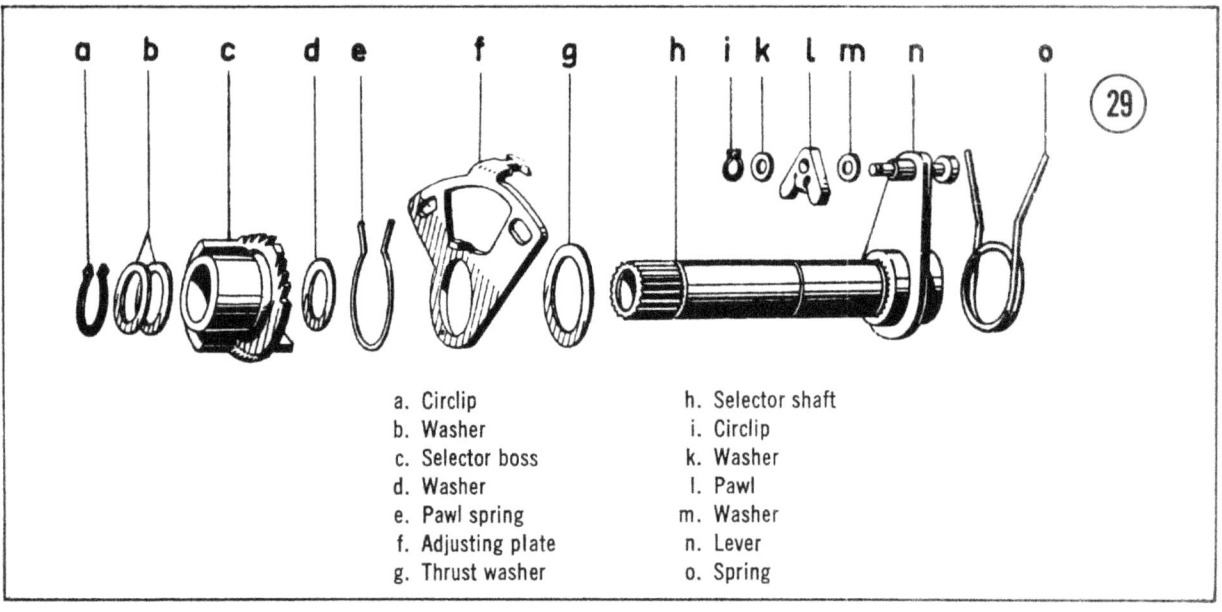

a. Circlip
b. Washer
c. Selector boss
d. Washer
e. Pawl spring
f. Adjusting plate
g. Thrust washer

h. Selector shaft
i. Circlip
k. Washer
l. Pawl
m. Washer
n. Lever
o. Spring

Assembly

1. Place a 0.5mm (0.020 in.) shim on the selector shaft and install the adjusting plate. Place a 0.5mm (0.020 in.) shim on the pawl and install the pawl with the spring tab facing inward. Add the outer shim and install the small circlip. The axial play of the pawl on the shaft should be 0.1mm (0.004 in.). Check it with a flat feeler gauge.

2. Install the pawl spring on the adjusting plate with the right end of the spring (offset) away from the plate. Cross the offset over the straight end of the spring and over the spring stop on the plate. The spring must also engage either side of the tab on the pawl (**Figure 30**).

3. Install the selector boss using appropriate shims so that the teeth of the boss line up accurately with the teeth of the pawl.

4. Fit shims to the selector shaft all the way to the circlip groove and install the circlip. There should be no perceptible axial play of the selector boss on the shaft. However, the boss must rotate freely on the shaft.

5. Install the large return spring on the inboard end of the selector shaft with the straight end toward the adjusting plate. Engage the straight end with the right side of the tab on the adjuster plate and cross the offset end over and engage it with the left side of the tab (**Figure 31**).

6. Install the shim and selector assembly on the kickstarter shaft and engage the pin on the selector lever with the pathway in the selector boss. Press the selector assembly all the way on.

7. Position the adjuster plate so the tapped holes in the case are in the center of the holes in the adjuster. Install the 2 Allen screws and tighten them (**Figure 32**).

8. Fit the gear selector pedal onto the shaft and check to see that it snaps back from both the raised and depressed positions.

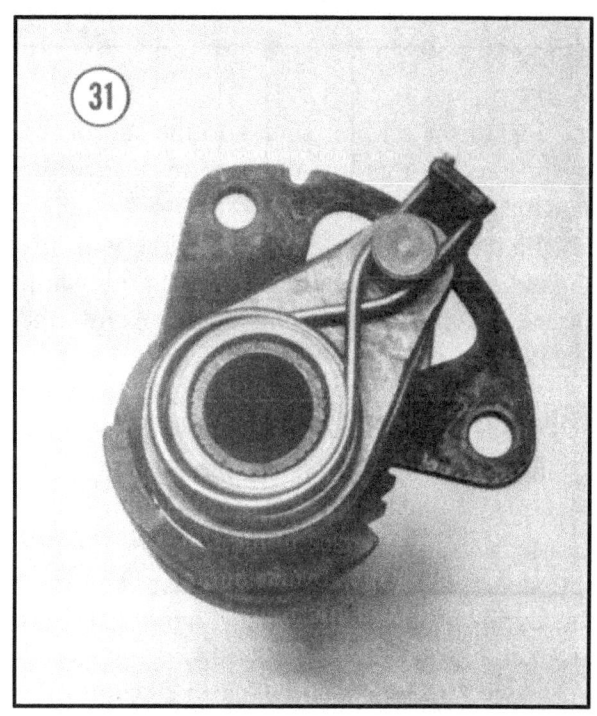

9. Screw the counter nut onto the selector rod and move the rod in or out by hand and engage third gear. You'll probably have to rotate the main shaft at the same time so that the gears will engage as the rod is moved.

10. Install the selector shoe into the end of the lever. The open end of the shoe must face the selector mechanism.

11. Fit the grooved nut into the shoe with the narrow shoulder on the nut facing outward. Screw the grooved nut all the way onto the selector rod but don't tighten it.

Adjustment

1. Install the selector pedal on the shaft and check to see that the transmission is in third gear.

2. Measure the distance between the mating surface of the crankcase (without a gasket) and the shaft of the selector shoe (**Figure 33**). This distance must be 23.2mm (0.914 in.). If necessary, screw the grooved nut in or out until the distance is correct.

3. Hold the grooved nut securely with a wrench and lock it with the counternut (**Figure 34**). Recheck the distance.

4. Shift the transmission into first gear and hold the selector pedal down, all the way against the

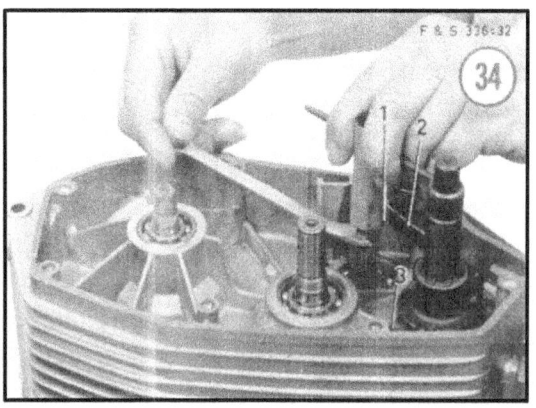

stop. You should be able to move the selector shoe in the nut groove (**Figure 35**). If not, loosen the Allen bolts which secure the adjusting plate to the case and rotate the stop cams as required until the selector shoe can be moved with the gear pedal pressed all the way to the bottom stop. Then tighten the Allen screws to 8.7-10.8 ft.-lb. (1.2-1.5 mkg). Shift the transmission into fifth gear and repeat the check.

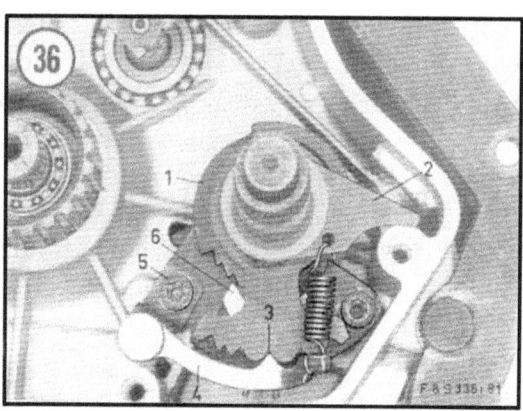

5. If the selector does not have a gear lock, the adjustment is complete. Reinstall the shims on the selector shaft and install the outer cover, gear selector pedal, and kickstart pedal as described in Chapter Four. If there is a gear lock on the selector, perform the following adjustment before reinstalling the cover.

Adjusting the Gear Lock

1. Install the selector pawl (4, **Figure 36**) so that its detent tip rests in the third-gear notch in the selector boss. Tighten the Allen screw (5) and install the spring between the plate (2) and the pawl.

2. Install the selector pedal on the shaft and push it downward, as though to engage second gear, and at the same time lift the rear tooth of the shifting pawl over the selector tooth with the tip of a small screwdriver so that the shifting pawl does not engage the selector but instead comes to rest against the rear stop. Note the position of lock pawl in the third gear notch in the lock plate.

3. Lift the selector pedal, as though to engage fourth gear, and lift the front tooth of the shifting pawl over the selector tooth so that the shifting pawl does not engage the selector tooth but instead comes to rest against the forward stop.

Note the position of the lock pawl in the third gear notch in the lock plate and compare it to its position in Step 2. If the gear lock is correctly adjusted, the lock pawl should rise an equal amount out of the recess in the lock plate in both directions.

4. If the lock pawl rose farther out of the notch in one direction, loosen the Allen screw (5, Figure 36) and center the pawl. For instance, if the pawl lifted farther out of the notch when the selector was pushed down (in the direction of second gear), move it slightly rearward and tighten the Allen screw. Recheck the action of the lock pawl as in Steps 2 and 3 and continue adjustment until the lock pawl rises out of the notch the same amount in both directions.

5. When the adjustment of the gear lock is correct, tighten the Allen screws to 8.7-10.8 ft.-lb. (1.2-1.5 mkg) and install the outer cover, selector pedal, and kickstarter as described in Chapter Four.

GEAR SELECTOR (TWO-PIECE)

Removal

Removal of the gear selector mechanism is described in Chapter Four.

Inspection

Inspection of the parts of the 2-piece selector assembly is the same as for the one-piece selector. Also, if the selector boss or shaft are to be replaced, they should be removed as described previously.

Assembly

1. If the selector assembly was disassembled, reassemble it in accordance with the instructions

79

presented previously for the selector system with the one-piece lever and proceed as follows.

2. Install the selector assembly onto the shaft and press the adjusting plate down to check the axial play. There should be no apparent play, but the selector must rotate freely. If play is present, remove the selector and add appropriate shims to the shaft. Then reinstall the selector assembly.

3. Pull the selector rod out until its end is flush with the mating surface of the case and the transmission is in first gear (**Figure 37**). It may be necessary to rotate the mainshaft to align the gears so they will mesh.

4. Loosen the nut on the selector lever (3, **Figure 38**) and install the the selector shoe in the end of the lever and onto the groove in the end of the selector rod. The open end of the shoe must face away from the selector shaft as shown in **Figure 39**.

5. Engage the pin in the rear half of the selector lever with the pathway in the selector boss. Press the selector boss down and line up the 2

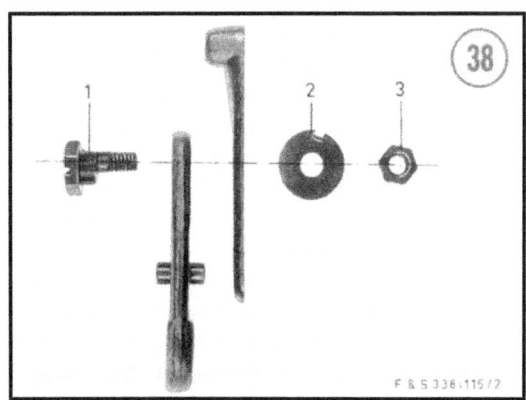

halves of the selector lever. Tighten the nut in the middle of the selector lever; make certain that the tab on the lockwasher engages the bore in the lever.

6. Install the 2. Allen screws and eccentric bushes in the adjuster plate. Turn the bushes outward and tighten the bolts (**Figure 40**).

7. Install the selector pedal and alternately depress and lift it and check to see that it snaps back to center from both directions.

Adjustment

1. Shift the transmission into first gear with the selector pedal and hold the pedal down against the bottom stop. Note the play of the selector pawl and the tooth on the selector boss (see **Figure 41**).

2. Shift the transmission into second gear and hold the pedal against the stop. Check the play of the forward selector pawl with the tooth on the selector boss. The play should be equal to the play observed in Step 1 (**Figure 42**).

3. If the play is unequal, loosen the nut in the center of the selector lever (1, **Figure 43**) and turn the eccentric bolt (4) clockwise or counterclockwise until the play between the ends of the selector pawl and the appropriate teeth in the selector boss is equal for both first and second gear, as described above. Then tighten the nut without turning the eccentric bolt and recheck the play. When the adjustment is correct, lock the nut with the tab washer.

NOTE: *The selector boss is not precisely machined. All that is necessary is to reach a reasonable compromise between the play of the front and rear pawls.*

NOTE: *If over- or under-shifting is experienced after the adjustments have been made, they can be corrected by further adjustment of the stops. If the selector undershifts in either direction, the appropriate stop should be rotated outward slightly to permit the pawl to travel farther. If the selector overshifts in either direction the appropriate stop should be rotated inward to reduce the travel of the pawl.*

6. Remove the selector pedal and add shims to the end of the shaft until the outer face of the shim is level with the mating surface of the crankcase (**Figure 45**).

4. Shift the transmission into first gear and hold the pedal against the stop. Loosen the Allen screw (4, **Figure 44**) and rotate the eccentric bushing (3) until it comes in contact with the selector pawl and tighten the screw to 8.7-10.8 ft.-lb. (1.2-1.5 mkg). Make sure the bushing does not rotate while the screw is being tightened.

5. Shift the transmission into second gear and hold the pedal against the stop. Loosen the Allen screw (2, Figure 44) and rotate the eccentric bushing (1) until it comes in contact with the selector pawl. Tighten the screw to 8.7-10.8 ft.-lb. (1.2-1.5 mkg), making sure the bushing does not rotate.

7. Install clutch and layshaft gear assembly, the outer cover, selector pedal, and kickstarter as described in Chapter Four.

SHIFTER SET-UP & ADJUSTMENT

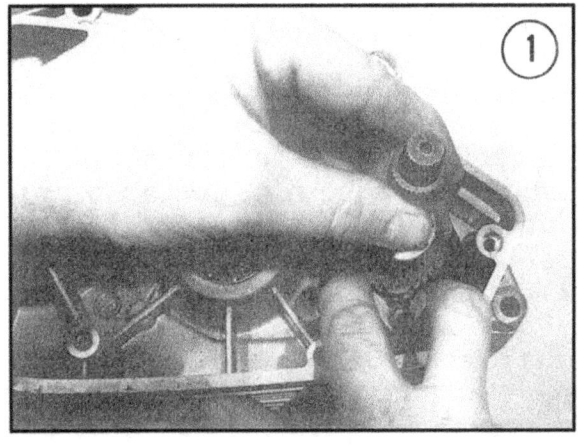

1. With the selector pedal on the shaft, move it first down and then up, allowing it to snap back each time. If the return spring is all right, the pedal will snap smartly back to center. Check the end play of the selector shaft and boss. There should be none. If you can see or feel any in-and-out movement you've already located some trouble.

2. Shift the transmission into first gear (the outer end of the selector draw rod should be level with the mating surface of the case). Unscrew the Allen screws from the adjuster plate and remove them along with their washers and eccentric bushes. Bend down the edge of the tab washer on the two-piece selector lever and unscrew the eccentric bolt and nut. Lift the selector lever and at the same time pull the selector assembly off of the starter shaft.

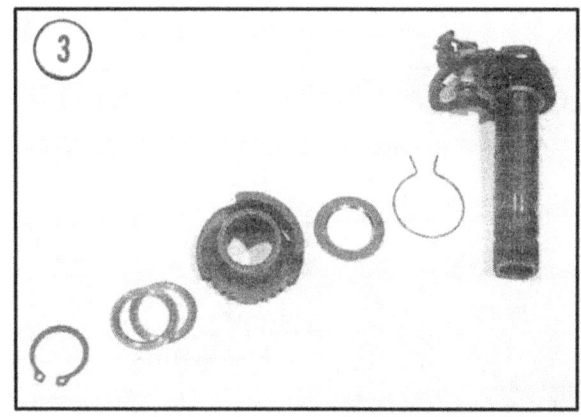

3. Check the spiral groove in the selector boss for wear. The edges must be sharp and even. Check the condition of the teeth. These too must be sharp. If there's any doubt about its condition, replace it. Remove the outer shim from the shaft, remove the circlip and the inner shims, the boss, the shim behind it, and the pawl spring. Pay close attention to the position of the pawl spring before you remove it; it has to go back in the same position with its ends crossed over one another, straddling the tang on the pawl and the tang on the adjuster plate.

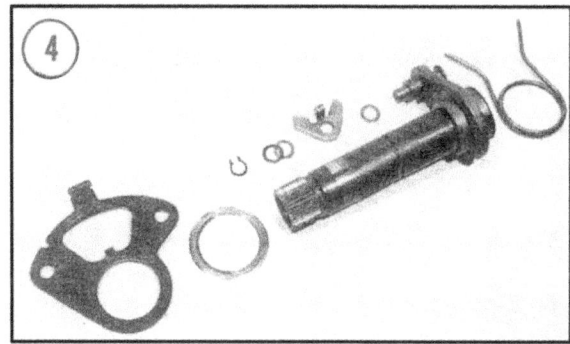

4. Remove the large return spring from the selector shaft. Check the teeth of the shifting pawl for wear. They must be sharp if the pawl is to do its job correctly. If they're not, replace it. If the pawl is in good condition you may not have to remove it but you do have to check its end play; it should be 0.1mm (0.0039 in.). The shim behind the pawl must be 0.5mm (0.020 in.). End

play can be corrected by substituting different size shims to the shaft ahead of the pawl. These shims are available through Sachs dealers in thicknesses of 0.2mm, 0.3mm, 0.5mm and 1.0mm. And while you're at it, get a new circlip.

5. If there was any end play apparent in the selector mechanism on the starter shaft it must be compensated with the shims shown here. These also are available through Sachs dealers in thicknesses of 0.2mm, 0.3mm, 0.5mm, and 1.0mm.

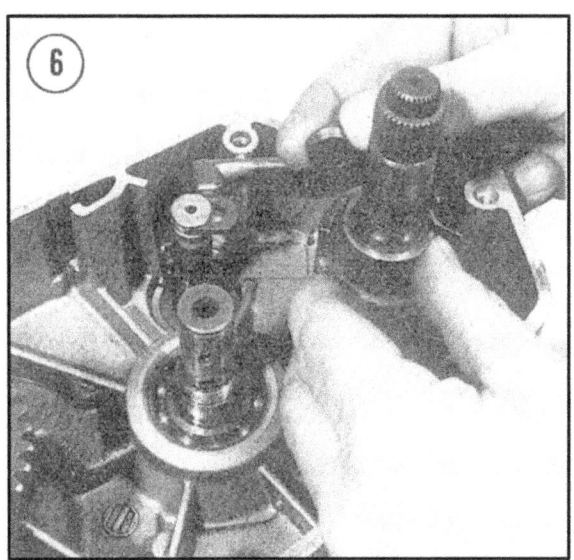

6. Reassemble the selector assembly and check the alignment of the teeth in the boss with the teeth of the pawl. They must line up exactly. If they do not, you must increase or decrease the thickness of the shim behind the selector boss. Place the selector shoe in the end of the selector boss and start the selector assembly onto the starter shaft. Line up the selector shoe with the groove in the selector rod and at the same time engage the pin in the selector lever with the beginning of the spiral groove in the boss. This sounds like a job for three hands, but actually all it requires is a little patience and coordination. When the selector assembly is in place, put a dab of grease on the tab washer that goes on the selector lever and set it in place, with the tang in the hole in the top of the lever. Reinstall the eccentric bolt and nut and tighten them securely but don't bend the washer over just yet.

7. Reinstall the Allen screws and eccentric bushes in the adjuster plate, rotating the bushes out as far as they will go. Tighten the screws. Install the selector pedal and check to see that it snaps back to center after it is raised and then depressed. Using the pedal, shift the transmission into first gear and carefully release it. Note the distance the pawl tooth rises out of the selector boss tooth.

8. Shift the transmission into second gear with the pedal and carefully release it. Again note the distance the pawl tooth rises out of the selector boss tooth. The return distance for both first and second gear engagement should be as nearly equal as possible.

9. The distances can be equalized by turning the eccentric bolt in the center of the selector lever clockwise or counterclockwise. Have a little patience and double check the distance in both gears until you're confident that it's as nearly equal as possible.

With your other hand, grasp the selector shoe and check its play in the groove in the selector rod. Then, shift the transmission into second gear, hold the pedal against the stop and check the play of the shoe in the groove. If the stop adjustment is correct, the play in the shoe should be about equal for both gears. Repeat this check between each gear pairing — first and second, second and third, third and fourth, fourth and fifth, fifth and sixth. Because the selector boss is not a precision machined part it's doubtful that the spacing set between first and second gear will work best for each pair up the line. You'll have to accept a compromise and it's going to take some time. Each time you make an adjustment with the eccentric bolt double check the shoe play in all of the gear pairings. Very soon, you should develop a "feel" for the best compromise in adjustment and when you're satisfied that you've reached it, stop.

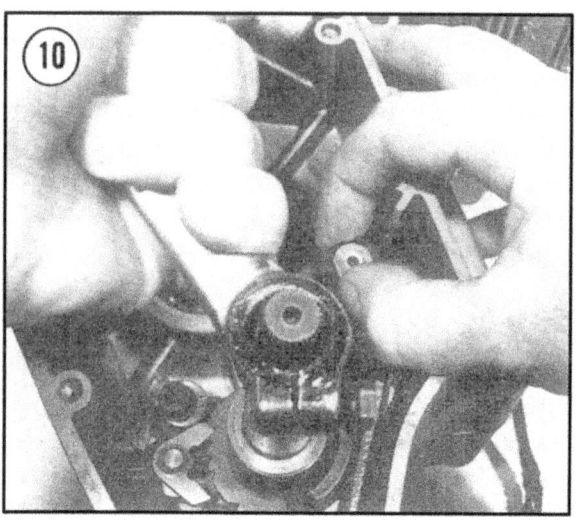

10. Once again shift the transmission into first gear but don't release the pedal; hold it firmly against the stop.

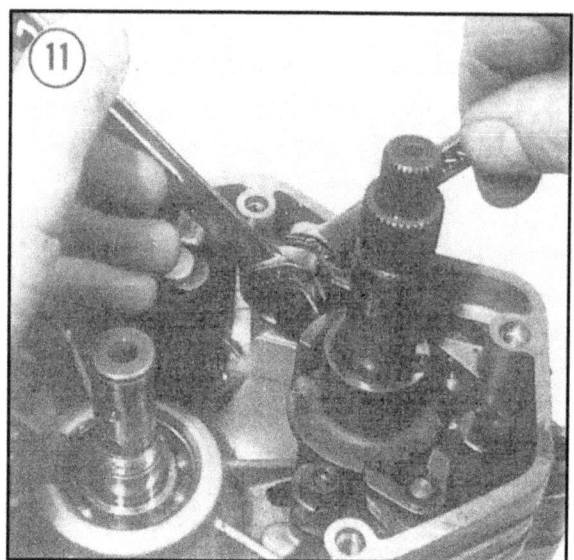

11. Retighten the nut on the eccentric bolt, without turning the bolt, and bend over the tab washer to lock everything neatly in place.

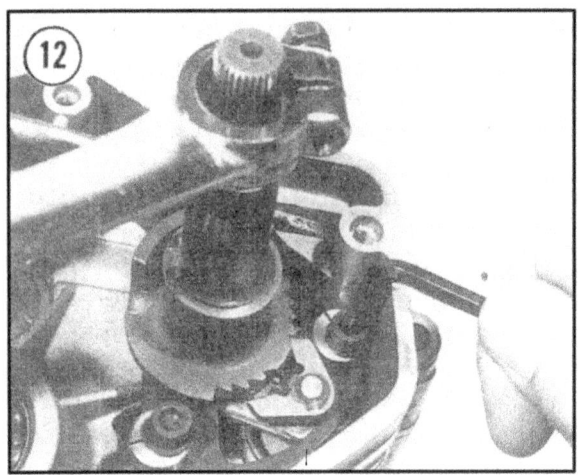

12. Now you're ready to adjust the overshift. Loosen the rear Allen screw in the adjuster plate. Shift the transmission into first gear and hold the lever against the stop. Rotate the rear eccentric bushing until it just contacts the selector pawl. Then, without moving the bushing, tighten the Allen screw to between 8.7 and 10.8 ft.-lb. (or 1.2 to 1.5 kpm, if you have a metric torque wrench).

13. Adjust the front overshift bushing in the same manner. Shift the transmission into second gear and hold it against the top. Rotate the eccentric bushing to contact the pawl and tighten the Allen screw without moving the bushing. The torque is the same.

14. Shim the outer end of the selector boss up to the level of the mating surface of the case. Reinstall the clutch (tighten the clutch hub nut to between 57.8 and 65 ft.-lb. – 8 to 9 kpm) making sure that all of the bits and pieces go back in the order they were removed. And while you're at it, you might check the axial play of the layshaft gear and clutch after you've installed the circlip. It should be 0.1mm (0.0039 in.). Coat the mating surfaces of the case and cover with gasket cement, install a new gasket over the alignment dowels, and set the cover in place. Tighten the cover screws to 6 to 7 ft.-lb., install the starter and gear selector pedals (don't forget the O-ring at the end of the selector shaft) and you're down the road!

CHAPTER SIX

CARBURETOR

For correct operation, a gasoline engine must be supplied with fuel and air mixed in proper proportions by weight. A mixture in which there is an excess of fuel is said to be rich. A lean mixture is one which contains an insufficient amount of fuel. It is the function of the carburetor to supply the correct fuel/air mixture to the engine under all operating conditions.

Sachs engines are equipped with Bing carburetors. The carburetor incorporates 4 subsystems; fuel feel, main control, idling, and starting.

OPERATION

The Bing carburetor is shown in exploded view in **Figure 1**, and in cutaway in **Figure 2**. These illustrations will be helpful in identifying individual components and their relationships.

Fuel Feed System

The fuel feed system consists of the float chamber, float, and needle valve. When fuel flowing into the float chamber reaches the correct operating level it lifts the float which raises the valve needle into the valve, cutting off the flow of fuel from the fuel tank.

As the engine consumes fuel, the level in the float chamber drops, causing the float to drop which lowers the valve needle and allows additional fuel to enter the float chamber. The needle valve serves only as a level regulator; it cannot positively shut off the fuel flow to the carburetor. Because of the likelihood of small particles becoming lodged between the needle and its seat and holding the valve open permitting a continuous flow of fuel into the float chamber, it's important that the fuel tap on the tank be closed when the engine is shut off and the motorcycle allowed to stand.

The float chamber incorporates a tickler which can be used to depress the float and allow the chamber to fill completely for cold-engine starts. This is not part of the starting system, however. The tickler tube and a hole in the top of the float chamber serve as atmospheric vents for the float chamber. If the vent hole becomes clogged, the tickler tube will act as a vent although the engine will experience fuel starvation until the vent hole is unblocked.

Main Control System

The main control system consists of the air control slide, needle, needle jet, mixing tube, and main jet. The amount of air drawn through the carburetor and into the engine is controlled by the air slide. As the slide is lifted the air flow through the carburetor increases creating a vacuum in the carburetor bore. The vacuum siphons fuel from the float chamber through the

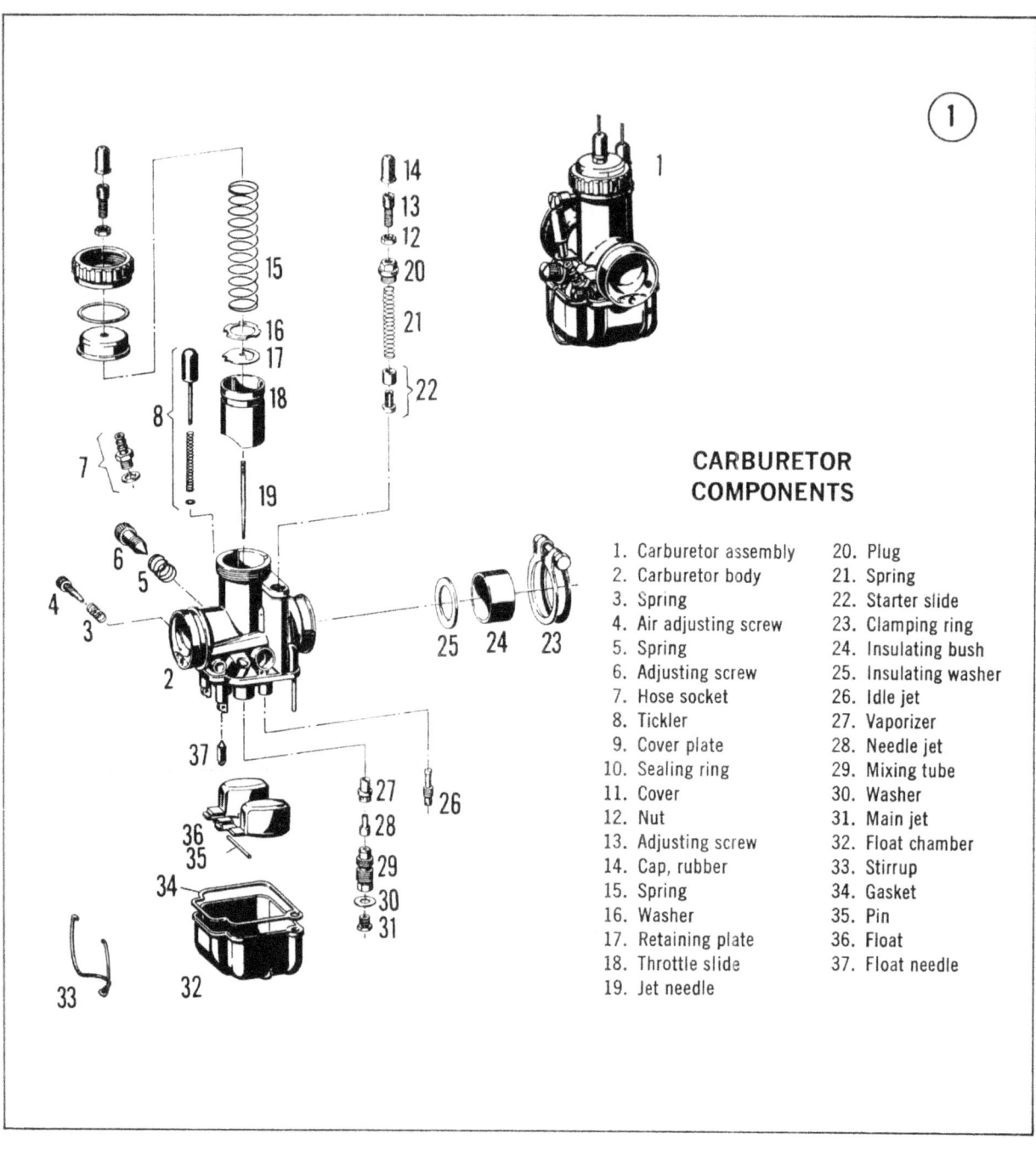

CARBURETOR COMPONENTS

1. Carburetor assembly
2. Carburetor body
3. Spring
4. Air adjusting screw
5. Spring
6. Adjusting screw
7. Hose socket
8. Tickler
9. Cover plate
10. Sealing ring
11. Cover
12. Nut
13. Adjusting screw
14. Cap, rubber
15. Spring
16. Washer
17. Retaining plate
18. Throttle slide
19. Jet needle
20. Plug
21. Spring
22. Starter slide
23. Clamping ring
24. Insulating bush
25. Insulating washer
26. Idle jet
27. Vaporizer
28. Needle jet
29. Mixing tube
30. Washer
31. Main jet
32. Float chamber
33. Stirrup
34. Gasket
35. Pin
36. Float
37. Float needle

jets where it is mixed with the incoming air. A portion of the incoming air is routed into the mixing tube where it helps to atomize the fuel passing through the jets and into the main chamber.

At partial throttle settings (from one-quarter to three-quarters full opening), fuel flow is controlled by the needle and needle jet. As the tapered needle is lifted in the needle jet, the effective flow area of the jet is increased to permit an increase of fuel flow into the incoming air stream.

At full throttle, the needle and needle jet are completely open, permitting the main jet to flow fuel at its full capacity.

Idling System

The idling system consists of an idling jet, adjustable air flow screw, and adjustable throttle stop screw.

With the air control slide closed, the vacuum in the main chamber is too low to siphon fuel through the needle jet. Air flow through the

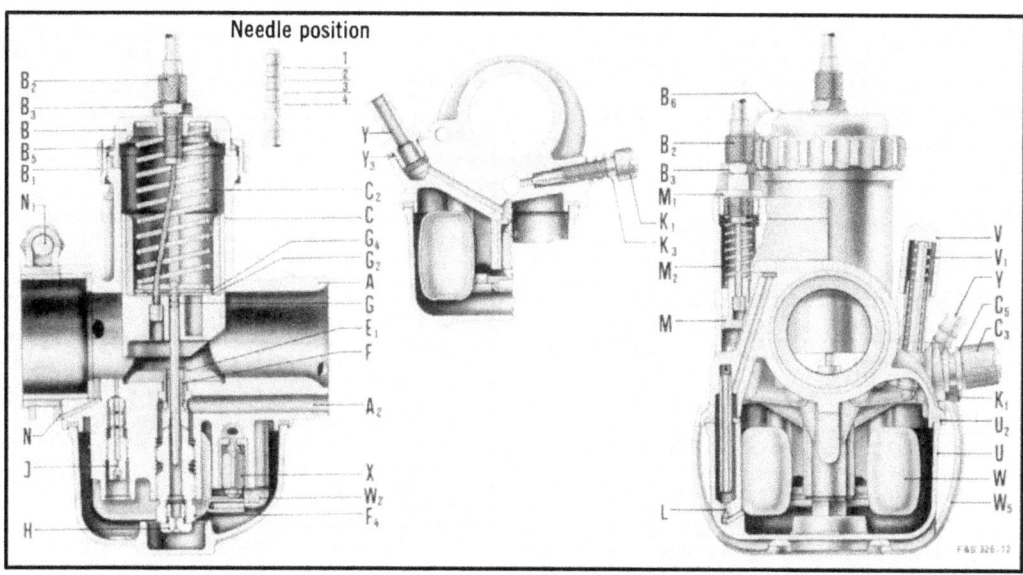

CARBURETOR COMPONENTS

A	Carburetor body	F	Needle jet
A_2	Compensating air passage	F_4	Mixing pipe
		G	Jet needle
B	Cover plate	G_2	Retaining plate
B_1	Screw cover	G_4	Washer
B_2	Adjusting screw	H	Main jet
B_3	Nut	J	Pilot jet
B_5	Washer	K_1	Air regulating screw
B_6	Safety spring	K_3	Spring
C	Throttle valve	L	Starting valve (fixed)
C_2	Throttle valve spring	M	Starting piston
C_3	Adjusting screw	M_1	Screw plug
C_5	Spring	M_2	Compression spring
E_1	Vaporiser		
N	Clamp ring		
N_1	Clamp screw		
U	Float chamber		
U_2	Gasket		
V	Priming device		
V_1	Spring for priming device		
W	Float		
W_2	Stud		
W_5	Spring clip		
X	Float needle		
Y	Hose fitting		
Y_3	Washer		

primary air hole in the bottom of the carburetor air intake passes by the air adjustment screw and through a drillway to the idling jet where it siphons fuel from the float chamber. The main air flow through the carburetor intake mixes with the fuel from the idling jet and the resulting air/fuel mixture is consumed by the engine.

Correct idling mixture is important to efficient engine operation and it must be achieved through careful adjustment of both the slide stop position and the amount of air flow to the idling jet.

Starting System

The starting system consists of a starting piston and a starting jet.

During starting, operation of the starting control lever lifts the starting piston to allow additional fuel to enter the main chamber through the starting jet. This creates a fuel-rich condition which is required for cold-engine starts.

CARBURETOR SERVICING

Major carburetor service intervals depend on use. A carburetor on a motorcycle that is used principally for transportation will usually not require attention for several thousand miles. At the extreme, for a motorcycle that is used weekly in rigorous competition, the carburetor should be serviced more frequently to ensure that it is always in top working order.

The disassembly, inspection, service, and reassembly procedures presented require that the carburetor be removed from the engine. The adjustments are carried out with the carburetor installed.

Disassembly

1. Unscrew the top ring from the carburetor and pull out the slide and needle (**Figure 3**).

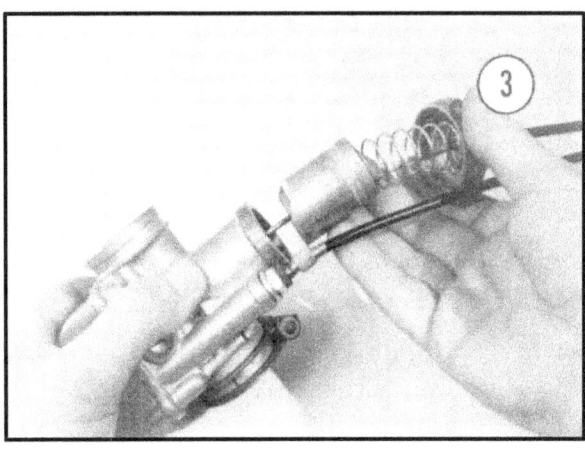

2. Note the position of the retaining plate on the needle and disassemble the cable, spring, cap, needle, and slide.

3. Unscrew the starting assembly and pull it out of the carburetor (**Figure 4**).

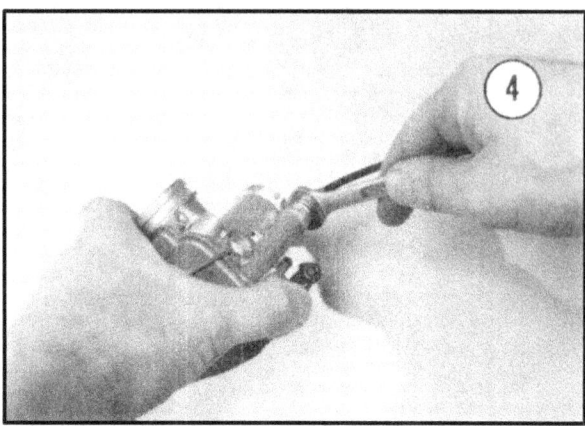

4. Unscrew the air adjusting screw and throttle stop screw (**Figure 5**).

5. Press the float chamber retaining clip forward with your thumbs and remove the float chamber (**Figure 6**).

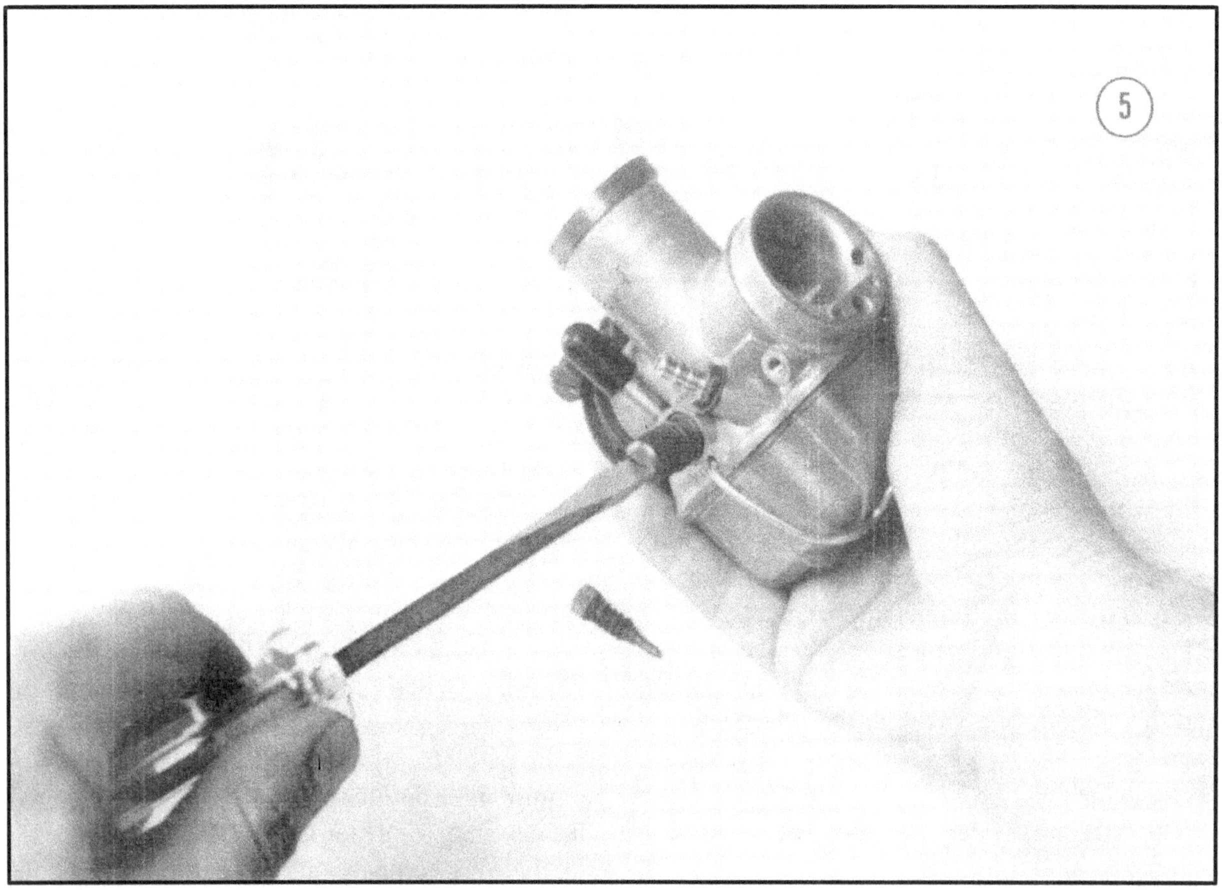

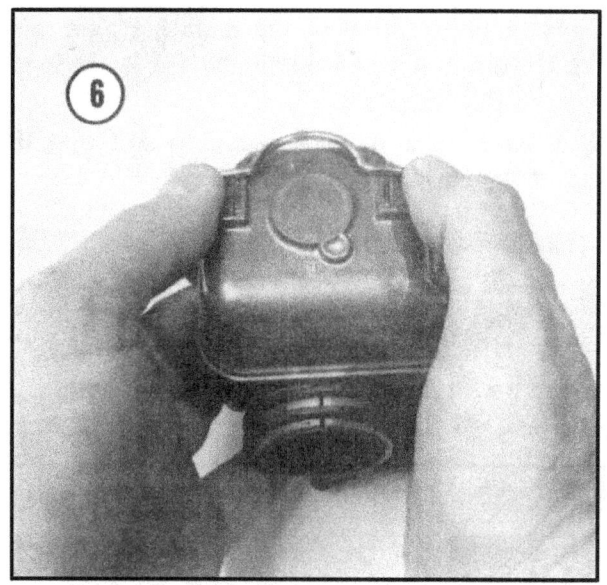

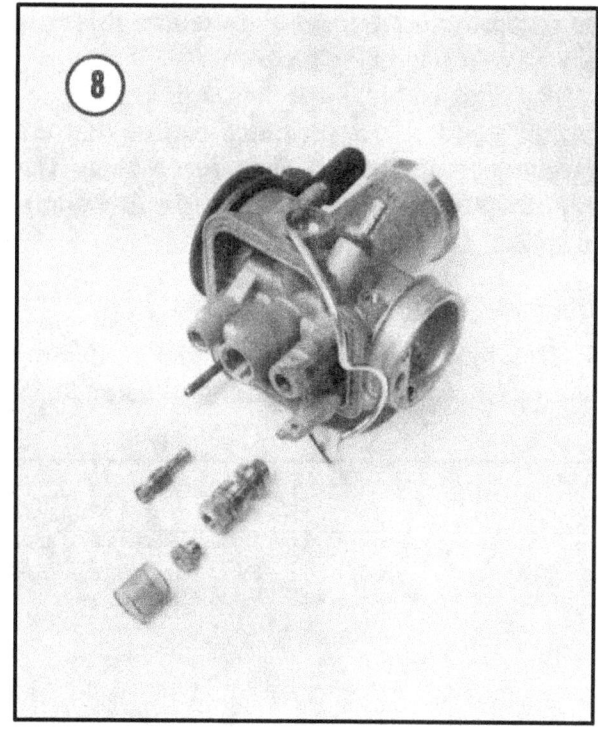

6. Slide the float hinge pin out to the side with a pair of needle-nose pliers and remove the float and needle valve (**Figure 7**).

7. Unscrew the main jet, mixing tube, and idling jet, noting their locations for reference during reassembly (**Figure 8**).

8. Push the vaporizer and needle jet out through the mixing tube port with your finger (**Figure 9**).

9. Unscrew the fuel hose nipple (**Figure 10**).

Cleaning and Inspection

1. Thoroughly clean and dry all the parts. If a special carburetor cleaning solution is used, the float, top-cap O-ring, and gaskets should be omitted from the bath and cleaned separately in common solvent.

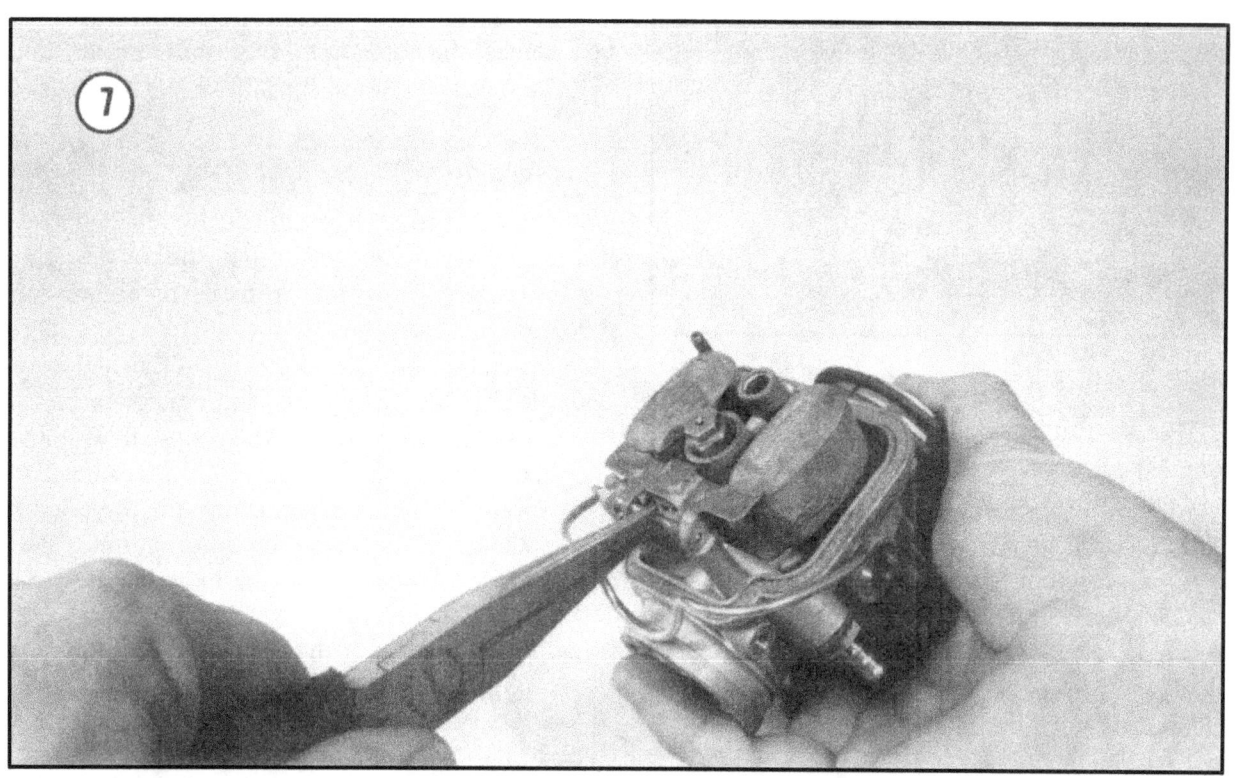

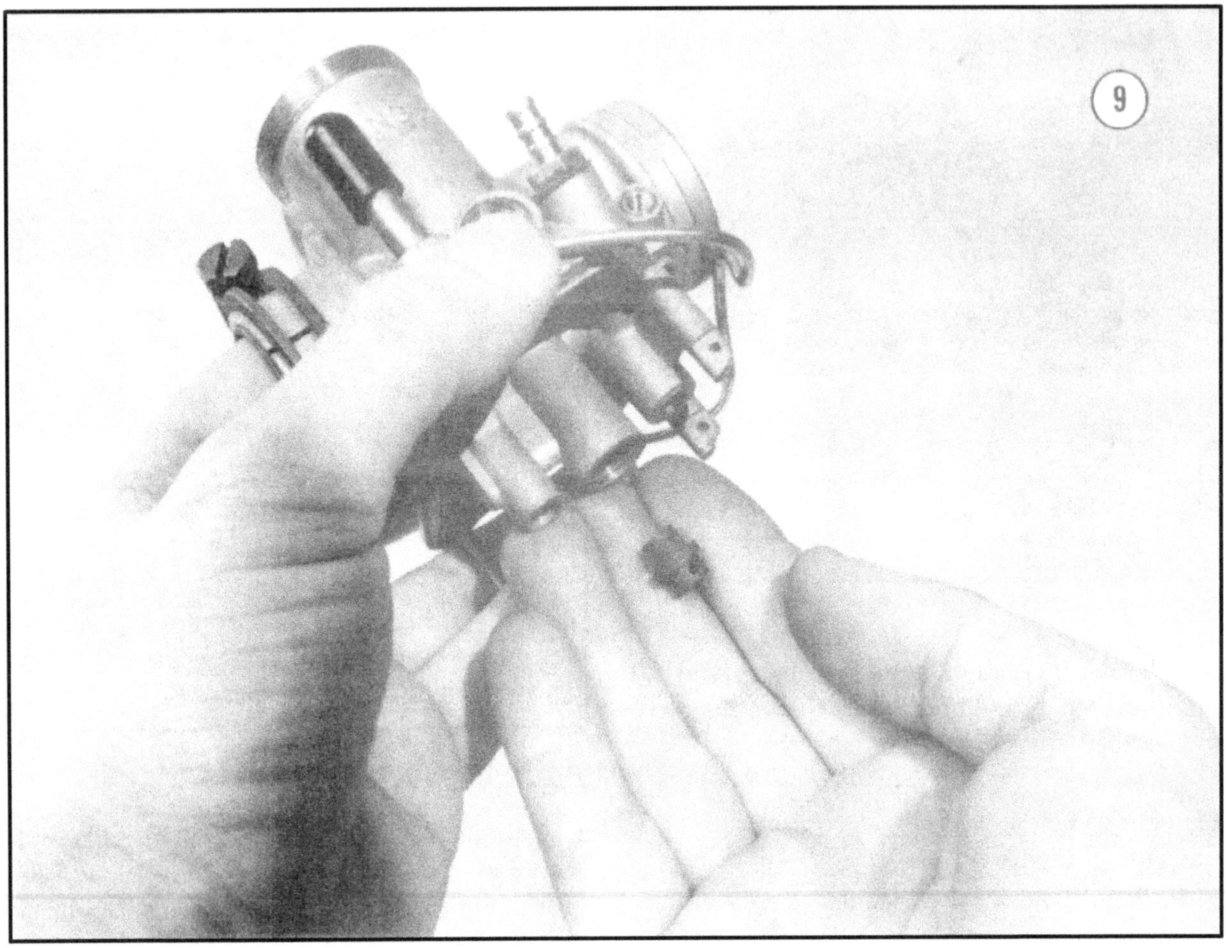

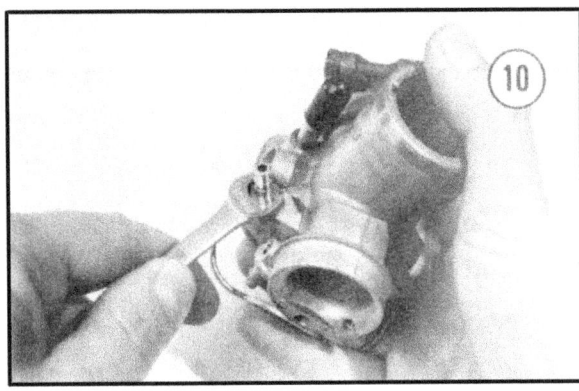

5. Check the slide for scoring and galling, and if it's excessive, replace the slide.

6. Check the top-cap O-ring and replace it if it's damaged or shows signs of deterioration.

Reassembly

The carburetor is assembled by reversing the order of disassembly. The jets should be tight, but be careful not to strip their threads or the threads in the carburetor body. The float chamber gasket and the sealing ring on the fuel hose nipple should be replaced with new ones.

With the float needle valve and float reinstalled, check the float level by inverting the carburetor on a level surface. With the needle fully seated in the valve bore, the bottom of the float should be parallel to the mating surface of the float chamber as shown in **Figure 11**. The ball in the bottom of the float needle should not be compressed into the needle. If necessary, the float level can be corrected by carefully bending the brass tab on the float.

2. Blow out all the passages and jets with compressed air. Don't use wire to clean any of the orifices.

3. Check the cone of the float needle and replace it if it is scored or pitted. Also, the spring-loaded ball in the bottom of the needle should move freely in and out of its bore.

4. If the float is all brass, shake it to determine if there is any fuel in it. If there is, replace it with a new float.

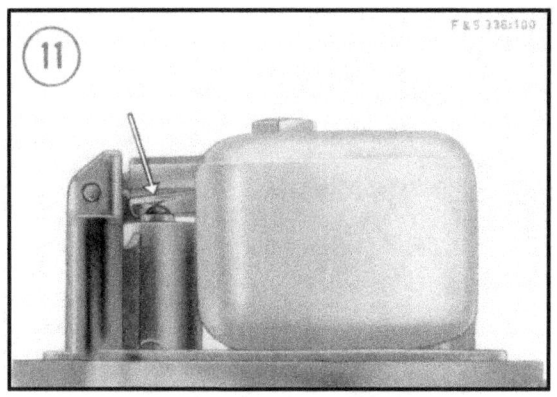

NOTE: *Late-model carburetors are fitted with an anti-surge screen at the bottom of the main jet. This device entraps gas around the main jet to prevent fuel starvation and surging when the motorcycle is operated at moderate and high speeds over undulating terrain. It's recommended that the screen be fitted in place of the flat washer on the main jet of earlier carburetors.*

When installing the slide assembly in the carburetor body, make sure the needle is seated in the needle jet and that the movement of the slide with the cap and ring installed is smooth throughout the length of the slide's travel.

Reinstall the carburetor on the engine, reconnect the control cables and fuel line, and reconnect the intake bellows between the carburetor and the air cleaner.

Carburetor Adjustment

Carburetor adjustments should be made with the engine warmed up to operating temperature.

1. Adjust the free-play in the throttle cable by turning the adjuster screw on the top of the carburetor in or out until the cable sheath can be pulled out of the carburetor top about 0.039 in. (1.0mm), **Figure 12**.

2. With the engine running, screw in the throttle stop screw (**Figure 13**) until engine speed increases slightly with the throttle completely closed.

3. Screw in the air adjustment screw (**Figure 14**) until the engine falters and then screw it out until the engine begins to run smoothly (about ½ turn).

4. Slowly unscrew the throttle stop screw to bring the engine to its lowest idle speed. For competition use, and particularly for observed trials, it's recommended that very little or no idling occur with the throttle closed.

AIR FILTER

There are two basic types of air filters used on Sachs-engine motorcycles—micronic paper element and oil-wetted foam. Service on both units is covered in the Penton workshop manual.

CHAPTER SEVEN

ELECTRICAL SYSTEM

Operating principles, service and repair procedures for the ignition, charging, and lighting systems are presented in this chapter. Two basic systems are used on Sachs engines: Bosch magneto-generator with mechanical contact breaker ignition, and Motoplat magneto-generator with electronic ignition. Both types are flywheel-mounted systems. The 2 types are shown in **Figures 1 and 2**.

MAGNETO IGNITION SYSTEM

A magneto is a mechanically driven alternating current generator which produces the electrical energy required to fire the spark plug. On models equipped with lights, additional coils in the magneto produce the energy required to charge the battery and power the lights.

Magneto Operation

Figure 3 illustrates a typical contact-breaker magneto ignition system. As the flywheel rotates, magnets located in the flywheel move past a stationary ignition source coil inducing a current in the coil. A contact breaker, controlled by a cam attached to the crankshaft, opens at the precise instant the piston reaches its firing position. The energy produced in the source coil is then discharged to the primary side of

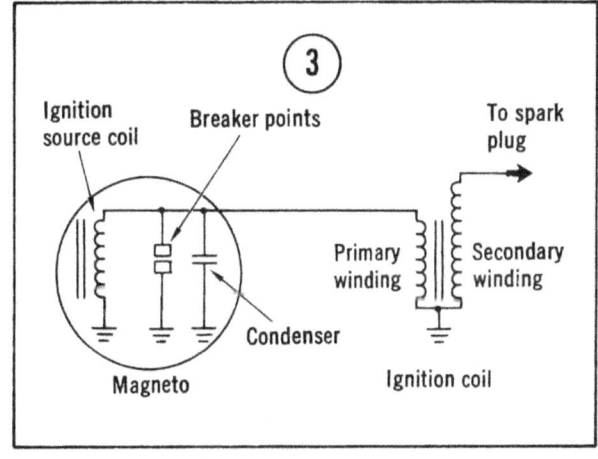

the high-voltage ignition coil where it is increased, or stepped up to a high enough voltage to jump the gap between the spark plus electrodes.

Breaker Points

The contact breaker for Bosch ignition systems is shown in **Figure 4**. During normal operation, the contact surfaces of the points gradually burn and erode away. If the points are not badly pitted, they can be dressed with a few strokes from a point file. Never use sandpaper or emery cloth for dressing the contacts; for maximum efficiency, the contact surfaces must be flat and parallel, and sandpaper will

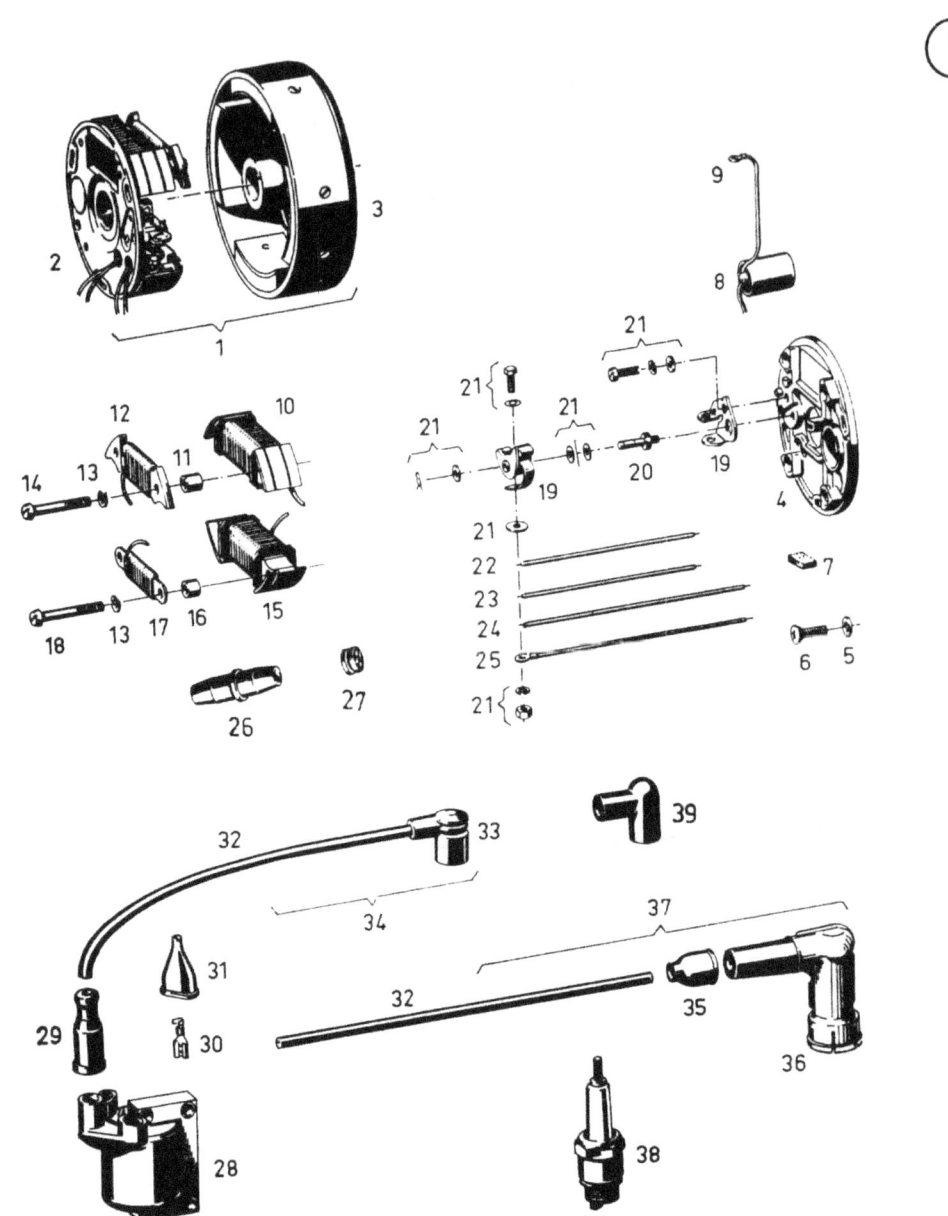

BOSCH IGNITION

1. Magneto-generator
2. Armature base plate
3. Flywheel
4. Armature base plate
5. Washer
6. Screw
7. Lubrication felt
8. Condenser
9. Cable
10. Ignition armature
11. Bush
12. Stop light armature
13. Spring washer
14. Screw, fillister head
15. Generating armature
16. Bush
17. Taillight armature
18. Screw, fillister head
19. Contact breaker set
20. Pivot pin
21. Set of spares for contact breaker
22. Lighting cable
23. Taillight cable
24. Stop light cable
25. Generating cable
26. Cable terminal
27. Rubber grommet
28. Ignition coil
29. Cap, protective
30. Cable terminal
31. Cap, protective
32. Ignition cable
33. Spark plug cap
34. Ignition cable
35. Cap, protective
36. Spark plug cap
37. Ignition cable
38. Spark plug

MOTOPLAT IGNITION

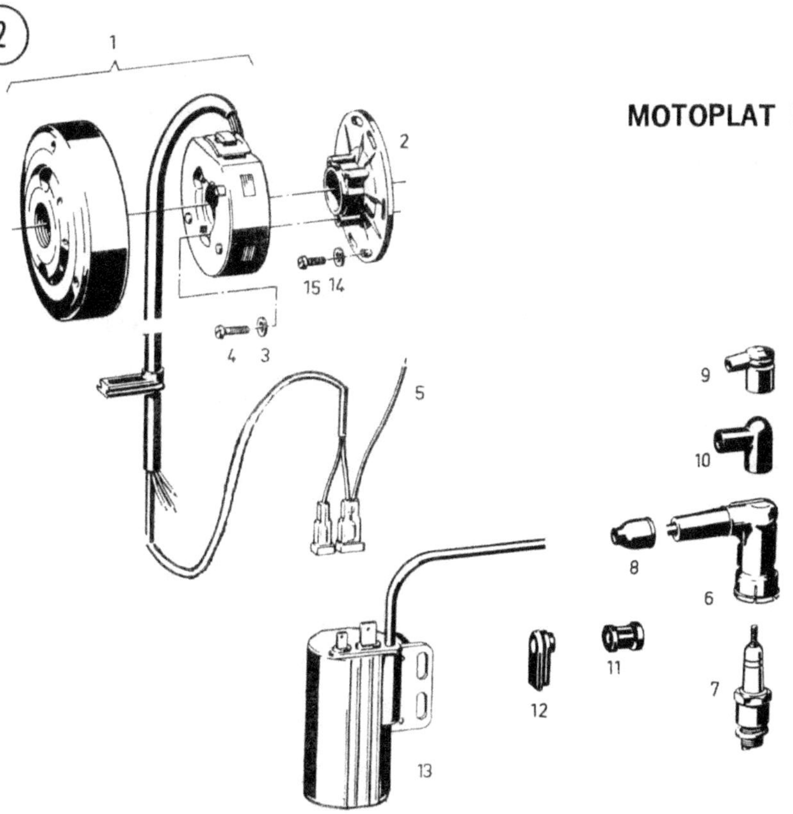

1. Magneto-generator
2. Base plate
3. Washer
4. Screw, fillister head
5. Short-circuit cable
6. Spark plug cap
7. Spark plug
8. Cap, protective
9. Spark plug connector
10. Spark plug connector
11. Rubber grommet
12. Rubber grommet
13. Ignition coil with cable
14. Washer
15. Screw, fillister head

round off the edges of the contacts and create the sort of condition you're attempting to correct (see **Figure 5**). If a few strokes won't correct the contact surfaces, replace the breaker assembly.

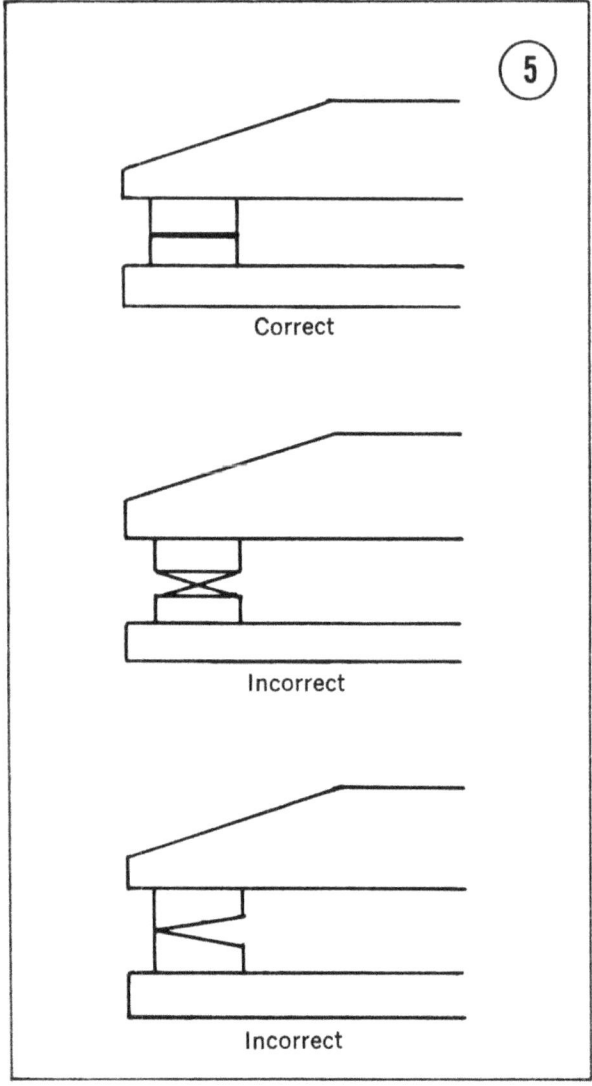

Always remove the contact breaker assembly before dressing the contacts. The time spent removing, reinstalling, and adjusting the points is preferable to risking small particles finding their way into the magneto.

Oil or dirt may get on the contacts, creating electrical resistance in them or resulting in their failure. These conditions can be caused by a defective crankshaft seal, incorrect breaker cam lubricant, or dirt getting into the magneto when the outer cover is removed. To correct these conditions, remove the contact breaker assembly and dress the contacts, clean the assembly in lacquer thinner, and lubricate the breaker cam with contact breaker lubricant. Never use oil or common grease; they break down under high temperature and frictional load and are likely to find their way to the contacts.

A weak breaker spring will allow the points to bounce at high engine speeds and cause misfiring. Usually, however, the spring will last for the life of the contacts.

Close the contacts on a piece of clean white paper, such as a business card, and pull it through the contacts. Continue to do this until no discoloration or residue remains on the card. Finally, rotate the engine and watch the contacts as they open and close. If they do not meet squarely, replace them.

Contact Breaker Replacement

1. Remove the right-side cover and the flywheel as discussed in Chapter Four.

2. Disconnect the ground (short-circuit) connection, noting the location of the insulation washers for reference during reassembly, as shown in **Figure 6**.

3. Remove the spring clip from the end of the pivot shaft. Pull off breaker arm and shims.

4. Remove the slotted screw and pull off the contact carrier (**Figure 7**).

5. Reverse the above steps to install a new breaker assembly. Grease the pivot shaft with contact breaker lubricant (Bosch Ft 1 v4 or an equivalent) before installing the breaker arm. With the breaker arm installed, check the alignment of the contacts and correct it if necessary by adding or removing shims. Knead the lubricating felt with contact breaker lubricant and apply some to the groove in the rubbing portion of the arm. Be sure the terminals are clean and tight and that there is no oil or grease between the contact carrier and the stator baseplate.

Condenser Replacement

The condenser should be routinely replaced with the points.

1. Unsolder the condenser leads (**Figure 8**).

2. Pull the condenser out of the stator baseplate (**Figure 9**).

99

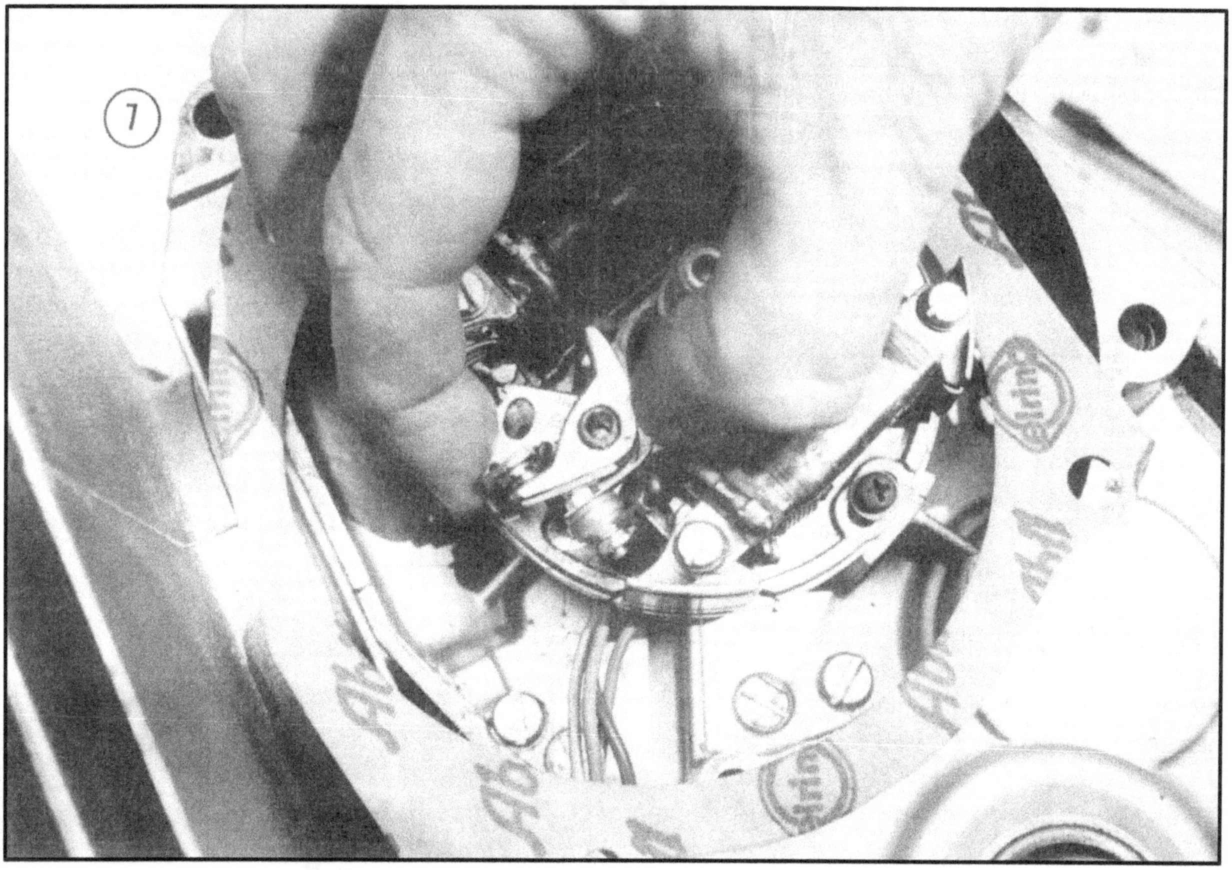

3. Remove any oxidation burrs from the condenser boss.

4. Install a new condenser in the boss and caulk it with silicone sealer (**Figure 10**).

5. Solder the condenser leads to the terminals.

Adjusting Contact Gap

The gap of the contact breaker is adjusted with the flywheel installed.

1. Rotate the flywheel counterclockwise and line up the timing mark "M" with the mark on the crankcase (**Figure 11**). The contacts should be closed.

2. Slowly rotate the flywheel clockwise. The contacts should begin to open immediately. If not, time the ignition in accordance with the instructions which follow.

3. Continue to rotate the flywheel clockwise until the contacts are at their maximum opening. Measure the gap with a flat feeler gauge. It should be 0.0014-0.0018 in. (0.35-0.45mm). If necessary, adjust the gap by loosening the locking screw (**Figure 12**) and moving the breaker plate as required.

4. Tighten the locking screw and recheck the adjustment.

5. Again check the ignition timing and adjust if necessary.

Ignition Timing

Any change in contact breaker gap, including that occuring through normal wear of the contacts and the rubbing block, will alter ignition timing. For this reason, ignition timing should be checked and corrected each time the contact breaker is serviced or replaced. Severe engine damage can result from a spark that is too far advanced, and a late or retarded spark can cause overheating and loss of power.

The ignition timing described employs a Sachs timing gauge (tool No. 14). However, a similar plunger or dial type timing gauge can be used.

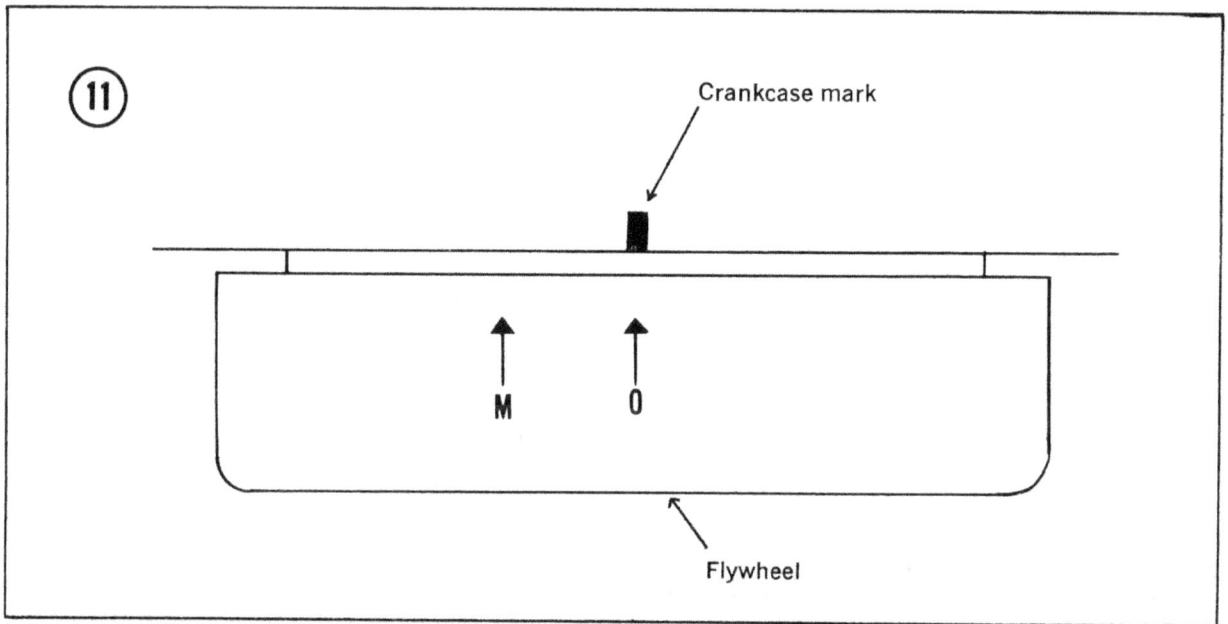

1. Remove the spark plug from the cylinder head and install the timing gauge (**Figure 13**). Remove the right-side engine cover.

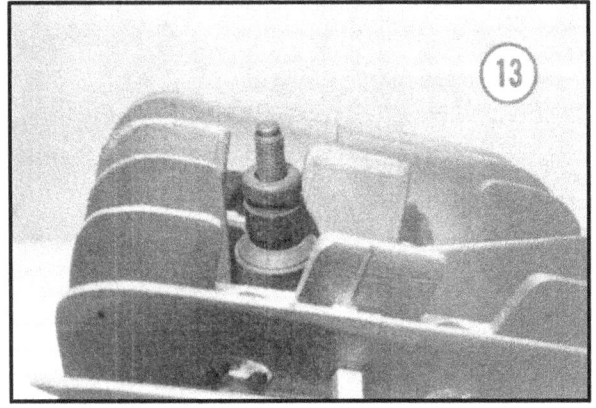

2. Rotate the flywheel counterclockwise as viewed from the ignition side to bring the piston to TDC as indicated by the timing gauge. The "O" mark on the flywheel should line up with the mark on the crankcase (**Figure 14**).

3. Continue to rotate the flywheel and line up the "M" mark on the flywheel with the mark on the crankcase (Figure 11). The contact breaker should be closed.

4. Slowly rotate the flywheel clockwise—in the direction of rotation during engine operation—and observe the contact breaker. If the timing is correct, the breaker should begin to open.

5. If the timing is not correct, loosen the 3 screws in the stator plate and rotate the plate as required. The screws can be loosened and tightened through the openings in the flywheel (**Figures 15A through 15C**). To advance the timing, rotate the stator counterclockwise. To retard it, rotate the stator plate clockwise. After adjusting the stator, tighten the screws.

Establishing Timing Marks

If the flywheel and crankcase do not have ignition timing marks, these should be established to facilitate future ignition servicing.

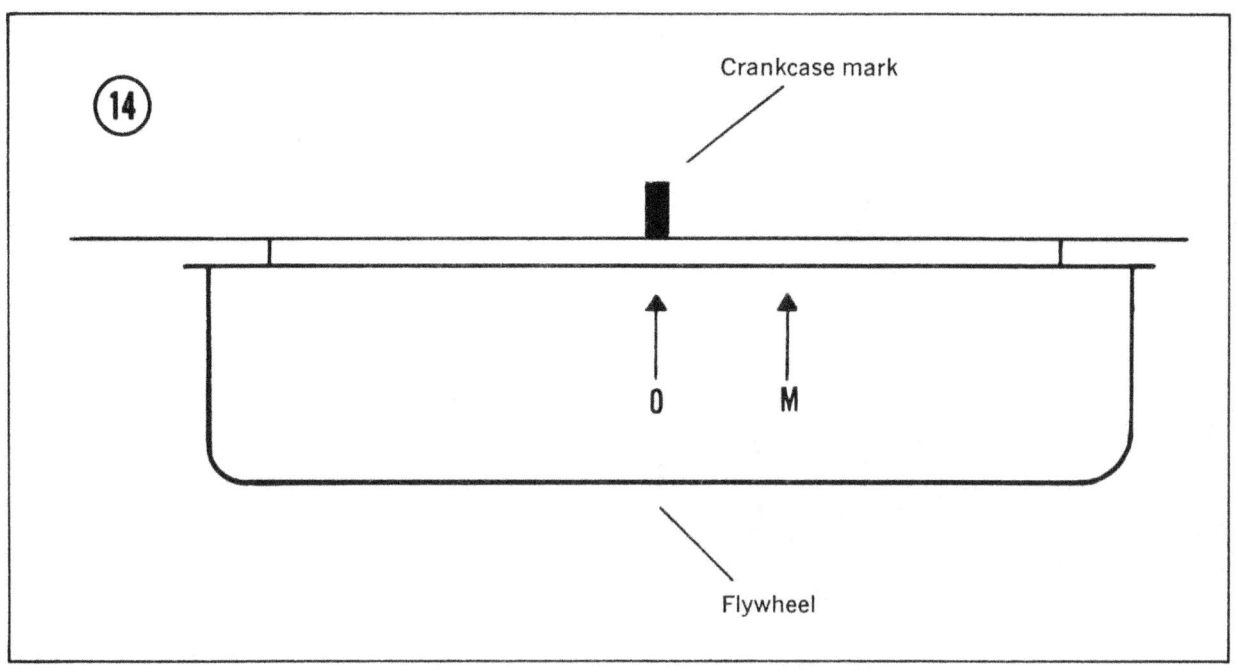

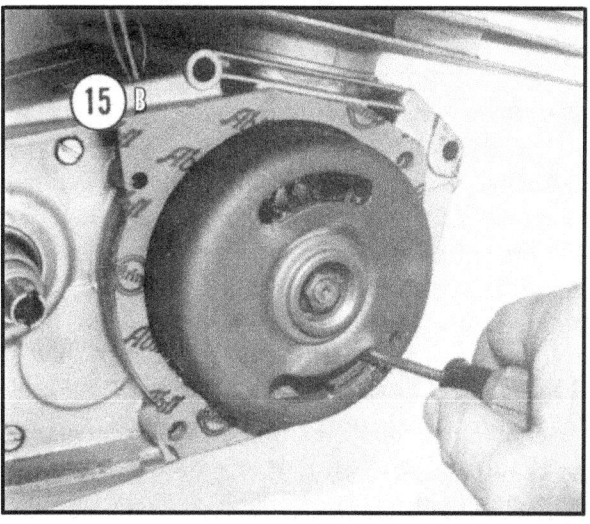

1. With a timing gauge installed in the spark plug bore in the head, rotate the crankshaft to bring the piston to TDC.

2. Make a mark on the crankcase and a corresponding mark on the flywheel with a chisel. Scribe an "O" on the flywheel at the mark. This establishes TDC.

3. Screw in the adjusting nut (see **Figure 16**) until it just touches the bushing.

4. Turn the nut back 2½ to 3 turns. This establishes the piston at the firing position before TDC. The firing position is 2.5-3.0mm (0.098-0.118 in.) before TDC. Each complete turn of the adjuster nut on the timing gauge corresponds

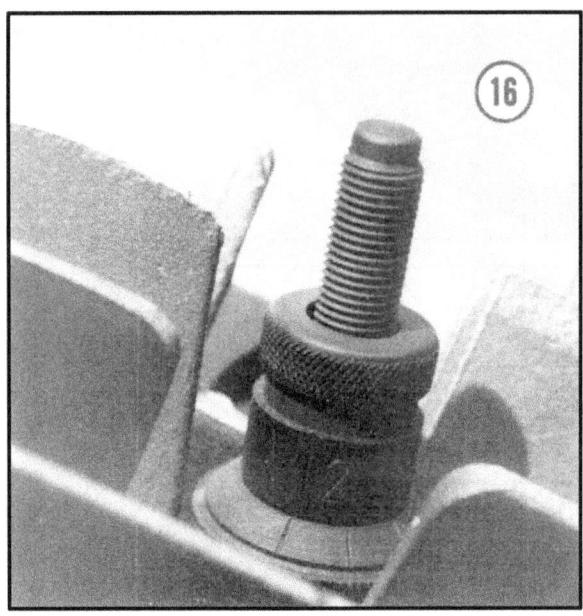

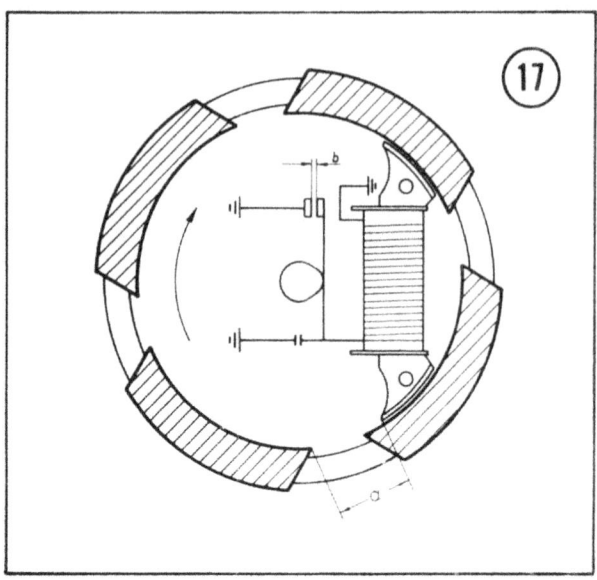

to 1.0mm (0.039 in.). The marks on the adjuster nut correspond to 0.25mm (0.00985 in.), and the marks on the bush correspond to 0.1mm (0.00394 in.).

5. Rotate the flywheel counterclockwise until the adjusting nut just touches the bush. Check to see that the piston is in contact with the rod in the timing gauge. Apply a chisel mark to the flywheel in line with the mark on the crankcase. This establishes the firing position.

Pole Shoe Gap

The pole shoe gap (a, **Figure 17**) should be 22-25mm (0.867-0.985 in.) with the flywheel set at the firing position ("M"). The pole shoe gap may be corrected by adjusting the contact breaker gap, within the limits of 0.0014-0.0018 in. (0.35-0.45mm) prescribed for the contact breaker gap.

Armature Replacement

If a functional test of the generator indicates that one or more of the 4 armatures is faulty, they may be replaced individually. However, armature replacement shouldn't be attempted unless you have access to a Bosch centering plate and ring; these special tools are required to accurately set the air gap between the armature cores and the magneto flywheel.

1. Remove the right-side cover and the flywheel as described in Chapter Four.

2. Remove the 3 Phillips-head screws which hold the stator baseplate in place (**Figure 18**) and carefully pull the wiring harness out of the hole in the crankcase.

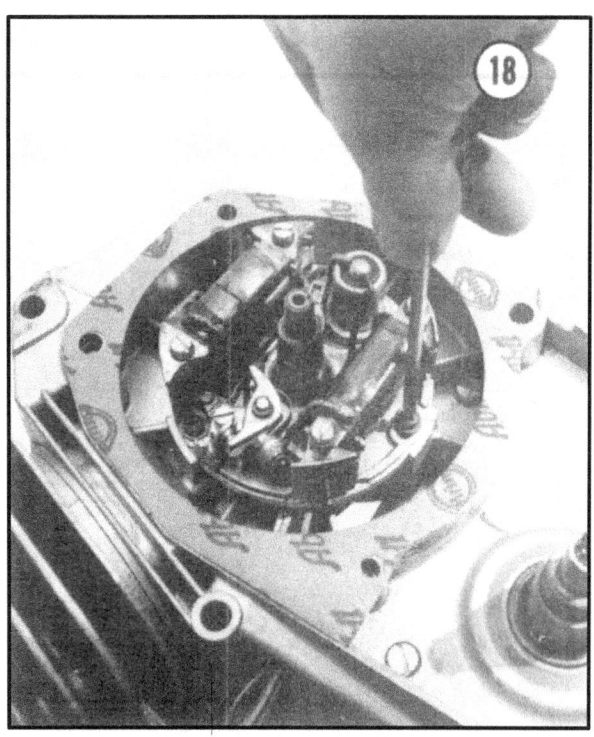

3. Pass the wiring harness through the hole in the centering plate and set the stator in place (**Figure 19**). Install the bolt in the centering tool and tighten it by hand.

4. Remove faulty armature cores and install new ones.

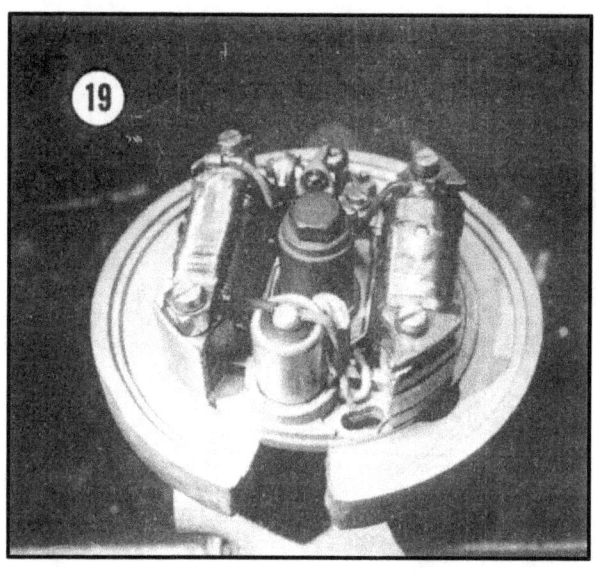

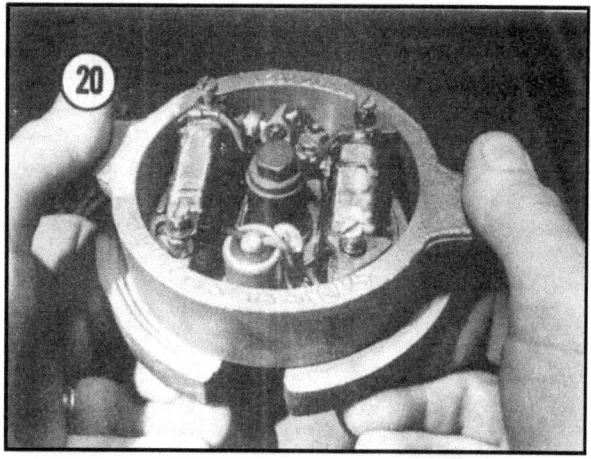

5. Set the centering ring in place (**Figure 20**). Press the armatures up tight against the ring and tighten the retaining screws.

6. Remove the ring, unscrew the centering bolt, and reinstall the stator on the engine, taking care to line up the timing mark. Reinstall the flywheel and check ignition timing as discussed earlier.

Ignition Coil

The ignition coil is a step-up transformer which increases the low voltage produced by the magneto to a high voltage required to jump the spark plug gap. The only service required is periodic inspection of the electrical leads to make sure they are clean and tight, and checking to see that the coil is mounted securely.

If the functional condition of the coil is in doubt, there are several checks which should be made.

1. Using an ohmmeter, measure the resistance between the primary wire and ground as shown in **Figure 21**. Resistance should be about 1 ohm.

2. Measure the resistance between the high-tension lead and ground as shown in **Figure 22**. It should be 3,000 ohms.

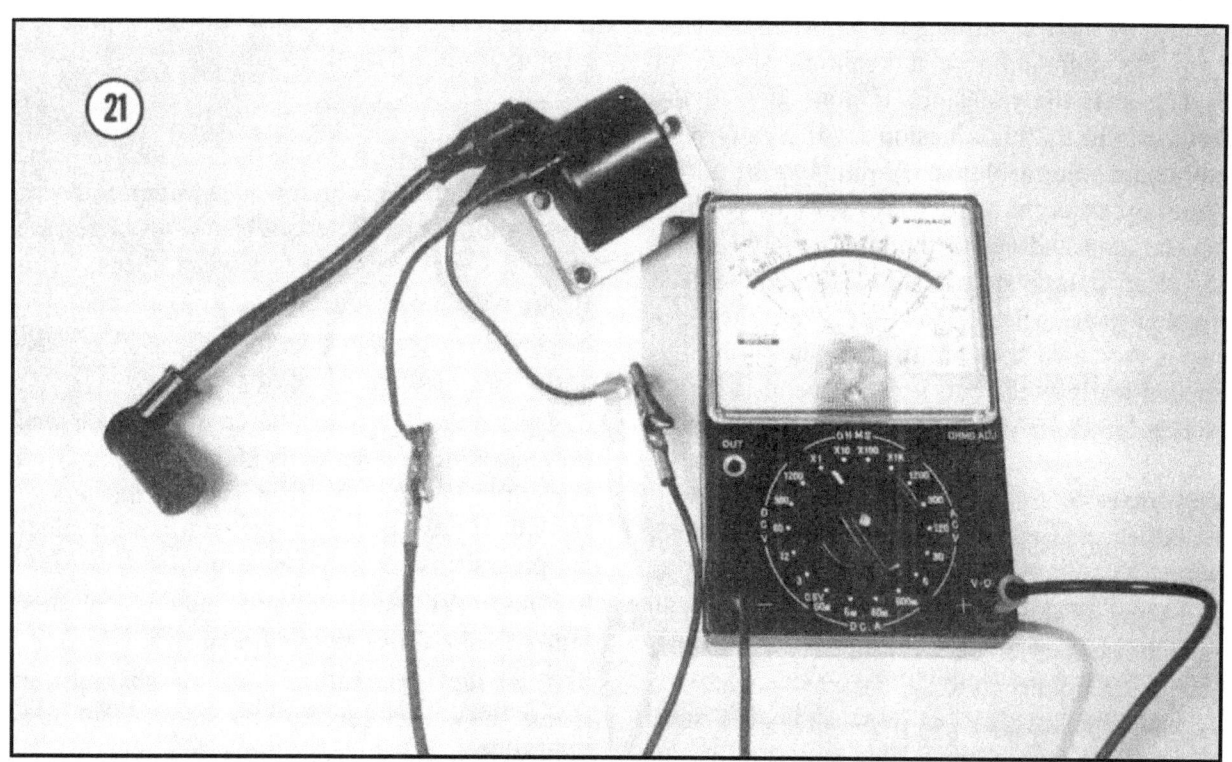

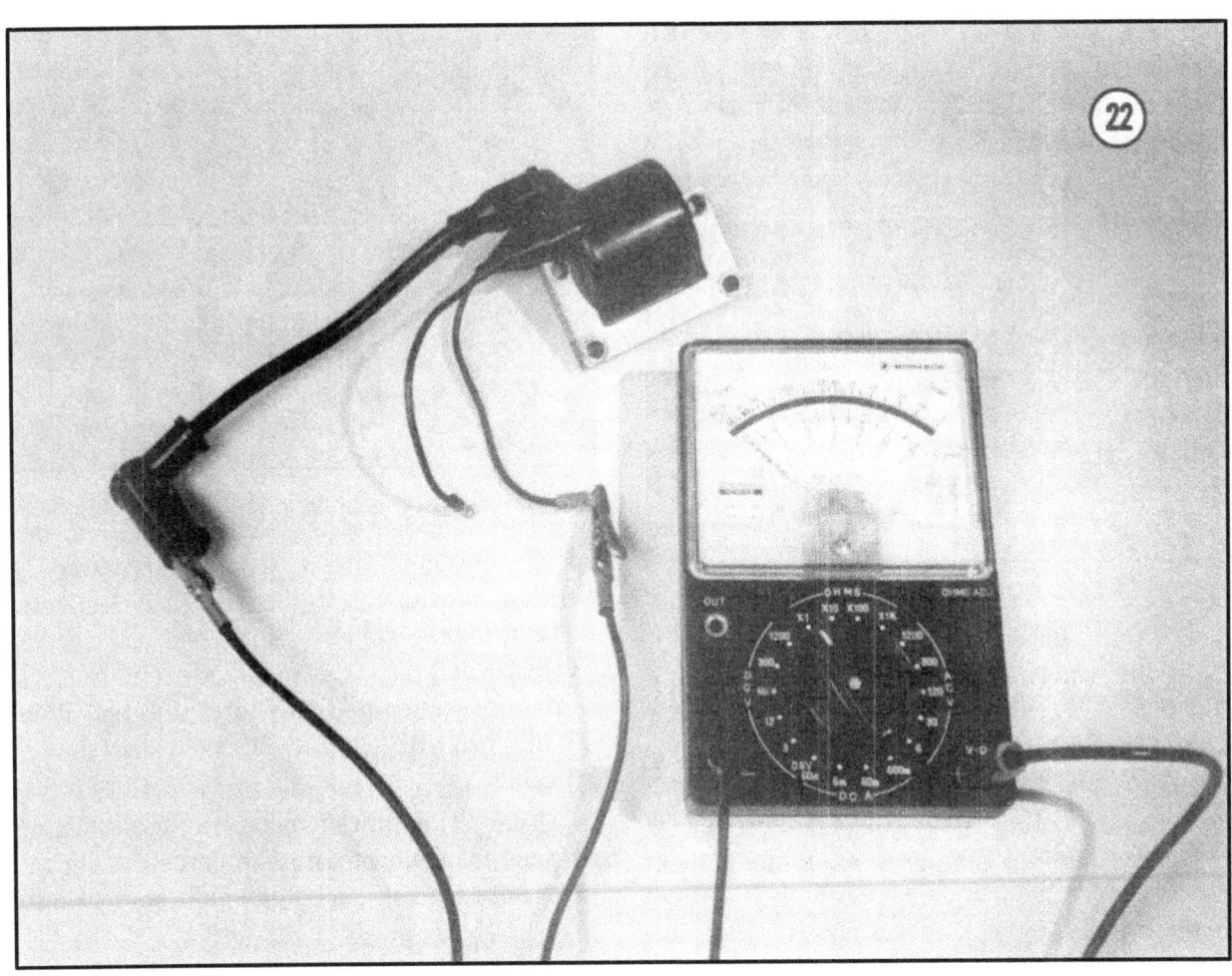

3. If the meter indicates an open circuit (no continuity) in Step 2, unplug the high-tension lead from the coil and test it again as shown in Figure 2. If the resistance is now correct, the trouble is in the high-tension lead. It may be a bad connection at the spark plug cap or an internal break in the wire. Make sure the connection is good and check the lead for continuity, and if an open circuit is still indicated, replace the high-tension lead. However, if an open circuit is indicated between the primary and high-tension leads of the coil itself, the coil is defective and must be replaced.

Condenser

The condenser requires no service other than checking to see that its connections are clean and tight. It should be routinely replaced each time the contact breaker is replaced. To test the condenser, connect it to the battery—negative to negative, positive to positive—and allow it to charge for a few seconds. Then, quickly disconnect it and touch one condenser lead to the other. If there is a spark, the condenser may be assumed to be all right.

Troubleshooting

The magneto-generator is a simple device which should give little trouble. If problems are suspected, perform the following checks with all the wiring disconnected.

1. Block the contact breaker open with a business card or similar piece of paper.

2. Disconnect both of the contact leads and with an ohmmeter set at its highest range, check that the movable breaker is not shorted to ground. If the ohmmeter registers at all, replace the points.

3. Check the condenser and replace it if there is any doubt about its condition.

4. Examine temperature coils for chafing and check them individually for shorts and continuity. Replace any coils that are faulty.

5. Check the flywheel for cracks or movement at the point where the cam is pressed into it. If the cam moves, the "E" gap (which ensures maximum energy from the primary ignition pulse) will not be correct and the flywheel must be replaced.

ELECTRONIC IGNITION SYSTEM

Some Sachs engines are equipped with Motoplat electronic ignition. This system has no mechanical contact breaker, cam, or any adjustable components. The system requires no servicing other than periodic checks of the connections to make sure they are clean and tight. It's virtually unaffected by dust and dampness but care should still be taken to keep it clean and dry when the right-side cover is removed from the engine.

The Motoplat electronic ignition system can be installed on Sachs engines currently fitted with conventional contact breaker ignition with no modifications.

System Operation

Figure 23 is a diagram of a typical electronic ignition system. Alternating current produced by a source coil located in the magneto is rectified to direct current by a diode in the electronic unit. This current charges a capacitor. A trigger pulse, produced by a signal coil in the magneto, is developed each time the piston reaches firing position. This pulse is the equivalent of the opening of a contact breaker. It is applied to the gate of a diode which connects the capacitor to the primary side of the high-voltage coil. The pulse to the gate of the diode signals the diode to conduct. It thus provides a discharge path for the capacitor to the coil primary. This voltage is then stepped up in the coil to a value which is sufficient to jump the spark plug gap.

Testing

The Motoplat electronic can be tested with an ohmmeter with a 0-10,000 ohm range. Always make sure the polarity is correct for a test hookup and never attempt to test the ignition components with a voltmeter.

The stator and coil need not be removed from the motorcycle to be tested, but the flat connectors must be disconnected from the coil,

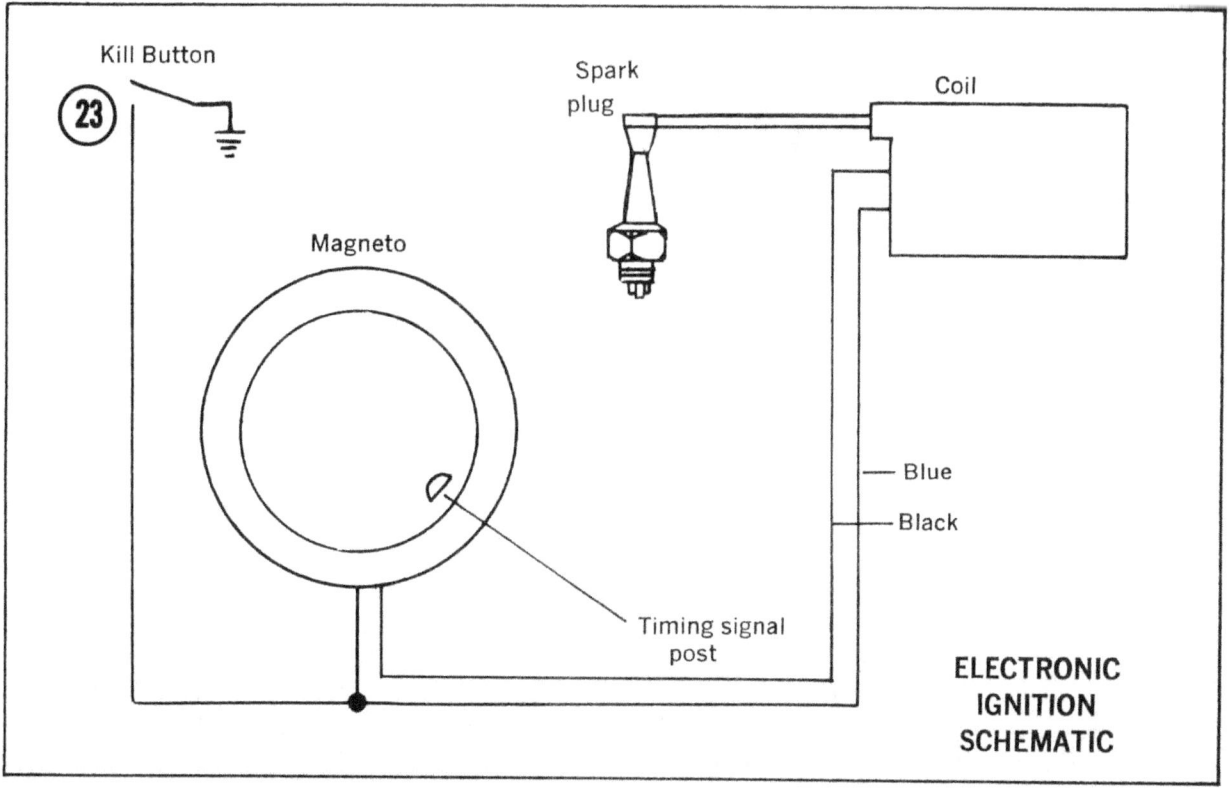

the spark plug cap removed from the high-tension lead, and the blue ignition lead disconnected from the No. 2 terminal of the ignition switch (or kill button).

1. Connect the ohmmeter test leads to the flat terminals on the ignition coil (**Figure 24**) and read the resistance of the primary winding. It should be 20-30 ohms. If it is not within this range, the coil is defective and should be replaced.

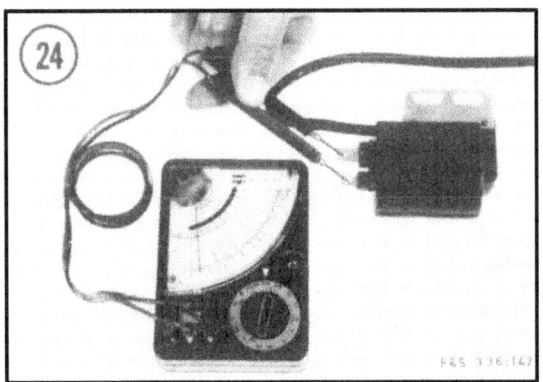

2. Test the coil secondary winding by connecting one test lead to ground and the other to the high-tension lead (**Figure 25**). The reading should be 7,000-9,000 ohms.

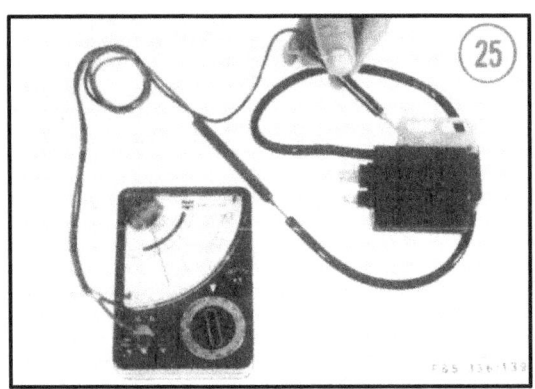

3. Connect one ohmmeter lead to the blue ignition wire and the other to ground (**Figure 26**). The meter should indicate either infinity or 8,000-9,000 ohms. Reverse the ohmmeter leads and the meter should read the opposite of the first reading; i.e., if the meter indicated infinity for the first polarity, it should indicate 8,000-9,000 ohms for the opposite polarity, and vice versa. If resistance is 0 in both directions, the diode is defective, and if it is infinity in both directions, there is a break in the stator. In

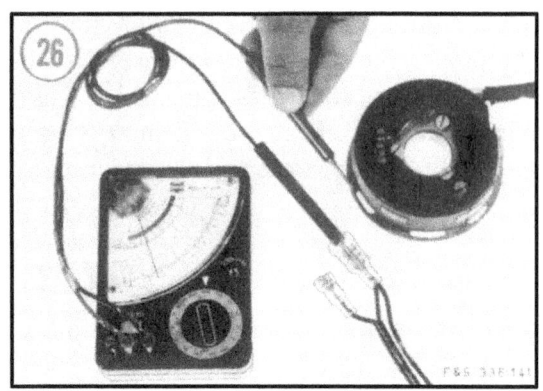

either case, both the stator and flywheel must be replaced as a set.

4. Test the ignition signal coil by connecting one ohmmeter lead to the blue ignition lead and the other ohmmeter lead to the black ignition lead (**Figure 27**). The reading should be approximately 20 ohms. If it is less, there is a short in the signal coil and the stator and flywheel must be replaced as a set.

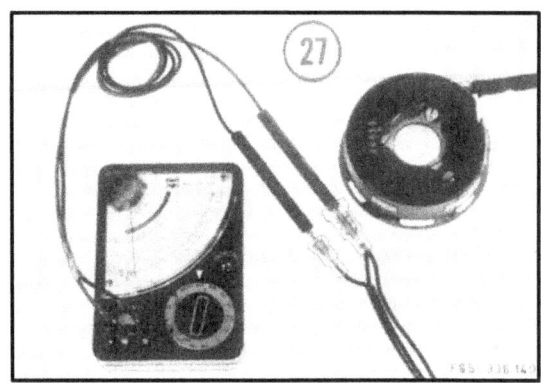

Timing

1. Rotate the flywheel to line up the "M" mark with the mark on the crankcase. Insert a timing pin (a bicycle spoke makes a good pin) into the timing hole in the flywheel (**Figure 28**). If the timing is correct, the pin should also enter the hole in the stator.

2. If the pin will not engage the hole in the stator, remove the flywheel and loosen the 3 screws (1) which hold the stator in place (see **Figure 29**).

3. Reinstall the flywheel on the shaft, put the timing pin into the hole in the flywheel and rotate it until the pin engages the hole in the stator. Rotate the flywheel and stator to line up the "M" mark with the crankcase mark.

4. Remove the flywheel without disturbing the position of the stator. Tighten the stator screws to 2.9-4.3 ft.-lb. (0.4-0.6 mkg) and reinstall the flywheel. Tighten the flywheel nut to 39-43 ft.-lb. (5.5-6.0 mkg) and recheck the timing with the pin as described in Step 1.

Establishing Timing Marks

If a new Motoplat ignition is being installed, either to replace an electronic unit that has failed or to update an engine previously equipped with a contact breaker ignition, the timing must be checked and set with the timing gauge as described for the contact breaker ignition and new timing marks established.

The firing point is the same for the electronic ignition as it is for the contact breaker type— 0.098-0.1118 in. (2.5-3.0mm) before TDC.

Install the Motoplat stator, leaving the 3 screws loose enough so the stator can be turned. Install the flywheel and line it up and lock with the stator with the timing pin. Then proceed to to time the ignition with the use of the timing gauge as described earlier and make a chisel mark on the crankcase to correspond with the "M" mark on the flywheel when the timing is correct.

MOTOPLAT IGNITION SYSTEM - INSTALLATION or REPLACEMENT

The technical conception of these breakerless magneto-generators, as compared with the conventional types provides a considerable improvement of the functioning and the reliability of the ignition system of the engine, since there are no wearing parts in it, such as breaker points, lubricating felt etc. Moreover, this new magneto with its ignition coil fitted outside of the engine is less sensitive to the effects of humidity and dust and does not require any maintenance or servicing.

Trouble shooting

We are listing various faults that are liable to occur, likewise as on the conventional magneto-generators, also on the electronically controlled magneto generators.

Check the electric connections and terminals.

Take care of bare, pinched, oxydized or wrongly connected cables.

Both electronic cables coming from the stator plate – blue and black – must on no account be cut for easing the removal or the installation and for connecting them afterwards with a terminal block.

This would create the risk that through dirt and humidity on the exposed terminals short-circuits occur and destroy the electronics.

The fitting strap of the ignition coil must be well grounded to the frame. The contact faces should be bright (watch for paint and rost).

When the spark plug is brought into ground contact and the starter activated, a spark must flash across the electrodes.

The electrode gap of the spark plug must be 0.4 + 0.1 mm (0.016 + 0.0039 in.).

The electronic magneto-generator must never be checked with conventional testing devices. Such attempts result in destroying the system.

Testing the electronic magneto-generator can only be carried out with a resistance testing device (Ohmmeter) with a testing capacity of 0 ... 10 000 Ω (Ω = Ohm).

Exchange and subsequent fitting of the MOTOPLAT ignition set

The electronic, breakerless MOTOPLAT magneto generator can also subsequently be fitted into previously sold SACHS engines 1001/1251.

For proceeding to such an exchange, take care of the following:
New ignition sets do not have marks. The top dead center and the firing point must be measured and marked anew.

Attention!

Replacement ignition sets have both marks "O" and "M" on the magneto flywheel.

The chisel mark on the crankcase, however, must in any case be measured and marked anew, using the spark advance timing gauge.

Delete the previous mark on the crankcase.

Short-circuiting button

On motorcycles with the conventional contact breaker ignition set, the engines had been short-circuited by the ignition-and lighting switch (B_1, see wiring diagram).

On introduction of the electronic ignition set, Messrs NHW (Nürnberger Hercules-Werke) have moved, for technical reasons, the short-circuiting device out of the head lamp to a short-circuiting button (B_9, see wiring diagram) at the handlebar.

When subsequently fitting an electronic magneto-generator, a short-circuiting button must on principle be fitted at the handlebar. The corresponding parts (short-circuiting button, clamp, cable etc,) are available from NHW/ZU under kit No. 927 380 30 02.

Instructions for fitting the rubber sliding piece

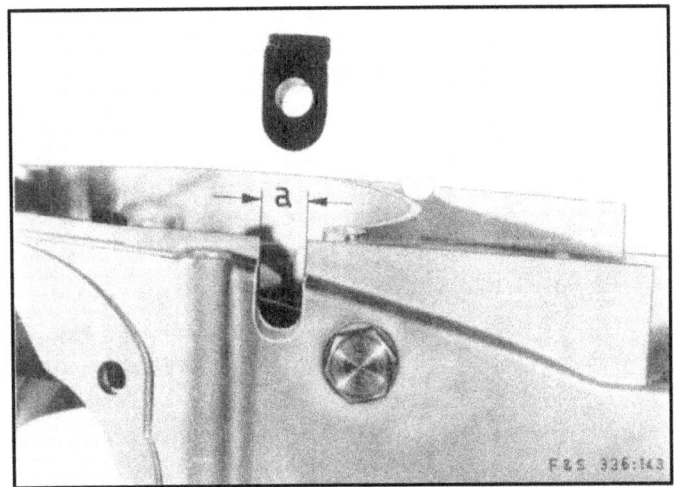

Engines that have previously been sold are provided with a round rubber grommet.

Fitting the set of cables can widely be eased by machining the crankcase as illustrated.

Dimension "a"
= 12 ± 0.1 mm
= 0.472 ± 0.0039 in.

Instead of the round rubber grommet 0665 119 001, fit the sliding rubber unit 0665 124 000, as illustrated.

INSTRUCTIONS AND WIRING DIAGRAM FOR MAGNETO GENERATOR
version BOSCH (controlled by contact breaker)

6 Volt 35 Watt with 5 Watt tail light and 18 Watt stop light armature and ignition coil fitted outside of the engine

Terminals:
On generating armature C_2 (yellow cable with red stripes)
    Head light 6 Volt 35 Watt
On tail light armature (inductive) C_5 (grey cable)
    direct connection without switch to the tail light 6 Volt 5 Watt
On stop light armature C_1 (green cable with red stripes)
One rectifier 15 Volt, 1 Amp (for example BOSCH-LIWI 4 Z 2 Z No. 3 107 320 011) for charging a battery 6 Volt 12 Ah, for connecting:
    1 stop light 6 Volt 18 Watt
    1 direct current signal horn 6 Volt
    1 directional signal 6 Volt 18 Watt on each side
On ignition armature (primary) C_6 (blue cable)
    ignition coil terminal 1

Switch positions

0   Off (ignition short-circuited)
I   Daylight driving
II   Driving lights on

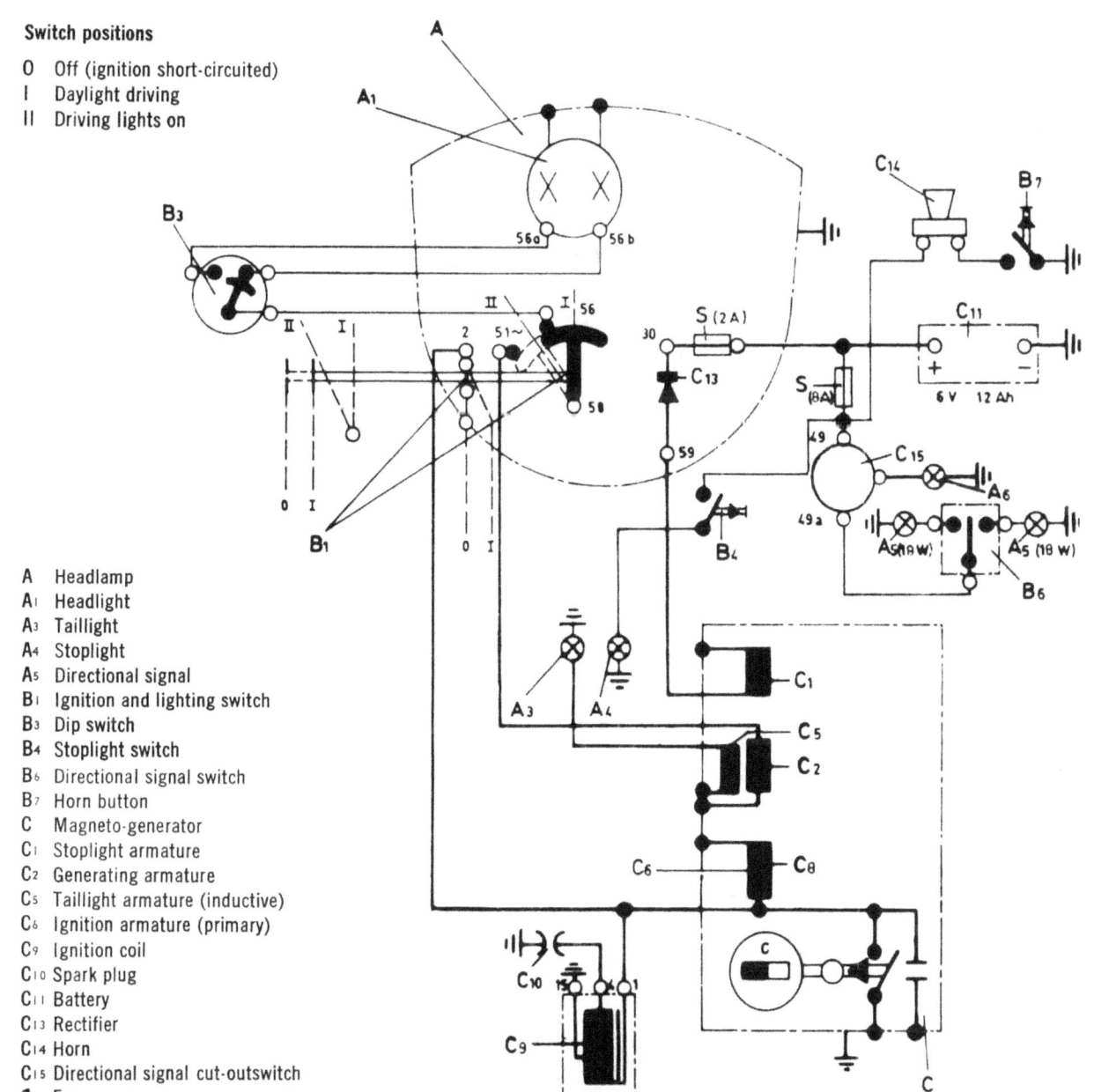

A   Headlamp
A_1 Headlight
A_3 Taillight
A_4 Stoplight
A_5 Directional signal
B_1 Ignition and lighting switch
B_3 Dip switch
B_4 Stoplight switch
B_6 Directional signal switch
B_7 Horn button
C   Magneto-generator
C_1 Stoplight armature
C_2 Generating armature
C_5 Taillight armature (inductive)
C_6 Ignition armature (primary)
C_9 Ignition coil
C_{10} Spark plug
C_{11} Battery
C_{13} Rectifier
C_{14} Horn
C_{15} Directional signal cut-outswitch
S   Fuse

INSTRUCTIONS AND WIRING DIAGRAM FOR MAGNETO GENERATOR
version MOTOPLAT (breakerless, electronic control)
6 Volt 35 - 5 - 18 Watt and ignition coil fitted outside of the engine

Terminals:
Lighting cable (yellow)
Head light 6 Volt 35 Watt
Tail light cable (red) direct connection without switch to the tail light 6 Volt 5 Watt
Stop light cable (green)
One rectifier for 15 Volt, 1 Amp (for example BOSCH-LIWI 4 Z 2 Z No. 3 107 320 011)
for charging a battery 6 Volt 12 Ah, for connecting:
1 stop light 6 Volt 18 Watt – 1 direct current signal horn 6 Volt – 1 directional signal 6 Volt 21 Watt (each side)
Electronic cable (black) small terminal of the ignition coil
Electronic cable (blue) large terminal of the ignition coil

Attention!
The blue short-circuiting cable coming off the large terminal must be installed direct
(without intermediate connecting blocks) to the short-circuiting button B_9 at the handlebar

Switch positions

- 0   Off (ignition short-circuited)
- I   Daylight driving
- II Driving lights on

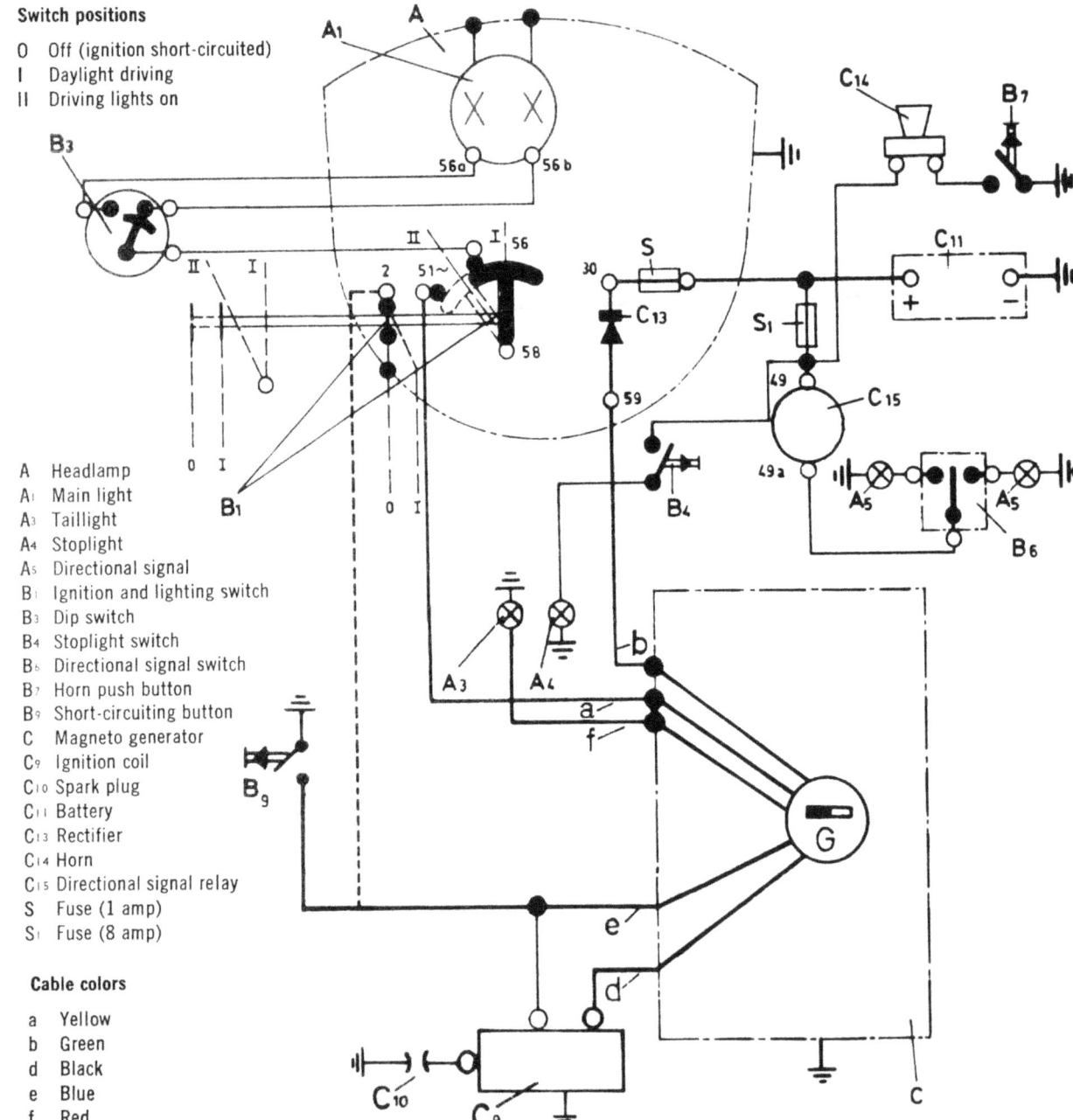

- A   Headlamp
- A_1 Main light
- A_3 Taillight
- A_4 Stoplight
- A_5 Directional signal
- B_1 Ignition and lighting switch
- B_3 Dip switch
- B_4 Stoplight switch
- B_5 Directional signal switch
- B_7 Horn push button
- B_9 Short-circuiting button
- C   Magneto generator
- C_9 Ignition coil
- C_{10} Spark plug
- C_{11} Battery
- C_{13} Rectifier
- C_{14} Horn
- C_{15} Directional signal relay
- S   Fuse (1 amp)
- S_1 Fuse (8 amp)

Cable colors

- a   Yellow
- b   Green
- d   Black
- e   Blue
- f   Red

CHAPTER EIGHT

SPECIFICATIONS

> This chapter contains specifications for the various Sachs engines and related components covered by this manual.
>
> However, since there are differences between the various models, be sure to consult the correct table for the engine in question.

SPECIFICATIONS — MODEL 1251/5 A
(Cast-iron cylinder, vertical-finned head)

Displacement	122cc (7.444 cu. in.)
Bore	2.126 in. (54mm)
Stroke	2.126 in. (54mm)
Compression ratio	9 to 1
Output	12.5 hp (DIN) at 7,300 rpm
Engine lubrication	Oil/gasoline mix 1:25
Primary reduction (engine/transmission)	2.10:1
Transmission ratios	
1st	4.60:1
2nd	2.73:1
3rd	1.95:1
4th	1.50:1
5th	1.24:1
Transmission lubrication	1.3 pints (600cc) SAE 80
Clutch	Multiple disc, oil bath
Ignition	
Bosch	Magneto-generator, contact breaker
Motoplat	Magneto-generator, electronic
Ignition timing	0.098-0.118 in. (2.5-3.0mm) BTDC
Contact breaker gap (Bosch ignition)	0.014-0.018 in. (0.35-0.45mm)
Pole shoe separation (Bosch ignition)	0.866-0.984 in. (22-25mm)
Spark plug	Bosch W 260 T1
Gap	0.016-0.020 in. (0.4-0.5mm)
Carburetor	Bing No. 1/24/153
Venturi diameter	0.945 in. (24mm)
Main jet	100
Needle jet	2.73
Needle	5
Idle jet	40
Idle adjustment screw	
Cold weather	½ turn open
Warm weather	¾ turn open
Air filter	Micronic paper element
Head pipe diameter	1.496 in. (38mm) inside diameter
Head pipe length	15.75 in. (400mm)

SPECIFICATIONS — MODEL 1001/5A
(Cast-iron cylinder, vertical-finned head)

Displacement	97cc (5.9 cu. in.)
Bore	1.89 in. (48mm)
Stroke	2.126 in. (54mm)
Compression ratio	9 to 1
Output	10 hp (DIN) at 7,300 rpm
Engine lubrication	Oil/gasoline mix 1:25
Primary reduction (engine/transmission)	2.10 to 1
Transmission ratios	
1st	4.60:1
2nd	2.73:1
3rd	1.95:1
4th	1.50:1
5th	1.24:1
Transmission lubrication	1.3 pints (600cc) SAE 80
Clutch	Multiple disc, oil bath
Ignition	
Bosch	Magneto-generator, contact breaker
Motoplat	Magneto-generator, electronic
Ignition timing	0.098-0.118 in. (2.5-3.0mm) BTDC
Contact breaker gap (Bosch ignition)	0.014-0.018 in. (0.35-0.45mm)
Pole shoe separation (Bosch ignition)	0.866-0.984 in. (22-25mm)
Spark plug	Bosch W 260 T1
Gap	0.016-0.020 in. (0.4-0.5mm)
Carburetor	Bing No. 1/24/158
Venturi diameter	0.945 in. (24mm)
Main jet	95
Needle jet	2.73
Needle	5
Idle jet	40
Idle adjustment screw	
Cold weather	½ turn open
Warm weather	¾ turn open
Air filter	Micronic paper element
Head pipe diameter	1.496 in. (38mm) inside diameter
Head pipe length	15.75 in. (400mm)

SPECIFICATIONS — MODEL 1001/5 A
(Aluminum cylinder, sunburst head)

Displacement	97cc (5.9 cu. in.)
Bore	1.89 in. (48mm)
Stroke	2.126 in. (54mm)
Compression ratio	10.8 to 1
Output	12 hp (DIN) at 7,400 rpm
Engine lubrication	Oil/gasoline mix 1:25
Primary reduction (engine/transmission)	2.10:1
Transmissioin ratios	
1st	4.60:1
2nd	2.73:1
3rd	1.95:1
4th	1.50:1
5th	1.24:1
Transmission lubrication	1.3 pints (600cc) SAE 80
Clutch	Multiple disc, oil bath
Ignition	
Bosch	Magneto-generator, contact breaker
Motoplat	Magneto-generator, electronic
Ignition timing	0.098-0.118 in. (2.5-3.0mm) BTDC
Contact breaker gap (Bosch ignition)	0.014-0.018 in. (0.35-0.45mm)
Pole shoe separation (Bosch ignition)	0.866-0.984 in. (22-25mm)
Spark plug	Bosch W 260 T1
Gap	0.016-0.020 in. (0.4-0.5mm)
Carburetor	Bing No. 1/26/115
Venturi diameter	1.024 in. (26mm)
Main jet	105
Needle jet	2.73
Needle	5
Idle jet	40
Idle adjusting screw	½ to 1 turn open
Air filter	Micronic paper element
Head pipe diameter	1.496 in. (38mm) inside diameter
Head pipe length	15.75 in. (400mm)

SPECIFICATIONS — MODEL 1251/5 A
(Aluminum cylinder, sunburst head)

Displacement	122cc (7.444 cu. in.)
Bore	2.126 in. (54mm)
Stroke	2.126 in. (54mm)
Compression ratio	10.8 to 1
Output	15 hp (DIN) at 7,400 rpm
Engine lubrication	Oil/gasoline mix 1:25
Primary reduction (engine/transmission)	2.10:1
Transmission ratios	
1st	4.60:1
2nd	2.73:1
3rd	1.95:1
4th	1.50:1
5th	1.24:1
Transmission lubrication	1.3 pints (600cc) SAE 80
Clutch	Multiple disc, oil bath
Ignition	
Bosch	Magneto-generator, contact breaker
Motoplat	Magneto-generator, electronic
Ignition timing	0.098-0.118 in. (2.5-3.0mm) BTDC
Contact breaker gap (Bosch ignition)	0.014-0.018 in. (0.35-0.45mm)
Pole shoe separation (Bosch ignition)	0.866-0.984 in. (22-25mm)
Spark plug	Bosch W 260 T1
Gap	0.016-0.020 in. (0.4-0.5mm)
Carburetor	Bing No. 1/26/115
Venturi diameter	1.024 in. (26mm)
Main jet	105
Needle jet	2.73
Needle	5
Idle jet	40
Idle adjustment screw	½ to 1 turn open
Air filter	Micronic paper element
Head pipe diameter	1.496 in. (38mm) inside diameter
Head pipe length	15.75 in. (400mm)

SPECIFICATIONS — MODEL 1001/6 A
(Aluminum cylinder, sunburst head)

Displacement	97cc (5.919 cu. in.)
Bore	1.89 in. (48mm)
Stroke	2.126 in. (54mm)
Compression ratio	10.8 to 1
Output	12 hp (DIN) at 7,400 rpm
Engine lubrication	Oil/gasoline mix 1:25
Primary reduction (engine/transmission)	2.10:1
Transmission ratios	
1st	4.60:1
2nd	2.93:1
3rd	2.16:1
4th	1.72:1
5th	1.43:1
6th	1.24:1
Transmission lubrication	1.3 pints (600cc) SAE 80
Clutch	Multiple disc, oil bath
Ignition	
Bosch	Magneto-generator, contact breaker
Motoplat	Magneto-generator, electronic
Ignition timing	0.098-0.118 in. (2.5-3.0mm) BTDC
Contact breaker gap (Bosch ignition)	0.014-0.018 in. (0.35-0.45mm)
Pole shoe separation (Bosch ignition)	0.866-0.984 in. (22-25mm)
Spark plug	Bosch W 260 T1
Gap	0.016-0.020 in. (0.4-0.5mm)
Carburetor	Bing No. 1/26/115
Venturi diameter	1.024 in. (26mm)
Main jet	105
Needle jet	2.73
Needle	5
Idle jet	40
Idle adjustment screw	½ to 1 turn open
Air filter	Micronic paper element
Head pipe diameter	1.496 in. (38mm) inside diameter
Head pipe length	15.75 in. (400mm)

SPECIFICATIONS — MODEL 1251/6 A
(Aluminum cylinder, sunburst head)

Displacement	122cc (7.444 cu. in.)
Bore	2.126 in. (54mm)
Stroke	2.126 in. (54mm)
Compression ratio	10.8 to 1
Output	15 hp (DIN) at 7,400 rpm
Engine lubrication	Oil/gasoline mix 1:25
Primary reduction (engine/transmission)	2.10:1
Transmission ratios	
1st	4.60:1
2nd	2.93:1
3rd	2.16:1
4th	1.72:1
5th	1.43:1
6th	1.24:1
Transmission lubrication	1.3 pints (600cc) SAE 80
Clutch	Multiple disc, oil bath
Ignition	
Bosch	Magneto-generator, contact breaker
Motoplat	Magneto-generator, electronic
Ignition timing	0.098-0.118 in. (2.5-3.0mm) BTDC
Contact breaker gap (Bosch ignition)	0.014-0.018 in. (0.35-0.45mm)
Pole shoe separation (Bosch ignition)	0.866-0.984 in. (22-25mm)
Spark plug	Bosch W 260 T1
Gap	0.016-0.020 in. (0.4-0.5mm)
Carburetor	Bing No. 1/26/115
Venturi diameter	1.024 in. (25mm)
Main jet	105
Needle jet	2.73
Needle	5
Idle jet	40
Idle adjustment screw	½ to 1 turn open
Air filter	Micronic paper element
Head pipe diameter	1.496 in. (38mm) inside diameter
Head pipe length	15.75 in. (400mm)

SPECIFICATIONS — MODEL 1001/6 B
(Aluminum cylinder, sunburst head)

Displacement	97cc (5.919 cu. in.)
Bore	1.890 in. (48mm)
Stroke	2.126 in. (54mm)
Compression ratio	10.8 to 1
Output	14 hp (DIN) at 8,500 rpm
Engine lubrication	Oil/gasoline mix 1:25
Primary reduction (engine/transmission)	2.10:1
Transmission ratios	
1st	4.60:1
2nd	2.93:1
3rd	2.16:1
4th	1.72:1
5th	1.43:1
6th	1.24:1
Transmission lubrication	1.3 pints (600cc) SAE 80
Clutch	Multiple disc, oil bath
Ignition	Motoplat, magneto-generator, electronic
Timing	0.098-0.118 in. (2.5-3.0mm) BTDC
Spark plug	Bosch W 260 T1
	Bosch W 290 T16 (for competition)
Gap	0.016-0.020 in. (0.4-0.5mm)
Carburetor	
NHW	Bing No. 1/27/26
Venturi diameter	1.064 in. (27mm)
Main jet	135
Needle jet	2.73
Needle	4
Idle jet	45
Idle adjustment screw	1 turn open
KTM	Bing No. 1/27/21
Venturi diameter	1.064 in. (27mm)
Main jet	130
Needle jet	2.73
Needle	4
Idle jet	45
Idle adjustment screw	1 turn open
Monark	Bing No. 1/27/23
Venturi diameter	1.064 in. (27mm)
Main jet	115
Needle jet	2.73
Needle	4
Idle jet	45
Idle adjustment screw	1 turn open
Air filter	Micronic paper element
Head pipe diameter	1.496 in. (38mm) inside diameter
Head pipe length	14.57 in. (370mm)

SPECIFICATIONS — MODEL 1251/6 B
(Aluminum cylinder, sunburst head)

Displacement	122cc (7.444 cu. in.)
Bore	2.126 in. (54mm)
Stroke	2.126 in. (54mm)
Compression ratio	12 to 1
Output	18 hp (DIN) at 8,500 rpm
Engine lubrication	Oil/gasoline mix 1:25
Primary reduction (engine/transmission)	2.10:1
Transmission ratios	
1st	4.60:1
2nd	2.93:1
3rd	2.16:1
4th	1.72:1
5th	1.43:1
6th	1.24:1
Transmission lubrication	1.3 pints (600cc) SAE 80
Clutch	Multiple disc, oil bath
Ignition	Motoplat, magneto-generator, electronic
Timing	0.098-0.118 in. (2.5-3.0mm) BTDC
Spark plug	Bosch W 260 T1
	Bosch W 290 T16 (for competition)
Gap	0.016-0.020 in. (0.4-0.5mm)
Carburetor	
NHW	Bing No. 1/27/19
Venturi diameter	1.064 in. (27mm)
Main jet	140
Needle jet	2.73
Needle	4
Idle jet	45
Idle adjustment screw	1 turn open
KTM	Bing No. 1/27/20
Venturi diameter	1.064 in. (27mm)
Main jet	140
Needle jet	2.70
Needle	4
Idle jet	45
Idle adjustment screw	1 turn open
Monark	Bing No. 1/27/22
Venturi diameter	1.064 in. (27mm)
Main jet	120
Needle jet	2.73
Needle	4
Idle jet	45
Idle adjustment screw	1 turn open
Air filter	Micronic paper element
Head pipe diameter	1.496 in. (38mm) inside diameter
Head pipe length	14.57 in. (370mm)

SPECIFICATIONS — MODEL 1251/6 C
(Aluminum cylinder, sunburst head)

Displacement	122cc (7.444 cu. in.)
Bore	2.126 in. (54mm)
Stroke	2.126 in. (54mm)
Compression ratio	11.8 to 1
Output	17 hp (DIN) at 7,500 rpm
Engine lubrication	Oil/gasoline mix 1:25
Primary reduction (engine/transmission)	2.10:1
Tranmission ratios	
1st	4.60:1
2nd	2.93:1
3rd	2.16:1
4th	1.72:1
5th	1.43:1
6th	1.24:1
Transmission lubrication	1.3 pints (600cc) SAE 80
Clutch	Multiple disc, oil bath
Ignition	Motoplat, magneto-generator, electronic
Timing	0.098-0.118 in. (2.5-3.0mm) BTDC
Spark plug	Bosch W 280 M1
Gap	0.016-0.020 in. (0.4-0.5mm)
Carburetor	Bing No. 1/27/25
Venturi diameter	1.064 in. (27mm)
Main jet	110
Needle jet	2.70
Needle	4
Idle jet	45
Idle adjustment screw	1 turn open
Air filter	Micronic paper element
Head pipe diameter	1.496 in. (38mm) inside diameter
Head pipe length	14.96 in. (380mm)

CHAPTER NINE

USEFUL FORMULAS AND TABLES

> It is often necessary to convert metric to American dimensions or vice versa. This chapter contains formulas for doing so, with typical examples worked out. Also in this chapter are other useful tables and formulas.

CONVERSIONS

Multiply	by	To obtain
Volume		
Cubic centimeters	0.061	Cubic inches
Cubic inches	16.387	Cubic centimeters
Liters	0.264	Gallons
Gallons	3.785	Liters
Liters	1.057	Quarts
Quarts	0.946	Liters
Cubic centimeters	0.0339	Fluid ounces
Fluid ounces	29.57	Cubic centimeters
Length		
Millimeters	0.03937	Inches
Inches	25.4	Millimeters
Centimeters	0.3937	Inches
Inches	2.54	Centimeters
Kilometers	0.6214	Miles
Miles	1.609	Kilometers
Meters	3.281	Feet
Feet	0.3048	Meters
Millimeters	0.10	Centimeters
Centimeters	10.0	Millimeters
Weight		
Kilograms	2.205	Pounds
Pounds	0.4536	Kilograms
Grams	0.03527	Ounces
Ounces	28.35	Grams
Other		
Metric horsepower	1.014	Brake horsepower
Brake horsepower	0.9859	Metric horsepower
Kilogram-meters	7.235	Foot-pounds
Foot-pounds	0.1383	Kilogram-meters
Kilometers per liter	2.352	Miles per gallon
Miles per gallon	0.4252	Kilometers per liter
Square millimeters	0.00155	Square inches
Square inches	645.2	Square millimeters
Square inches	6.452	Square centimeters
Square centimeters	0.155	Square inches
Kilometers per hour	0.6214	Miles per hour
Miles per hour	1.609	Kilometers per hour
Foot-pounds	0.1383	Kilogram-meters
Kilogram-meters	7.233	Foot-pounds
Pounds per square inch	0.0703	Kilograms per square centimeter
Kilograms per square centimeter	14.22	Pounds per square inch
Miles per hour	88	Feet per minute
Feet per minute	0.01136	Miles per hour
Miles per hour	1.467	Feet per second

Table 1   FUEL AND OIL MIXTURES

Fuel U.S. Gallons	SAE 40 Motor Oil		Two-Stroke Oil	
	Oz.	(cc)	Oz.	(cc)
0.1	0.6	18	0.5	15
0.2	1.3	39	1.1	33
0.3	1.9	57	1.6	48
0.4	2.6	78	2.1	63
0.5	3.2	96	2.6	78
0.6	3.9	117	3.2	96
0.7	4.5	135	3.7	111
0.8	5.2	156	4.2	126
0.9	5.8	174	4.8	144
1.0	6.4	192	5.3	159
1.1	7.0	210	5.8	192
1.2	7.7	231	6.4	174
1.3	8.3	249	6.9	207
1.4	9.0	270	7.4	222
1.5	9.6	288	7.9	237
1.6	10.3	309	8.5	255
1.7	10.9	327	9.0	270
1.8	11.6	348	9.5	285
1.9	12.2	366	10.6	303
2.0	12.8	384	11.1	318
2.1	13.5	405	11.3	333
2.2	14.1	423	11.6	348
2.3	14.8	444	12.1	363
2.4	15.4	480	12.6	378
2.5	16.0	462	13.1	393
2.6	16.7	501	13.7	411
2.7	17.3	519	14.2	426
2.8	17.9	537	14.7	441

LUBRICANTS AND SEALANTS

required for rebuilding the engines

Lubricant or sealant	Suppliers/addresses
Molykote-Paste	DOW CORNING GmbH D-8000 München 54 Pelkoven Str. 152
Sealant No. 40 F & S Part No. 0999 107 000)	FICHTEL & SACHS AG D-8720 Schweinfurt
Sealant "Diamant" Typ OW	Schleifmittelwerk Kahl Artur GLÖCKLER D-8756 Kahl a. M. Postfach 80
Loctite AAV	LOCTITIE TECHNIK D-8000 München Arabella Str. 5
Alvania 3 (High melting point grease)	SHELL D-8500 Nürnberg Postfach 567
BOSCH grease Ft 1 v 4 Ft 1 v 8	Robert BOSCH GmbH D-7022 Leinfelden/Stuttgart Max-Lang-Str. 40–46 BOSCH agents

TIGHTENING TORQUES FOR BOLTS AND NUTS

Bolts

F&S Part No.	Qty.	used for	Dimension	Tightening torque kpm	Tightening torque ft lb
0940 119 102	6	Crankcase	M 6 x 60	0,8 ... 1,0	5.78 ... 7.23
0940 128 202	4	Crankcase	M 6 x 75	0,8 ... 1,0	5.78 ... 7.23
0640 005 005	1	Crankcase (kickstarter stop)	M 12	2,5 ... 3,0	18.08 ... 21.70
0240 100 000	1	Crankcase (oil drain)	M 10 x 1	1,3 ... 1,5	9.40 ... 10.85
0240 133 100	1	Selector lever	M 12 x 1	1,5	10.85
0240 106 100	3	Stator plate (version BOSCH)	M 4 x 14	0,4 ... 0,6	2.89 ... 4.34
0241 028 001	3	Base plate	M 4 x 12	0,4 ... 0,6	2.89 ... 4.34
2840 002 001	3	Stator plate (version MOTOPLAT)	M 4 x 20	0,4 ... 0,6	2.89 ... 4.34
1940 108 000	2	Selector adjusting plate	M 6 x 20	1,2 ... 1,5	8.68 ... 10.85
1940 114 000	2	Selector adjusting plate with stop bushes	M 6 x 25	1,2 ... 1,5	8.68 ... 10.85
0640 011 102	4	Crankcase cover, clutch side	M 6 x 65	0,8 ... 1,0	5.78 ... 7.23
0241 040 001	2	Crankcase cover, clutch side	M 6 x 38	0,8 ... 1,0	5.78 ... 7.23
0240 120 002	1	Crankcase cover, clutch side	M 6 x 52	0,8 ... 1,0	5.78 ... 7.23
0940 119 102	4	Crankcase cover, magneto side	M 6 x 60	0,8 ... 1,0	5.78 ... 7.23
2740 024 000	3	Clutch case on layshaft wheel	M 6 x 15	1,1 ... 1,2	7.95 ... 8.68
0941 049 006	4	Cylinder head on cast iron cylinder	M 8 x 40	3,0 ... 3,2	21.70 ... 23.15

Nuts

F&S Part No.	Qty.	used for	Dimension	Tightening torque kpm	Tightening torque ft lb
0642 105 001	1	Crankshaft, drive side	M 14 x 1,5	7,0 ... 7,5	50.63 ... 54.25
0242 106 005	1	Clutch hub	M 18 x 1	8,0 ... 9,0	57.86 ... 65.10
0942 067 100	4	Cast iron cylinder and aluminium cylinder on SACHS 1251/5 B	M 8	2,4 ... 2,6	17.36 ... 18.80
2842 003 004	4	Cylinder head on SACHS 1251/5 B	M 8	3,0 ... 3,2	21.70 ... 23.15
0942 072 110	1	Crankshaft, magneto-side (BOSCH magneto flywheel)	M 10 x 1 L	3,8 ... 4,0	27.48 ... 28.93
0942 072 110	1	Crankshaft, magneto-side (MOTOPLAT magneto flyhweel)	M 10 x 1 L	5,5 ... 6,0	39.78 ... 43.40
0642 103 001	1	Sprocket	M 20 x 1 L	7,0 ... 7,5	50.63 ... 54.25
0642 107 001	4	Cylinder and cylinder head (alu)	M 8 x 45	2,5 ... 3,0	18.08 ... 21.70
0316 057 003	3	Clutch case on layshaft wheel	M 6	0,5 ... 0,6	3.62 ... 4.34

NOTES

CHAPTER TEN

ILUSTRATED PARTS LIST

SACHS 1001/5A
1001/6A

1251/5A
1251/5A L
1251/5B

1251/6A
1251/6B

(June 1974)

FICHTEL & SACHS AG · D-8720 SCHWEINFURT

Cylinder, Piston, Crankshaft, Crankcase

Crankcase, Crankshaft, Cylinder

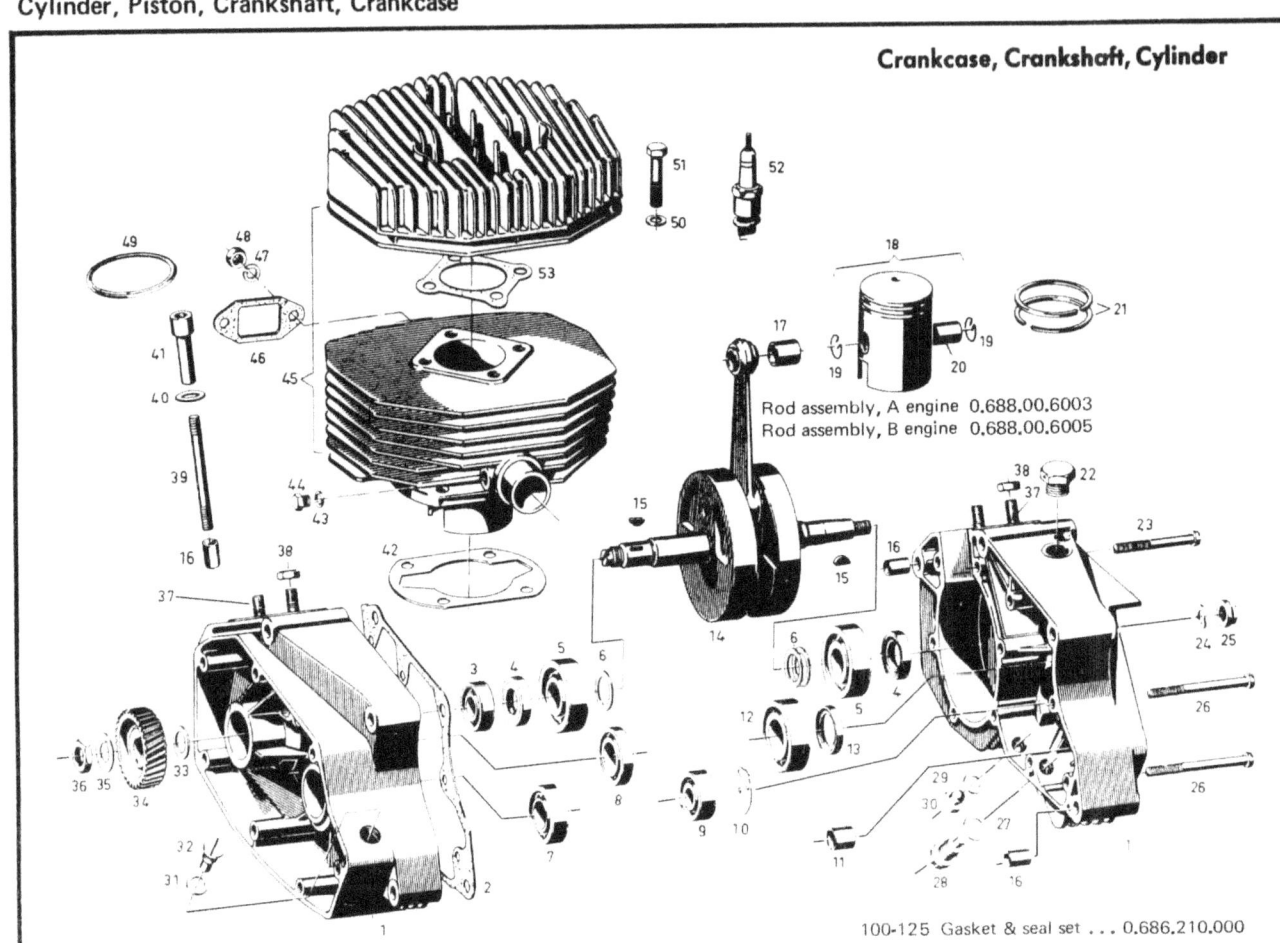

100-125 Gasket & seal set ... 0.686.210.000

Rod assembly, A engine 0.688.00.6003
Rod assembly, B engine 0.688.00.6005

Illustr. No.	Part No.	Description	1001/5 A	1251/5 A	1251/5 A L	1001/6 A	1251/6 A	1251/6 B
1	see page 30	Crankcase ass'y., incl. ill. 2, 16 + 17						
2	0650 105 100	Gasket	1	1	1	1	1	
	•0650 105 101	Gasket						1
3	0232 120 001	Grooved ball bearing 6202 C3 DIN 625 (15 x 35 x 11)	1	1	1	1	1	1
4	0230 002 000	Oil seal 18.6 x 35 x 8	2	2	2	2	2	2
5	0932 063 001	Ball bearing M 20 DIN 615 (20 x 52 x 15)	2	2	2	2	2	2
6	0944 046 000	Shim 20.5 x 28.5	x	x	x	x	x	
	•0644 117 000	Shim 20.5 x 28.5 x 1.0						x
7	0232 126 001	Grooved ball bearing 6004 C3 DIN 625 for layshaft	1	1	1	1	1	1
8	0232 130 001	Grooved ball bearing 16004 C3 DIN 625 20 x 42 x 8 for mainshaft up to engine No. 6318 754	1	1	1			
	2732 006 000	Grooved ball bearing 16005 DIN 625 25 x 47 x 8 for engine No. 6318 755 on	1	1	1	1	1	1
9	0632 110 001	Grooved ball bearing 6301 C3 DIN 625 for layshaft	1	1	1	1	1	1
10	0644 109 100	Profile washer	1	1	1	1	1	1
11	0232 129 000	Bush 12 x 16 x 14.5	1	1	1	1	1	1
12	0632 017 201	Cylindrical roller bearing NJ 205 E C3 ZS for mainshaft	1	1	1	1	1	1
13	0630 001 000	Oil seal 23.4 x 34 x 5	1	1	1	1	1	1
14	0688 005 100	Crankshaft (aluminium connect. rod)	1	1	1			
	0688 005 001	Crankshaft (steel connecting rod)				1	1	
	•0688 005 003	Crankshaft (steel connecting rod)						1
15	0246 005 000	Key 3 x 3.7	2	2	2	2	2	2
16	0249 120 000	Dowel sleeve 10 x 15	4	4	4	4	4	4
	•1949 011 000	Dowel sleeve 12 x 22 for front crankcase fitting						1
17	0932 061 005	Bush 15 x 18.9 x 17 (alu con-rod)	1	1	1			
	0632 111 000	Needle cage K 15 x 19 x 20 (steel con-rod)				1	1	1
18	see table	Piston ass'y.						
19	0945 063 000	Circlip	2	2	2	2	2	2
20	0616 101 000	Gudgeon pin 9 x 15 x 41	1	1	1			

Illustr. No.	Part No.	Description	1001/5 A	1251/5 A	1251/5 A L	1001/6 A	1251/6 A	1251/6 B
21	0616 100 000	Gudgeon pin 9 x 15 x 46				1	1	1
22	see table	Piston ring,						
23	0241 048 000	Plug screw M 16 x 1.25 x 6	1	1	1	1	1	1
24	0940 119 102	Screw, fillister head M 6 x 60	6	6	6	6	6	6
25	0245 022 000	Spring washer for M 10	1	1	1	1	1	1
26	0942 072 110	Collar nut M 10 x 1 (left-hand thread)	1	1	1	1	1	1
27	0940 128 202	Screw, fillister head M 6 x 75	4	4	4	4	4	4
28	0650 004 000	Sealing washer 12.2 x 20 x 1	1	1	1	1	1	1
29	0640 005 005	Stop screw M 12	1	1	1	1	1	1
30	1950 023 000	Sealing washer 10.2 x 15.9 x 1	1	1	1	1	1	1
31	0240 100 000	Oil drain plug M 10 x 1	1	1	1	1	1	1
32	0250 118 000	Sealing washer 12.2 x 15.4 x 1.5	1	1	1	1	1	1
33	0240 133 100	Pivot screw M 12 x 1	1	1	1	1	1	1
34	0246 009 006	Washer 15.2 x 20.3 x 1.5	1	1	1	1	1	1
35	0634 112 000	Driving pinion	1	1	1	1	1	1
36	0645 102 000	Tab washer	1	1	1	1	1	1
	0642 105 001	Nut M 14 x 1.5, height 6 mm	1	1	1	1	1	
	•0942 020 100	Nut M 14 x 1.5, height 8 mm						1
37	0940 017 101	Stud M 8 x 20 — for fitting the grey-cast cylinder	4	4	4			
38	0942 067 100	Nut M 8	4	4	4			
	•0944 003 005	Washer 8.4 x 14 x 1.5						
39	0640 108 001	Stud M 8 x 90 — for fitting the aluminium cylinder head				4	4	4
40	0244 075 008	Washer 13.2 x 20 x 1.7				4	4	4
41	0642 107 001	Nut M 8 x 45				4	4	4
42	0650 107 200	Gasket	1	1	1	1	1	
43	1950 024 000	Sealing ring 8.4 x 11.5 x 1						1
44	2015 008 000	Plug M 8 x 1						1
45	see table	Cylinder head and cylinder,	1	1	1	1	1	1
46	0650 108 000	Gasket	1	1	1	1	1	1
47	0245 023 003	Spring washer for M 8 — for fitting the muffler	2	2	2	2	2	2
48	0642 104 101	Nut M 8, height 36 mm	2	2	2	2	2	2
49	0650 112 000	Sealing ring 40 x 47 x 2.5, for fitting the muffler to the aluminium cyl.				1	1	1
50	0244 124 001	Washer 8.4 x 17 x 2	4	4	4			
51	0941 049 006	Screw, hexagon head, M 8 x 40	4	4	4			
	2842 003 004	Nut M 8						
52		Spark plug,						
53	0650 113 000	Gasket Ø 48 — for aluminium cylinders only				1	1	
	0650 114 000	Gasket Ø 54						1

x = as needed

Gearbox, Selecting

Gear-changing lever, Main shaft, Gearbox for SACHS 1001/5 A up to engine No. 5692 842
for SACHS 1251/5 A and 1251/5 A L up to engine No. 6318 754

I

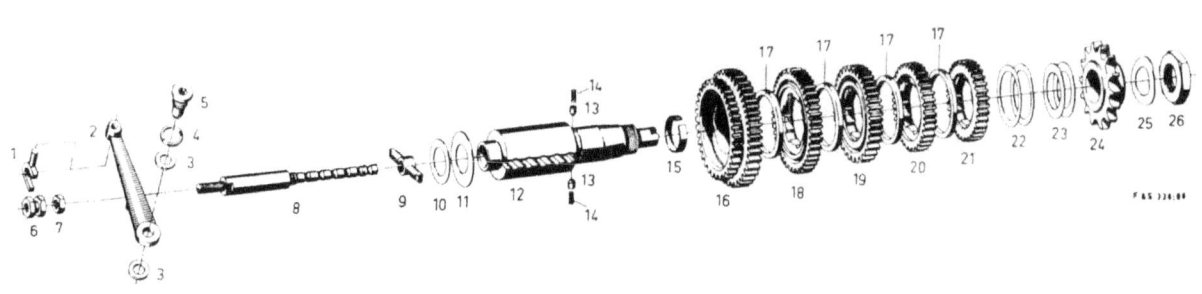

for SACHS 1001/5 A from engine No. 5692 843 up
for SACHS 1251/5 A and 1251/5 A L from engine No. 6318/755 up

II

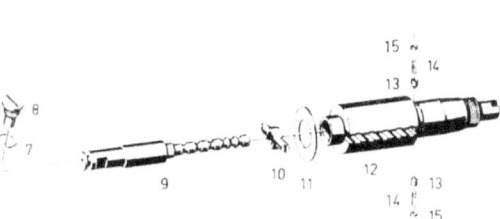
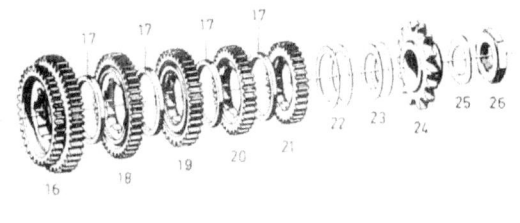

Illustr. No.	Part No.	Description	1001/5 A	1251/5 A	1251/5 A L	1001/6 A	1251/6 3
			\multicolumn{5}{c}{Qty.}				
I		**Gear changing lever, Main shaft Gearbox**					
1	0248 135 100	Selector fork	1	1	1		
2	0248 131 100	Selector lever	1	1	1		
3	0944 003 000	Shim 8.4 x 14	x	x	x		
4	0250 118 000	Sealing ring 12.2 x 15.4 x 1.5	1	1	1		
5	0240 133 100	Pivot screw M 12 x 1 (see Fig. II/8)	1	1	1		
6	0242 103 100	Nut M 6, with groove	1	1	1		
7	0242 109 000	Nut M 6	1	1	1		
8	0237 120 200	Selector rod M 8 x 1	1	1	1		
9	0619 001 000	Selector key	1	1	1		
10	0244 118 001	Washer 20.2 x 32 x 0.8	1	1	1		
11	0644 103 000	Washer 20.2 x 39 x 1.0	1	1	1		
12	0637 102 000	Main shaft					
	0685 102 000	Main shaft ass'y., including	1	1	1		
		1 x 0637 102 000 main shaft					
		1 x 0237 120 200 selector rod					
		1 x 0619 001 000 selector key					
		2 x 0649 105 000 cup					
		2 x 0639 100 100 pressure spring					
		1 x 0639 101 000 spring ring					
13	0649 105 000	Cup	2	2	2		
14	0639 100 100	Pressure spring	2	2	2		
15	0639 101 000	Spring ring	1	1	1		
16	0634 106 000	Selector gear 1st speed (46 and 34 teeth)	1	1	1		
17	0647 101 000	Ring 42 x 49 x 3	4	4	4		
18	0634 107 000	Selector gear 2nd speed (41 teeth)	1	1	1		
19	0634 108 000	Selector gear 3rd speed (37 teeth)	1	1	1		
20	0634 109 000	Selector gear 4th speed (33 teeth)	1	1	1		
21	0634 110 000	Selector gear 5th speed (31 teeth)	1	1	1		
22	0644 104 000	Shim 35.2 x 44	x	x	x		
23	0644 105 000	Shim 25.2 x 39	x	x	x		
24	0636 106 000	Sprocket 14 teeth	1	1	1		
	0636 107 000	Sprocket 13 teeth	1				
25	0944 019 000	Spring washer for Ø 20	1	1	1		
26	0642 103 001	Nut M 20 x 1 (left-hand thread)	1	1	1		

Illustr. No.	Part No.	Description	1001/5 A	1251/5 A	1251/5 A L	1001/6 A	1251/6 A	1251/6 B
			\multicolumn{6}{c}{Qty.}					
II		**Gear changing lever, Main shaft, Gearbox**						
1	0248 135 100	Selector fork	1	1	1			
2	0648 106 000	Selector lever, upper part	1	1	1			
3	0640 110 000	Eccentric screw M 6	1	1	1			
4	0648 105 100	Selector lever, lower part	1	1	1			
5	1445 017 000	Lock washer with inner tab	1	1	1			
6	0642 108 000	Nut M 6	1	1	1			
7	0250 118 000	Sealing ring 12.2 x 15.4 x 1.5	1	1	1			
8	0240 133 100	Pivot screw M 12 x 1	1	1	1			
9	0619 004 000	Selector rod M 10 x 1	1	1	1			
10	0619 001 100	Selector key	1	1	1			
11	0644 105 104	Washer 25.2 x 39 x 1	1	1	1			
12	0637 102 100	Main shaft						
	0685 102 100	Main shaft ass'y., including illustr. 9, 10 and 12 ... 15	1	1	1			
13	0649 105 000	Cup	2	2	2			
14	0639 100 100	Pressure spring	2	2	2			
15	0663 002 000	Plug	2	2	2			
16	0634 106 100	Selector gear, 1st (46 and 34 teeth)	1	1	1			
17	0647 101 000	Ring 42 x 49 x 3	4	4	4			
18	0634 107 000	Selector gear, 2nd (41 teeth)	1	1	1			
19	0634 108 000	Selector gear, 3rd (37 teeth)	1	1	1			
	•0634 108 003	Selector gear, 3rd (37 teeth)						
20	0634 109 000	Selector gear, 4th (33 teeth)	1	1	1			
	•0634 109 002	Selector gear, 4th (32 teeth)						
21	0634 110 000	Selector gear, 5th (31 teeth)	1	1	1			
	•0634 110 002	Selector gear, 5th (30 teeth)						
22	0644 104 000	Shim 35.2 x 44	x	x	x			
23	0644 105 000	Shim 25.2 x 39	x	x	x			
24	0636 106 000	Sprocket 14 teeth	1	1	1			
	0636 107 000	Sprocket 13 teeth	1	1	1			
25	0944 019 000	Spring washer for Ø 20	1	1	1			
26	0642 103 001	Nut M 20 x 1 (left-hand thread)	1	1	1			

x = as needed

Gearbox, Selecting and Starting device

I — Gear changing lever, Main shaft, Gearbox
for SACHS 1001/6 A from engine No. 5692 843 up
for SACHS 1251/6 A from engine No. 6320 501 up

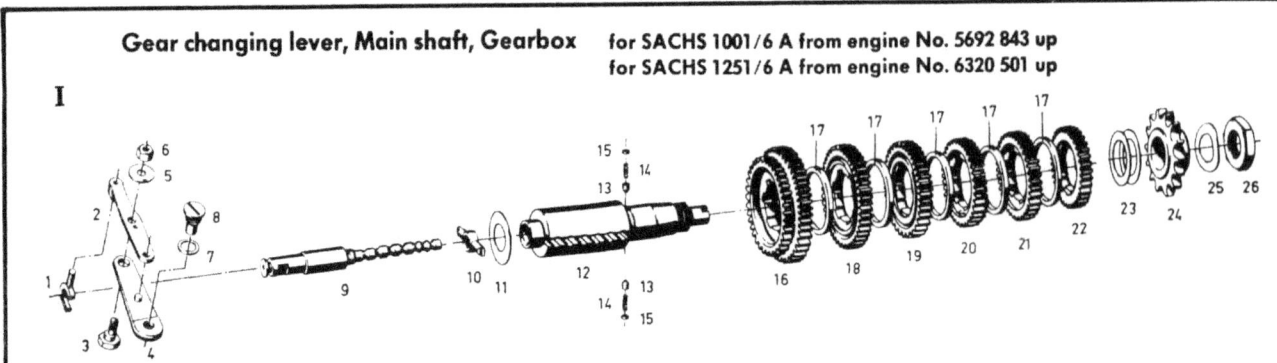

II — Starting and gear changing devices
for SACHS 1001/5 A, 1001/6 A and 1251/6 A
for SACHS 1251/5 A and 1251/5 A L
for SACHS 1251/5 B and
for SACHS 1251/6 B

from engine No. 5692 843 up
from engine No. 6318 543 up
from engine No. 6319 316 up
from engine No. 7103 005 up

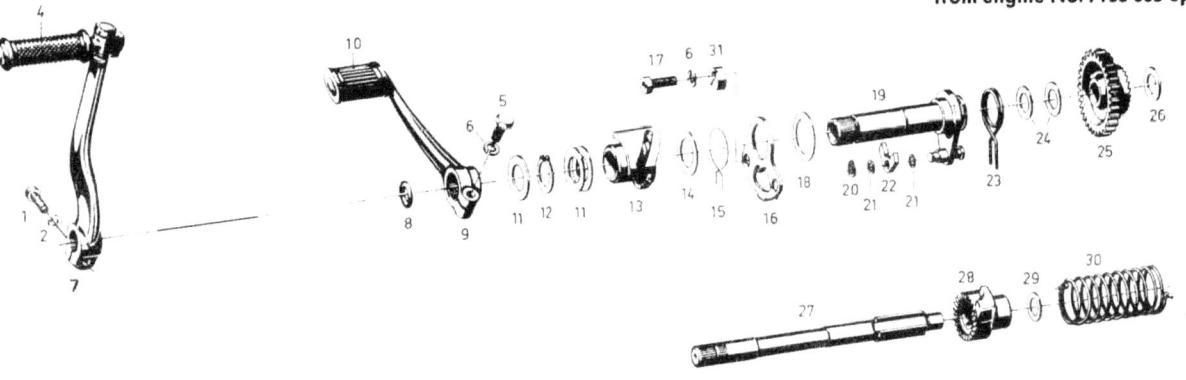

Illustr. No.	Part No.	Description	1001/5 A	1251/5 A	1251/5 A L	1001/6 A	1251/6 A	1251/6 B
I		**Gear changing lever, Main shaft, Gearbox**						
1	0248 135 100	Selector fork				1	1	1
2	0648 106 000	Selector lever, upper part				1	1	1
3	0640 110 000	Eccentric screw M 6				1	1	1
4	0648 105 100	Selector lever, lower part				1	1	1
5	1445 017 000	Lock washer with inner tab				1	1	1
6	0642 108 000	Nut M 6				1	1	1
7	0250 118 000	Sealing ring 12.2 x 15.4 x 1.5				1	1	1
8	0240 133 100	Pivot screw M 12 x 1				1	1	1
9	0619 004 001	Selector rod				1	1	1
10	0619 001 100	Selector key				1	1	1
11	0644 105 103	Shim 15.2 x 39				1	1	1
12	0637 102 101	Main shaft	x	x	x			
	0685 102 101	Main shaft ass'y., including illustr. 9, 10 and 12...15				1	1	1
13	0649 105 000	Cup	2	2	2			
14	0639 100 100	Pressure spring	2	2	2			
15	0663 002 000	Plug	2	2	2			
16	0634 106 201	Selector gear, 1st (46 and 34 teeth)				1	1	1
17	0647 101 001	Ring 42 x 49 x 2.7						
	0647 101 002	Ring 42 x 49 x 2.6	x	x	x			
	0647 101 003	Ring 42 x 49 x 2.5						
18	0634 107 001	Selector gear, 2nd (41 teeth)				1	1	1
19	0634 108 001	Selector gear, 3rd (39 teeth)				1	1	1
20	0634 108 002	Selector gear, 4th (36 teeth)				1	1	1
21	0634 109 001	Selector gear, 5th (33 teeth)				1	1	1
22	0634 110 001	Selector gear, 6th (31 teeth)				1	1	1
23	0644 105 000	Shim 25.2 x 39	x	x	x			
24	0636 106 000	Sprocket 14 teeth				1	1	1
	0636 107 000	Sprocket 13 teeth						
25	0944 019 000	Spring washer for Ø 20				1	1	1
26	0642 103 001	Nut M 20 x 1 (left-hand thread)				1	1	1
II		**Starting and gear changing devices**						
1	1940 106 101	Screw, hex. socket head, M 8 x 22	1	1	1	1	1	
2	0245 023 003	Spring washer for M 8	1	1	1	1	1	

Illustr. No.	Part No.	Description	1001/5 A	1251/5 A	1251/5 A L	1001/6 A	1251/6 A	1251/6 B
4	0260 017 000	Rubber sleeve	1	1	1	1	1	1
5	0240 005 002	Screw, hexagon head, M 6 x 20	1	1				
6	0245 023 002	Spring washer for M 6	3	3	3	3	3	3
7	0289 028 020	Kickstarter crank ass'y.	1	1	1	1	1	1
8	0250 148 000	Sealing ring 11.3 x 2.4	1	1	1	1	1	1
9	0248 144 101	Selector pedal	1	1	1	1	1	1
	0248 144 101	Selector foot lever						
10	0660 000 000	Rubber sleeve	1	1	1	1	1	1
11	0944 046 000	Shim 20.5 x 28.5	x	x	x	x	x	x
12	0945 064 000	Circlip	1	1	1	1	1	1
13	0286 317 000	Selector boss	1	1	1			
	0286 317 021	Selector boss				1	1	1
14	0244 118 000	Shim 20.2 x 32	x	x	x	x	x	x
15	0239 119 000	Spring	1	1	1	1	1	1
16	0248 133 001	Selector adjusting plate	1	1	1	1	1	1
17	1940 114 000	Screw, hex. socket head, M 6 x 25	2	2	2	2	2	1
18	0246 008 001	Washer 25.3 x 34 x 0.5	1	1	1	1	1	1
19	0290 106 211	Selector shaft ass'y., with locking lever (illustr. 19...22)	1	1	1	1	1	1
20	0945 105 000	Circlip	1	1	1	1	1	1
21	0244 100 000	Shim 6.2 x 10	x	x	x	x	x	x
22	0248 136 000	Selector pawl	1	1	1	1	1	1
23	0239 120 000	Spring	1	1	1	1	1	1
24	0240 055 000	Shim 14.5 x 24	x	x	x	x	x	x
25	0634 111 000	Starter gear	1	1	1	1	1	1
26	0244 055 002	Washer 14.5 x 24 x 1.0	1	1	1	1	1	1
27	0237 122 200	Starter shaft	1	1	1	1	1	1
28	0634 005 001	Ratchet wheel	1	1	1	1	1	1
29	0244 102 102	Washer 12.1 x 18.5 x 1.0	1	1	1	1	1	1
30	0239 122 000	Spring	1	1	1	1	1	1
31	0647 103 000	Stopping bush for gear lock	2	2	2	2	2	2
	0690 002 000	Gear changing device ass'y., consisting of: illustr. 11...16 and 18...23				1	1	
	0690 002 001	Gear changing device ass'y., consisting of: illustr. 11...16 and 18...23			1			1

x = as needed

Gearbox, Selecting and Starting device

Starting device, Gear change mechanism without and with gear lock
for SACHS 1001/5 A, 1251/5 A and 1251/5 A L up to engine No. 6318 754

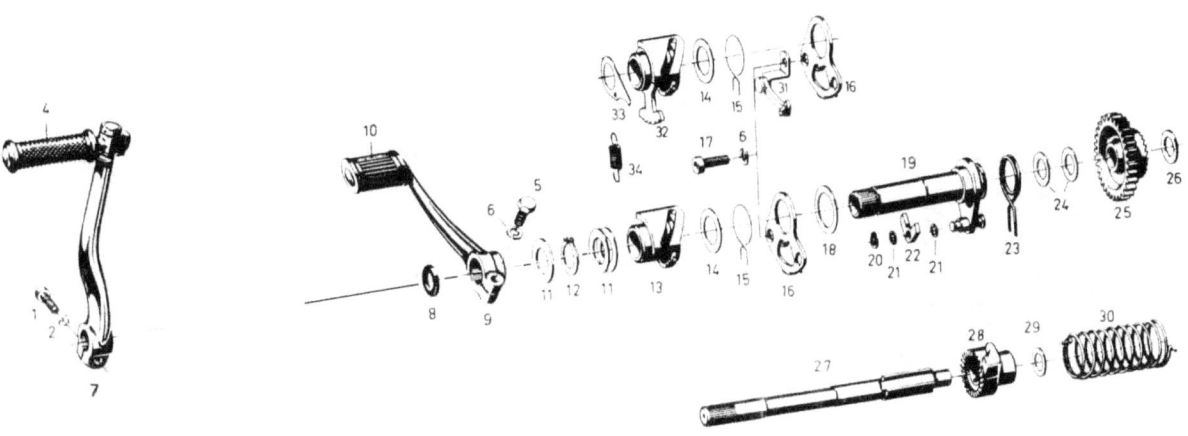

Illustr. No.	Part No.	Description	1001/5 A	1251/5 A	1251/5 A L	1001/6 A	1251 6 A	1251 6 B
			Qty.					
1	1940 106 101	Screw, hex. socket head, M 8 x 22	1	1	1			
2	0245 023 003	Spring washer for M 8	1	1	1			
4	0260 017 000	Rubber sleeve	1	1	1			
5	0240 005 002	Screw, hexagon head, M 6 x 20	1	1	1			
6	0245 023 002	Spring washer for M 6	3	3	3			
7	0289 028 020	Kickstarter lever ass'y., with illustr. 4, 5 and 6			1			
8	0250 148 000	Sealing ring, round, 11.3 x 2.4	1	1	1			
9	0248 144 101	Gear-changing pedal	1	1	1			
10	0660 000 000	Rubber sleeve	1	1	1			
11	0944 046 000	Shim 20.5 x 28.5	x	x	x			
12	0945 064 000	Circlip for ⌀ 20	1	1	1			
13	0286 317 000	Selector boss	1	1	1			
14	0244 118 000	Shim 20.2 x 32	x	x	x			
15	0239 119 000	Pawl spring	1	1	1			
16	0248 133 000	Selector adjusting plate	1	1	1			
17	1940 134 001	Screw hex. socket head M 6 x 20	2	2	2			
18	0246 008 001	Washer 25.3 x 34 x 0.5 for locking lever 6.0 mm thick	1	1	1			
	0246 008 000	Washer 25.3 x 34 x 1.0 for locking lever 4.5 mm thick	1	1	1			
19	0290 106 211	Selector shaft ass'y. with locking lever with illustr. 20...22	1	1	1			
20	0945 105 000	Circlip for ⌀ 6	1	1	1			
21	0244 100 000	Shim 6.2 x 10	x	x	x			
22	0248 136 000	Selector pawl	1	1	1			
23	0239 120 000	Torsion spring	1	1	1			
24	0244 055 000	Shim 14.5 x 24	x	x	x			
25	0634 111 000	Starter gear	1	1	1			
26	0244 055 002	Washer 14.5 x 24 x 1.0	1	1	1			
27	0237 122 200	Starter shaft (to be fitted together with 1 x 0250 148 000 sealing ring, round)	1	1	1			
28	0634 005 001	Ratchet wheel	1	1	1			
29	0244 102 102	Washer 12.1 x 18.5 x 1.0	1	1	1			
30	0239 122 000	Torsion spring	1	1	1			
31	0686 211 000	Bracket	1	1	1			
32	0286 317 020	Selector boss } for gear lock	1	1	1			
33	0644 112 000	Plate	1	1	1			
34	0639 003 000	Spring	1	1	1			
	0290 112 101	Gear changing ass'y. version without gear lock, with illustr. 11...16 and 18...23	1	1	1			

x = as needed

Crankcase cover, Table of Pistons and Piston Rings

Magneto side crankcase cover, Speedometer drive

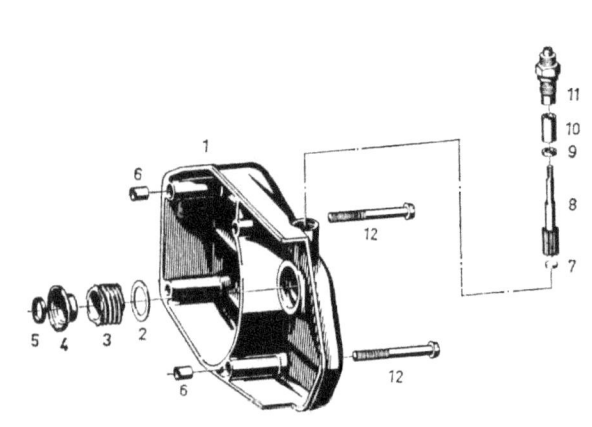

Illustr. No.	Part No.	Description	1001/5 A	1251/5 A	1251/5 A L	1001/6 A	1251/6 A	1251/6 B
					Qty.			
1	0611 113 200	Cover, magneto side (SACHS)	1	1		1	1	1
	•0611 113 204	Cover, magneto side (SACHS)						
	•0677 002 002	Cover ass'y., magneto side (SACHS), with speedometer drive i = 7:12						
	0677 002 000	Cover ass'y., magneto side (SACHS), with speedometer drive i = 7:12 consisting of: illustr. 1...5, 7, 9...11 and spiral pinion 0234 070 111 (12 teeth)	1	1		1	1	1
	0677 002 003	Cover ass'y., magneto side (SACHS), with speedometer drive i = 7:11 consisting of: ill. 1...5, 7, 9...11 and spiral pinion 0234 070 110 (11 teeth) version HERCULES	1	1		1	1	1
	0611 113 202	Cover, magneto side (DKW)	1	1		1	1	1
	•0677 002 001	Cover ass'y., magneto side (DKW)	1	1		1	1	1
	•0611 113 206	Cover ass'y., magneto side (DKW) shortened version	1	1		1	1	1
	•0677 002 105	Cover ass'y., magneto side (DKW) shortened version	1	1		1	1	1
2	0244 082 002	Washer 15.7 x 24.8 x 0.5	1	1		1	1	1
3	0234 071 000	Spiral gear	1	1		1	1	1
4	0246 052 000	Cup	1	1		1	1	1
5	0650 017 000	Sealing ring 13.8 x 19 x 2.5	1	1		1	1	1
6	0949 090 000	Dowel sleeve 8.5 x 10	2	2		2	2	2
7	0644 017 000	Washer 8.8 x 2				1	1	1
8	0234 070 111	Spiral pinion (12 teeth)	1	1		1	1	1
	0234 070 110	Spiral pinion (11 teeth)						
9	0246 047 000	Washer 6 x 9 x 1	1	1		1	1	1
10	0232 151 000	Bush	1	1		1	1	1
11	0241 049 100	Connecting screw M 12 x 1	1	1		1	1	1
	0260 041 000	Cap, rubber	1	1		1	1	1
	0240 095 105	Connecting screw M 12 x 1 (without speedometer drive)	1	1		1	1	1
12	0940 119 102	Screw, fillister head M 6 x 60 with speedometer drive i = 7:12	4	4		4	4	4

Pistons and piston rings

Piston Piston rings	Part Number / Remark	1001/5 A	1251/5 A	1251/5 A L	1001/6 A	1251/6 A	1251/6 B	Part Number / Remark	1001/5 A	1251/5 A	1251/5 A L	1001/6 A	1251/6 A	1251/6 B
	0686 208 005 Piston ass'y. ⌀ 48.0	1						0686 208 015 Piston ass'y. ⌀ 48.0				1		
	0686 208 006 Piston ass'y. ⌀ 48.5	1						0686 208 016 Piston ass'y. ⌀ 48.5				1		
	0686 208 007 Piston ass'y. ⌀ 49.0	1						0686 208 017 Piston ass'y. ⌀ 49.0				1		
	0686 208 008 Piston ass'y. ⌀ 49.5	1						0686 208 018 Piston ass'y. ⌀ 49.5				1		
	0615 102 000 Piston ring, L, ⌀ 48.0	1						•+ 0615 102 105 Piston ring, L, ⌀ 48.0 } 2nd vers.				1		
	0615 102 001 Piston ring, L, ⌀ 48.5	1						+ 0615 102 106 Piston ring, L, ⌀ 48.5				1		
	0615 102 002 Piston ring, L, ⌀ 49.0	1						+ 0615 102 107 Piston ring, L, ⌀ 49.0				1		
	0615 102 003 Piston ring, L, ⌀ 49.5	1						+ 0615 102 108 Piston ring, L, ⌀ 49.5				1		
	0615 104 000 Piston ring, rect., ⌀ 48.0	1						*0615 102 005 Piston ring, L, ⌀ 48.0 } 1st vers.				1		
	0615 104 001 Piston ring, rect., ⌀ 48.5	1						*0615 102 006 Piston ring, L, ⌀ 48.5				1		
	0615 104 002 Piston ring, rect., ⌀ 49.0	1						*0615 102 007 Piston ring, L, ⌀ 49.0				1		
	0615 104 003 Piston ring, rect., ⌀ 49.5	1						*0615 102 008 Piston ring, L, ⌀ 49.5				1		
	for grey cast cylinder							0615 104 005 Piston ring, rect., ⌀ 48.0				1		
	0686 207 005 Piston ass'y. ⌀ 54.0		1	1				0615 104 006 Piston ring, rect., ⌀ 48.5				1		
	0686 207 006 Piston ass'y. ⌀ 54.5		1	1				0615 104 007 Piston ring, rect., ⌀ 49.0				1		
	0686 207 007 Piston ass'y. ⌀ 55.0		1	1				0615 104 008 Piston ring, rect., ⌀ 49.5				1		
	0686 207 008 Piston ass'y. ⌀ 55.5		1	1				**for aluminium cylinder**						
	0615 103 000 Piston ring, L, ⌀ 54.0		1	1				0686 207 025 Piston ass'y. ⌀ 54.0		1			1	1
	0615 103 001 Piston ring, L, ⌀ 54.5		1	1				0686 207 026 Piston ass'y. ⌀ 54.5		1			1	1
	0615 103 002 Piston ring, L, ⌀ 55.0		1	1				0686 207 027 Piston ass'y. ⌀ 55.0		1			1	1
	0615 103 003 Piston ring, L, ⌀ 55.5		1	1				0686 207 028 Piston ass'y. ⌀ 55.5		1			1	1
	0615 101 000 Piston ring, rect., ⌀ 54.0		1	1				0615 103 005 Piston ring, L, ⌀ 54.0		1			1	1
	0615 101 001 Piston ring, rect., ⌀ 54.5		1	1				0615 103 006 Piston ring, L, ⌀ 54.5		1			1	1
	0615 101 002 Piston ring, rect., ⌀ 55.0		1	1				0615 103 007 Piston ring, L, ⌀ 55.0		1			1	1
	0615 101 003 Piston ring, rect., ⌀ 55.5		1	1				0615 103 008 Piston ring, L, ⌀ 55.5		1			1	1
	for grey cast cylinder							0615 101 005 Piston ring, rect., ⌀ 54.0		1			1	1
								0615 101 006 Piston ring, rect., ⌀ 54.5		1			1	1
								0615 101 007 Piston ring, rect., ⌀ 55.0		1			1	1
								0615 101 008 Piston ring, rect., ⌀ 55.5		1			1	1
								for aluminium cylinder						

+ Profile thickness 2.2 mm } not inter-
* Profile thickness 1.9 mm } changeable

Crankcase cover, Clutch

Clutch side crankcase cover, Clutch, Layshaft

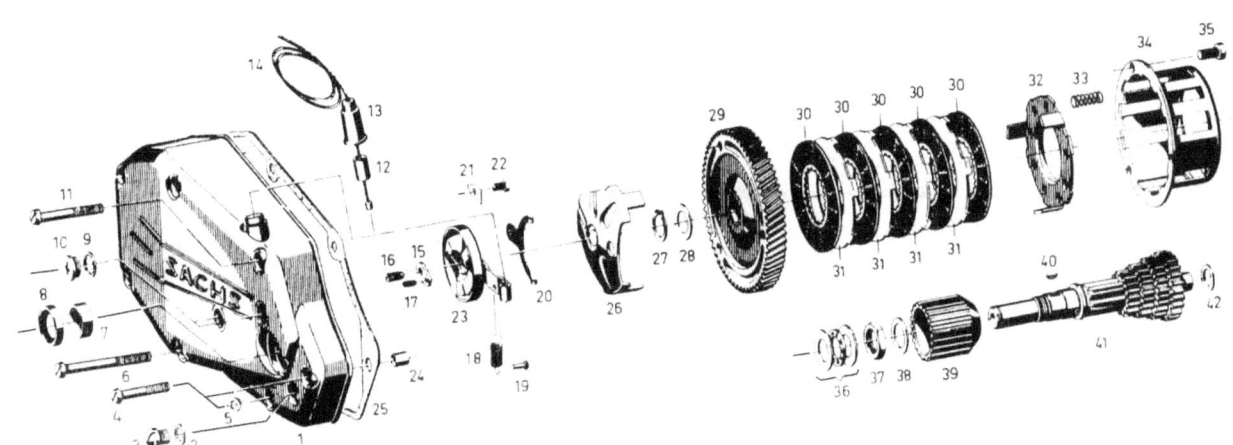

Illustr. No.	Part No.	Description	1001/5 A	1251/5 A	1251/5 A L	1001/6 A	1251/6 A	1251/6 B
			Qty.					
1	0611 114 100	Cover, clutch side (SACHS), up to engine No. 6318 754, to be used together with: 1 x 0658 002 100 clutch case 9 x 0639 106 000 thrust spring 1 x 0684 003 000 cam cup	1	1	1	1	1	1
	0677 001 100	Cover ass'y., clutch side (SACHS) consisting of: illustr. 1, 5, 7...10, 12...23	1	1	1	1	1	1
	•0611 114 104	Cover, clutch side (DKW)	1	1	1	1	1	1
	•0677 001 102	Zsb. Cover ass'y., clutch side (DKW)	1	1	1	1	1	1
2	0230 015 000	Sealing ring 10 x 14 x 1.5	1	1	1	1	1	1
3	0241 053 100	Screw M 10 x 10	1	1	1	1	1	1
4	0241 040 001	Screw, fillister head, M 6 x 38	2	2	2	2	2	2
5	0250 112 100	Sealing ring 6.5 x 11 x 1	1	1	1	1	1	1
6	0640 011 102	Screw, fillister head, M 6 x 65	4	4	4	4	4	4
7	0232 131 000	Bush 20 x 24 x 9	1	1	1	1	1	1
8	0250 128 000	Oil seal 29 x 28 x 4	1	1	1	1	1	1
9	0250 131 000	Sealing ring 14.1 x 17.2 x 0.5	2	2	2	2	2	2
10	0240 140 000	Screw plug M 14 x 1	2	2	2	2	2	2
11	0240 120 002	Screw, fillister head, M 6 x 52	1	1	1	1	1	1
12	0299 141 000	Nipple 14.5 x 15	1	1	1	1	1	1
13	0260 125 000	Cap, protective	1	1	1	1	1	1
14	0291 007 000	Wire with solder nipple	1	1	1	1	1	1
15	0251 107 000	Locking plate with tap M 4 and tap M 6	1	1	1			
	0251 107 001	Locking plate with tap M 4 and tap M 8 x 1				1	1	1
16	0240 043 002	Adjusting screw M 6 x 12	1	1	1			
	0640 107 000	Adjusting screw M 8 x 1 x 13.5				1	1	1
17	0240 139 000	Grub screw M 4 x 6	1	1	1	1	1	1
18	0239 123 000	Spring	1	1	1	1	1	1
19	0949 003 002	Grooved pin 3 x 8	1	1	1	1	1	1
20	0239 126 000	Fork	1	1	1	1	1	1
21	0245 112 000	Locking plate	1	1	1	1	1	1
22	0941 087 000	Screw, hexagon head, M 5 x 10	1	1	1	1	1	1
23	0286 324 200	Cam cup with thread M 6	1	1	1			
	▲ 0286 324 201	Cam cup with thread M 8 x 1				1	1	1
	+ 0684 003 000	Cam cup with thread M 8 x 1				1	1	1
24	0949 090 000	Dowel sleeve 8.5 x 10	2	2	2	2	2	2
25	0650 106 000	Gasket	1	1	1	1	1	1
26	0684 002 000	Thrust plate	1	1	1	1	1	1
27	0245 020 005	Circlip	1	1	1	1	1	1
28	0246 015 000	Shim 16.3 x 25.8	x	x	x	x	x	x
29	0685 100 101	Layshaft wheel with bush 0632 113 000	1	1	1	1	1	1
30	0284 007 000	Inner plate	5	5	5	5	5	5
31	0259 109 000	Outer plate	4	4	4	4	4	4
32	0658 003 000	Thrust plate	1	1	1	1	1	1
33	▲ 0239 015 000	Thrust spring ⌀ 8.5 length 21 mm	9	9	9			
	+ 0639 106 000	Thrust spring ⌀ 9.5 length 22.3 mm	9	9	9	9	9	9
34	▲ 0658 002 000	Clutch case, 39.5 mm high	1	1	1			
	+ 0658 002 100	Clutch case, 41.5 mm high	1	1	1	1	1	1
	+ 0684 001 100	Clutch ass'y., consisting of illustr. 29...35 and 3 x 0316 057 003 nut M 6	1	1	1	1	1	1
35	2740 024 002	Screw, hexagon socket head, M 6 x 16	3	3	3	3	3	3
	0316 057 003	Nut M 6 for illustr. 35	3	3	3	3	3	3
36	0686 209 000	Ball cage with 2 washers	1	1	1	1	1	1
37	0242 106 005	Nut M 18 x 1	1	1	1	1	1	1
38	0644 106 000	Washer 18.3 x 27 x 2	1	1	1	1	1	1
39	0658 001 000	Clutch hub	1	1	1	1	1	1
40	0246 005 000	Key 3 x 3.7	1	1	1	1	1	1
41	0685 101 100	Layshaft	1	1	1			
	0685 101 001	Layshaft				1	1	1
	•0685 101 102	Layshaft						
42	0244 102 000	Shim 12.1 x 18.5	x	x	x	x	x	x

▲ = up to engine No. 6318 754
+ = from engine No. 6318 755 up

x = as needed

Carburetor

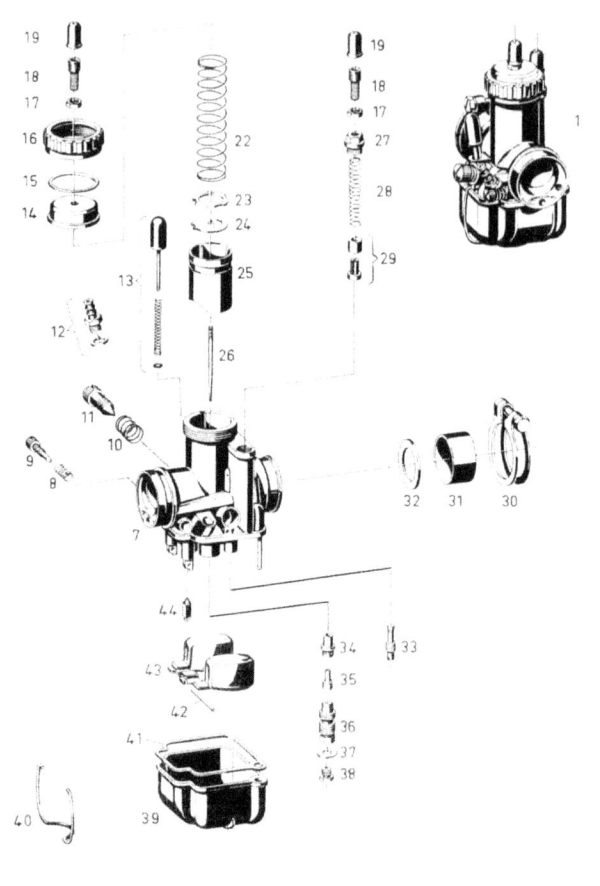

Illustr. No.	Part No.	Description	1001/5 A	1251/5 A	1251/5 B	1001/6 A	1251/6 A	1251/6 B
			Qty.					
1	see table	Carburettor ass'y						
7		Carburettor body available only as ill. 1 carburettor ass'y.						
8	0961 067 000	Spring	1	1	1	1	1	1
9	0640 105 000	Air adjusting screw	1	1	1	1	1	1
10	0639 103 000	Spring	1	1	1	1	1	1
11	0640 106 000	Adjusting screw	1	1	1	1	1	1
12	0986 432 000	Hose fitting ass'y	1	1	1	1	1	1
13	0661 110 000	Priming device	1	1	1	1	1	1
14	0661 119 000	Cover plate	1	1	1	1	1	1
15	0650 111 000	Sealing ring	1	1	1	1	1	1
16	0642 106 000	Cover, to be screwed	1	1	1	1	1	1
17	0961 018 001	Nut	2	2	2	2	2	2
18	0961 081 000	Adjusting screw	2	2	2	2	2	2
19	0260 024 001	Cap, rubber	2	2	2	2	2	2
20	0291 004 000	Wire with solder nipple 0291 003 000 for starter and throttles control — quote required length	2	2	2	2	2	2
21	0299 042 000	Outer casing, black	2	2	2	2	2	2
	0299 042 010	Outer casing, silver colour						
22	0639 105 000	Spring	1	1	1	1	1	1
23	0644 111 000	Washer	1	1	1	1	1	1
24	0661 113 000	Retaining plate	1	1	1	1	1	1
	•0639 107 000	Spring for carb 1/24/170, 1/27/19, 1/27/22		1				1
25	0661 120 000	Throttle slide for carb 1/24/153, 1/24/158, 1/24/161, 1/24/166, 1/26/115, 1/26/117, 1/26/120, 1/26/127, 1/27/16 and 1/27/17	1	1		1	1	
	•0661 120 001	Throttle slide for carb 1/24/170, 1/27/19, 1/27/20 and 1/27/22		1				1
	•0661 127 000	Throttle slide for carb 2/26/66, 2/67	1					
26	0661 114 000	Jet needle for carb 1/24/153, 1/24/158, 1/24/161, 1/24/166, 1/26/115, 1/26/117, 1/26/120, 1/26/127, 1/27/16 and 1/27/17	1	1		1	1	
	0661 114 001	Jet needle for carburettor 1/24/170		1				
	0661 114 002	Jet needle for carburettor 1/27/19, 1/27/20 and 1/27/22		1				1
27	0661 007 000	Plug	1	1	1	1	1	1
28	0661 005 000	Spring	1	1	1	1	1	1
29	0686 100 000	Starter slide with sleeve	1	1	1	1	1	1
30	0651 102 000	Clamping ring	1	1	1	1	1	1
31	0647 102 000	Insulating bush for carb 1/24/153, 1/24/158, 1/24/161, 1/24/166, 1/24/170, 1/26/117, 1/26/127 and 1/27/16	1	1		1	1	
	0947 125 000	Insulating bush for carb 1/26/115, 1/26/120, 1/27/17, 1/27/19, 1/27/20 and 1/27/22	1	1				1
32	0644 110 000	Insulating washer for carb 1/24/153, 1/24/158, 1/24/161, 1/24/166, 1/24/170		1				
	0644 110 001	Insulating washer for carb 1/26/115, 1/26/117, 1/26/120, 1/26/127, 1/27/16 and 1/27/19	1	1		1	1	
	0644 110 002	Insulating washer for carb 1/27/17, 1/27/17, 1/27/20, 1/27/22						
33	0661 118 000	Idle jet, quote required size	1	1	1	1	1	1
34	0661 115 000	Vaporizer for carburettor 1/24/153, 1/24/158, 1/24/161, 1/24/166, 1/24/170, 1/26/115, 1/26/117, 1/26/120, 1/26/127, 1/27/16, 1/27/17	1	1		1	1	
	•0661 115 001	Vaporizer for carburettor 1/27/19, 1/27/20 and 1/27/22		1				1
35	0661 116 000	Needle jet 2.73	1	1		1	1	1
	0661 116 001	Needle jet 2.76				1		1
	•0661 116 002	Needle jet 2.70						1
36	0661 117 000	Mixing tube	1	1	1	1	1	1
37	0962 083 000	Washer	1	1	1	1	1	1
	•0661 126 000	Strainer for carburettor 1/27/19, 1/27/20 and 1/27/22 for illustr. 38		1				1
38	0961 106 000	Main jet, quote required size	1	1	1	1	1	1
39	0661 122 000	Float chamber for carb 1/24/153, 1/24/158, 1/24/161, 1/24/166, 1/24/170, 1/26/115, 1/26/117, 1/26/120, 1/26/127, 1/27/16 and 1/27/17	1	1		1	1	
	•0661 122 001	Float chamber for carburettor 1/27/19, 1/27/20 and 1/27/22		1				1
	•0661 122 002	Float chamber for carburettor 2/26/66, 2/26/67	1					
40	0639 104 000	Stirrup	1	1	1	1	1	1
41	0650 110 000	Gasket	1	1	1	1	1	1
42	0649 103 000	Pin for float	1	1	1	1	1	1
43	0661 121 000	Float	1	1	1	1	1	1
44	0661 112 000	Float needle	1	1	1	1	1	1

Part No.	BING Ref.	Needle position	Needle jet	Main jet	Idle jet	Idle air adjustment screw: turns open	Mixing tube	Remarks	1001/5 A	1251/5 A	1251/5 A L B	1001/6 A	1251/6 A	1251/6 B
0681 005 001	1/26/115	III	2.73	105	40	½ ... 1	45-420	* with 2 contr. wires	1			1		
0681 005 109	1/26/127	II	2.76	140	45	1½	45-420	* with 2 contr. wires * for aluminium cylinder		1				1
•0681 005 113	1/27/17	III	2.76	140	45	1	45-420	* with 2 contr. wires		1			1	
•0681 005 115	1/27/20	II	2.70	140	45	1	45-420	* with 2 contr. wires		1				1

Ignition

Magneto-generator (BOSCH)

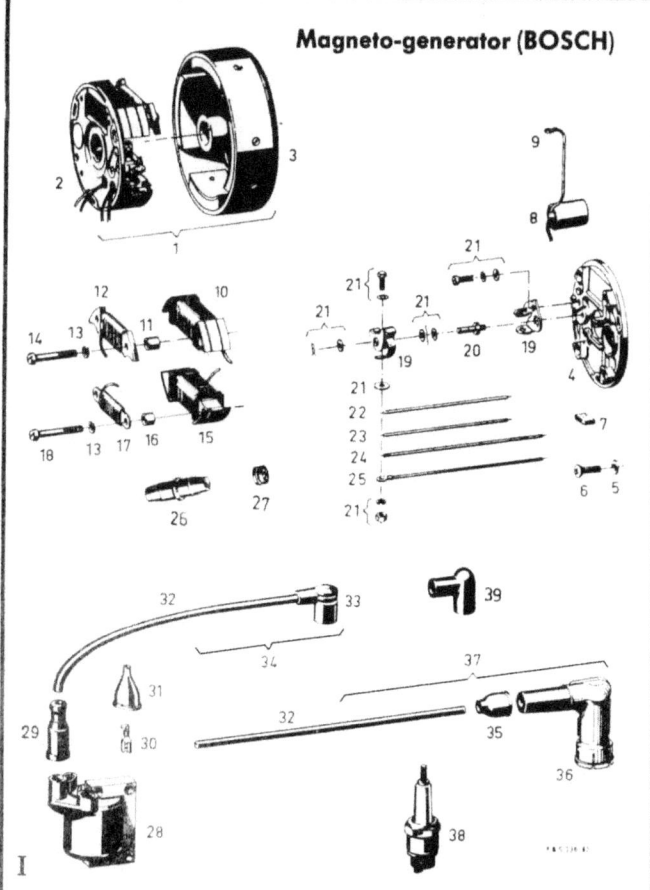

Magneto-generator (MOTOPLAT)

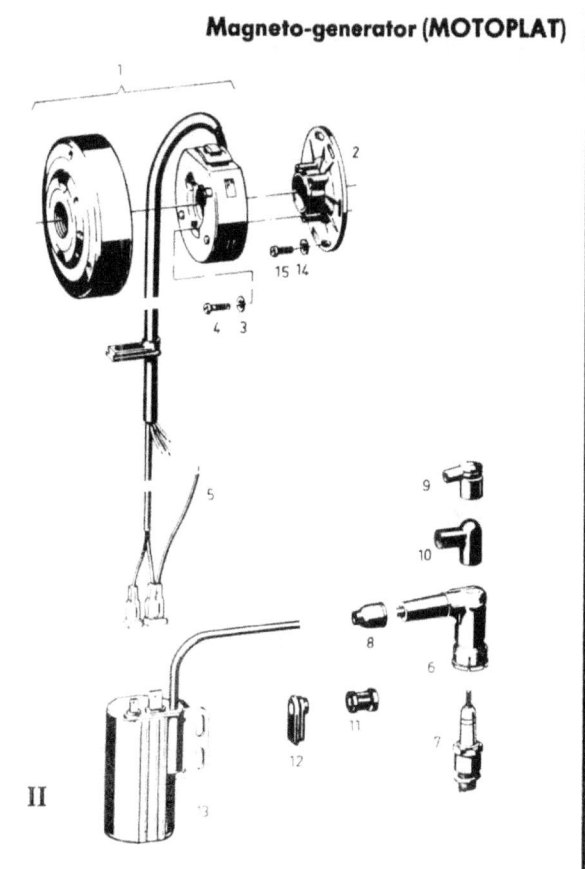

Illustr. No.	Part No.	Description	100W/5 A	125W/5 A	125W/5 A L	100W/6 A	125W/6 A	125W/6 B
			Qty.					
I		**Magneto – generator (BOSCH)**						
1	0283 100 402	Magneto-generator ass'y. 6 Volt 35-5/18 Watt (BOSCH: 0212 124 014)	1	1		1	1	
	0283 100 403	Magneto-generator ass'y. 6 Volt 35-5/18 Watt (BOSCH: MZ 9/94 H 33)			1			
2	0283 105 017	Armature base plate ass'y.	1	1	1	1	1	
3	0283 108 018	Flywheel for 0283 100 402	1	1		1	1	
	0283 108 021	Flywheel with 2 tapped holes M 6			1			
	0283 108 023	Flywheel with welded hub (BOSCH: 1215 254 402/S) version KTM						
4	0265 140 009	Armature base plate	1	1	1	1	1	
5	0244 108 000	Washer 4.1 x 9 x 1.2	3	3	3	3	3	
6	0240 106 100	Screw M 4 x 14	3	3	3	3	3	
7	2865 008 000	Lubrication felt	1	1	1	1	1	
8	0965 091 000	Condenser	1	1	1	1	1	
9	0265 077 001	Cable	1	1	1	1	1	
10	0265 139 012	Ignition armature	1	1	1	1	1	
11	0247 106 002	Bush 4.2 x 8 x 8	2	2	2	2	2	
12	0265 139 014	Stop light armature	1	1	1	1	1	
13	0245 023 000	Spring washer for M 4	4	4	4	4	4	
14	0240 122 002	Screw, fillister head, M 4 x 30	2	2	2	2	2	
15	0265 141 004	Generating armature	1	1	1	1	1	
16	0247 106 001	Bush 4.2 x 8 x 2	2	2	2	2	2	
17	0265 139 013	Taillight armature	1	1	1	1	1	
18	0240 153 000	Screw, fillister head, M 4 x 32	2	2	2	2	2	
19	0283 101 100	Contact breaker set	1	1	1	1	1	
20	0240 066 009	Pivot pin	1	1	1	1	1	
21	0283 107 000	Set of spares for contact breaker	1	1	1	1	1	
22	0299 059 009	Lighting cable	1	1	1	1	1	
23	0299 059 016	Taillight cable } quote	1	1	1	1	1	
24	0299 059 026	Stop light cable } required length	1	1	1	1	1	
25	0265 137 002	Generating cable	1	1	1	1	1	
26	0265 073 000	Cable terminal	2	2	2	2	2	
27	0665 119 000	Rubber grommet	1	1	1	1	1	
28	0283 109 000	Ignition coil	1	1	1	1	1	
29	0265 150 000	Cap, protective	1	1	1	1	1	

Illustr. No.	Part No.	Description	100W/5 A	125W/5 A	125W/5 A L	100W/6 A	125W/6 A	125W/6 B
			Qty.					
30	0265 152 000	Cable terminal	2	2	2	2	2	
31	0265 151 000	Cap, protective	2	2	2	2	2	
32	0665 016 101	Ignition cable ⌀ 7	1	1	1	1	1	
33	0288 091 000	Spark plug cap, not suppressed			1			
34	0283 110 006	Ignition cable ass'y.			1			
35	0265 109 000	Cap, protective	1	1		1	1	
36	0265 100 002	Spark plug cap, partly suppressed	1	1		1	1	
37	0283 110 005	Ignition cable ass'y.	1	1		1	1	
38	0298 087 011	Spark plug W 260 T 1	1	1		1	1	
	0298 087 009	Spark plug W 225 T 1			1			
	0665 120 001	Spark plug W 290 T 16 for CROSS-COUNTRY	1	1				
39	1465 011 001	Spark plug connector (rubber), not suppressed	1	1				
	0283 110 002	Ignition cable ass'y., including illustr. 39	1	1		1	1	
II		**Magneto – generator (MOTOPLAT)**						
1	0683 006 103	Magneto-generator ass'y. 6 Volt 35-5/18 Watt (MOTOPLAT: 9600 160)	1	1		1	1	1
2	0265 163 000	Base plate						
3	0644 031 000	Washer 4.3 x 8 x 0.5	3	3		3	3	3
4	2840 002 001	Screw, fillister head, M 4 x 20	3	3		3	3	3
5	0965 108 001	Short-circuit cable	1	1		1	1	1
6	0265 100 002	Spark plug cap, partly suppressed	1	1		1	1	1
7	0298 087 011	Spark plug W 260 T 1	1	1		1	1	1
	0665 120 001	Spark plug W 290 T 16 for CROSS-CONTRY	1	1				
8	2765 013 000	Cap, protective	1	1		1	1	1
9	0288 091 000	Spark plug connector (plastics), not suppressed	1	1		1	1	1
10	1465 011 001	Spark plug connector (rubber), not suppressed	1	1		1	1	1
11	0665 119 001	Rubber grommet	1	1		1	1	1
12	0665 124 000	Rubber grommet	1	1		1	1	1
13	0283 124 000	Ignition coil with cable	1	1		1	1	1
14	0244 108 000	Washer 4.1 x 9 x 1.2	3	3		3	3	3
15	0241 028 001	Screw, fillister head, M 4 x 12	3	3		3	3	3

Serial Number Identification

Serial numbers of engines for crankcases

0687 107 101 Crankcase ass'y.
for units with BOSCH magneto ignition, grey-cast cylinder, up to engine No. 5692 842 for SACHS 1001/5 A   6318 754 for SACHS 1251/5 A and 1251/5 AL

0687 107 401 Crankcase ass'y.
for units with BOSCH magneto ignition, grey-cast cylinder, reinforced front mounting eye, to be used in conjunction with 1ea. 1949 011 000 dowel sleeve 12 x 22 mm from engine No. 5692 843 for SACHS 1001/5 A 6318 755 for SACHS 1251/5 A and 1251/5 AL

0687 107 205 Crankcase ass'y.
for units with BOSCH magneto ignition and aluminium cylinder up to engine No. 5692 842 for SACHS 1001/5 A   6318 754 for SACHS 1251/5 A

0687 107 405 Crankcase ass'y.
for units with BOSCH magneto ignition and aluminium cylinder, to be used in conjunction with 1ea. 1949 011 000 dowel sleeve 12 x 22 mm from engine No. 5692 843 for SACHS 1001/5 A   5693 001 for SACHS 1001/6 A 6318 755 for SACHS 1251/5 A   6320 501 for SACHS 1251/6 A

0687 107 505 Crankcase ass'y.
for units with MOTOPLAT ignition systems and aluminium cylinders, to be used in conjunction with 1ea. 0665 124 000 rubber boot for SACHS 1001/5 A for SACHS 1251/5 A

0687 107 407 Crankcase ass'y.
for units with BOSCH magneto ignition and aluminium cylinder, to be used in conjunction with 1ea. 1949 011 000 dowel sleeve 12 x 22 mm from engine No. 6319 316 for SACHS 1251/5 B

0687 107 409 Crankcase ass'y.
for units with BOSCH magneto ignition and aluminium cylinder, to be used in conjunction with 1ea. 1949 011 000 dowel sleeve 12 x 22 mm for SACHS 1251/6 A (NHW – USA)

0687 107 509 Crankcase ass'y.
for units with MOTOPLAT ignition systems and aluminium cylinders, to be used in conjunction with 1ea. 0665 124 000 rubber boot from engine No. 9033 893 for SACHS 1251/6 B   (NHW – USA)

Engine plates

Description of engine plate	Engine model	Description of engine plate	Engine model
FICHTEL & SACHS AG SCHWEINFURT 97 TYP SACHS 1001/5A 316	SACHS 1001/5 A	FICHTEL & SACHS AG SCHWEINFURT 122 TYP SACHS 1251/5A Typz 10412 320	SACHS 1251/5 A
FICHTEL & SACHS AG SCHWEINFURT 97 TYP SACHS 1001/5A Typz 10413 317	SACHS 1001/5 A	FICHTEL & SACHS AG SCHWEINFURT 122 TYP SACHS 1251/5AL 9PS 321	SACHS 1251/5 A L
FICHTEL & SACHS AG SCHWEINFURT 97 TYP SACHS 1001/5A 10PS 318	SACHS 1001/5 A	FICHTEL & SACHS AG SCHWEINFURT TYP SACHS 1251/5AL 9PS	SACHS 1251/5 A L
FICHTEL & SACHS AG SCHWEINFURT 97 TYP SACHS 1001/6A 438	SACHS 1001/6 A	FICHTEL & SACHS AG SCHWEINFURT 122 TYP SACHS 1251/6A 439	SACHS 1251/6 A
FICHTEL & SACHS AG SCHWEINFURT 122 TYP SACHS 1251/5A 319	SACHS 1251/5 A	FICHTEL & SACHS AG SCHWEINFURT 122 TYP SACHS 1251/6B 493	SACHS 1251/6 B

Table for cylinder heads and cylinders

Cylinder head / Cylinder	Part Number / Description	1001/5 A	1251/5 A	1251/5 A L	1001/6 A	1251/6 A	1251/6 B	Cylinder head / Cylinder	Part Number / Description	1001/5 A	1251/5 A	1251/5 A L	1001/6 A	1251/6 A	1251/6 B
315	0613 109 000 Cylinder head 0687 109 000 Cylinder ass'y. (grey-cast) bore 48 mm dia. with 2 studs 1940 101 101 M 8 x 30	1 1						315	0613 109 002 Cylinder head 0687 109 000 Cylinder ass'y. (grey-cast) bore 48 mm dia. with 2 studs 1940 101 101 M 8 x 30 Version: CROSS-COUNTRY	1 1					
315	0613 106 000 Cylinder head 0687 108 000 Cylinder ass'y. (grey-cast) bore 54 mm dia. with 2 studs 1940 101 101 M 8 x 30		1 1					503	0613 106 102 Cylinder head 0687 108 000 Cylinder ass'y. (grey-cast) bore 54 mm dia. with 2 studs 1940 101 101 M 8 x 30 Version: CROSS-COUNTRY		1 1				
314	0613 109 005 Cylinder head 0687 109 015 Cylinder ass'y. (aluminium) bore 48 mm dia. with 2 studs 0640 109 001 M 8 x 30 Version: PENTON 0.613.111.000 Cylinder liner for 100cc Penton	1 1		1 1				314	*0613 106 006 Cylinder head 0687 108 225 Cylinder ass'y. (aluminium) bore 54 mm dia. with 2 studs 0640 109 001 M 8 x 30 Version: PENTON 0.613.110.200 Cylinder liner for 125cc Penton					1 1 1	1 1
314	0613 109 004 Cylinder head 0687 109 017 Cylinder ass'y. (aluminium) bore 48 mm dia. with 2 studs 0640 109 001 M 8 x 30 Vers. for damping rubber 0960 000 100 (24 off) Version: Fed. Rep. of Germany	1 1			1 1			314	0613 106 004 Cylinder head 0687 108 227 Cylinder ass'y. (aluminium) bore 54 mm dia. with 2 studs 0640 109 001 M 8 x 30 Vers. for damping rubber 0960 000 100 (24 off) Version: Fed. Rep. of Germany		1 1			1 1	
440	0613 109 004 Cylinder head 0687 109 030 Cylinder ass'y. (aluminium) bore 48 mm with 2 studs 0640 109 001 M 8 x 30 Version: USA Mark: the lower 3 fins are shorter	1 1						440	0613 106 004 Cylinder head 0687 108 250 Cylinder ass'y. (aluminium) bore 54 mm dia. with 2 studs 0640.109 001 M 8 x 30 Version: USA Mark: the lower 3 fins are shorter		1 1			1 1	1 1

Dimensions of Washers

Part-No.	Size	Part-No.	Size	Part-No.	Size	Part-No.	Size
0244 055 000	14.5 × 24 × 0.2	0244 118 000	20.2 × 32 × 1.0	0644 104 000	35.2 × 44 × 0.3	0944 003 000	8.4 × 14 × 0.3
0244 055 001	14.5 × 24 × 0.5	0244 118 001	20.2 × 32 × 0.8	0644 104 001	35.2 × 44 × 0.5	0944 003 001	8.4 × 14 × 0.5
0244 055 002	14.5 × 24 × 1.0	0244 118 002	20.2 × 32 × 0.5	0644 104 002	35.2 × 44 × 0.6	0944 003 002	8.4 × 14 × 0.6
0244 055 003	14.5 × 24 × 0.3	0244 118 003	20.2 × 32 × 0.3	0644 104 003	35.2 × 44 × 0.8	0944 003 003	8.4 × 14 × 1.0
		0244 118 004	20.2 × 32 × 0.15	0644 104 004	35.2 × 44 × 1.0	0944 003 004	8.4 × 14 × 0.4
0244 100 000	6.2 × 10 × 0.2						
0244 100 001	6.2 × 10 × 0.3	0246 015 000	16.3 × 25.8 × 0.3	0644 105 000	25.2 × 39 × 0.2	0944 046 000	20.5 × 28.5 × 0.2
0244 100 002	6.2 × 10 × 0.5	0246 015 001	16.3 × 25.8 × 0.5	0644 105 001	25.2 × 39 × 0.3	0944 046 001	20.5 × 28.5 × 0.3
0244 100 003	6.2 × 10 × 1.0	0246 015 002	16.3 × 25.8 × 1.0	0644 105 002	25.2 × 39 × 0.5	0944 046 002	20.5 × 28.5 × 0.5
		0246 015 003	16.3 × 25.8 × 0.15	0644 105 003	25.2 × 39 × 0.8	0944 046 003	20.5 × 28.5 × 0.4
0244 102 000	12.1 × 18.5 × 0.2			0644 105 004	25.2 × 39 × 1.0	0944 046 004	20.5 × 28.5 × 0.8
0244 102 001	12.1 × 18.5 × 0.5					0944 046 005	20.5 × 28.5 × 0.15
0244 102 102	12.1 × 18.5 × 1.0					0944 046 006	20.5 × 28.5 × 1.0
0244 102 003	12.1 × 18.5 × 1.5						

NOTES

CHAPTER ELEVEN

ILUSTRATED PARTS LISTS

PENTON - KTM

FRAME & COMPONENTS PARTS LIST (1968-1969)

Fork Assembly

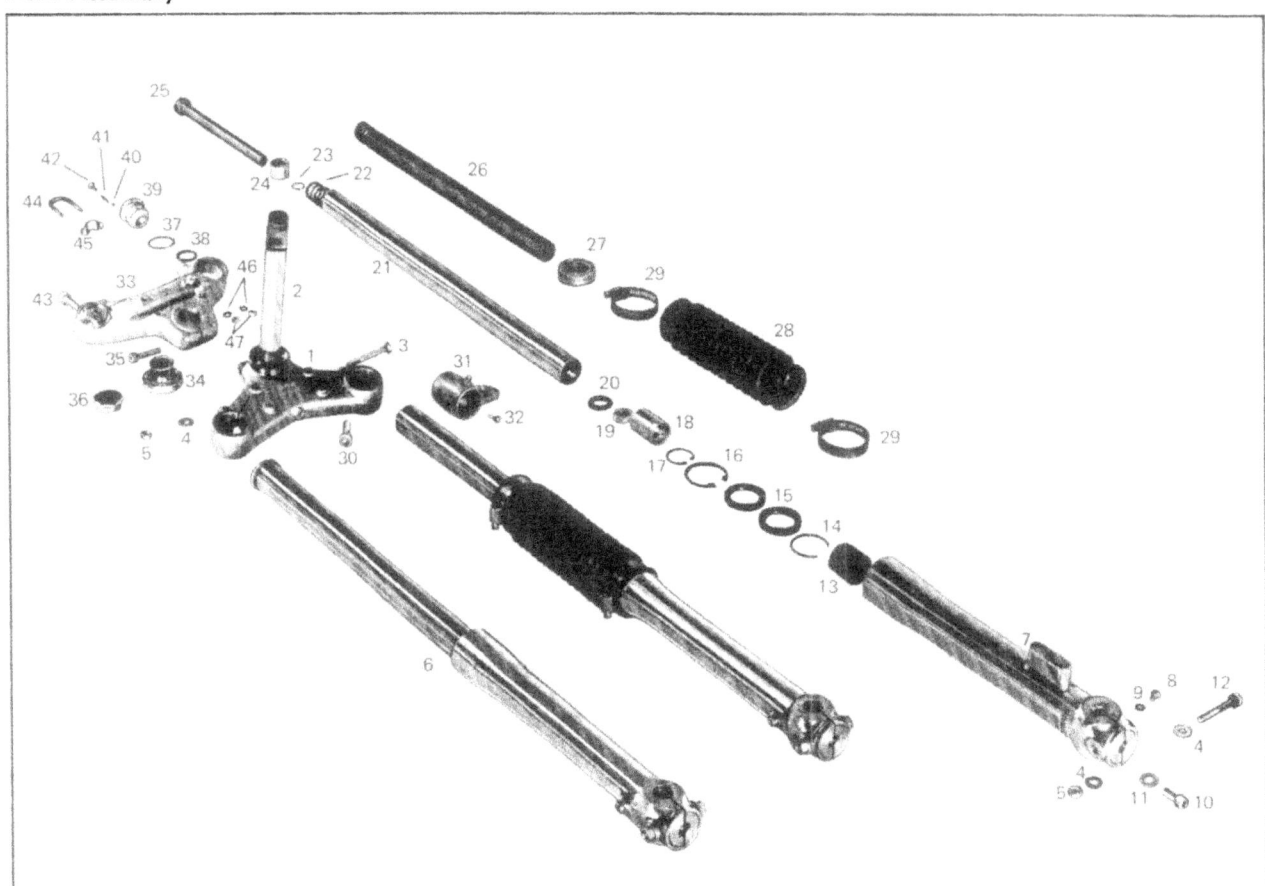

FIG. NO.	PART NO.	DESCRIPTION	100 Pieces	125 Pieces	FIG. NO.	PART NO.	DESCRIPTION	100 Pieces	125 Pieces
1	1-1.000	Fork stem	1	1	24	1-24.000	Bushing	2	2
2	Not Sold	Not available (sold only as unit item 1)	–	–	25	1-25.000	Stop valve	2	2
3	HH8x65	Pinch bolt - size [HH8x65]	1	1	26	1-26.000	Fork spring - long	2	2
4	FW8x20	Flat washer - size [FW8x20]	5	5	27	1-27.000	Boot collar	2	2
5	HH8	Nut - size [HH8-13]	3	3	28	1-28.000	Fork boot - rubber	2	2
6	1-6.000	Fork tube assm. - left side	1	1	29	1-29.000	Boot clamp	4	4
	1-6.001	Fork tube assm. - right side	1	1	30	AH10x30	Screw - allen head [AH10x30]	2	2
7	1-7.000	Fork leg - left side	1	1	31	1-31.000	Bracket - number plate - headlight	2	2
	1-7.001	Fork leg - right side	1	1	32	AH5x15	Screw - allen head [AH5x15]	4	4
8	1-8.000	Drain plug	2	2	33	1-33.000	Plate - top fork	1	1
9	1-9.000	Washer - drain plug	2	2	34	1-34.000	Nut - bearing	1	1
10	AH8x20	Screw - allen head [AH8x20]	2	2	35	AH8x35	Screw - allen head [AH8x35]	1	1
11	1-11.000	Washer - [special]	2	2	36	1-36.000	Nut - top fork plate	1	1
12	HH8x60	Bolt - size [HH8x60] axle security	2	2	37	1-37.000	Washer - [special]	2	2
13	1-13.000	Bushing - lower	2	2	38	1-38.000	"O" ring	2	2
14	1-14.000	Snap ring	2	2	39	1-39.000	Nut - fork tube	2	2
15	1-15.000	Seal	4	4	40	R.B.6	Ball - size [RB6]	2	2
16	1-16.000	Circlip - size [special]	2	2	41	1-41.000	Spring	2	2
17	1-17.000	Circlip - size [special]	2	2	42	TH6x6	Screw [TH6x6]	2	2
18	1-18.000	Bushing - upper	2	2	43	AH10x30	Bolt - allen head [AH10x30]	2	2
19	1-19.000	Valve bushing	2	2	44	2-4.000	Clamp - handlebar	2	2
20	1-20.000	Seal	2	2	45	2-3.000	Saddle - handlebar	2	2
21	1-21.000	Fork tube	2	2	46	FW6x10	Washer - [FW6x10]	4	4
22	1-22.000	Fork spring - short	2	2	47	HH6	Nut - size [HH6-10]	4	4
23	1-23.000	Circlip - size [special]	2	2					

Fork assembly, Headlight, Controls

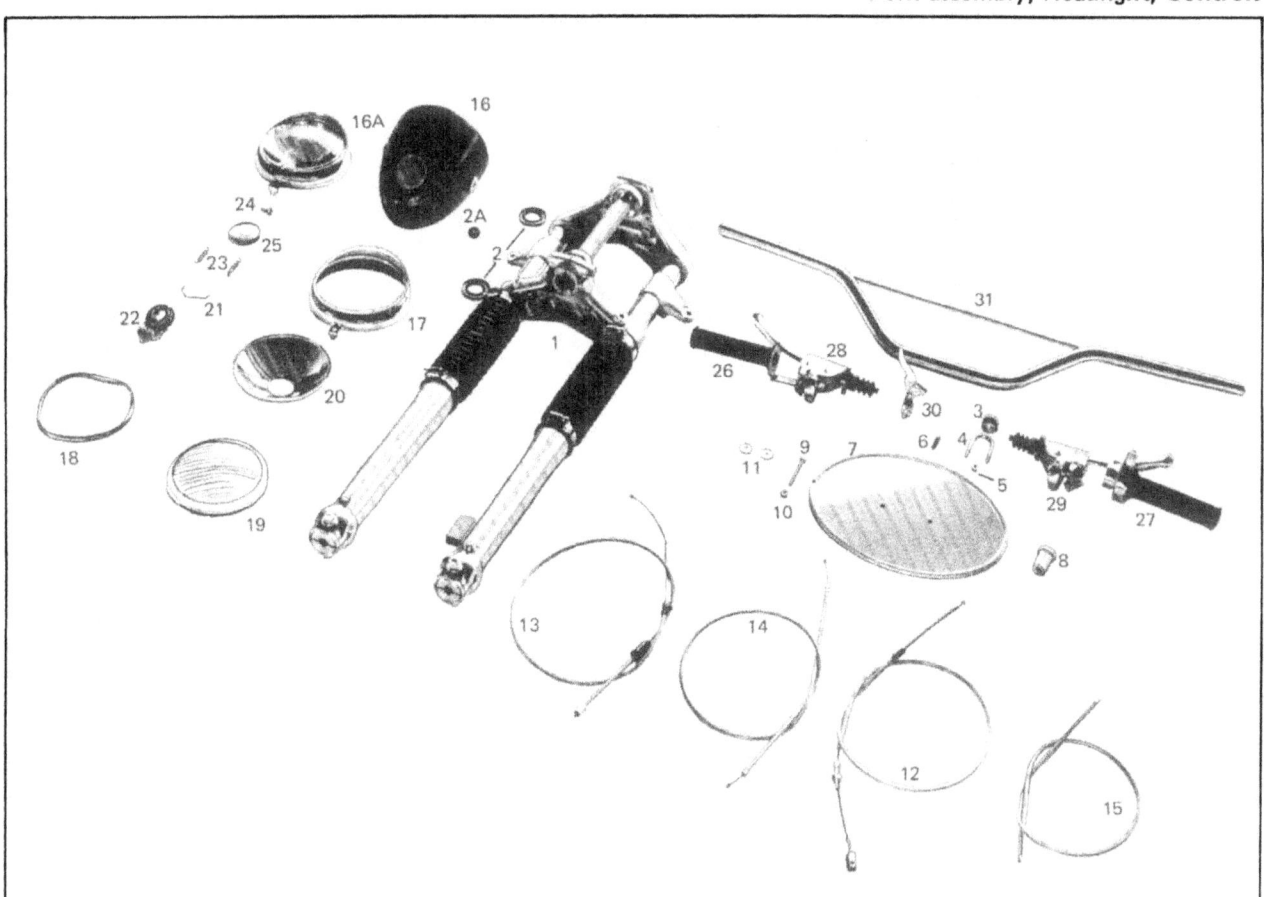

FIG. NO.	PART NO.	DESCRIPTION	100	125
			Pieces	
1	2-1.000	Fork assm complete	1	1
2	2-2.000	Bearing race - top & bottom	2	2
2A	2-2.000A	Ball - size [RB8]	34	34
3	2-3.000	Saddle - handlebar	2	2
4	2-4.000	Clamp - handlebar	2	2
5	HH6	Nut - size [HH6-10]	4	4
6	2-6.000	Split pin - handlebar	1	1
7	2-7.000	Number plate	3	3
8	2-8.000	Spacer - number plate	2	2
9	FH6x50	Screw - size [FH6x50]	2	2
10	1-47.000	Nut [HH6-10]	2	2
11	FW6x20	Washer [FW6x20]	2	2
12	2-12.000	Cable - front brake	1	1
13	2-13.000	Cable - clutch	1	1
14	2-14.000	Cable - throttle	1	1
15	2-15.000	Cable - choke	1	1
16	2-16.000	Headlight shell [green]		1
	2-16.001	Headlight shell [red]	1	
16A	2-16.000A	Headlight unit compl. [green]		1
	2-16.001A	Headlight unit compl. [red]	1	
17	2-17.000	Headlight rim [chrome]	1	1
18	2-18.000	Seal gasket - headlight	1	1
19	2-19.000	Lens - headlight	1	1
20	2-20.000	Reflector	1	1
21	2-21.000	Spring clip	4	4
22	2-22.000	Bulb holder	1	1
23	2-23.000	Spring	2	2
24	FH6x20	Screw [FH6x20]	1	1
25	2-25.000	Plug - rubber	1	1
26	2-26.000	Grip - L/S	1	1
27	2-27.000	Twist grip assm. R/S	1	1
28	2-28.000	Lever holder assm. L/S	1	1
29	2-29.000	Lever holder assm. R/S	1	1
30	2-30.000	Lever assm. - choke	1	1
31	2-31.000	Handlebar	1	1

Controls

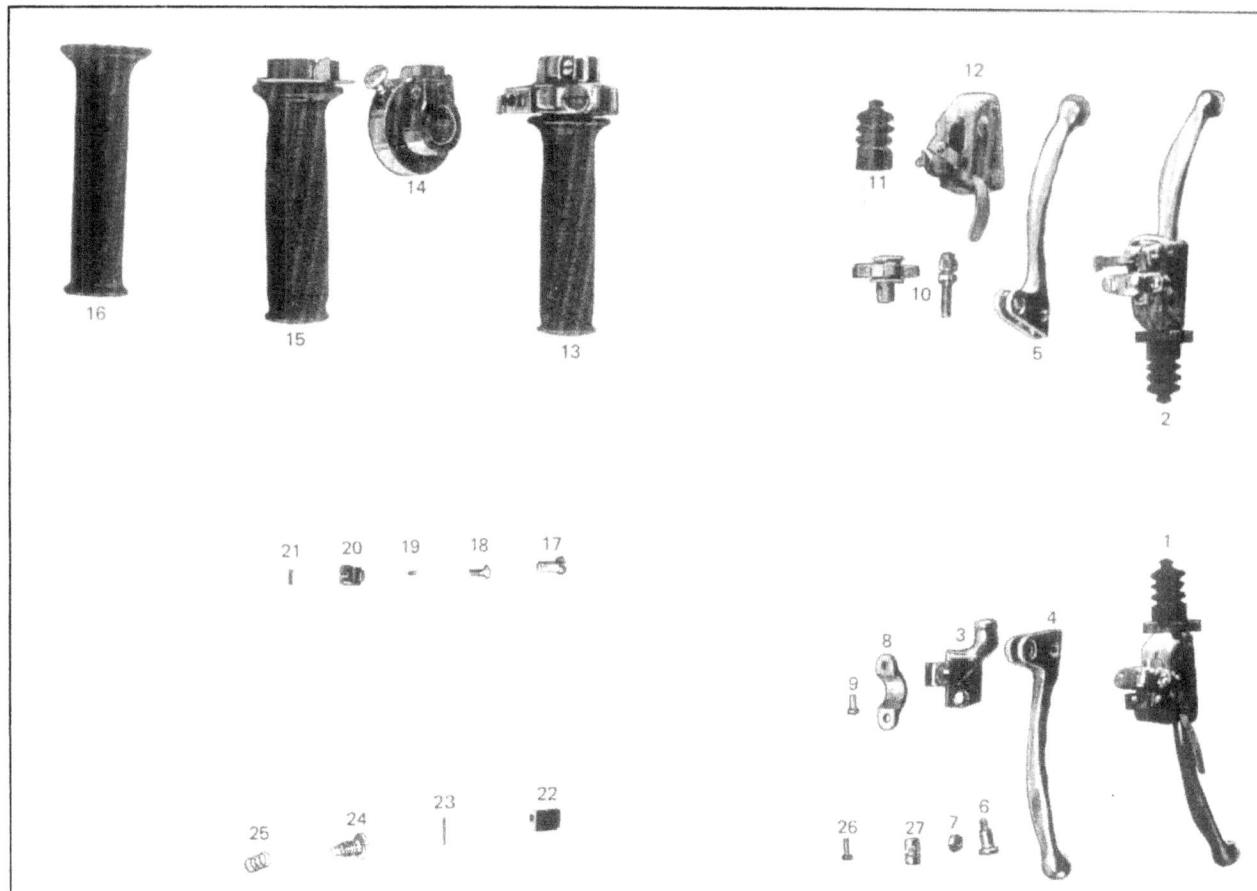

FIG. NO.	PART NO.	DESCRIPTION	100	125
			Pieces	
1	2-29.000	Lever assm. complete R/S	1	1
2	2-28.000	Lever assm. complete L/S	1	1
3	3.3.000	Lever holder	2	2
4	3-4.000	Lever - front brake	1	1
5	3-5.000	Lever - clutch	1	1
6	3-6.000	Pivot pin - levers	2	2
7	HH6	Nut - size (HH6-10)	2	2
8	3-8.000	Lever holder saddle	2	2
9	FH5x9	Screw (FH5x9)	4	4
10	3-10.000	Adjuster cable	2	2
11	3-11.000	Boot - cable cover	2	2
12	3-12.000	Cover - lever holder	2	2
13	2-27.000	Twist grip assm. compl.	1	1
14	3-14.000	Drum - twist grip	1	1
15	3-15.000	Twist grip tube	1	1
16	2-26.000	Rubber - twist grip L/S	1	1
17	FH6x15	Screw - (FH6x15)	1	1
18	TH3x12	Screw - (TH3x12)	1	1
19	3-19.000	Pin	1	1
20	3-20.000	Yoke cable	1	1
21	3-21.000	Pin	1	1
22	3-22.000	Cover	1	1
23	3-23.000	Pin - cover hinge	1	1
24	3-24.000	Screw - throttle tension	1	1
25	3-25.000	Spring	1	1
26	3-26.000	Cable end	2	2
27	3-27.000	Cable Saddle	2	2

Frame assembly

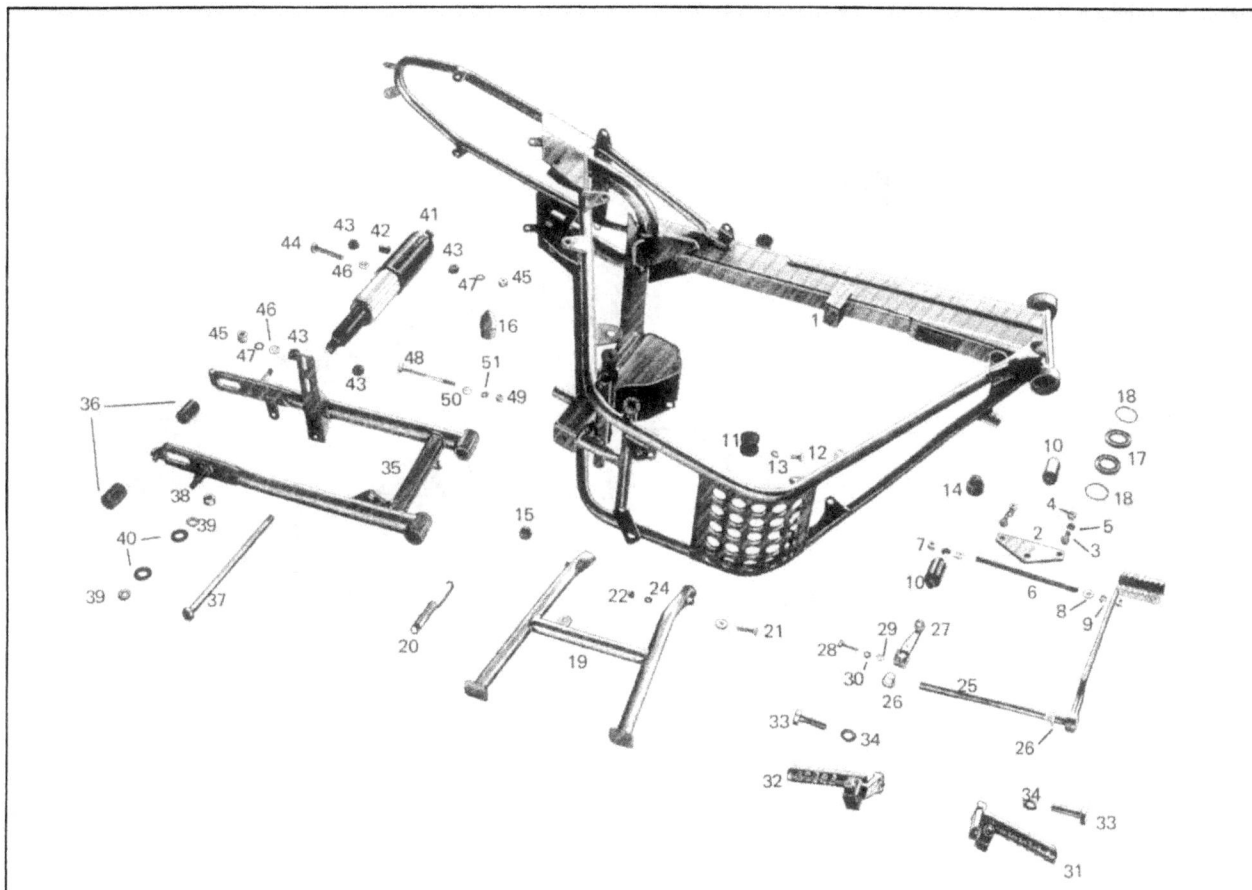

FIG. NO	PART NO.	DESCRIPTION	100 Pieces	125 Pieces	FIG. NO.	PART NO.	DESCRIPTION	100 Pieces	125 Pieces
1	4-1.000	Frame - complete	1	1	26	4-26.000	Bushing - nylon	2	2
					27	4-27.000	Arm - rear brake-front actuating	1	1
2	4-2.000	Plate - front eng. mt.	2	2	28	HH6x25	Bolt - size [HH6x25]	1	1
3	4-3.000	Bolt - size [HH8x15]	4	4	29	FW6x12	Washer [FW6x12]	1	1
4	HH8	Nut - size [HH8-13]	4	4	30	LW6	Lock washer [FW6]	1	1
5	LW8	Lock washer [LW8]	4	4	31	4-31.000	Foot rest Assm R/S	1	1
6	4-6.000	Bolt - front eng. mt.	1	1	32	4-32.000	Foot rest Assm L/S	1	1
7	HH8	Nut - size [HH8-13]	2	2	33	HH12x40	Bolt - size [HH12x40]	2	2
8	FW8x18	Washer - [FW8x18]	2	2	34	LW12	Lock washer [LW12]	2	2
9	LW8	Lock washer [LW8]	2	2	35	4-35.000	Swing arm section	1	1
10	4-10.000	Tank mount bushing	2	2	36	4-36.000	Bushing - swing arm	2	2
11	4-11.000	Bushing - rubber	1	1	37	4-37.000	Bolt - swing arm pivot	1	1
12	HH8x15	Bolt - size [HH8x15]	1	1	38	HH12SL	Nut - size [HH12-17]	1	1
13	LW8	Washer - locking [LW8]	1	1	39	FW12x20	Washer [FW12x20]	2	2
14	4-14.000	Bumper - fork stop	2	2	40	4-40.000	Washer - rubber	2	2
15	4-15.000	Bumper rubber - center stand	1	1	41	4-41.000	Rear shock assm [green]		2
16	4-16.000	Plug - frame	2	2		4-41.001	Rear shock assm [red]	2	
17	4-17.000	Bearing race - top & bottom	2	2	42	4-42.000	Bushing - top shock	2	2
18	4-18.000	"O" ring	2	2	43	4-43.000	Bushing - rubber	8	8
19	4-19.000	Stand	1	1	44	HH10x60	Bolt - size [HH10x60]	2	2
20	4-20.000	Spring - main stand	1	1	45	HH10	Nut [HH10-17]	2	2
21	HH6x25	Bolt - size [HH6x25]	2	2	46	FW10x18	Washer [FW10x18]	2	2
22	HH6	Nut - size [HH6-10]	2	2	47	LW10	Lock Washer [LW10]	2	2
23	FW6x18	Washer [FW6x18]	2	2	48	HH8x100	Bolt - size [HH8x100] rear eng. mt	2	2
24	LW6	Washer - locking [LW6]	2	2	49	HH8	Nut - size [HH8-13]	2	2
25	4-25.000	Brake pedal - rear	1	1	50	FW8	Washer [FW8x18]	2	2
					51	LW8	Lock washer [LW8]	2	2

Fenders, Exhaust, Gas tank, Seat, Air filter assembly

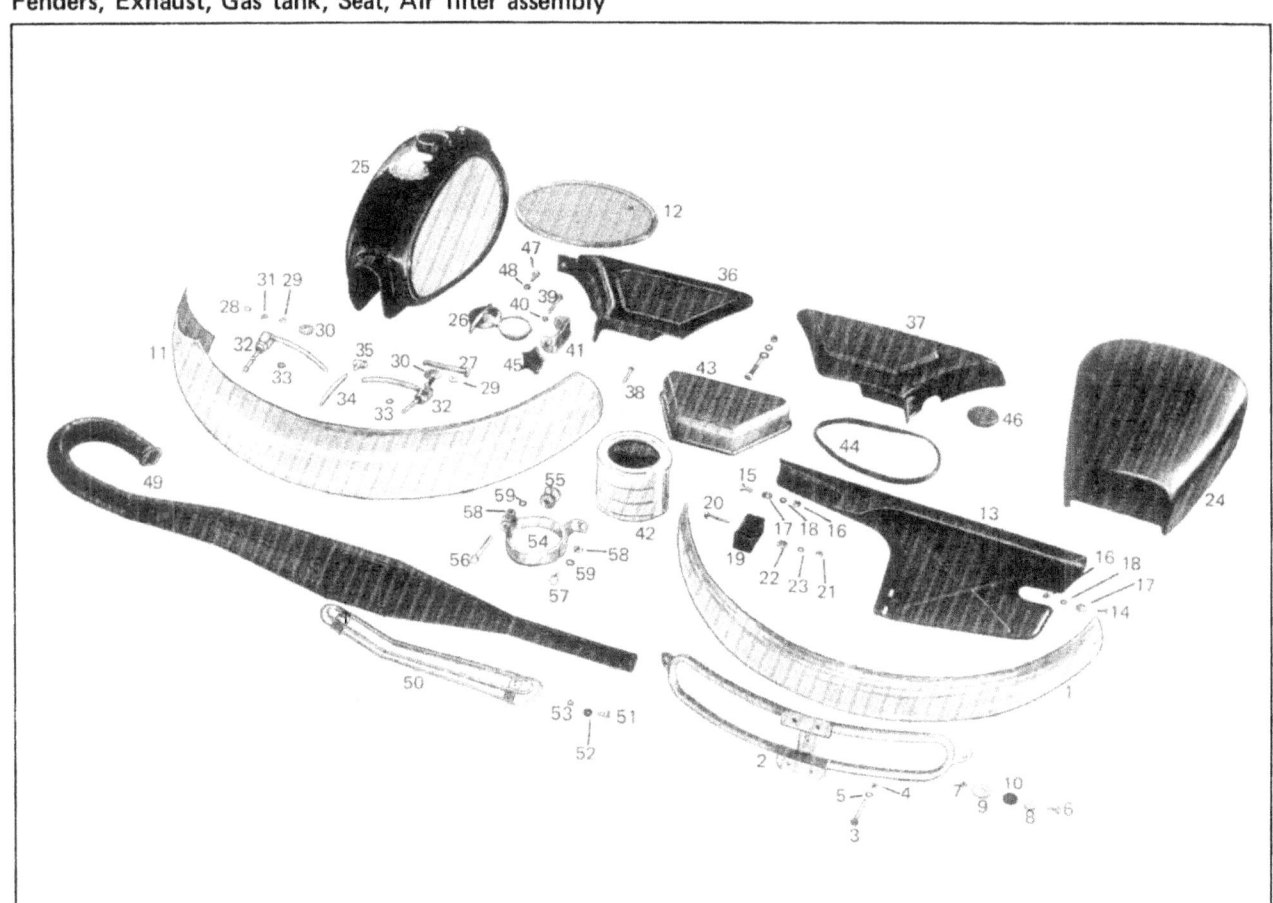

FIG. NO.	PART NO.	DESCRIPTION	100 Pieces	125 Pieces	FIG. NO.	PART NO.	DESCRIPTION	100 Pieces	125 Pieces
1	5-1.000	Front fender	1	1	31	LW8	Lock washer [LW8]	2	2
2	5-2.000	Stay - fr. fender	1	1	32	5-32.000	Petrol tap	2	2
3	5-3.000	Bolt - size [HH6x45]	4	4	33	5-33.000	Washer - fiber	2	2
4	5-4.000	Nut - [HH6-10]	4	4	34	5-34.000	Fuel line - 12" length only	1	1
5	LW6	Lock washer [LW6]	4	4	35	5-35.000	Fuel line junction	1	1
6	HH6x15	Bolt - size [HH6x15]	2	2	36	5-36.000	Cover - air cleaner L/S [green]		1
7	HH6SL	Nut - [HH6-10SL]	4	4		5-36.001	Cover - air cleaner L/S [red]	1	
8	FW6x18	Washer [FW6x18]	4	4	37	5-37.000	Cover - air cleaner R/S [green]		1
9	FW6x30	Washer [FW6x30]	5	5		5-37.001	Cover - air cleaner R/S [red]	1	
10	5-10.000	Washer - rubber	4	4	38	FH6x50	Screw [FH6-50]	3	3
11	5-11.000	Fender - rear	1	1	39	FH6x20	Screw [FH6x20]	2	2
12	2-7.000	Number plate	3	3	40	HH6-SL	Nut - size [HH6-10]	2	2
13	5-13.000	Chain guard	1	1	41	5-41.000	Bracket	1	1
14	FH6x15	Screw [FH6x15]	1	1	42	5-42.000	Filter - air cleaner - Filtron	1	1
15	HH6x15	Bolt - size [HH6x15]	1	1	43	5-43.000	Cover - air cleaner	1	1
16	HH6	Nut [HH6-10]	2	2	44	5-44.000	Gasket - air cleaner cover	1	1
17	FW6x18	Washer [FW6x18]	2	2	45	5-45.000	Knob - air cleaner cover	1	1
18	LW6	Lock washer [LW6]	2	2	46	5-46.000	Plug - rubber	1	1
19	5-19.000	Chain guide - nylon	1	1	47	HH6x20	Bolt - size [HH6x20]	1	1
20	HH6x35	Bolt - size [FH6x35]	2	2	48	LW6	Washer - locking [LW6]	1	1
21	HH6	Nut [HH6-10]	2	2	49	5-49.000	Exhaust pipe assm. - specify outlet size	1	1
22	FW6X	Washer [FW6x18]	2	2	50	5-50.000	Heat shield	1	1
23	LW6	Lock washer [LW6]	2	2	51	HH5x12	Bolt - size [HH5x12]	2	2
24	5-24.000	Seat	1	1	52	FW6x12	Washer [FW6x12]	2	2
25	5-25.000	Fuel tank [green]		1	53	LW6	Washer - locking	2	2
	5-25.001	Fuel tank [red]	1		54	5-54.000	Bracket - exhaust hanger	1	1
26	5-26.000	Cap - fuel tank	1	1	55	5-55.000	Spacer	1	1
27	HH8x75	Bolt - tank mount - [HH8x75]	2	2	56	HH8x25	Bolt - size [HH8x25]	1	1
28	HH8	Nut [HH8-13]	2	2	57	HH8x15	Bolt - size [HH8x15]	1	1
29	FW8x20	Washer [FW8x20]	2	2	58	HH8	Nut - size [HH8-13]	3	3
30	FW8x30	Washer [FW8x30]	2	2	59	LW8	Washer [LW8]	2	2

Front and Rear wheel assemblies

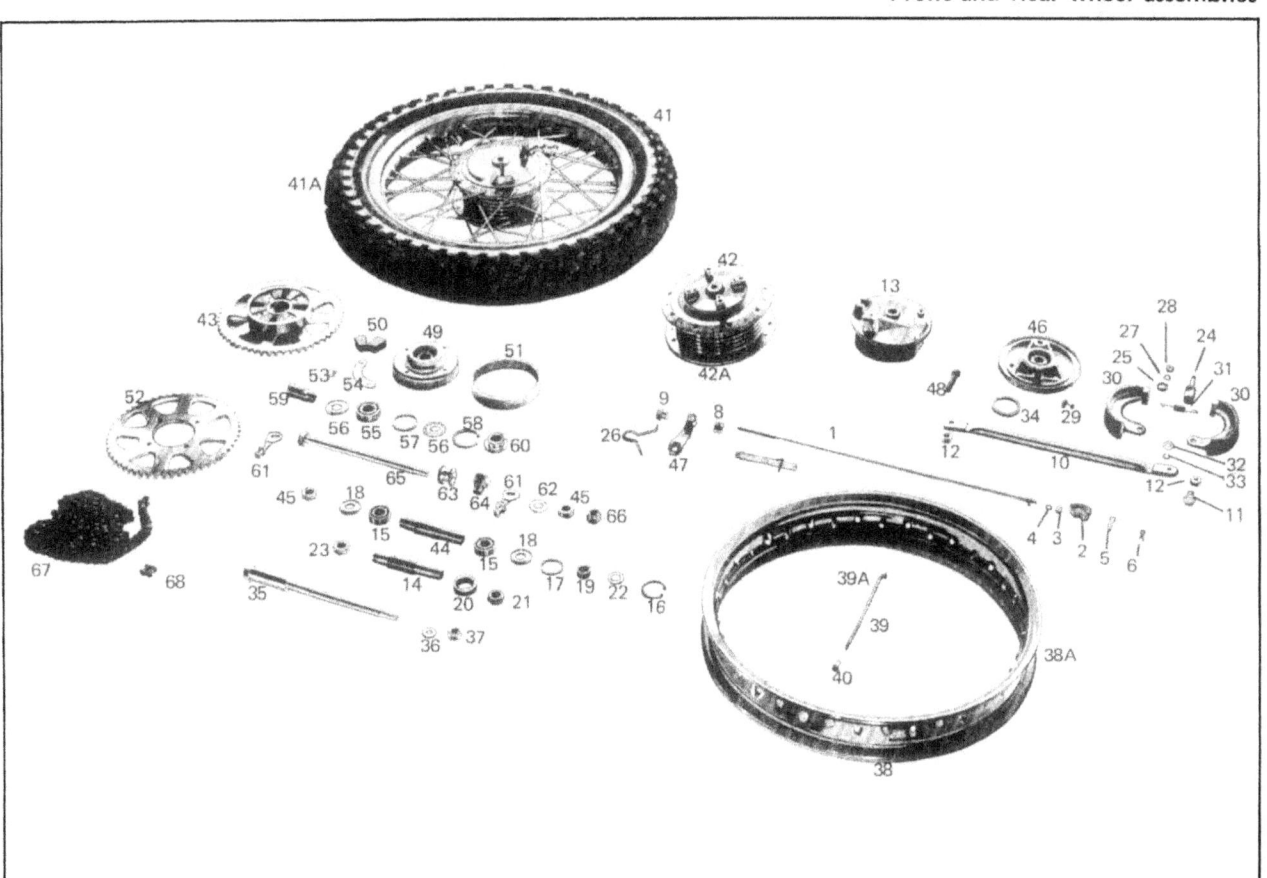

FIG. NO.	PART NO.	DESCRIPTION	100	125
			Pieces	
1	6-1.000	Brake rod - rear	1	1
2	6-2.000	Yoke - rear br. rod	1	1
3	HH6	Nut - size [HH6-10]	1	1
4	LW6	Lock washer [LW6]	1	1
5	6-5.000	Pin - yoke	1	1
6	6-6.000	Clip - spring	1	1
7	6-7.000	Spring	1	1
8	6-8.000	Shoe	1	1
9	6-9.000	Nut - brake rod adjusting	1	1
10	6-10.000	Strap - brake anchor	1	1
11	HH10x20	Bolt - size [HH10x20]	1	1
12	HH10SL	Nut - size [HH10-17]	2	2
13	6-13.000	Brake plate - front wheel	1	1
14	6-14.000	Spacer tube - fr axle	1	1
15	6-15.000	Bearing - no [6003]	4	4
16	6-16.000	Circlip	1	1
17	6-17.000	Spacer	1	1
18	6-18.000	Dust cover	2	2
19	6-19.000	Spacer	1	1
20	6-20.000	Seal	1	1
21	6-21.000	Nut - size [special]	1	1
22	6-22.000	Washer [special]	1	1
23	6-23.000	Nut - size [special]	1	1
24	6-24.000	Cam - rear br. shoes	1	1
25	6-25.000	Seal	1	1
26	6-26.000	Spring	1	1
27	LW8	Washer [LW8]	1	1
28	HH8	Nut - size [HH8-14]	1	1
29	6-29.000	Grease fitting	1	1
30	6-30.000	Brake shoe	4	4
31	6-31.000	Brake shoe spring	2	2
32	6-32.000	Washer	2	2
33	6-33.000	Circlip	2	2
34	6-34.000	Dust seal	2	2
35	6-35.000	Axle - front	1	1
36	FW12x22	Washer - fr. axle [FW12x22]	1	1
37	6-37.000SL	Nut - fr. axle - size [HH12-19SL]	1	1
38	6-38.000	Rim - rear wheel 350x18 alloy - MZ	1	1
	6-38.001	Rim - rear wheel 350x18 alloy - Borrani	1	1
	6-38.002	Rim - rear wheel 350x18 steel	1	1
38A	6-38.000A	Rim - front wheel 300x21 alloy - MZ	1	1
	6-38.001A	Rim - front wheel 300x21 alloy - Borrani	1	1
39	6-38.002A	Rim - front wheel 300x21 steel	1	1
	6-39.000	Spoke - rear [for alloy MZ or Borrani rim]	36	36
39A	6-39.000A	Spoke - front [for Borrani alloy rim]	36	36
	6-39.001A	Spoke - front [for MZ alloy rim]	36	36
40	6-40.000	Nipple	72	72
41	Not Sold	Tire - rear 350x18 [not sold]	1	1
41A	Not Sold	Tire - front 300x21 [not sold]	1	1
42	6-42.000	Hub - rear - complete only	1	1
42A	6-42.000A	Hub - front - complete only	1	1
43	6-43.000	Sprocket - rear wheel 57T [sprocket assm. only]	1	1
44	6-44.000	Spacer tube - rear axle	1	1
45	6-45.000	Nut - size [special]	2	2
46	6-46.000	Brake plate - rear wheel	1	1
47	6-47.000	Brake arm - rear wheel	1	1
48	HH10x40	Bolt - size [HH10x40]	1	1
49	6-49.000	Drive plate	1	1
50	6-50.000	Cushion drive - rubber		
51		Ring - [not available - sold only as unit #49]	4	4
52	6-52.000	Sprocket - rear wheel 60T-57T-5HT [specify no. of teeth]	1	1
53		Bolt - sprocket fixing - size [HH8x]	4	4
54	6-54.000	Locking plate - rear sprocket	2	2
55	6-53.000	Bearing [6004]	1	1
56	6-56.000	Dust cover	2	2
57	6-57.000	Spacer ring	1	1
58	6-58.000	Circlip	1	1
59	6-59.000	Bushing - sprocket hub	1	1
60	6-60.000	Spacer - sprocket hub	1	1
61	6-61.000	Adjuster - rear wheel	2	2
62	6-62.000	Washer [special]	1	1
63	6-63.000	Spacer - rear axle	1	1
64	6-64.000	Leading bolt - L/S	1	1
65	6-65.000	Axle - rear	1	1
66	6-66.000SL	Nut - rear axle	1	1
67	6-67.000	Chain - rear drive [120 links]	1	1
68	6-68.000	Master link	1	1

NOTES

PENTON - KTM

FRAME & COMPONENTS PARTS LIST (1970-1971)

Frame, Swing arm, Components

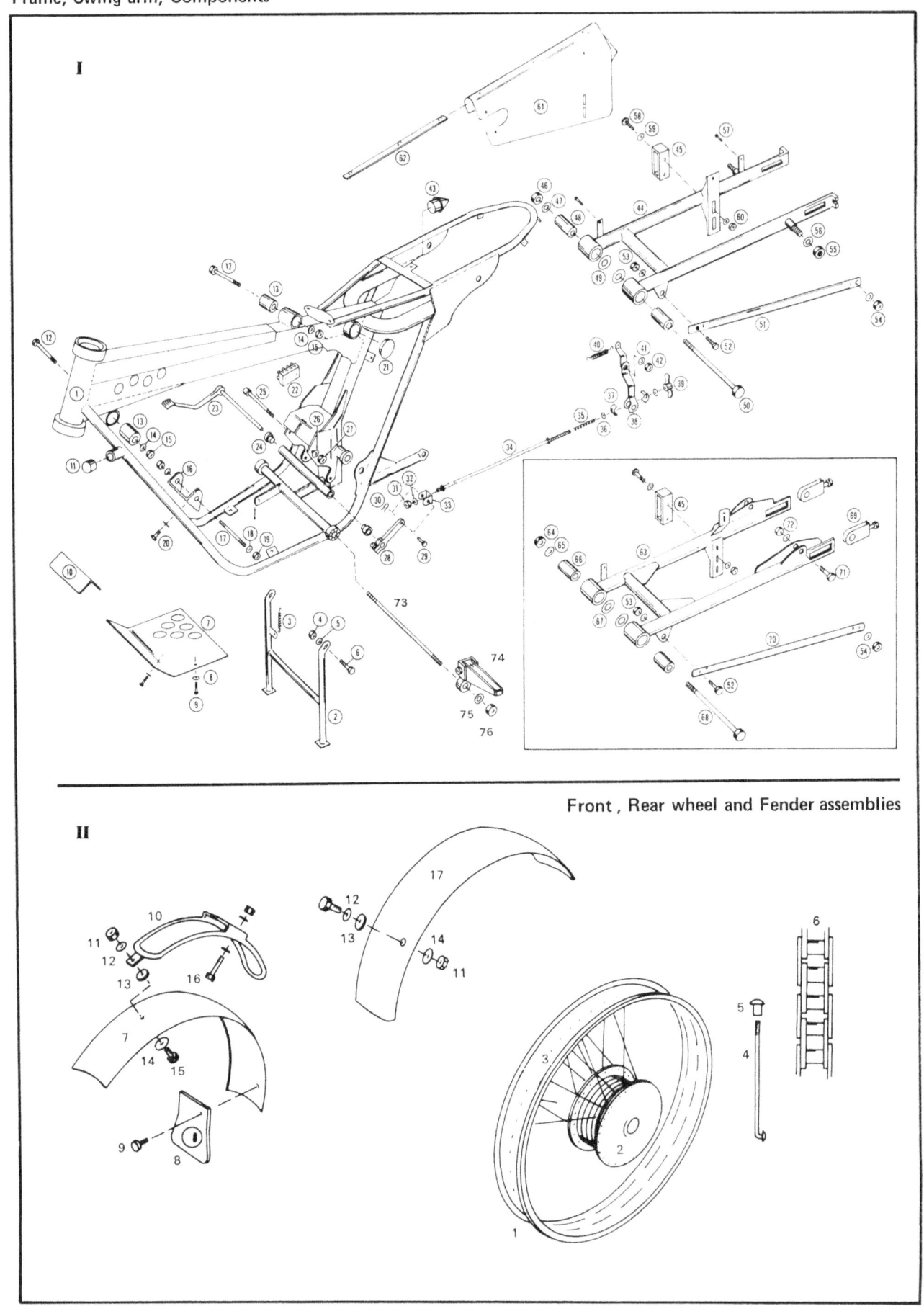

Front, Rear wheel and Fender assemblies

150

Frame, Swing arm, Components

FIG. NO.	PART NO.	DESCRIPTION	100 Pieces	125 Pieces
I				
1	4- 1.000	FRAME	1	1
2	4-19.000	CENTER STAND	1	1
3	4-20.000	SPRING - CENTER STAND	1	1
4	2-59.000	NUT (HH 8)	2	2
5	2-62.000	LOCK WASHER (FW 6 x 20)	4	4
	2-65.000	WASHER (LW 6)	2	2
6	2-63.000	BOLT (HH 6 x 25)	2	2
7	4- 5.000	SKID PLATE	1	1
8	2-75.000	LOCK WASHER (LW 8 x 28)	4	4
9	2-63.000	BOLT (HH 6 x 25)	4	4
10	4- 7.000	SPLASH GUARD	1	1
11	4-14.000	BUMPER - FORK STOP	2	2
12	2-85.000	BOLT - TANK MOUNT (HH 8 x 75)	2	2
13	4-10.000	TANK MOUNT BUSHING	2	2
14	2-58.000	WASHER (FW 8 x 20)	4	4
	2-75.000	LOCK WASHER (LW 8)	2	2
15	2-59.000	NUT (HH 8)	2	2
16	4- 4.000	FRONT ENGINE MOUNT BRACKET	1	1
17	4- 6.000	BOLT - ENGINE MOUNT	1	1
18	2-58.000	WASHER (FW 8 x 20)	2	2
	2-75.000	LOCK WASHER (LW 8)	2	2
19	2-59.000	NUT (HH 8)	2	2
20	2-64.000	BOLT (HH 8 x 20)	2	2
	2-75.000	LOCK WASHER (LW 8)	2	2
21	5-46.000	FRAME PLUG	1	1
22	5-47.000	TERMINAL - WIRE	1	1
23	4-25.000	BRAKE PEDAL	1	1
24	4-26.000	BUSHING - NYLON	2	2
25	4- 8.000	BOLT (HH 8 x 100) REAR ENGINE MOUNT	2	2
26	2-58.000	WASHER (FW 8 x 20)	2	2
	2-75.000	LOCK WASHER (LW 8)	2	2
27	2-59.000	NUT (HH 8)	2	2
28	4-27.000	ARM - BRAKE ACTUATING FRONT	1	1
29	6- 5.000	PIN	1	1
30	6- 6.000	COTTER PIN	1	1
31	2-61.000	NUT (HH 6)	1	1
32	2-65.000	LOCK WASHER (LW 6)	1	1
33	6- 2.000	YOKE - BRAKE ROD	1	1
34	6- 1.000	BRAKE ROD	1	1
35	6- 7.000	SPRING	1	1
36	2-66.000	WASHER (FW 6 x 10)	2	2
37	6- 8.000	SHOE	2	2
38	6-83.000	BRAKE ARM - REAR	1	1
39	6- 9.000	WING NUT	1	1
40	6-84.000	BRAKE SPRING	1	1
41	2-75.000	WASHER (LW 8)	1	1
42	2-59.000	NUT (HH 8)	1	1
43	4-16.000	PLUG - FRAME	2	2
44	4-35.000	SWING ARM	1	1
45	5-19.000	CHAIN GUIDE - NYLON	1	1
46	6-66.000	NUT (HH 12)	1	1
47	2-67.000	WASHER (FW 12 x 20)	2	2
48	4-36.000	BUSHING - SWING ARM	2	2
49	4-40.000	WASHER - RUBBER	2	2
50	4-37.000	BOLT - SWING ARM	1	1
51	6-10.000	BRAKE ANCHOR ARM	1	1
52	2-68.000	BOLT (HH 10 x 20)	1	1
53	2-69.000	NUT (HH 10)	1	1
54	2-69.000	NUT (HH 10)	1	1
55	2-69.000	NUT (HH 10)	2	2
56	2-67.000	WASHER (FW 12 x 20)	2	2
57	2- 7.000	SCREW (FH 6 x 15)	2	2
58	2-71.000	BOLT (FH 6 x 35)	2	2
59	2-66.000	WASHER (FW 6 x 10)	2	2
	2-65.000	LOCK WASHER (LW 6 x 10)	4	4
60	2-61.000	NUT (HH 6 x 10)	2	2
61	5-13.000	CHAIN GUARD	1	1
62	5-14.000	RUBBER CHAIN GUARD	1	1
63	4-35.001	SWING ARM - NEW STYLE	1	1
64		NUT	1	1
65		WASHER	1	1
66	4-36.001	BUSHING - SWING ARM	2	2
67	4-40.001	WASHER	2	2
68	4-37.001	BOLT - SWING ARM	1	1
69	6-61.001	CHAIN ADJUSTER	2	2
70	6-10.001	BRAKE ANCHOR ARM	1	1
71		BOLT	2	2
72		NUT	2	2
		WASHER	4	4
		LOCK WASHER	2	2
73	2-33.000	FOOT PEG BOLT	1	1
74	4-31.000	FOOT PEG	2	2
75		LOCK WASHER (LW 10 x 18)	2	2
76	6-37.000SL	NUT	2	2
II				
1	6-90.000	WHEEL COMPLETE (FRONT)	1	1
	6-95.000	WHEEL COMPLETE (REAR)	1	1
2	6-92.000	HUB COMPLETE (FRONT)	1	1
	6-69.000	HUB COMPLETE (REAR)	1	1
3	6-38.002	21" STEEL RIM	1	1
	6-38.000	18" STEEL RIM	1	1
4	6-39.000	SPOKES - REAR 18"	36	36
	6-39.001	SPOKES - FRONT 21"	36	36
5	6-40.000	NIPPLES		
6	6-67.000	CHAIN (1/2 x 5/16 - 120 LINKS)	1	1
	6-68.000	MASTER LINK (1/2 x 5/16)		
7	5- 1.000	FRONT FENDER	1	1
8	5- 5.000	MUD FLAP	1	1
9	5- 6.000	COTTER PIN	2	2
10	5- 2.000	FENDER BRACKET	1	1
11	2-61.000	NUT (HH 6)	10	10
12	2-65.000	WASHER (LW 6 x 10)	14	14
13	5-10.000	RUBBER WASHER	6	6
14	2-62.000	WASHER (FW 6 x 20)	6	6
15	2-79.000	BOLT (HH 6 x 20)	6	6
16	2-80.000	BOLT (HH 6 x 40)	4	4
17	5-11.000	REAR FENDER	1	1

Dimensions of washer, Nuts, Bolts

PART NO.	SIZE	TYPE
1-12.000	HH 8 x 60	BOLT
2-58.000	FW 8 x 20	WASHER
2-59.000	HH 8	NUT
2-60.000	HH 6 x 50	BOLT
2-61.000	HH 6	NUT
2-62.000	FW 6 x 20	WASHER
2-63.000	HH 6 x 25	BOLT
2-64.000	HH 8 x 20	BOLT
2-65.000	LW 6 x 10	WASHER
2-66.000	FW 6 x 10	WASHER
2-67.000	FW 12 x 20	WASHER
2-68.000	HH 10 x 20	BOLT
2-69.000	HH 10 SL	NUT
2-70.000	FW 6 x 15	WASHER
2-71.000	HH 6 x 35	BOLT
2-72.000	FW 10 x 20	WASHER
2-73.000	HH 10 x 40	BOLT
2-74.000	FW 8	WASHER
2-75.000	LW 8	WASHER
2-76.000	HH 8 x 30	BOLT
2-77.000	FW 12 x 22	WASHER
2-78.000	AH 5 x 15	ALLEN BOLT
2-79.000	HH 6 x 20	BOLT
2-80.000	HH 6 x 40	BOLT

Fork assembly, Steering crown, Rear shocks

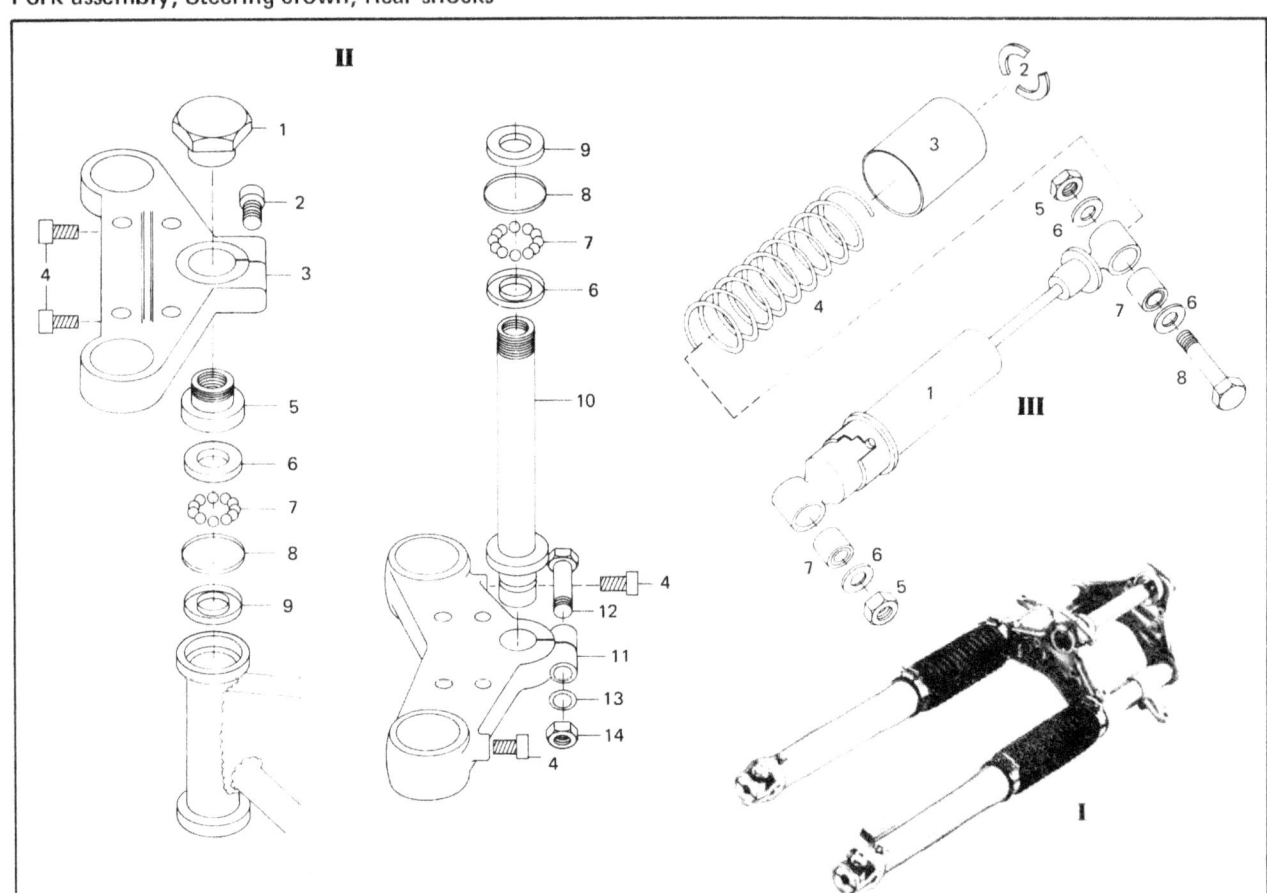

FIG. NO.	PART NO.	DESCRIPTION	100 Pieces	125 Pieces
I				
1	2-1.000	FORK ASSEMBLY COMPLETE	1	1
II				
1	2-47.000	NUT - TOP FORK PLATE	1	1
2	2-49.000	ALLEN SCREW PINCH BOLT (AH8 x 35)	1	1
3	2-56.000	TOP FORK PLATE	1	1
4	2-46.000	ALLEN SCREW PINCH BOLTS (AH 10 x 30)	4	4
5	2-48.000	NUT BEARING	1	1
6	2-50.000	BEARING RACE	2	2
7	2-51.000	BALL BEARINGS (RB 8)	34	34
8	2-52.000	"O"-RING	2	2
9	2-53.000	BEARING RACE	2	2
10	2-54.000	FORK STEM	1	1
11	2-55.000	BOTTOM FORK PLATE	1	1
12	2-57.000	BOLT (HH 8 x 65)	1	1
13	2-58.000	WASHER (FW 8 x 20)	1	1
14	2-59.000	NUT (HH 8)	1	1

FIG. NO.	PART NO.	DESCRIPTION	100 Pieces	125 Pieces
III				
1	4-41.000	SHOCK COMPLETE	2	2
2	4-45.000	RETAINER CLIPS	4	4
3	4-46.000	DUST COVER	2	2
4	4-47.000	SPRING	2	2
5	2-69.000	NUT (HH 10 SL)	2	2
6	2-72.000	WASHER (FW 10 x 20)	3	3
7	4-48.000	RUBBER GROMMET	2	2
8	2-82.000	BOLT (HH 10 x 60)	2	2

Front fork legs

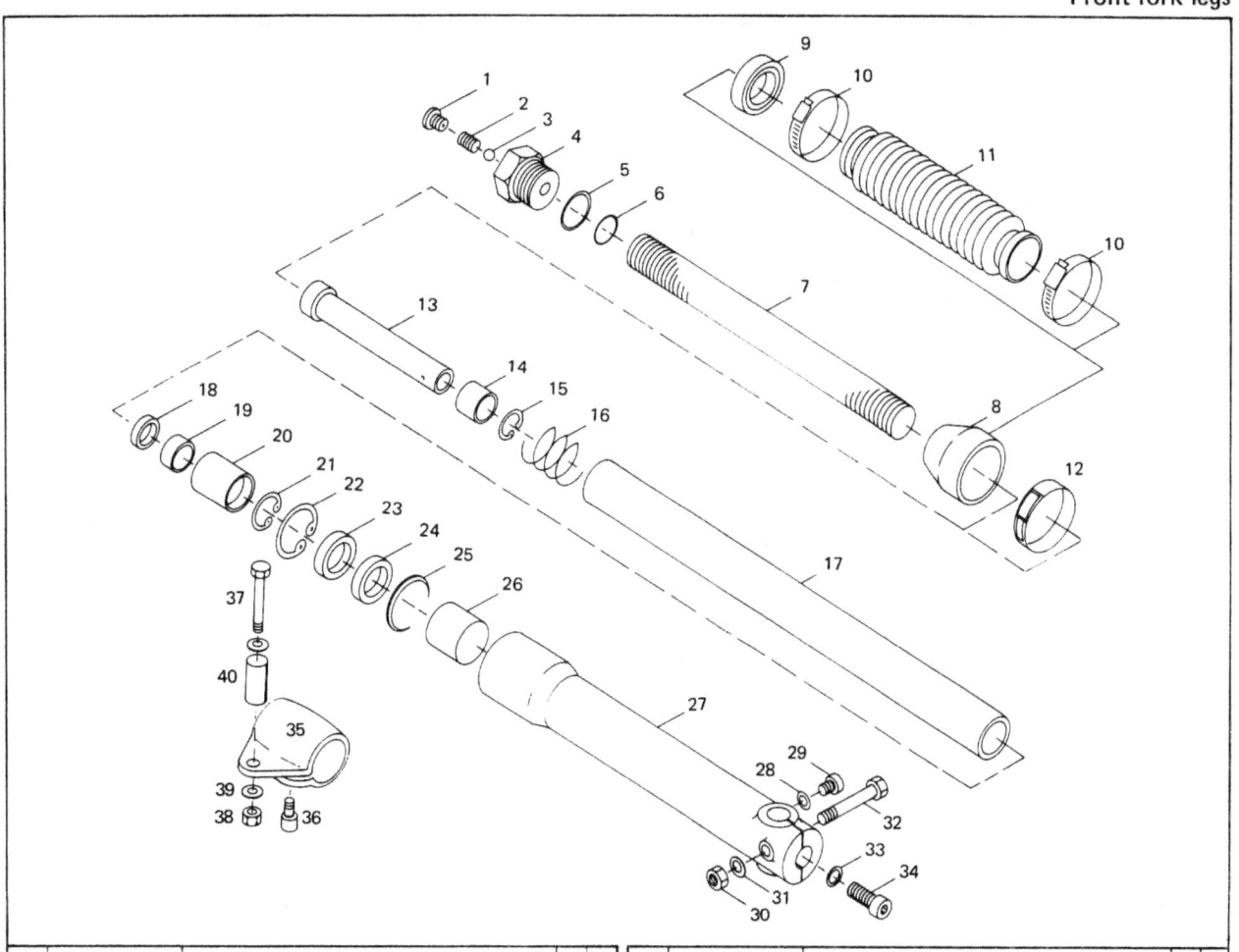

FIG. NO.	PART NO.	DESCRIPTION	100 Pieces	125 Pieces	FIG. NO.	PART NO.	DESCRIPTION	100 Pieces	125 Pieces
1	1-43.000	SCREW (TH 6 x 6)	2	2	21	1-17.000	CIRCLIP (SPECIAL)	2	2
2	1-41.000	SPRING	2	2	22	1-16.000	CIRCLIP (SPECIAL)	2	2
3	1-42.000	BALL (RB 6)	2	2	23	1-15.000	SEAL	4	4
4	1-39.000	NUT - FORK TUBE	2	2	24	1-15.000	SEAL	4	4
5	1-37.000	WASHER (SPECIAL)	2	2	25	1-14.000	SNAP RING	2	2
6	1-38.000	"O"-RING	2	2	26	1-13.000	LOWER BUSHING	2	2
7	1-26.000	FORK SPRING - LONG	2	2	27	1-7.000	FORK LEG - LEFT SIDE	1	1
8	1-48.000	FORK BOOT	2	2		1-7.001	FORK LEG - RIGHT SIDE	1	1
9	1-27.000	BOOT COLLAR	2	2	28	1-9.000	WASHER - DRAIN PLUG	2	2
10	1-29.000	BOOT CLAMP	4	4	29	1-8.000	DRAIN PLUG	2	2
11	1-28.000	FORK BOOT - RUBBER	2	2	30	2-59.000	NUT (HH 8 - 13)	2	2
12	1-49.000	BOOT CLAMP	2	2	31	2-58.000	WASHER (FW 8 x 20)	4	4
13	1-25.000	STOP VALVE	2	2	32	1-12.000	BOLT (HH 8 x 60) AXEL SEC'	2	2
14	1-24.000	BUSHING	2	2	33	1-11.000	WASHER (SPECIAL)	2	2
15	1-23.000	CIRCLIP (SPECIAL)	2	2	34	1-10.000	SCREW - ALLEN HEAD (AH 8 x 20)	2	2
16	1-22.000	FORK SPRING - SHORT	2	2	35	1-31.000	BRACKET - FORK LEG	2	2
17	1-21.000	FORK TUBE	2	2	36	2-78.000	SCREW - ALLEN HEAD (AH 5 x 15)	4	4
18	1-20.000	SEAL	2	2	37	2-60.000	BOLT HH 6 x 50)	2	2
19	1-19.000	VALVE BUSHING	2	2	38	2-61.000	NUT (HH 6)	2	2
20	1-18.000	BUSHING - UPPER	2	2	39	2-62.000	WASHER (FW 6 x 20)	4	4
					40	2-8.000	SLEEVE	2	2

Front wheel hub

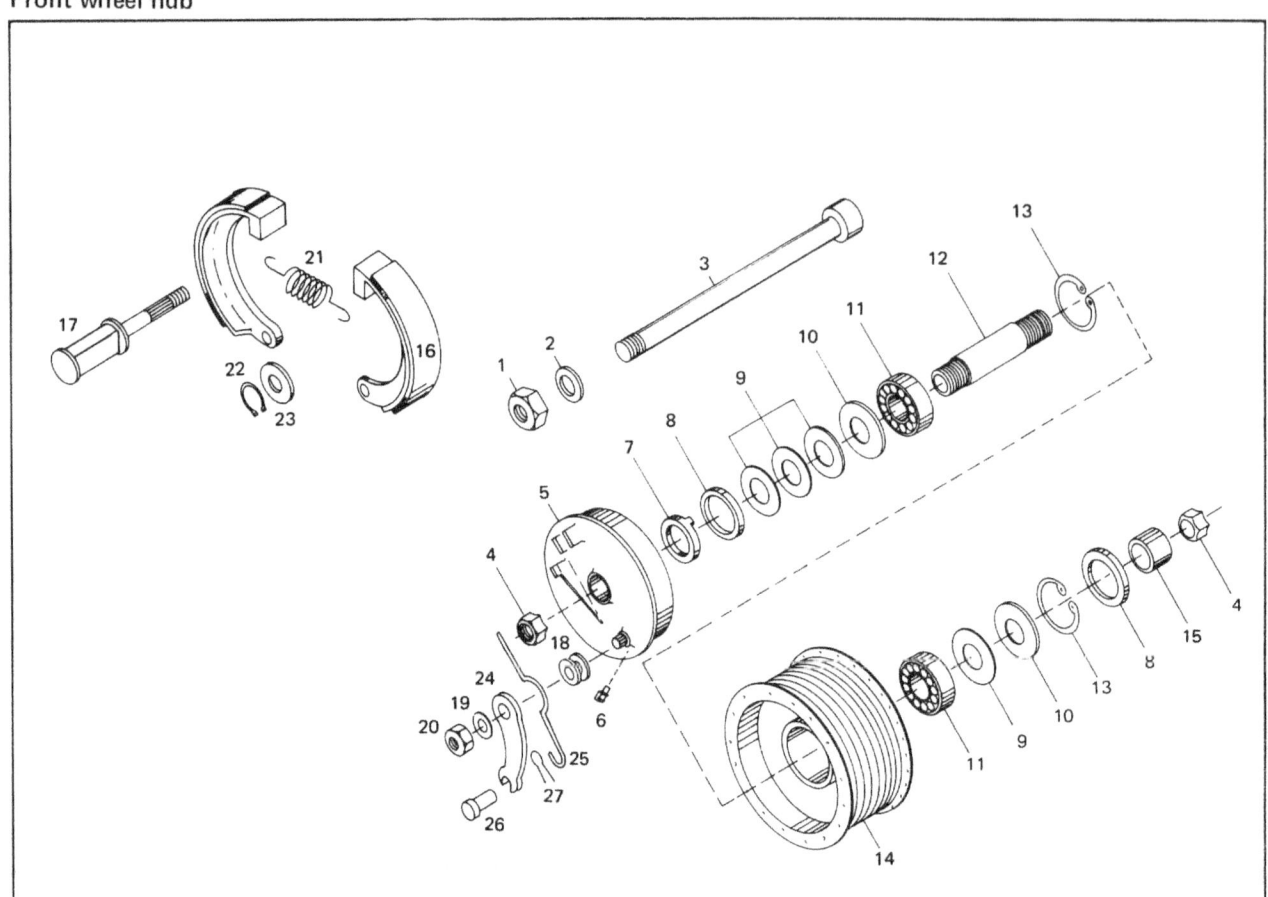

FIG. NO.	PART NO.	DESCRIPTION	100 Pieces	125 Pieces	FIG. NO.	PART NO.	DESCRIPTION	100 Pieces	125 Pieces
1	6-37.000 SL	AXEL NUT	1	1	15	6-19.000	BUSHING	1	1
2	2-77.000	WASHER (FW 12 - 22)	1	1	16	6-30.000	BRAKE SHOE	2	2
3	6-35.000	AXEL	1	1	17	6-24.000	CAM BOLT	1	1
4	6-23.000	NUT	2	2	18	6-25.000	RUBBER WASHER	2	2
5	6-13.000	BRAKE PLATE	1	1	19	2-75.000	WASHER		
6	6-29.000	GREASE FITTING	1	1	20	2-59.000	NUT		
7		SPEEDOMETER BUSHING (NOT USED)	1	1	21	6-31.000	RETURN SPRING (BRAKE SHOE)	1	1
8	6-34.000	SEAL	2	2	22	6-33.000	CIRCLIP	1	1
9	6-86.000	SHIMMING WASHERS			23	6-32.000	WASHER		
10	6-18.000	DUST COVER	2	2	24	6-47.000 A	BRAKE ARM	1	1
11	6-15.000	BEARINGS	2	2	25	6-26.000	BRAKE ARM SPRING	1	1
12	6-14.000	SPACER TUBE	1	1	26	6-48.000	PIN - CABLE	1	1
13	6-16.000	CIRCLIP	2	2	27	6- 6.000	COTTER KEY	1	1
14	6-42.000	HUB	1	1					

Rear wheel hub

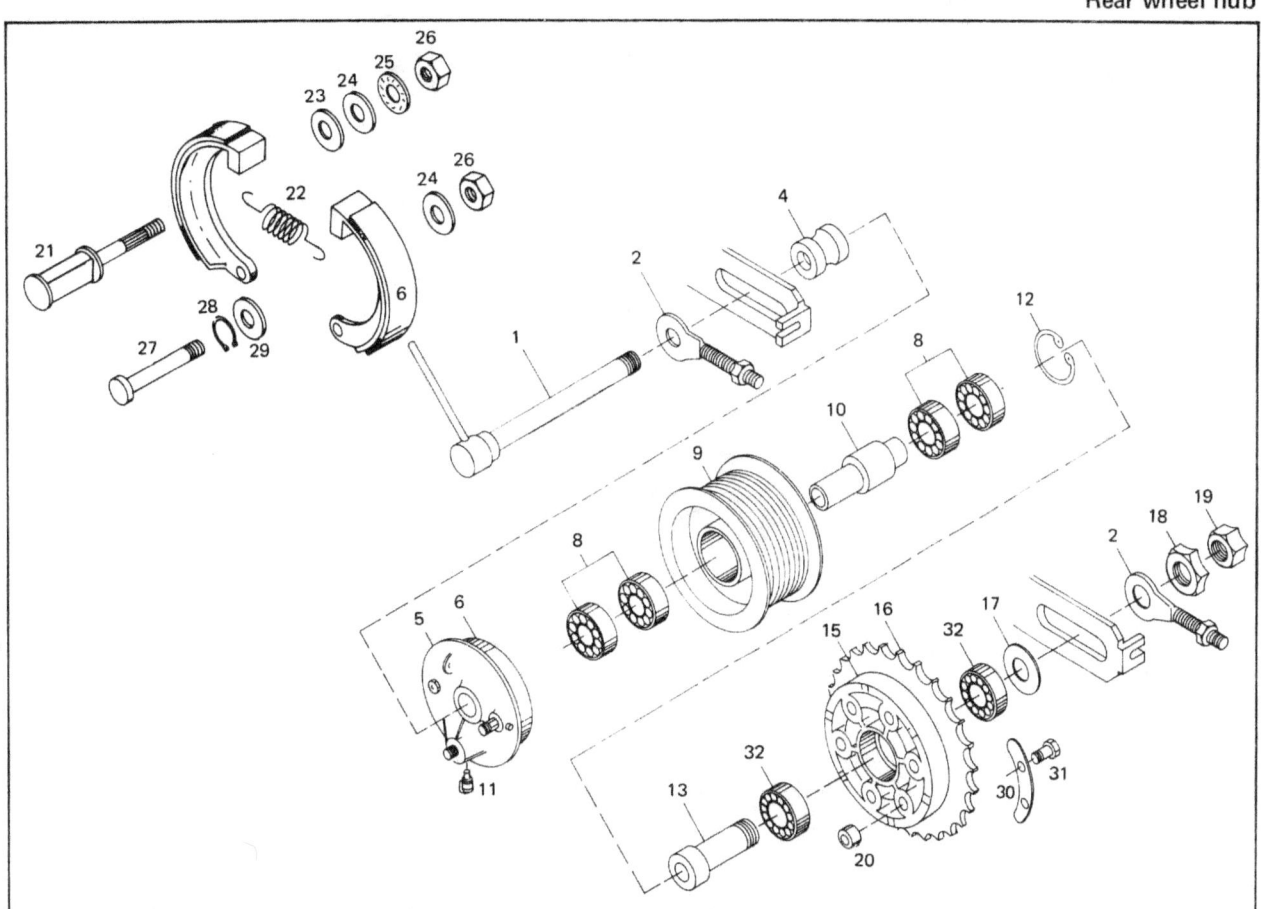

FIG. NO.	PART NO.	DESCRIPTION	100	125
			Pieces	
1	6-85.000	AXEL	1	1
2	6-61.000	ADJUSTER	2	2
4	6-63.000	SPACER	1	1
		SPACER (NEW SWING ARM)	1	1
5	6-82.000	BRAKE PLATE	1	1
6	6-30.000	BRAKE SHOES	2	2
8	6-72.001	BEARINGS	4	4
9	6-70.000	HUB	1	1
10	6-71.000	AXEL SPACER TUBE	1	1
11	6-29.000	GREASE FITTING	1	1
12	6-16.000	CIRCLIP	1	1
13	6-80.000	SPROCKET AXEL	1	1
15	6-74.000	SPROCKET HUB	1	1
16	6-78.000	SPROCKET (SPECIFY SIZE)	1	1
17	6-60.000	WASHER	1	1
18	6-45.000	SPROCKET NUT	1	1
19	6-66.000 SL	AXEL NUT	1	1
20	6-75.000	RUBBER SHOCKS	6	6
21	6-24.000	CAM BOLT	1	1
22	6-31.000	BRAKE SHOE SPRING	1	1
23	6-25.000	RUBBER WASHER	1	1
24	2-74.000	WASHER (FW 8)	1	1
25	2-75.000	LOCK WASHER (LW 8)	1	1
26	2-59.000	NUT (HH 8)	2	2
27	2-73.000	BRAKE SHOE BOLT (HH 10 x 40)	1	1
28	6-33.000	CIRCLIP	1	1
29	6-32.000	WASHER	1	1
30	6-54.000	SPROCKET LOCKING PLATE	3	3
31	2-76.000	BOLT (HH 8 x)	6	6
32	6-76.000	BEARING 6004	2	2

Controls, Gas tank, Seat, Number plates

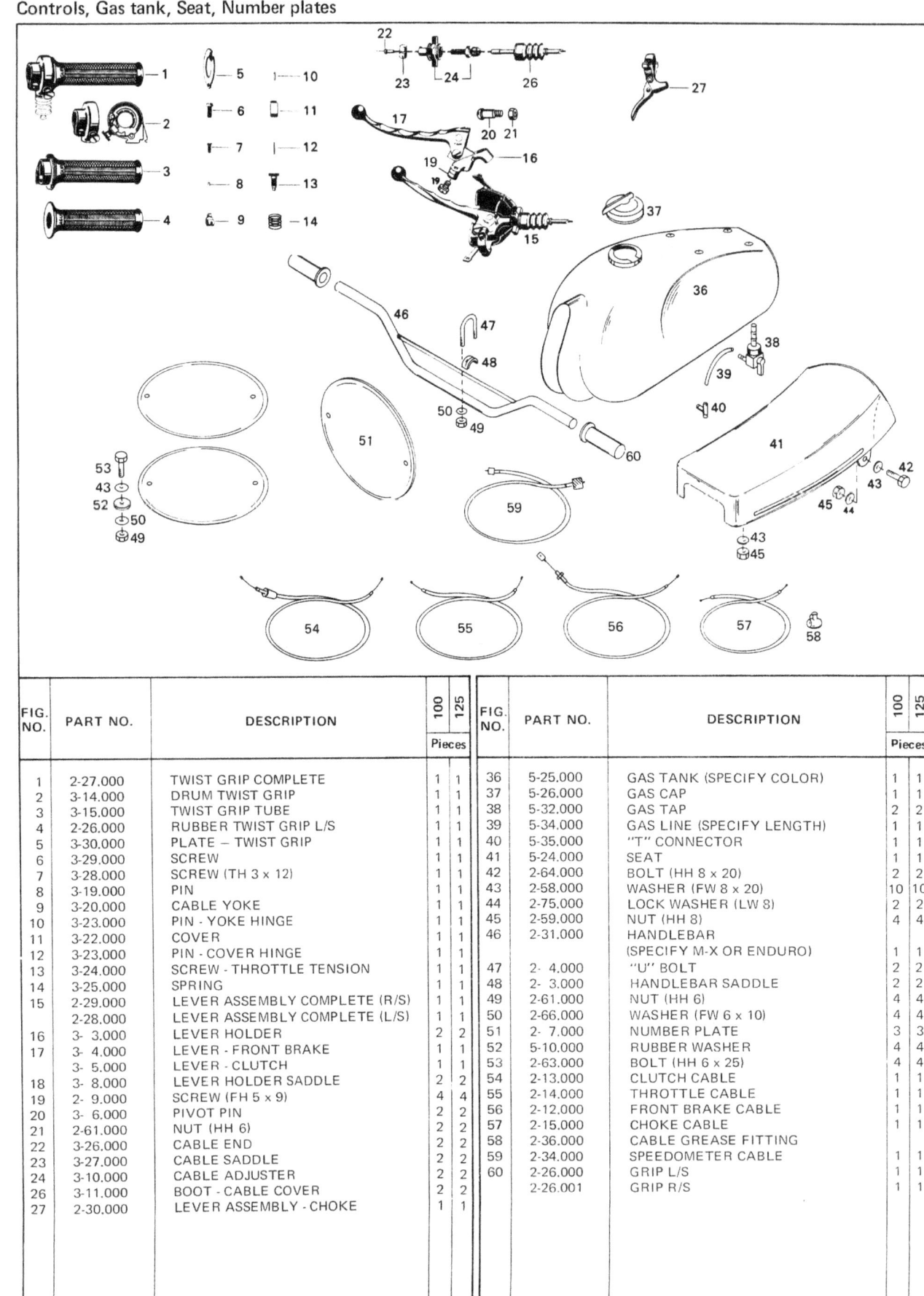

FIG. NO.	PART NO.	DESCRIPTION	100	125
			Pieces	
1	2-27.000	TWIST GRIP COMPLETE	1	1
2	3-14.000	DRUM TWIST GRIP	1	1
3	3-15.000	TWIST GRIP TUBE	1	1
4	2-26.000	RUBBER TWIST GRIP L/S	1	1
5	3-30.000	PLATE – TWIST GRIP	1	1
6	3-29.000	SCREW	1	1
7	3-28.000	SCREW (TH 3 x 12)	1	1
8	3-19.000	PIN	1	1
9	3-20.000	CABLE YOKE	1	1
10	3-23.000	PIN - YOKE HINGE	1	1
11	3-22.000	COVER	1	1
12	3-23.000	PIN - COVER HINGE	1	1
13	3-24.000	SCREW - THROTTLE TENSION	1	1
14	3-25.000	SPRING	1	1
15	2-29.000	LEVER ASSEMBLY COMPLETE (R/S)	1	1
	2-28.000	LEVER ASSEMBLY COMPLETE (L/S)	1	1
16	3- 3.000	LEVER HOLDER	2	2
17	3- 4.000	LEVER - FRONT BRAKE	1	1
	3- 5.000	LEVER - CLUTCH	1	1
18	3- 8.000	LEVER HOLDER SADDLE	2	2
19	2- 9.000	SCREW (FH 5 x 9)	4	4
20	3- 6.000	PIVOT PIN	2	2
21	2-61.000	NUT (HH 6)	2	2
22	3-26.000	CABLE END	2	2
23	3-27.000	CABLE SADDLE	2	2
24	3-10.000	CABLE ADJUSTER	2	2
26	3-11.000	BOOT - CABLE COVER	2	2
27	2-30.000	LEVER ASSEMBLY - CHOKE	1	1

FIG. NO.	PART NO.	DESCRIPTION	100	125
			Pieces	
36	5-25.000	GAS TANK (SPECIFY COLOR)	1	1
37	5-26.000	GAS CAP	1	1
38	5-32.000	GAS TAP	2	2
39	5-34.000	GAS LINE (SPECIFY LENGTH)	1	1
40	5-35.000	"T" CONNECTOR	1	1
41	5-24.000	SEAT	1	1
42	2-64.000	BOLT (HH 8 x 20)	2	2
43	2-58.000	WASHER (FW 8 x 20)	10	10
44	2-75.000	LOCK WASHER (LW 8)	2	2
45	2-59.000	NUT (HH 8)	4	4
46	2-31.000	HANDLEBAR (SPECIFY M-X OR ENDURO)	1	1
47	2- 4.000	"U" BOLT	2	2
48	2- 3.000	HANDLEBAR SADDLE	2	2
49	2-61.000	NUT (HH 6)	4	4
50	2-66.000	WASHER (FW 6 x 10)	4	4
51	2- 7.000	NUMBER PLATE	3	3
52	5-10.000	RUBBER WASHER	4	4
53	2-63.000	BOLT (HH 6 x 25)	4	4
54	2-13.000	CLUTCH CABLE	1	1
55	2-14.000	THROTTLE CABLE	1	1
56	2-12.000	FRONT BRAKE CABLE	1	1
57	2-15.000	CHOKE CABLE	1	1
58	2-36.000	CABLE GREASE FITTING		
59	2-34.000	SPEEDOMETER CABLE	1	1
60	2-26.000	GRIP L/S	1	1
	2-26.001	GRIP R/S	1	1

Air cleaner, Lights, Speedometer bracket, Exhaust

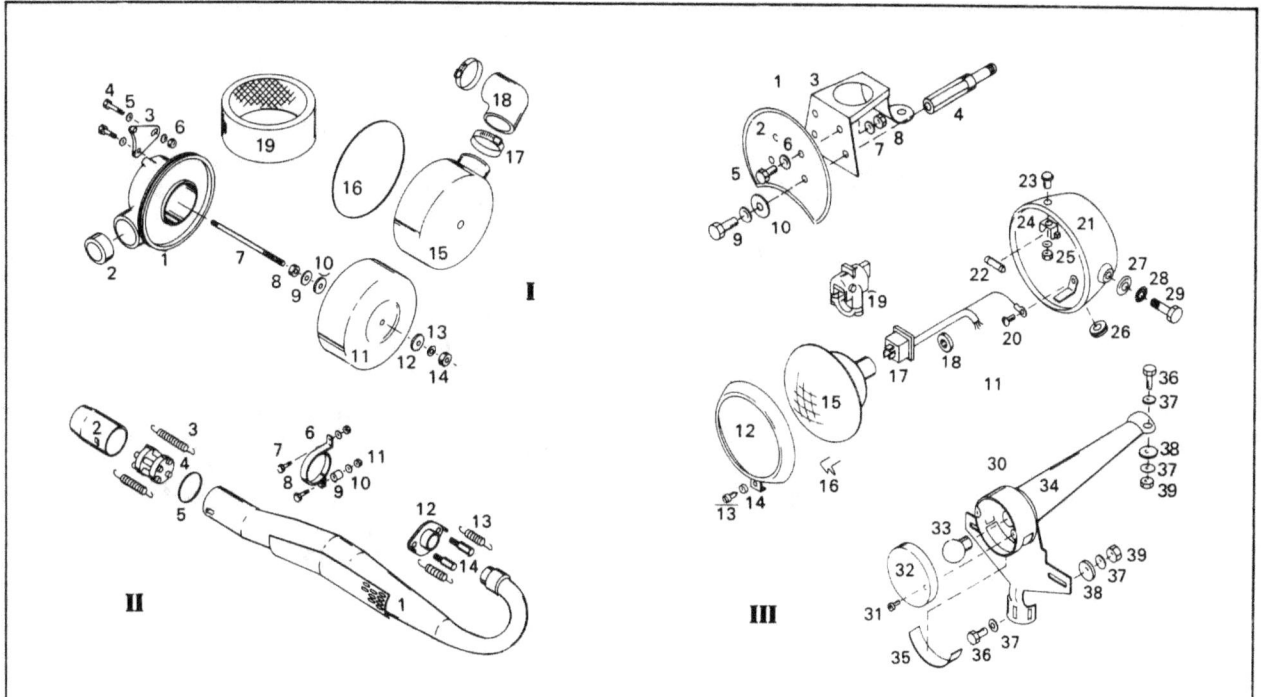

FIG. NO.	PART NO.	DESCRIPTION	100	125
			Pieces	
1	5-61.000	AIR CLEANER HOUSING	1	1
2	5-63.000	RUBBER BUSHING	1	1
3	5-64.000	BRACKET	1	1
4	1-12.000	BOLT (HH 8 x 60)	1	1
5	2-62.000	WASHWE (FW 6 x 20)	6	6
6	2-59.000	NUT (H110)	1	1
7	2-71.000	BOLT (HH 6 x 35)	1	1
8	2-59.000	NUT (HH 8)	1	1
9	2-58.000	WASHER (FW 8 x 20)	1	1
10	5-10.000	RUBBER WASHER	1	1
11	5-62.000	MOTO-CROSS COVER	1	1
12	2-58.000	WASHER (FW 8 x 20)	1	1
13	2-75.000	LOCK WASHER (LW 8)	1	1
14	2-59.000	NUT (HH 8)	1	1
15	5-62.001	ENDURO COVER	1	1
16	5-67.000	"O"-RING	1	1
17	5-70.000	CLAMP	2	2
18	5-69.000	AIR FILTER HOSE	1	1
19	5-66.000	FILTRON FILTER	1	1
	5-66.001	PAPER FILTER	1	1
II				
1	5-49.000	EXHAUST COMPLETE (1 - 5)	1	1
	5-49.001	EXHAUST COMPLETE W/SQUARE FLANGE (OLD STYLE)	1	1
2	5-50.001	MUFFLER END	1	1
3	5-51.000	SPRING	3	3
4	5-50.002	BAFFLE	1	1
5	5-52.000	GASKET	1	1
6	5-54.000	BRACKET	1	1
7	2-64.000	BOLT (HH 8 x 20)	1	1
8	1-12.000	BOLT (HH 8 x 60)	1	1
9	5-55.000	SPACER	1	1
10	2-75.000	WASHER (LW 8)	2	2
11	2-59.000	NUT (HH 8)	2	2
12	5-49.003	ENGINE EXHAUST FLANGE	1	1
13	5-49.002	SPRING	2	2
14	0642104101	HEX HEAD BOLT	2	2

FIG. NO.	PART NO.	DESCRIPTION	100	125
			Pieces	
III				
1	2-33.000	SPEEDOMETER BRACKET COMPLETE	1	1
2	2- 7.001	NUMBER PLATE - FRONT	1	1
3	2-33.002	SPEEDOMETER BRACKET	1	1
4	2-33.001	BOLT (SPECIAL)	2	2
5	2-63.000	BOLT	2	2
6	2-62.000	WASHER	6	6
7	2-65.000	LOCK WASHER	2	2
8	2-61.000	NUT	2	2
9	2-64.000	BOLT	2	2
10	2-58.000	WASHER	2	2
11	2-16.000	HEADLIGHT ASSEMBLY COMPLETE	1	1
12	2-17.000	RIM	1	1
13	2-11.000	SCREW	1	1
14	2-41.001	RUBBER WASHER	1	1
15	2-19.001	SEAL BEAM	1	1
16	2-21.000	RETAINING CLIPS	1	1
17	2-22.001	PLUG	1	1
18	2-24.001	RUBBER GROMMET	1	1
19	2-32.000	DIPPER SWITCH	1	1
20	2-24.000	SCREW	1	1
21	2-16.001	HEADLIGHT HOUSING	1	1
22	2-37.000	INDICATOR BULB	1	1
23	2-38.000	INDICATOR LENS	1	1
24	2-39.000	INDICATOR BRACKET	1	1
25	2-40.000	NUT	1	1
26	2-41.000	RUBBER GROMMET	2	2
27	2-42.000	WASHER (SPECIAL)	2	2
28	2-75.000	LOCK WASHER	2	2
29	2-64.000	BOLT	2	2
30	5-56.000	TAIL LIGHT ASSEMBLY COMPLETE	1	1
31	5-71.000	SCREW	2	2
32	5-72.000	TAIL LIGHT LENS	1	1
33	5-73.000	BULB	1	1
34	5-75.000	HOUSING	1	1
35	5-74.000	LICENSE PLATE LENS	1	1
36	2-63.000	BOLT	4	4
37	2-62.000	WASHER	4	4
38	5-10.000	RUBBER WASHER	4	4
39	2-61.000	NUT	4	4

Lights

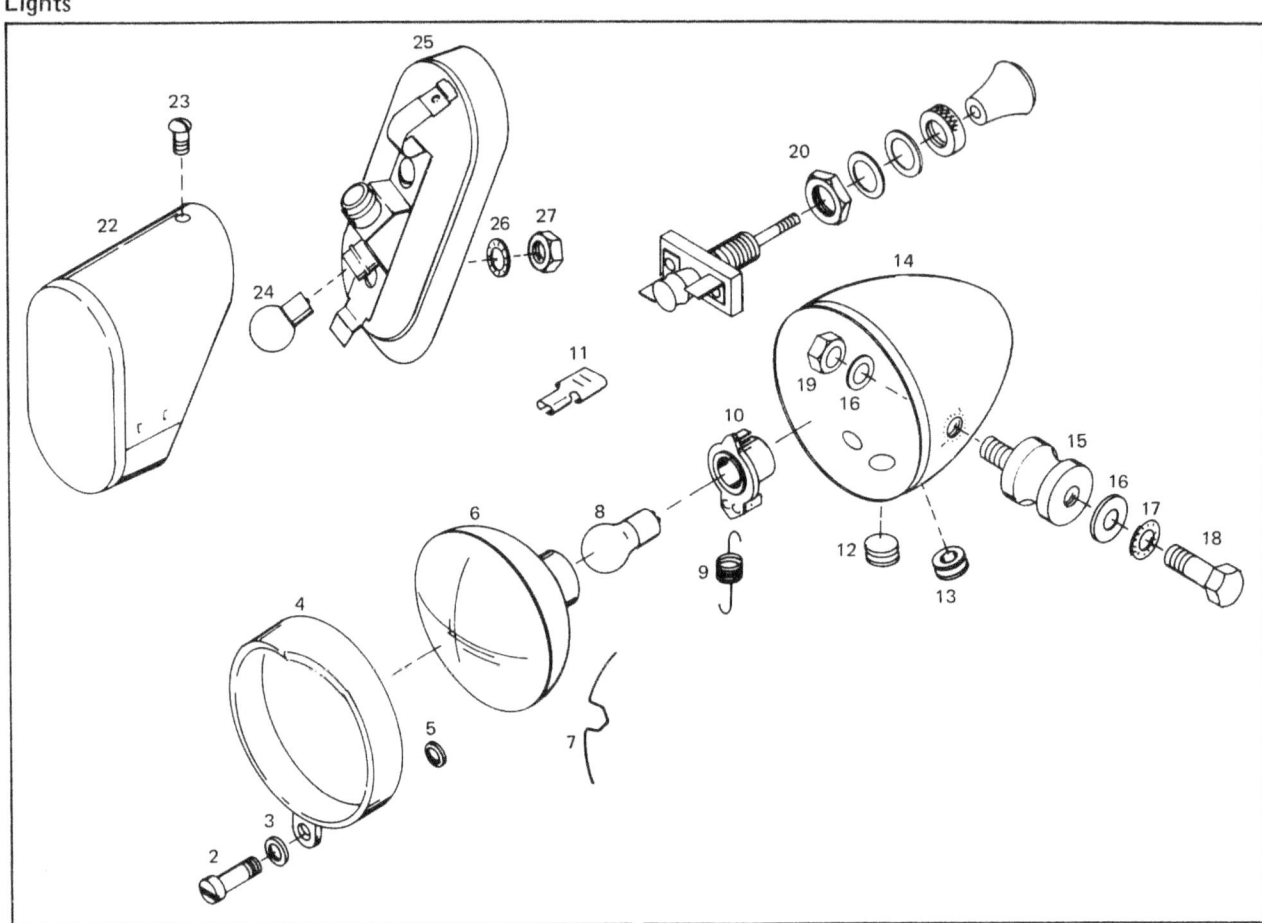

FIG. NO.	PART NO.	DESCRIPTION	100	125
			Pieces	
1	7- 1.000	HEADLIGHT COMPLETE	1	1
2	7- 2.000	SCREW, HEADLIGHT RIM	1	1
3	7- 3.000	WASHER	1	1
4	7- 4.000	RIM	1	1
5	7- 5.000	WASHER, FIBER	1	1
6	7- 6.000	GLASS REFLECTOR	1	1
7	7- 7.000	SPRING CLIP	4	4
8	7- 8.000	BULB, 6V - 15, 15W	1	1
9	7- 9.000	SPRING	1	1
10	7-10.000	BULB SOCKET	1	1
11	7-11.000	WIRE CONNECTOR	2	2
12	7-12.000	RUBBER GROMMET	1	1
13	7-13.000	RUBBER GROMMET	1	1
14	7-14.000	HEADLIGHT SHELL	1	1
15	4-11.000	RUBBER GROMMET	2	2
16	2-58.000	WASHER 8 x 20	4	4
17	2-75.000	LOCK WASHER 8 x 20	2	2
18	2-64.000	BOLT 8 x 20	2	2
19	2-59.000	NUT 8 mm	2	2
20	7-15.000	SWITCH (COMPLETE ONLY)	1	1
21	7-16.000	TAIL LIGHT COMPLETE	1	1
22	7-17.000	LENS & SHIELD	1	1
23	7-18.000	SCREW	1	1
24	7-19.000	BULB, 6V - 4, 5W	2	2
25	7-20.000	TAIL LIGHT BASE COMPLETE	1	1
26	2-65.000	WASHER, 6 x 10	2	2
27	2-61.000	NUT, 6 mm	2	2

PENTON - KTM

FRAME & COMPONENTS PARTS LIST (1972-1975)

Frame, Brake Assembly, Engine Mounts

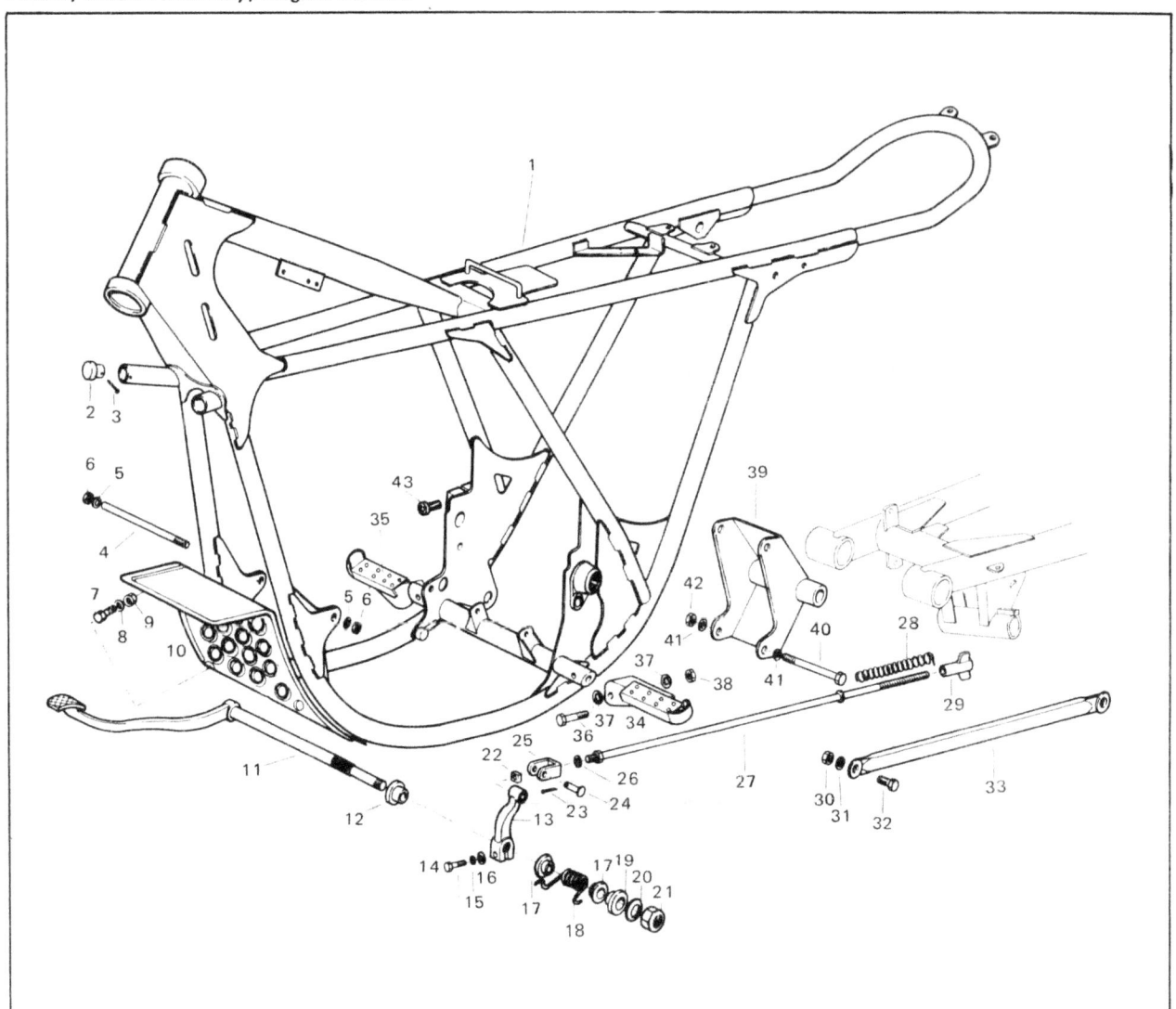

FIG. NO.	PART NO.	DESCRIPTION	Pieces	FIG. NO.	PART NO.	DESCRIPTION	Pieces
1	51.03.001.000	Frame	1	23	6.6000	Cotter pin (PIN 1.5 x 12)	1
2	51.03.090.000	Fork bumper	2	24	51.03.064.000	Pin	1
3	51.03.089.000	Fork bumper pin	2	25	51.03.071.100	Yoke, brake rod	1
4	51.03.011.000	Bolt engine mount	1	26	LW 6 x 4	Lock washer (LW 6 x 4)	1
5	2.58.000	Washer (FW 8 x 20)	6	27	51.03.070.000	Brake rod	1
6	SLN 8	Nut, self-locking (M 8)	6	28	51.03.073.000	Pressure spring	1
7	HH 6 x 10	Bolt (M 6 x 10)	4	29	51.03.076.000	Wing nut	1
8	LW 6 x 4	Lock washer (J 6 x 4)	6	30	2.69.000	Nut, self-locking (SLN 10)	1
9	2.61.000	Nut (HH 6)	4	31	FW 10 x 5	Washer (FW 10 x 5)	1
10	51.03.012.000	Skid plate	1	32	2.68.000	Bolt (HH 10 x 20)	1
11	51.03.060.000	Brake pedal	1	33	51.03.078.000	Rear brake anchor rod	1
12	51.03.066.100	Nylon bushing (right)	1	34	51.03.040.000	Foot peg (L/S)	1
13	51.03.063.000	Brake actuating arm	1	35	51.03.140.000	Foot peg (R/S)	1
14	HH 6 x 25	Bolt (M 6 x 25)	1	36	HH 8 x 40	Bolt (M 8 x 40)	2
15	LW 6 x 4	Lock washer	1	37	FW 8 x 4	Washer (FW 8 x 4)	4
16	FW 6 x 4	Washer (FW 6 x 4)	1	38	SLN 8	Nut, self-locking (M 8)	2
17	51.03.067.000	Brake spring bushing	2	39	51.03.042.000	Engine mount	1
18	51.03.062.000	Brake pedal spring	1	40	HH 8 x 100	Engine bolt (M 8 x 100)	2
19	51.03.061.000	Nylon bushing (left)	1	41	VS M 8	Washer (VS M 8)	4
20	FW 10 x 5	Washer (FW 10 x 5)	1	42	SLN 8	Nut, self-locking (M 8)	2
21	2.69.000	Nut, self locking (SLN 10)	1	43	AH 10 x 30	Allen head bolt (M 10 x 30)	1
22	2.61.000	Nut (HH 6)	1				

Tank, Seat and Swing Arm

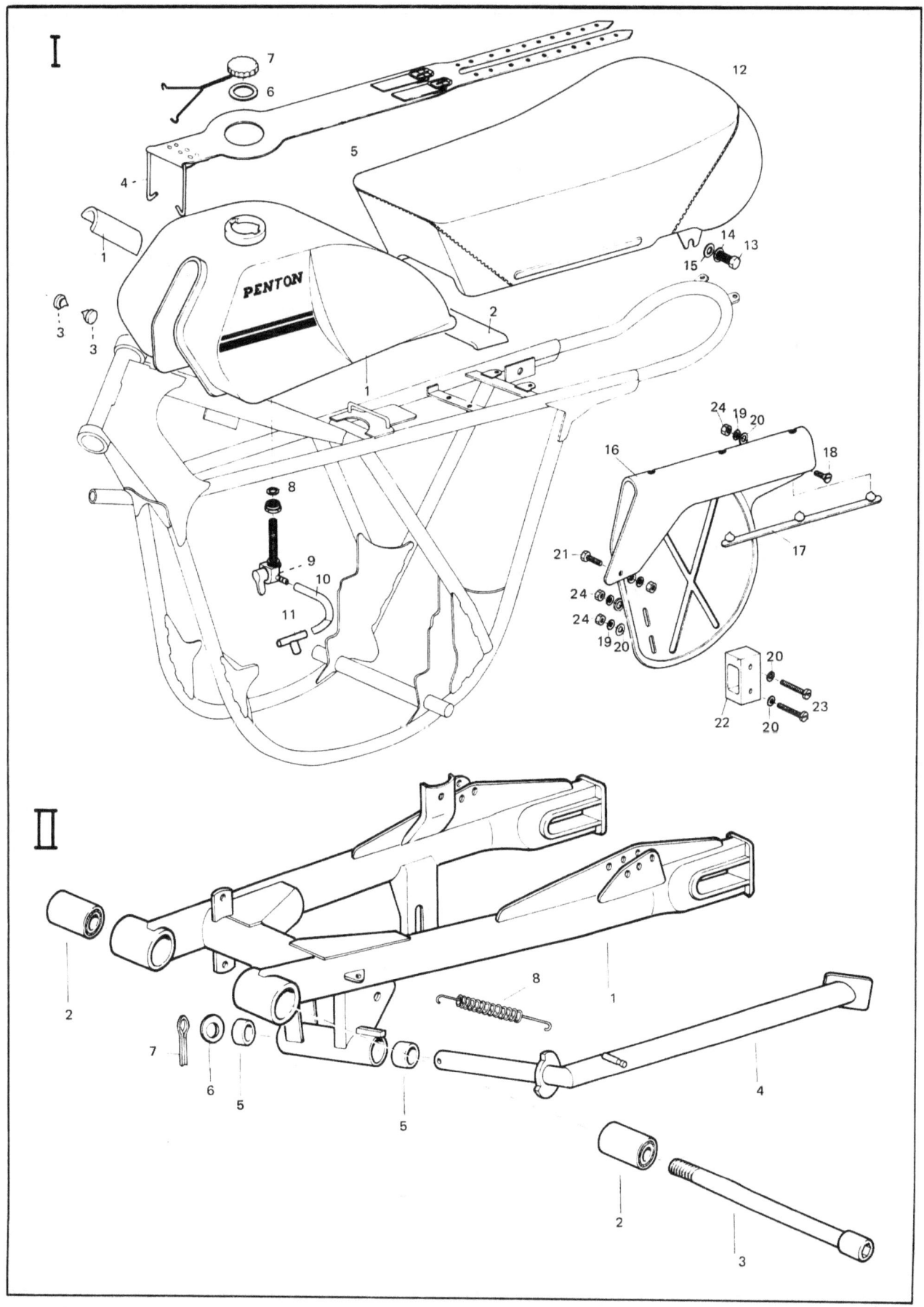

Fenders

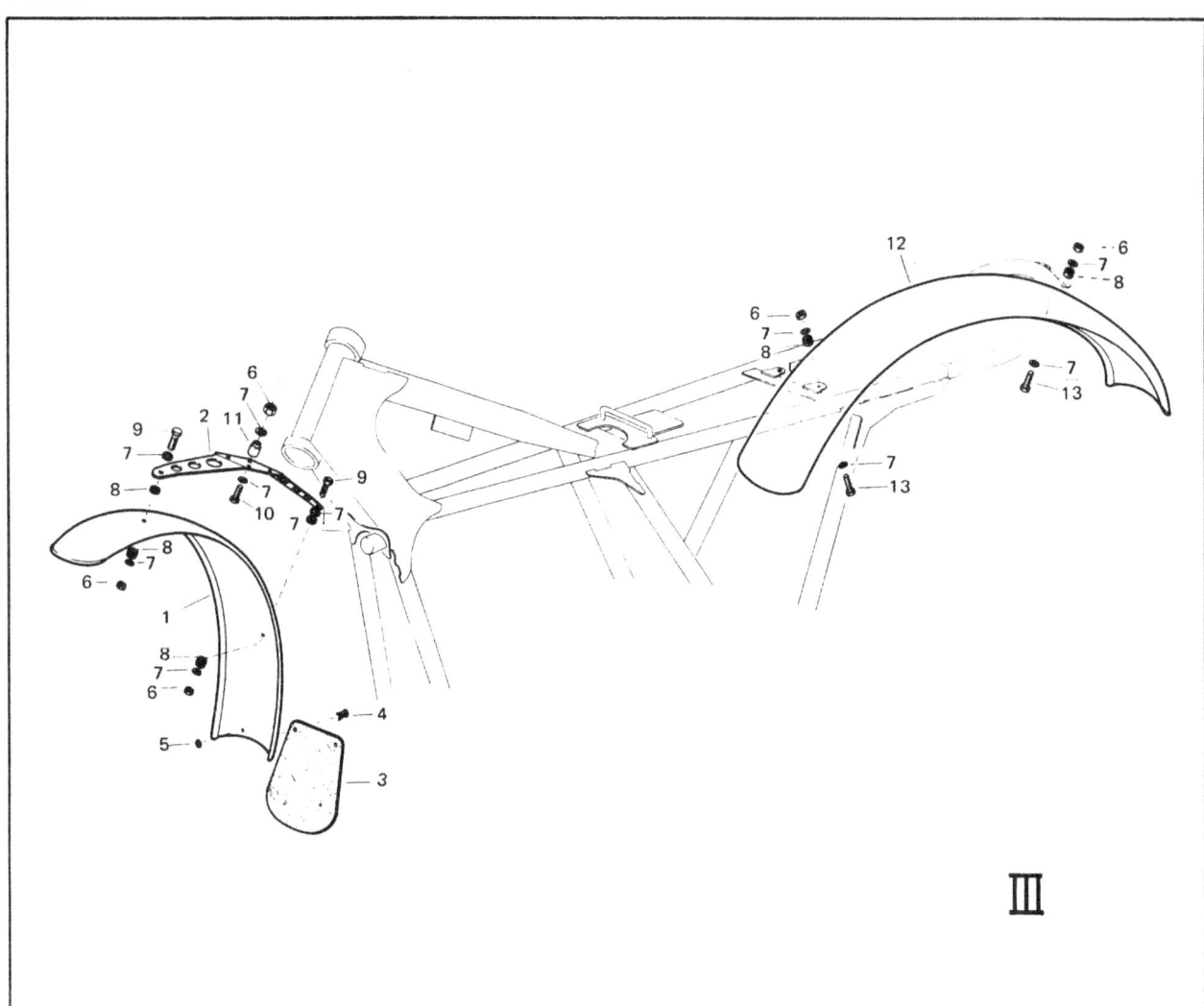

FIG. NO.	PART NO.	DESCRIPTION	Pieces
	I		
1	51.07.001.000	Gas tank (green)	
	50.07.001.000	Gas Tank (red)	1
2	51.07.010.000	Felt pads	2
3	51.07.069.100	Rubber tank shocks	2
4	51.07.014.200	Bracket for strap	1
5	51.07.011.000	Leather strap	1
6	51.07.009.000	Gas cap gasket	1
7	51.07.008.000	Gas cap w/chain	1
8	31.07.006.000	Washer fiber	2
9	31.07.005.000	Gas tap	2
10	31.07.007.000	Fuel line (specify length)	3
11	51.07.015.000	"T" Connector	1
12	51.07.040.000	Seat	1
13	HH 8 x 20	Bolt (M 8 x 20)	2
14	LW 8 x 4	Lock washer (J 8 x 4)	2
15	FW 8 x 4	Washer (FW 8 x 4)	2
16	51.07.060.000	Chain guard	1
17	51.07.064.000	Rubber chain guard	1
18	FH 6 x 10	Flat head screw (M 6 x 10)	1
19	LW 6 x 4	Lock washer (J 6 x 4)	
20	FW 6 x 4	Washer (FW 6 x 4)	
21	HH 6 x 10	Bolt (M 6 x 10)	1
22	51.07.066.000	Chain guide	1
23	FH 6 x 45	Flat head screw (M 6 x 45)	2
24	HN 6	Nut	4

FIG. NO.	PART NO.	DESCRIPTION	Pieces
	II		
1	51.03.030.000	Swing arm (complete)	1
2	51.03.031.000	Swing arm bushings	2
3	51.03.033.000	Swing arm bolt	1
4	51.03.023.000	Side stand (complete)	1
5	10.03.041.000	Side stand bushings	2
6	FW 17	Washer (FW 17)	1
7	PIN 3 x 28	Cotter pin (PIN 3 x 28)	1
8	51.03.021.000	Side stand spring	1
	III		
1	51.08.010.000	Front fender	1
2	51.08.011.000	Fender bracket	1
3	51.08.012.000	Mud flap	1
4	PIN	Cotter pin	2
5	FW 4 x 3	Washer (FW 4 x 3)	2
6	SLN 10	Nut, self-locking (M 10)	
7	FW 6 x 4	Washer (FW 6 x 4)	
8	RW	Rubber washer	
9	HH 6 x 25	Bolt (M 6 x 25)	
10	HH 6 x 45	Bolt (M 6 x 45)	4
11	51.08.015.000	Spacer	4
12	51.08.013.000	Rear fender	1
13	HH 6 x 15	Bolt	3

Air Filter Assembly, Exhaust Assembly

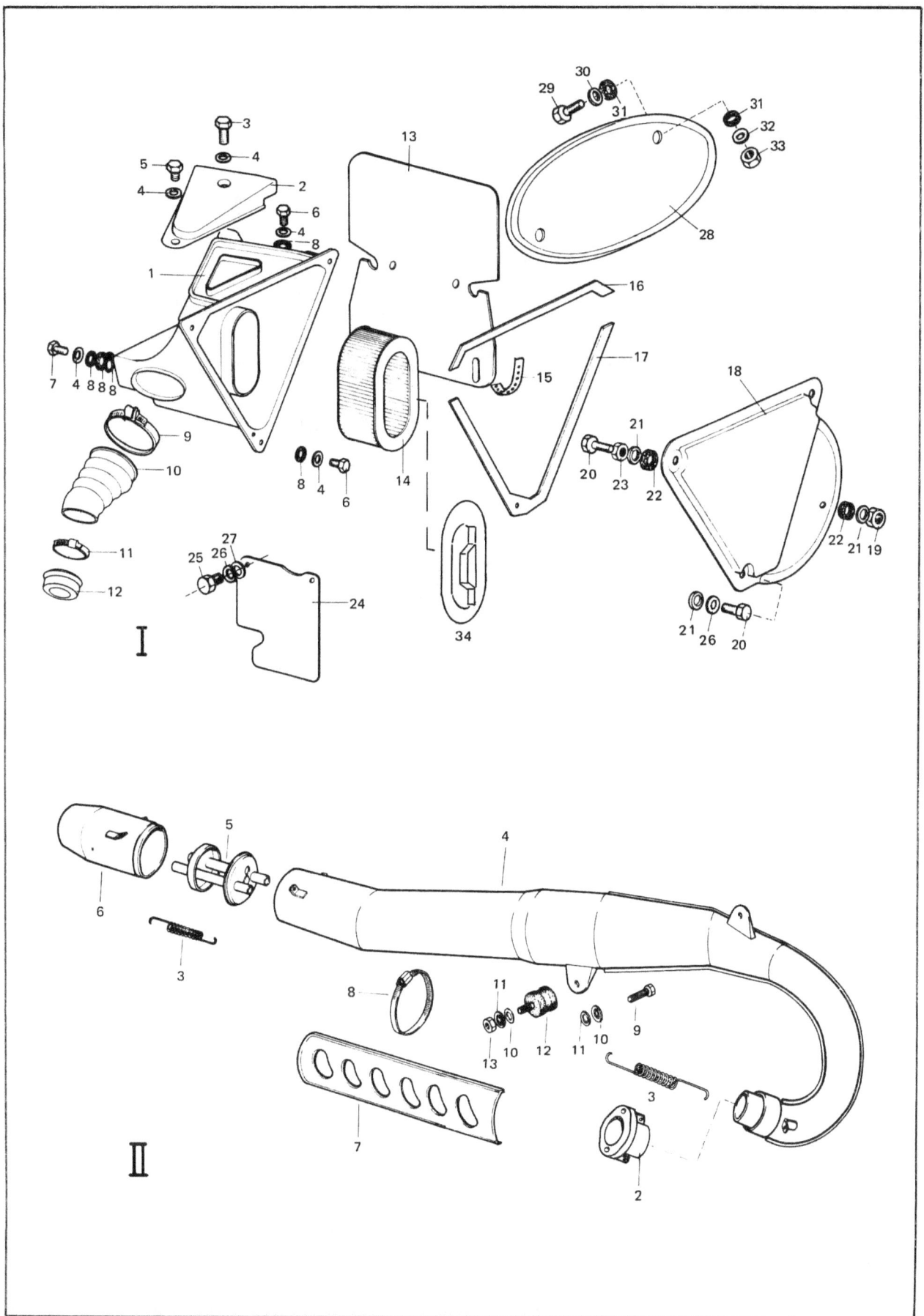

Handlebar, Controls, Cables

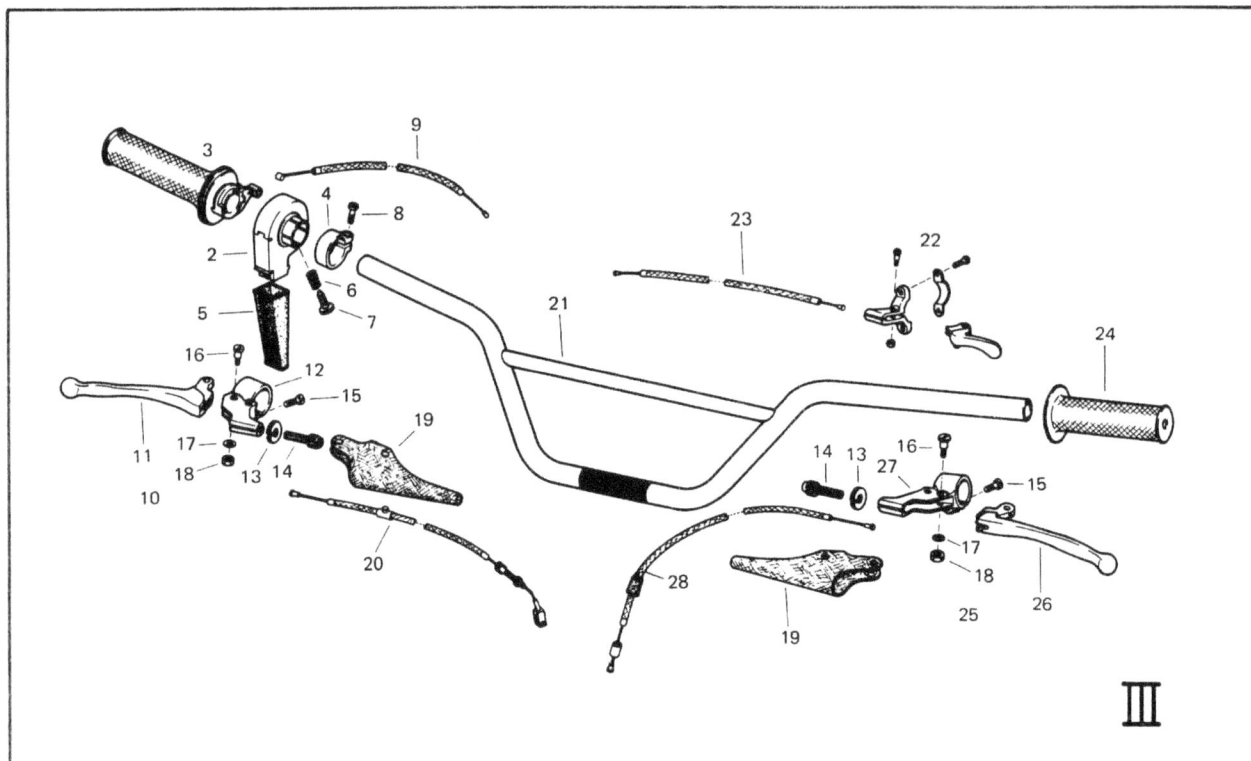

FIG. NO.	PART NO.	DESCRIPTION	Pieces
1	51.06.001.000	Air filter box (specify color)	1
2	51.06.043.100	Air filter top	1
3	HH 6 x 35	Bolt (M 6 x 35)	1
4	FW 6 x 4	Washer (FW 6 x 4)	1
5	HH 6 x 10	Bolt (M 6 x 10)	1
6	HH 6 x 20	Bolt (M 6 x 20)	1
7	HH 6 x 25	Bolt (M 6 x 25)	1
8	RW	Rubber Washer	1
9	51.06.028.000	Clamp	1
10	51.06.026.000	Air filter boot	1
11	51.06.027.000	Clamp	1
12	51.06.029.000	Rubber bushing	1
13	51.06.061.000	Splash guard	1
14	51.06.015.000	Air filter	1
15	51.06.076.000	Plastic bands	2
16	51.06.040.000	Gasket	1
17	51.06.039.000	Gasket	1
18	51.06.041.100	Air filter cover (specify color)	1
19	SLN 6	Nut, self-locking (M 6)	1
20	HH 6 x 25	Bolt (M 6 x 25)	3
21	FW 6 x 4	Washer (FW 6 x 4)	1
22	RW	Rubber washer	1
23	HN 6	Nut (M 6)	1
24	51.06.062.000	Splash guard	1
25	HH 6 x 10	Bolt (M 6 x 10)	2
26	LW 6 x 4	Lock washer (J 6 x 4)	2
27	FW 6 x 4	Washer (FW 6 x 4)	2
28	51.06.087.000	Number plate (right)	1
29	HH 6 x 20	Bolt (M 6 x 20)	2
30	FW 6 x 4	Washer (FW 6 x 4)	2
31	RW	Rubber washer	1
32	LW 6 x 4	Lock washer (LW 6 x 4)	2
33	HN 6	Nut (M 6)	2
34	51.06.017.000	Spring loaded air filter cover	1

II

FIG. NO.	PART NO.	DESCRIPTION	Pieces
1	51.05.070.000	Exhaust complete with baffle and muffler end	1
2	51.05.051.000	Engine exhaust flange	1
3	51.05.063.000	Exhaust spring	5
4	51.05.053.000	Exhaust pipe	1
5	51.05.072.000	Baffle	1
6	51.05.071.000	Muffler end	1
7	51.05.075.000	Leg guard	1
8	51.05.064.000	Clamp (90 mm)	2
9	HH 8 x 10	Bolt (M 8 x 10)	3
10	LW 8 x 4	Lock washer (J 8 x 4)	6
11	FW 8 x 4	Washer (FW 8 x 4)	6
12	51.05.062.000	Rubber bolt block	3
13	HN 8	Nut (M 8)	3

III

FIG. NO.	PART NO.	DESCRIPTION	Pieces
1	51.02.010.000	Throttle twist grip (complete)	1
2	51.02.015.000	Twist grip drum	1
3	51.02.018.000	Twist grip tube	1
4	51.02.019.000	Twist grip clamp	1
5	51.02.016.000	Twist grip rubber	1
6	51.02.017.000	Pressure spring	1
7	51.02.021.000	Screw, throttle tension	1
8	51.02.020.000	Screw	1
9	52.02.091.000	Throttle cable	1
10	51.02.031.000	Lever assembly complete (R/S)	1
11	51.02.022.000	Lever brake	1
12	51.02.023.000	Lever holder	1
13	51.02.024.000	Adjuster nut	2
14	51.02.025.000	Adjuster screw	2
15	51.02.027.000	Bolt (M 6 x 15)	2
16	51.02.028.000	Pivot pin screw	2
17	LW 6.4	Lock washer (J 6.4)	2
18	HN 6	Hex nut (M 6)	2
19	51.02.026.000	Dust cover	1
20	51.02.092.000	Front brake cable	1
21	51.02.001.000	Handlebar specify M-X or Enduro	1
22	51.02.059.000	Choke lever (complete only)	1
23	51.02.095.000	Choke cable	1
24	51.02.052.000	Rubber twist grip (L/S)	1
25	51.02.040.000	Lever assembly complete (L/S)	1
26	51.02.055.000	Clutch lever	1
27	51.02.045.000	Lever holder	1
28	51.02.090.000	Clutch cable	1

Front Wheel and Hub Assembly

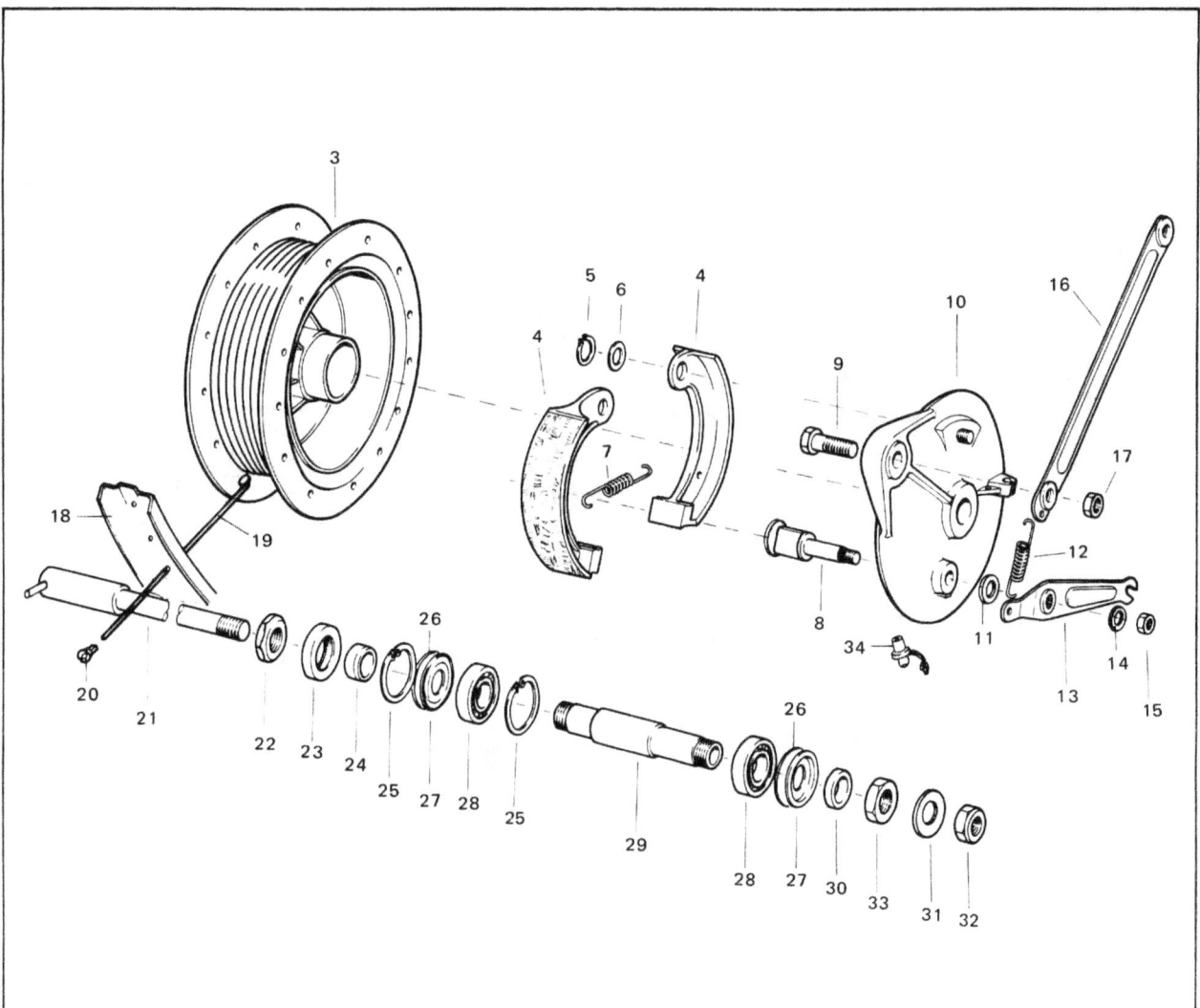

FIG. NO.	PART NO.	DESCRIPTION	Pieces
1	6-90.000	Wheel complete (front)	1
2	6-92.000	Hub complete (front)	1
3	31.09.010.000	Hub	1
4	31.09.035.000	Brake shoe	2
5	C 12 x 1	Circlip (12 x 1)	1
6	31.09.037.000	Flat washer	1
7	31.09.036.000	Spring	1
8	31.09.031.000	Cam	1
9	HH 10 x 35	Bolt (M 10 x 35)	1
10	31.09.030.000	Brake plate	1
11	31.09.032.000	PVC washer	1
12	51.10.040.000	Spring	1
13	51.09.033.100	Brake arm - front hub	1
14	LW 8 x 4	Lock washer (J 8 x 4)	1
15	HN 8 x 1	Nut (M 8 x 1)	1
16	51.09.042.000	Front brake anchor	1
17	SLN 10	Nut, self-locking (M 10)	1
18	51.09.070.000	Steel rim (21")	1
19	51.09.071.000	Spoke	36
20	51.09.072.000	Nipples	36
21	51.09.081.000	Axle - front hub	1
22	31.09.018.000	Nut	1
23	6.20.000	Seal	1
24	31.09.016.000	Bushing	1
25	C 35 x 1.5	Circlip (35 x 1.5)	2
26	31.09.014.000	Spacer	2
27	31.09.015.000	Dust shield	2
28	6.72.00	Ball bearing	2
29	51.09.011.000	Axle	1
30	31.09.085.000	Spacer	1
31	FW 13	Washer (13)	1
32	SLN 12	Nut, self-locking	1
33	HN 16 x 1	Nut	1
34	31.09.039.000	Grease fitting	1

Rear Wheel and Hub Assembly

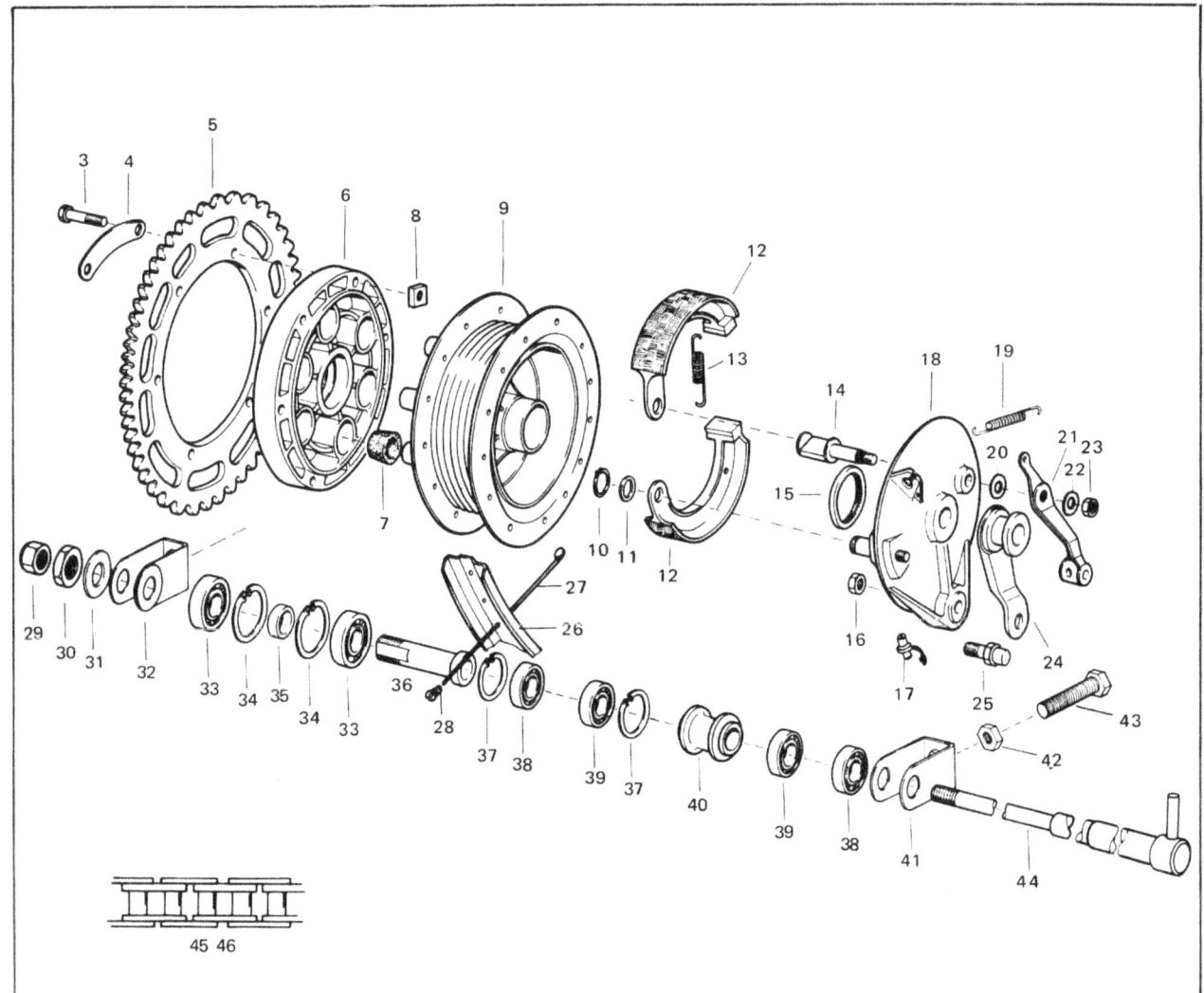

FIG. NO.	PART NO.	DESCRIPTION	Pieces
1	6-95.000	Wheel complete	1
2	6-69.000	Hub complete	1
3	HH 8 x 35	Bolt (M 8 x 35)	6
4	51.10.052.000	Sprocket locking plate	3
5	51.10.051.000	Sprocket (48, 52, 54, 57 and 60T) specify	1
6	51.10.050.000	Sprocket carrier	1
7	51.10.059.000	Rubber shocks	6
8	SN 8	Nut (M 8)	6
9	51.10.010.000	Hub	1
10	C 12 x 1	Circlip (12 x 1)	1
11	31.09.037.000	Washer	1
12	31.09.035.000	Brake shoe	2
13	31.09.036.000	Spring	1
14	31.09.031.000	Cam	1
15	634.000	Seal	1
16	SLN 10	Nut, self-locking (M 10)	1
17	31.09.039.000	Grease nipple	1
18	51.09.030.000	Brake plate	1
19	51.10.040.000	Return spring	1
20	31.09.032.000	PVC washer	1
21	51.10.033.000	Brake arm	1
22	FW 8 x 4	Washer (FW 8 x 4)	1
23	HN 8 x 1	Nut (8 x 1)	1
24	51.10.087.000	Spacer	1
25	51.10.034.000	Brake anchor arm bolt	1
26	51.10.070.000	Steel rim (18")	1
27	51.10.071.000	Spoke	36
28	51.09.072.000	Nipple	36
29	SLN 12	Nut, self locking (SLN 12)	1
30	HN 20	Nut, M 20 x 1	1
31	51.10.038.000	Washer	1
32	51.10.184.000	Chain adjuster (R/S)	1
33	6.76.000	Ball bearing	2
34	C 42 x 1.75	Circlip (42 x 1.75)	2
35	51.10.057.000	Distance bushing	1
36	51.10.054.100	Sprocket axle	1
37	C 35 x 1.5	Circlip (C 35 x 1.5)	2
38	6.72.001	Ball bearing	2
39	6.72.001	Ball bearing	2
40	51.10.011.000	Spacer	1
41	51.10.084.000	Chain adjuster (L/S)	1
42	HN 8	Nut (M 8)	1
43	HH 8 x 50	Bolt (8 x 50)	2
44	51.10.085.000	Rear axle	1
45	51.10.065.000	Chain 125 links (1/2 x 5/16)	1
46	51.10.066.000	Master link	

Front Fork Assembly

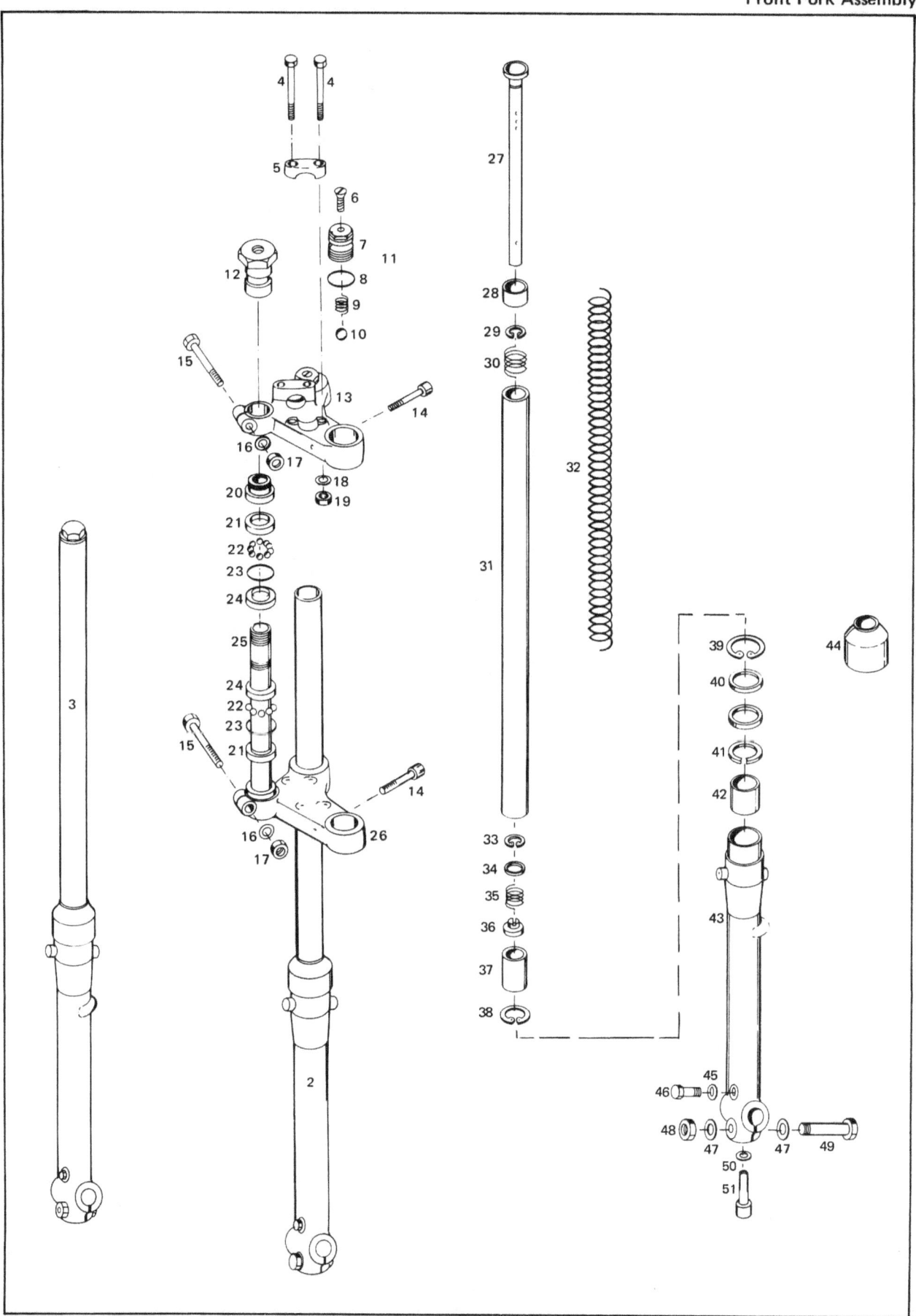

Rear Shock Assembly

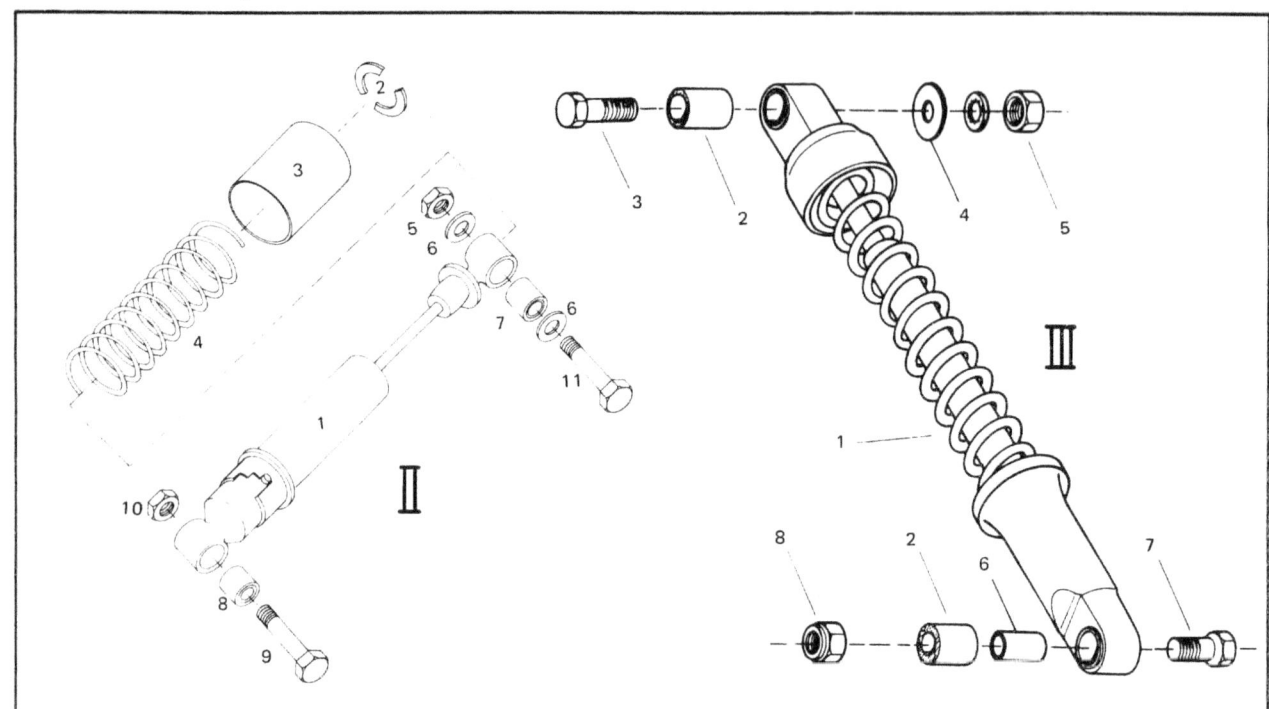

FIG. NO.	PART NO.	DESCRIPTION	Pieces
	I		
1	ES 1.579	Fork assembly complete	1
2	1.519.08.01	Fork leg (clutch side)	1
3	1.519.07.01	Fork leg (throttle side)	1
4	1.503.013	Bolt, handlebar	4
5	1.211/1.012	Handlebar saddle	2
6	1.503.022	Screw	2
7	1.503.021	Fork tube nut	2
8	1.503.027	"O" Ring	2
9	1.503.023	Spring	2
10	1.88.043	Ball	2
11	1.503.021.01	Fork tube nut complete	2
12	1.541.032	Nut, top fork plate	1
13	1.503.011	Top fork plate	1
14	1.503.015	Allen screw	4
15	1.98.0612	Bolt, pinch	2
16	1.69.024	Washer	2
17	1.42.05.01.07	Nut	2
18	1.55/1.01.02.2	Washer	4
19	1.55/1.01.02.3	Nut	4
20	1.541.033	Nut bearing	1
21	2.50.000	Bearing race	2
22	2.51.000	Ball Bearing (RB 8)	34
23	2.52.000	"O" Ring	2
24	2.53.000	Bearing race	2
25	1.541.031	Fork stem	1
26	1.519.041	Fork plate, bottom	1
27	1.519.061	Stop valve	2
28	1.503.067	Bushing	2
29	1.503.068	Circlip	2
30	1.503.069	Spring	2
31	1.519.05	Fork tube	2
32	1.519.10	Fork spring (long)	2
33	1.503.0655	Circlip	2
34	1.503.0652	Seal	2
35	1.503.0653	Spring	2
36	1.503.0654	Valve	2
37	1.503.0651	Bushing	2
38	1.503.066	Circlip	2
39	1.503.092	Circlip	2
40	1.503.091	Seal	2
41	1.503.075	Snap ring	2
42	1.503.074	Bushing	2
43	1.519.07	Fork leg lower (throttle side)	1
	1.519.08	Fork leg lower (clutch side)	1
44	1.503.093	Fork boot	2
45	1.88.0512	Washer	2
46	1.88.0511	Screw	2
47	1.69.024	Washer	4
48	1.42.05.01.07	Nut	2
49	1.98.0612	Bolt	2
50	1.503.077	Washer	2
51	1.503.076	Allen screw	2
	II		
1	ES 2.496	Shock complete	2
2	2.207.094	Retainer clips	4
3	2.8.02.01/2	Dust cover	2
4	2.350/2.092	Spring	2
5	HH 10	Nut (Self-locking M10)	4
6	FW 10 x 5	Washer (FW 10 x 5)	2
7	2.496.10.1	Bushing	2
8	2.496.10.2	Bushing	2
9	HH 8 x 35	Bolt (M 8 x 35)	2
10	SLN 8	Nut, Self-locking (M 8)	2
11	HH 10 x 55	Bolt	2
	III		
1	51.04.010.000	Rear shock assembly	2
2	51.04.028.000	Bushing	4
3	HH 10 x 55	Bolt (M 10 x 55)	2
4	FW 10 x 5	Washer (FW 10 x 5)	2
5	HH 10	Nut (M 10)	2
6	51.04.029.000	Distance bushing	2
7	HH 8 x 35	Bolt (M 8 x 35)	2
8	SLN 8	Nut, self-locking (M 8)	2

Plate 16 Lighting Equipment

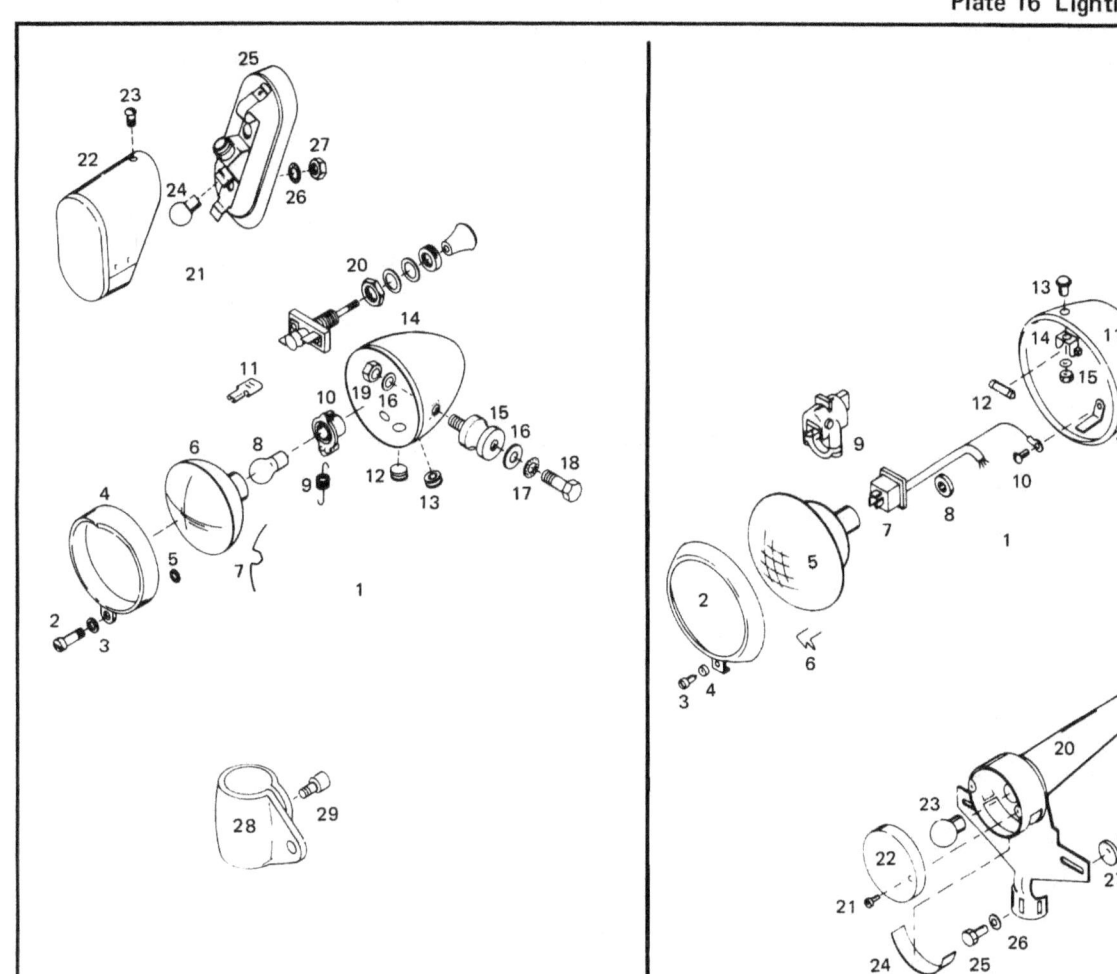

FIG. NO.	PART NO.	DESCRIPTION	Pieces
1	7.1.000	Headlight complete	1
2	7.2.000	Screw, headlight rim	1
3	7.3.000	Washer	1
4	7.4.000	Rim	1
5	7.5.000	Washer, fiber	1
6	7.6.000	Glass reflector	1
7	7.7.000	Spring clip	4
8	7.8.000	Bulb, 6V-15,15W	1
9	7.9.000	Spring	1
10	7.10.000	Bulb socket	1
11	7.11.000	Wire connector	2
12	7.12.000	Rubber grommet	1
13	7.13.000	Rubber grommet	1
14	7.14.000	Headlight shell	1
15	4.11.000	Rubber grommet	2
16	FW 8 x 20	Washer	4
17	LW 8 x 20	Lock washer	2
18	HH 8 x 20	Bolt	2
19	HH 8	Nut	2
20	7.15.000	Switch, complete only	1
21	7.16.000	Tail light complete	1
22	7.17.000	Lens & shield	1
23	7.18.000	Screw	1
24	7.19.000	Bulb, 6V-4,5W	2
25	7.20.000	Tail light base complete	1
26	LW 6 x 10	Washer	2
27	HH 6	Nut	2
28	1.343.08	Bracket	2
29	1.343.09	Allen screw	2

FIG. NO.	PART NO.	DESCRIPTION	Pieces
1	2.16.000	Headlight assembly complete	1
2	2.17.000	Rim	1
3	2.11.000	Screw	1
4	2.41.000	Rubber washer	1
5	2.19.001	Seal beam	1
6	2.21.000	Retaining clips	x
7	2.22.000	Plug	1
8	2.24.000	Rubber grommet	1
9	2.32.000	Dipper switch	1
10	2.24.000	Screw	1
11	2.16.001	Headlight housing	1
12	2.37.000	Indicator bulb	1
13	2.38.000	Indicator lens	1
14	2.39.000	Indicator bracket	1
15	2.40.000	Nut	1
16	2.41.000	Rubber grommet	2
17	2.42.000	Washer (special)	2
18	LW 8	Lock washer (LW 8)	2
19	HH 8 x 20	Bolt (HH 8 x 20)	2
20	5.56.000	Tail light assembly complete	1
21	5.71.000	Screw	2
22	5.72.000	Tail light lens	1
23	5.73.000	Bulb	1
24	5.74.000	License plate lens	1
25	HH 6 x 25	Bolt	4
26	FW 6 x 20	Flat washer (FW 6 x 20)	4
27	5.10.000	Rubber washer	4
28	HH 6	Nut	4

VELOCEPRESS MANUALS – MOTORCYCLE BY MAKE

AJS 1932-1948 SINGLES & TWINS 250cc THRU 1000cc (BOOK OF)
AJS 1945-1960 SINGLES 350cc & 500cc MODELS 16 & 18 (BOOK OF)
AJS 1955-1965 SINGLES 350cc & 500cc (BOOK OF)
AJS 1957-1966 FACTORY WSM - ALL SINGLES & TWINS
ARIEL UP TO 1932 (BOOK OF)
ARIEL 1932-1939 PREWAR MODELS (BOOK OF)
ARIEL 1933-1951 (WORKSHOP MANUAL)
ARIEL 1939-1960 4 STROKE SINGLES (BOOK OF)
ARIEL 1958-1964 LEADER & ARROW FACTORY WSM & PARTS LIST
ARIEL 1958-1964 LEADER & ARROW (BOOK OF)
BMW R26 R27 (1956-1967) FACTORY WORKSHOP MANUAL
BMW R50 R50S R60 R69S (1955-1969) FACTORY WORKSHOP MANUAL
BMW R50/5 R60/5 R75/5 (1969-1973) FACTORY WORKSHOP MANUAL
BRIDGESTONE 90 SERIES FACTORY WSM & PARTS CATALOGUE
BRIDGESTONE 175 SERIES FACTORY WSM & PARTS CATALOGUE
BRIDGESTONE 350 SERIES FACTORY WSM & PARTS CATALOGUES
BSA SERVICE SHEETS MASTER CATALOGUE ALL MODELS 1945-1967
BSA BANTAM D1 TO D7 1948-1966 FACTORY SERVICE SHEETS MANUAL
BSA BANTAM ALL MODELS FROM 1948 ONWARDS (BOOK OF)
BSA BANTAM D14 FACTORY SERVICE MANUAL
BSA DANDY FACTORY WORKSHOP MANUAL (COMPILATION)
BSA SINGLES & V-TWINS UP TO 1926 inc. 1927 SUPPLEMENT (BOOK OF)
BSA SINGLES & V-TWINS UP TO 1930 (BOOK OF)
BSA SINGLES & V-TWINS UP TO 1935 (BOOK OF)
BSA SINGLES & V-TWINS 1936-1939 (BOOK OF)
BSA C10, C11 & C12 1945-1958 FACTORY SERVICE SHEETS MANUAL
BSA OHV & SV SINGLES 250-600cc 1945-1959 (BOOK OF)
BSA C15 & B40 1958-1967 FACTORY SERVICE SHEETS MANUAL
BSA OHV & SV SINGLES 250cc (ONLY) 1954-1970 (BOOK OF)
BSA B31, B32, B33 & B34 1945-60 FACTORY SERVICE SHEETS MANUAL
BSA OHV SINGLES 350 & 500cc 1955-1967 (BOOK OF)
BSA M20, M21 & M33 1945-1963 FACTORY SERVICE SHEETS MANUAL
BSA TWINS A7 & A10 1948-1962 FACTORY SERVICE SHEETS MANUAL
BSA TWINS A7 & A10 1948-1962 (BOOK OF)
BSA TWINS A50 & A65 1962-1965 FACTORY WORKSHOP MANUAL
BSA TWINS A50 & A65 1962-1969 (SECOND BOOK OF)
DOUGLAS 1929-1939 PREWAR ALL MODELS (BOOK OF)
DOUGLAS 1948-1957 POSTWAR ALL MODELS FACTORY SHOP MANUAL
DUCATI 160cc, 250cc & 350cc OHC MODELS FACTORY SHOP MANUAL
HONDA 50cc ALL MODELS UP TO 1970 INC MONKEY & TRAIL (BOOK OF)
HONDA 90cc ALL MODELS UP TO 1966 (BOOK OF)
HONDA TWINS & SINGLES 50cc THRU 305cc 1960-1966 (BOOK OF)
HONDA TWINS ALL MODELS 125cc THRU 450cc UP TO 1968 (BOOK OF)
HONDA C100 50cc SUPER CUB O.H.C. 1959-1962 FACTORY WSM
HONDA C110 50cc SPORT CUB O.H.C. 1960-1962 FACTORY WSM
HONDA 50-65-70-90cc O.H.C. SINGLES 1959-1983 WSM
HONDA 100-125cc SINGLES CB/CD/CL/SL/TL 1970-1984 FACTORY WSM
HONDA 125-150cc TWINS C/CS/CB/CA 1959-1966 FACTORY WSM
HONDA 125-160-175-200cc TWINS 1965-1978 WORKSHOP MANUAL
HONDA 250-305cc TWINS C/CS/CB 1961-1968 FACTORY WSM
HOHDA 250-350cc TWINS CB/CL/SL 1968-1973 FACTORY WSM
HONDA 250-360cc TWINS CB/CL/CJ 1974-1977 FACTORY WSM
HONDA 350F & 400F 4-CYLINDER 1972-1977 FACTORY WSM
HONDA 450cc TWINS CB/CL 1965-1974 K0 TO K7 WORKSHOP MANUAL
HONDA 500cc & 550cc 4-CYL 1971-1978 FACTORY WORKSHOP MANUAL
HONDA 750cc SHOC 4-CYL 1969-1978 K0~K8 WORKSHOP MANUAL
INDIAN PONYBIKE, BOY RACER & PAPOOSE ILL PARTS LIST & SALES LIT

J.A.P. ENGINES 1927-1952 & MOTORCYCLES 1934-1952 (BOOK OF)
MATCHLESS 1931-1939 ALL MODELS 250cc THRU 990cc (BOOK OF)
MATCHLESS 1945-1956 350 & 500cc SINGLES (BOOK OF)
MATCHLESS 1955-1966 350 & 500cc SINGLES (BOOK OF)
MATCHLESS 1957-1966 FACTORY WSM - ALL SINGLES & TWINS
NEW IMPERIAL ALL SV & OHV FROM 1935 ONWARDS (BOOK OF)
NORTON 1932-1939 PREWAR MODELS (BOOK OF)
NORTON 1932-1947 (BOOK OF)
NORTON 1938-1956 (BOOK OF)
NORTON 1945-1963 MODELS 16H, Big4, ES2, 19 & 50 WSM'S & PARTS
NORTON 1955-1963 MODELS 19, 50 & ES2 (BOOK OF)
NORTON 1948-1970 DOMINATOR TWINS FACTORY WSM'S & PARTS
NORTON 1955-1965 DOMINATOR TWINS (BOOK OF)
NORTON 1960-1970 TWIN CYLINDER FACTORY WORKSHOP MANUAL
NORTON 1970-1975 COMMANDO 850 & 750cc FACTORY WSM
NORTON 1975-1978 MK 3 COMMANDO 850 cc FACTORY WSM
PANTHER 1932-1958 LIGHTWEIGHT MODELS 250 & 350cc (BOOK OF)
PANTHER 1938-1966 HEAVYWEIGHT MODELS 600 & 650cc (BOOK OF)
PENTON-KTM-SACHS 1968-1975 100cc & 125cc WORKSHOP MANUAL
RALEIGH MOTORCYCLES 1919-1933 (BOOK OF)
ROYAL ENFIELD 1934-1946 SINGLES & V TWINS (BOOK OF)
ROYAL ENFIELD 1937-1953 SINGLES & V TWINS (BOOK OF)
ROYAL ENFIELD 1946-1962 SINGLES (BOOK OF)
ROYAL ENFIELD 1948-1963 500cc TWINS FACTORY WORKSHOP MANUAL
ROYAL ENFIELD 1952-1963 700cc TWINS FACTORY WORKSHOP MANUAL
ROYAL ENFIELD 1956-1966 250cc CRUSADER & 350cc NEW BULLET WSM
ROYAL ENFIELD 1958-1966 250cc & 350cc SINGLES (SECOND BOOK OF)
ROYAL ENFIELD 1962-1970 INTERCEPTOR WSM'S & PARTS (Compilation)
RUDGE 1933-1939 (BOOK OF)
SACHS 1968-1975 100cc & 125cc ENGINES WSM & M/CYCLE PARTS LIST
SUNBEAM 1928-1939 (BOOK OF)
SUNBEAM 1946 1957 S7 & S8 (BOOK OF)
SUZUKI 50cc & 80cc UP TO 1966 (BOOK OF)
SUZUKI T10 1963-1967 FACTORY WORKSHOP MANUAL
SUZUKI T20 & T200 1965-1969 FACTORY WORKSHOP MANUAL
SUZUKI TWINS 1962 ONWARDS 125-500cc WORKSHOP MANUAL
TRIUMPH 1935-1949 SINGLES & TWINS (BOOK OF)
TRIUMPH 1937-1961 SINGLES SV & OHV 250cc-600cc + TERRIER & CUB
TRIUMPH 1945-1955 PRE-UNIT 350cc, 500cc & 650cc TWINS WSM No.11
TRIUMPH 1945-1959 TWINS (BOOK OF)
TRIUMPH 1956-1969 TWINS (BOOK OF)
TRIUMPH 1956-1962 PRE-UNIT 500cc & 650cc TWINS WSM No.17
TRIUMPH 1957-1963 UNIT CONSTRUCTION 350-500cc WSM No.4
TRIUMPH 1963-1974 UNIT CONSTRUCTION 350-500cc FACTORY WSM
TRIUMPH 1963-1970 UNIT CONSTRUCTION 650cc FACTORY WSM
TRIUMPH 1968-1974 TRIDENT T150 & T150V FACTORY WSM
TRIUMPH 1971-1973 650cc OIL-IN-FRAME FACTORY WSM
TRIUMPH 1973-1978 750cc BONNEVILLE & TIGER FACTORY WSM
TRIUMPH 1979-1983 750cc T140, TR7 & TR65 FACTORY WSM
VELOCETTE 1925-1970 ALL SINGLES & TWINS (BOOK OF)
VELOCETTE 1933-1952 MOV-MAC-MSS RIGID FRAME FACTORY WSM
VELOCETTE 1954-1971 MSS-VENOM-THRUXTON-VIPER FACTORY WSM
VILLIERS ENGINE UP TO 1959 INC. 3 WHEELERS (BOOK OF)
VILLIERS ENGINE UP TO 1969 (BOOK OF)
VINCENT 1935-1955 (WORKSHOP MANUAL)
YAMAHA 1961-1967 YA5 & YA6 (WORKSHOP MANUAL)
YAMAHA 1971-1972 JT1 & JT2 (WORKSHOP MANUAL & ILL PARTS LIST)

VELOCEPRESS MANUALS – SCOOTERS BY MAKE

BSA SUNBEAM SCOOTER WORKSHOP MANUAL 1959-1965
BSA SUNBEAM SCOOTER 1959-1965 (BOOK OF)
LAMBRETTA 1947-1957 ALL 125 & 150cc MODELS (BOOK OF)
LAMBRETTA 1957-1970 LI & TV MODELS (SECOND BOOK OF)
NSU PRIMA 1956-1964 ALL MODELS (BOOK OF)
TRIUMPH TIGRESS SCOOTER WORKSHOP MANUAL 1959-1965
TRIUMPH TIGRESS SCOOTER (BOOK OF)
VESPA 1951-1961 (BOOK OF)
VESPA 1955-1963 125 & 150cc & GS MODELS (SECOND BOOK OF)
VESPA 1955-1968 GS & SS (BOOK OF)
VESPA 1963-1972 90, 125 & 150cc (THIRD BOOK OF)

VELOCEPRESS MANUALS – MOPEDS & MOTORIZED BICYCLES

CYCLEMOTOR (BOOK OF)
NSU QUICKLY 1953-1963 ALL MODELS (BOOK OF)
PUCH MAXI N & S MAINTENANCE & REPAIR (3 MANUAL COMPILATION)
RALEIGH MOPEDS 1960-1969 (BOOK OF)

VELOCEPRESS MANUALS - THREE WHEELER'S

BOND MINICAR THREE WHEELER 1948-1967 (BOOK OF)
BMW ISETTA FACTORY WORKSHOP MANUAL
BSA THREE WHEELER (BOOK OF)
RELIANT REGAL THREE WHEELER 1952-1973 (BOOK OF)
VINTAGE MORGAN THREE WHEELER (BOOK OF)

VELOCEPRESS TECHNICAL BOOKS – MOTORCYCLE

1930'S BRITISH MOTORCYCLE CARBS & ELEC COMPONENTS (BOOK OF)
1930'S BRITISH MOTORCYCLE ENGINES (OVERHAUL & MAINTENANCE)
1930'S BRITISH MOTORCYCLE GEARBOXES & CLUTCHES (BOOK OF)
CATALOG OF BRITISH MOTORCYCLES (1951 MODELS)
LUCAS ELECTRONICS BRITISH M/CYCLES REPAIR & PARTS (1950-1977)
MOTORCYCLE ENGINEERING (P.E. Irving)
MOTORCYCLE ROAD TESTS 1949-1953 (Motor Cycle Magazine UK)
SPEED AND HOW TO OBTAIN IT (Motor Cycle Magazine UK)
TUNING FOR SPEED (P.E. Irving)
WIPAC (COMBO) MANUAL NUMBER 3 + M/CYCLE & SCOOTER MANUAL

www.VelocePress.com

www.ingramcontent.com/pod-product-compliance
Lightning Source LLC
Chambersburg PA
CBHW080738300426
44114CB00019B/2622